OUR FIFTH-SUNDAY
HYMN SERVICES

To Kimberley[1]

[1] who said when we had met on Pulborough Station on 5.5.11 after I had found the station car park full and consequently had just missed my train to London, and with whom I had enjoyed a very interesting conversation during our subsequent drive to her destination in Brighton, from where I went on to London by car, that she would "look out for my book". Well, here it is at last!

I had been obliged to park the car on the verge of the main road near the station, where other people had left theirs, so I wasn't too happy to leave it there all day and quite ready to drive to London instead. As we walked back through the subway she asked me why I was going to London, so I said I was going to lunch with someone who had joined a society I belonged to two months before I was born. "What society was that?" "The Society for Psychical Research" "I'm a bit sceptical about such things." "So am I." made a good start to our conversation. Another topic we discussed was what I was going to say at our Hymns Service at the end of that month, and I mentioned William James's "Higamous, Hogamous . . ." couplet (see page 189) that he was reported to have uttered under the influence of nitrous oxide. Later that same day I too was breathing nitrous oxide, having tripped up outside the SPR premises and dislocated my shoulder, when it was put back for me by a surgeon at the Chelsea and Westminster Hospital. And the coincidences didn't end there, for my follow-up appointment at St Richard's Hospital, Chichester, happened to be on the afternoon of the day a special service was being held at the Cathedral for our parish of St Mary's West Chiltington. Not only could Tony give me a lift to the hospital, but I was able to walk to the Cathedral after I had been seen to, arriving with five minutes to spare. David Beal, our Rector, read the Old Testament lesson, which was from the Book of Job and included a reference to a dislocated shoulder! [Job Chapter 31, v.21: "if I have raised my hand against the innocent, knowing that men would side with me in court, then may my shoulder-blade be torn from my shoulder, my arm be wrenched out of its socket!" (*NEB*)]. There are some days in our lives that we recall for years afterwards, and I think this lends credence to the accounts of significant incidents described in the Gospels, even though these were recorded many years later. *DJE*

Our Fifth-Sunday Hymn Services

by David Ellis, Peter Evans
Tony Hills and Philip Newman

55

Simple Services, With Hymns

held at St Mary's Church, West Chiltington

30th November 2003
to
29th January 2017

on 5th Sundays at 6 p.m.

DE

D. J. ELLIS

PULBOROUGH

2019

ACKNOWLEDGEMENTS

These services were started in November 2003 by permission of Revd Kevin O'Donnell, Rector from 1999 to 2008, who gave us a 'slot' on 5th Sundays at 6 p.m., and continued with the permission and much encouragement of Revd David Beal, our Rector from 2009 to 2016. We are especially grateful also to Graham Barnes, Churchwarden, for commending our format to the Parochial Church Council, to his wife Anne, for suggesting that our talks be published in the Parish Magazine, and to David Burnett, Editor, for duly including them. Mrs Jean Peace attended the services until she moved to Bognor Regis in 2010, and her appreciation of our sending her the printed records of all the subsequent ones has encouraged us to think that other people might find these of interest. We also thank the permissions staff of the publishers we contacted for their courteous and friendly service.

ISBN 978 0 9554944 1 3

First published March 2019

For copyright reasons this book is not for sale outside the United Kingdom.

Published by

David J. Ellis

Fernwood, Nightingales, West Chiltington
PULBOROUGH,   West Sussex,   RH20 2QT

British Library Cataloguing-in-Publication Data

A catalogue record for this book
is available from the British Library.

Covers printed and laminated by Kenads Limited, Goring by Sea, West Sussex
Printed and Bound in Great Britain by Lanes (South East) Limited, Broadstairs, Kent

Preface

This book is an attempt to present in a convenient and portable form the records of a series of evening services held in a West Sussex village church over a period of some thirteen years, put together by a group of friends who shared the belief that the Christian religion, being basically simple, could be expressed in a straightforward format that they could put together themselves, with input from the people who might be willing to attend. Straightforward enough to be non-denominational, and simple enough not to deter people of good will who might not otherwise think of attending the usual run of services.

Input from the people attending derived from requesting them to tell us what hymns they would like to sing, thus reversing the usual process of prescribing hymns to go with a service. The hymns were selected from the requests to hand, and listed in advance in the Parish Magazine.

When the rest of the service was compiled, the hymns were put between the other items in what seemed their most logical order. We selected suitable readings to go with them, taking note of where we were in the Church's year.

From the outset we included provision for what we have always called a brief chat, making quite clear that it was not intended to be a sermon so as not to be bound by any church regulations regarding 'unlicensed preachers'.

Our initial plan was to produce a little book from just these talks, but however interesting and even challenging they may have been in themselves, these comprised only a small part of our efforts to put together a service that had some 'outreach' value in this increasingly secular country, in which the Christian faith seems to have been progressively eliminated from the teaching and practice in our schools. Examination of the material we have used raises the hope that we might possibly inspire lay people in other churches to follow our formula, or to adapt it as they saw fit. Besides which, people who would not normally have attended any conventional service could browse through at random and might come across something to inspire or cheer them.

So although anyone could look up the biblical passages we chose from the references provided, we have included them to save the reader the trouble. The printed Order of Service serves to introduce each one, listing the hymns and who did what, followed by the words for any hymn not in our usual hymn book, and then the text of my informal welcoming introduction.

There is a reference section at the end of the book, listing the hymns whose words are included, the talks, and poems and other items quoted.

DJE

ABOUT THE CONTRIBUTORS[1]

David Ellis attended grammar schools in Rye, Horsham, Winchester and Brighton, from which he won a minor scholarship in Natural Sciences to Gonville & Caius College, Cambridge. After six years in an industrial research laboratory he took up a studentship in psychical research. From 1974 he has been self-employed in the printing trade, specializing in books and journals. He was PCC Secretary 2009–2015, and PCC Treasurer 2013–2017.

Peter Evans retired early from the Church Commissioners and then worked locally as Parish Clerk. As a CPFA he continues to audit local authority accounts. He has served at St Mary's West Chiltington for over thirty years and was PCC Treasurer in the late 1990s.

Tony Hills chose a technical education in preference to a grammar-school one, and then became a student apprentice to the Ministry of Defence Royal Small Arms Factory at Enfield. After two years' National Service with the RAF as a ground electrician, he worked at the National Physical Laboratory at Teddington in the Aerodynamics Division. He was a Churchwarden near where he lived before moving to West Chiltington.

Philip Newman was a Sales Representative (Print), latterly with Robert Maxwell's (!) Group: British Printing & Communications Corporation.

---

[1] All the services in this volume were held in St Mary's Church, West Chiltington, on the dates specified in the text. On no occasion were any expenses claimed, either for the printing of the service material or for any refreshments provided after the services.

The publication of this book is intended as outlined in the Preface and any surplus or profits will be donated to the Royal National Lifeboat Institution. *See also page 195.*

Initial notice in Parish Magazine for November 2003. See also account on page 99.

COME AND SING SOME HYMNS

What better way to affirm what one believes than to join in singing a hymn whose words one can endorse and whose tune one likes?

We think so, anyway, so after the success of the Songs of Praise services to help raise money for the Millennium project we asked Kevin if we could do something similar on a more regular basis. He said we could have the fifth Sundays, instead of Evensong.

So the first one will be on **Sunday, 30th November, at 6 p.m.**

We are aiming for something very simple — half a dozen hymns, a reading or two (not necessarily both biblical), and a few short prayers to conclude with. Should there be any sort of address, talk, etc., it will not last more than five minutes. The whole service will not take too much of your time: about 30–35 minutes in total.

All those attending will be handed a sheet with which to tell us their own favourite hymns for the next service; if you each list up to eight rather than just one, we shall be able to work out which ones most people want. Suggestions for readings also welcomed.

'Voting with your feet' normally has a negative connotation, as it refers to people leaving some organization because they do not like the way it is run and have no other way of making their views known. Please make it *positive* for us — vote with *your* feet by *coming,* and bringing your family and friends. And tell us what you want. All we ask for is your readiness to sing!

For the first occasion we have chosen some of the hymns *we* like:–

> *On Jordan's bank the Baptist's cry ***
> *God is working His purpose out*
> *O Jesus I have promised*
> *Onward Christian soldiers*
> *I vow to thee, my country*
> *O come, O come, Emmanuel ***

David Ellis   (Fernwood, Nightingales. Tel: 813001)

Peter Evans   * 30th November is Advent Sunday

SING SOME HYMNS

30th November 2003

Order of Service

Welcome (Kevin)

Hymn 49 (Tune: Veni Emmanuel)
O come, O come, Emmanuel

Introduction (David)

Hymn 629 (Tune: *St Gertrude*)
Onward Christian soldiers

First reading (Peter) St Matthew, Chapter 5, Verses 1–16 *(NEB)*

Hymn 331 (Tune: *Thornbury*)
O Jesus I have promised

Second reading "The Ballad of East and West" *by Rudyard Kipling* (i)

Hymn 579 (Tune: *Thaxted*)
I vow to thee, my country

Second reading "The Ballad of East and West" *by Rudyard Kipling* (ii)

Hymn 271 (Tune: *Benson*)
God is working His purpose out

Prayers (Peter)

Hymn 50 (Tune: *Winchester New*)
On Jordan's bank the Baptist's cry

The service will proceed without announcements. All the hymns this time are in *Hymns Ancient & Modern Revised.*

Thank you for coming. Please use the attached voting form to list your own favourite hymns for a subsequent service.

SING SOME HYMNS   30 NOVEMBER 2003
INTRODUCTION

This service is very much an experiment. Peter Evans and I have tried to put together a very simple service, for the simple reason that we think that Christianity is—or should be—a very simple religion. Simple, that is, to state, and simple to understand, even if it is by no means always simple to put into practice.

We have chosen hymns we like—and we hope later to be selecting hymns you like. If there is any theme linking the non-Advent hymns, it is a slight bias towards the attitude associated with the putting-into-practice part of our religion.

You may be wondering why the second reading is in two parts. We put in the Parish magazine that the readings would not necessarily both be biblical, and this one is not. In fact, we have no excuse whatsoever for including it, except that it is—or was—a well-known poem by a much loved poet, and we like it! I wouldn't say that it has no message at all, but it is at least ninety per cent entertainment. We hope you will enjoy the story and enjoy the poet's command of words, and accept it as our way of saying thank you for coming. It's just a little long, so that's why it's in two parts. While thanking people, may I thank Peter Knowles for his work on the organ and Kevin for his support; but please do not hold either of them responsible for what follows!

We intend the service to proceed slickly and smoothly without any announcements, like the Nine Lessons and Carols; we think the hymns will not need any introduction, given that today, as you know, is Advent Sunday—and if you think the first verse of *I Vow to Thee My Country* is a little over the top with regard to its currently non-PC patriotism, I might add that today, as you may not all know, happens to be Winston Churchill's birthday.

The next hymn has personal memories for me of a Petworth & Pulborough District Scout St George's Day service I was involved in some twenty years ago.[1] I put a note on the service sheet saying, "Come on Scouts, don't leave all the singing to the Cubs!" and Basil Maltin, the Pulborough Rector, himself a former Scout, made some encouraging remarks as well. As the organ struck up I was wondering, would they sing? With the first verse the answer came: *yes they would!*

---

[1] Further details of this service can be found on pages 74–83.

4

Matthew 5, 1–16

When he saw the crowds he went up the hill. There he took his seat, and when his disciples had gathered round him he began to address them. And this is the teaching he gave:–

"How blest are those who know that they are poor; the kingdom of Heaven is theirs.

"How blest are the sorrowful; they shall find consolation.

"How blest are those of a gentle spirit; they shall have the earth for their possession.

"How blest are those who hunger and thirst to see right prevail ; they shall be satisfied.

"How blest are those who show mercy; mercy shall be shown to them.

"How blest are those whose hearts are pure; they shall see God.

"How blest are the peacemakers; God shall call them his sons.

"How blest are those who have suffered persecution for the cause of right; the kingdom of Heaven is theirs.

"How blest you are, when you suffer insults and persecution and every kind of calumny for my sake. Accept it with gladness and exultation, for you have a rich reward in heaven; in the same way they persecuted the prophets before you.

"You are salt to the world. And if salt becomes tasteless, how is its saltness to be restored? It is now good for nothing but to be thrown away and trodden underfoot.

"You are light for all the world. A town that stands on a hill cannot be hidden. When a lamp is lit, it is not put under the meal-tub, but on the lamp-stand, where it gives light to everyone in the house. And you, like the lamp, must shed light among your fellows, so that, when they see the good you do, they may give praise to your Father in heaven."

The Ballad of East and West

Oh, East is East, and West is West, and never the twain shall meet,
Till Earth and Sky stand presently at God's great Judgment Seat;
But there is neither East nor West, Border, nor Breed, nor Birth,
When two strong men stand face to face, though they come from the ends of
the earth!

Kamal is out with twenty men to raise the Border-side,
And he has lifted the Colonel's mare that is the Colonel's pride.
He has lifted her out of the stable-door between the dawn and the day,
And turned the calkins upon her feet, and ridden her far away.
Then up and spoke the Colonel's son that led a troop of the Guides:
"Is there never a man of all my men can say where Kamal hides?"
Then up and spoke Mohammed Khan, the son of the Ressaldar:
"If ye know the track of the morning-mist, ye know where his pickets are.
"At dusk he harries the Abazai—at dawn he is into Bonair,
"But he must go by Fort Bukloh to his own place to fare.
"So if ye gallop to Fort Bukloh as fast as a bird can fly,
"By the favour of God ye may cut him off ere he win to the Tongue of Jagai.
"But if he be past the Tongue of Jagai, right swiftly turn ye then,
"For the length and the breadth of that grisly plain is sown with Kamal's men.
"There is rock to the left, and rock to the right, and low lean thorn between,
"And ye may hear a breech-bolt snick where never a man is seen."
The Colonel's son has taken horse, and a raw rough dun was he,
With the mouth of a bell and the heart of Hell and the head of the gallows-tree.
The Colonel's son to the Fort has won, they bid him stay to eat—
Who rides at the tail of a Border thief, he sits not long at his meat.
He's up and away from Fort Bukloh as fast as he can fly,
Till he was aware of his father's mare in the gut of the Tongue of Jagai,
Till he was aware of his father's mare with Kamal upon her back,
And when he could spy the white of her eye, he made the pistol crack.
He has fired once, he has fired twice, but the whistling ball went wide.
"Ye shoot like a soldier," Kamal said. "Show now if ye can ride!"
It's up and over the Tongue of Jagai, as blown dust-devils go,
The dun he fled like a stag of ten, but the mare like a barren doe.
The dun he leaned against the bit and slugged his head above,
But the red mare played with the snaffle-bars, as a maiden plays with a glove.
There was rock to the left and rock to the right, and low lean thorn between,
And thrice he heard a breech-bolt snick tho' never a man was seen.
They have ridden the low moon out of the sky, their hoofs drum up the dawn,
The dun he went like a wounded bull, but the mare like a new-roused fawn.
The dun he fell at a water-course—in a woeful heap fell he,
And Kamal has turned the red mare back, and pulled the rider free.

He has knocked the pistol out of his hand—small room was there to strive,
" 'Twas only by favour of mine," quoth he, "ye rode so long alive:
"There was not a rock for twenty mile, there was not a clump of tree,
"But covered a man of my own men with his rifle cocked on his knee.
"If I had raised my bridle-hand, as I have held it low,
"The little jackals that flee so fast were feasting all in a row.
"If I had bowed my head on my breast, as I have held it high,
"The kite that whistles above us now were gorged till she could not fly."

Lightly answered the Colonel's son: "Do good to bird and beast,
"But count who come for the broken meats before thou makest a feast.
"If there should follow a thousand swords to carry my bones away,
"Belike the price of a jackal's meal were more than a thief could pay.
"They will feed their horse on the standing crop, their men on the garnered grain.
"The thatch of the byres will serve their fires when all the cattle are slain.
"But if thou thinkest the price be fair,—thy brethren wait to sup,
"The hound is kin to the jackal-spawn,—howl, dog, and call them up!
"And if thou thinkest the price be high, in steer and gear and stack,
"Give me my father's mare again, and I'll fight my own way back!"
Kamal has gripped him by the hand and set him upon his feet.
"No talk shall be of dogs," said he, "when wolf and grey wolf meet.
"May I eat dirt if thou hast hurt of me in deed or breath;
"What dam of lances brought thee forth to jest at the dawn with Death?"
Lightly answered the Colonel's son: "I hold by the blood of my clan:
"Take up the mare for my father's gift—by God, she has carried a man!"
The red mare ran to the Colonel's son, and nuzzled against his breast;
"We be two strong men," said Kamal then, "but she loveth the younger best.
"So she shall go with a lifter's dower, my turquoise-studded rein,
"My 'broidered saddle and saddle-cloth, and silver stirrups twain."
The Colonel's son a pistol drew, and held it muzzle-end,
"Ye have taken the one from a foe," said he. "Will ye take the mate from a friend?"
"A gift for a gift," said Kamal straight; "a limb for the risk of a limb.
"Thy father has sent his son to me, I'll send my son to him!"
With that he whistled his only son, that dropped from a mountain crest—
He trod the ling like a buck in spring, and he looked like a lance in rest.

"Now here is thy master," Kamal said, "who leads a troop of the Guides,
"And thou must ride at his left side as shield on shoulder rides.
"Till Death or I cut loose the tie, at camp and board and bed,
"Thy life is his—thy fate it is to guard him with thy head.
"So, thou must eat the White Queen's meat, and all her foes are thine,
"And thou must harry thy father's hold for the peace of the Border-line.
"And thou must make a trooper tough and hack thy way to power—
"Belike they will raise thee to Ressaldar when I am hanged in Peshawur!"

They have looked each other between the eyes, and there they found no fault.
They have taken the Oath of the Brother-in-Blood on leavened bread and salt:
They have taken the Oath of the Brother-in-Blood on fire and fresh-cut sod,
On the hilt and the haft of the Khyber knife, and the Wondrous Names of God.
The Colonel's son he rides the mare and Kamal's boy the dun,
And two have come back to Fort Bukloh where there went forth but one.
And when they drew to the Quarter-Guard, full twenty swords flew clear—
There was not a man but carried his feud with the blood of the mountaineer.
"Ha' done! ha' done!" said the Colonel's son. "Put up the steel at your sides!
"Last night ye had struck at a Border thief—to-night 'tis a man of the Guides!"

Oh, East is East, and West is West, and never the twain shall meet,
Till Earth and Sky stand presently at God's great Judgment Seat;
But there is neither East nor West, Border, nor Breed, nor Birth,
When two strong men stand face to face, though they come from the ends of
*   the earth!*

Rudyard Kipling[1]

(1865–1936)

This poem tells a true story of India's North-West Frontier; it is dated 1889, so the 'White Queen' is Queen Victoria, and the Guides are not the Girl Guides.

In those far-off days there were no tanks, and no bombers, suicide or otherwise; the British soldiers keeping the peace could be humiliated merely by someone nicking their commanding officer's favourite horse . . .

[1] See page 29 for a brief note about Rudyard Kipling. His poems in this book are taken from *The Definitive Edition of Rudyard Kipling's Verse*. London: Hodder & Stoughton, 1940, May 1996 reprint.

Prayers [1]

Teach us, good Lord, to serve thee as thou deservest; to give and not to count the cost; to fight and not to heed the wounds; to toil and not to seek for rest; to labour and not to ask for any reward save that of knowing that we do thy will.   *Amen.*

O God, our Father, by whose will we dwell together in families, let thy blessing rest upon our homes. Bless our parents, our children, and all the members of our families. Give them health and strength of soul and body, and unite us all in love for thee; through Jesus Christ our Lord.   *Amen.*

† Lighten our darkness, we beseech thee, O Lord; and by thy great mercy defend us from all perils and dangers of this night; for the love of thy only son, our Saviour, Jesus Christ.   *Amen.*

A few moments' silence for your own prayers.

The Lord's Prayer.

May the blessing of almighty God rest upon us and upon all our work; may he give us light to guide us, courage to support us, and love to unite us, now and evermore.   *Amen.*

---

[1] Many of the prayers used in our services were selected from *Prayers for Use in the Brotherhood of Scouts*, published in 1927 (revised 1963 and reprinted 1965) by what was then The Boy Scouts Association (since 1966 The Scout Association).

We have permission to use those taken from The Book of Common Prayer (see p.vi) and these are marked †, but we apologize to anyone who still holds copyright of any of the many other prayers included.

SING SOME MORE HYMNS

29th February 2004

Order of Service

Welcome & Notices (Kevin)

    Hymn 92 (Tune: *Heinlein*)
        Forty days and forty nights

Brief introduction (David)

    Hymn 235 (Tune: *Down Ampney*)
        Come down, O Love divine

First reading (Peter) Matthew, Chapter 6, Verses 19–34 *(NEB)*

    Hymn 293 (Tune: *Monks Gate*)
        Who would true valour see

Second reading (Peter) *from* "Neighbours" *by Rudyard Kipling*

    Hymn 51 (*Mission Praise;* words overleaf. Tune: *Slane*)
        Be Thou my vision

Brief chat (David)

    Hymn 290 (Tune: *Wiltshire*)
        Through all the changing scenes of life

Prayers (Peter)

    Hymn 269 (Tune: *Little Cornard*)
        Hills of the North, rejoice

The service will proceed without announcements. All the hymns except one (words opposite)[1] are in *Hymns Ancient & Modern Revised.*

Thank you for coming. Please use the voting form overleaf to list your own favourite hymns for a subsequent service.

---

[1] All our service sheets comprised a single sheet of A4, folded to four pages on A5. A cover page bore the title and date, and the Order of Service was on the left-hand page inside. The right-hand page could include the words of a hymn not in the hymn book, or a choice form. In this book we have left in that original note of where the words of a hymn could be found. Where they are in this book is stated in the Order of Service.

Be Thou my vision

Be Thou my vision, O Lord of my heart;
naught be all else to me, save that Thou art –
Thou my best thought, by day or by night,
waking or sleeping, Thy presence my light.

Be Thou my wisdom, Thou my true Word;
I ever with Thee, Thou with me, Lord;
Thou my great Father, I Thy true son;
Thou in me dwelling, and I with Thee one.

Be Thou my battle-shield, sword for the fight,
be Thou my dignity, Thou my delight.
Thou my soul's shelter, Thou my high tower:
raise Thou me heavenward, O Power of my power.

Riches I heed not, nor man's empty praise,
Thou mine inheritance, now and always:
Thou and Thou only, first in my heart,
High King of heaven, my treasure Thou art.

High King of heaven, after victory won,
may I reach heaven's joys, O bright heaven's Sun!
Heart of my own heart, whatever befall,
still be my vision, O ruler of all.

From *The Poem Book of the Gael* (8th century)
translated by Mary Elizabeth Byrne (1880–1931)
versified by Eleanor Henrietta Hull (1860–1935)

This is the second of these services; the support for the first one has encouraged us to think that they will be viable. We hope we didn't put anyone off in November with our long and unusual second reading. The next one, all being well, is due in May.

As I said last time, the aim is to have a very simple service, the hymns being the most important part, but the way we fill the gaps between them is intended to be constructive as well. Our hope is that we shall in due course attract not only church members who like singing hymns, but friends, relatives, neighbours and other people of good will who might not otherwise think of darkening the church's door.

My brother, Robert, worked out recently that the Evensong Choir has now been going for twenty years; he reckons it started on 19th February 1984. Let us thank the choir members for their loyal service over this period, as well as for their help for these services. And thanks, of course, to Peter Knowles and the others who have played the organ.

As before, we shall proceed without announcements, but I need to say a brief word about the fourth hymn, *Be Thou my vision*. I must warn you that there are **two versions** of the words and music. Against Peter Knowles's better judgement, I have chosen the words from *Mission Praise* rather than those from *Hymns for Today*, because I think they are neater and less cumbersome. The tune we shall sing is almost, **but not quite**, the same as for *Lord of all Hopefulness*. It has the same melody, but the rhythm is a little different, and needs some care if we are to get it to scan. It has **ten beats to every line**, rather than one line of ten and then three of eleven. The most important difference is that there is no twiddly bit at the start of the second line; it just goes "Naught be all else to me". Listen to it as it is played through, and try thinking "One, two, three-ee, four, five; o-one, two, three, four, five" or "One, two, three-ee, four, five, six; one, two, three, four" as appropriate!

Matthew 6, 19–34

"Do not store up for yourselves treasure on earth, where it grows rusty and moth-eaten, and thieves break in to steal it. Store up treasure in heaven, where there is no moth and no rust to spoil it, no thieves to break in and steal. For where your wealth is, there will your heart be also.

"The lamp of the body is the eye. If your eyes are sound, you will have light for your whole body; if the eyes are bad, your whole body will be in darkness. If then the only light you have is darkness, the darkness is doubly dark.

"No servant can be slave to two masters; for either he will hate the first and love the second, or he will be devoted to the first and think nothing of the second. You cannot serve God and Money.

"Therefore I bid you put away anxious thoughts about food and drink to keep you alive, and clothes to cover your body. Surely life is more than food, the body more than clothes. Look at the birds of the air; they do not sow and reap and store in barns, yet your heavenly Father feeds them. You are worth more than the birds! Is there a man of you who by anxious thought can add a foot to his height? And why be anxious about clothes? Consider how the lilies grow in the fields; they do not work, they do not spin; and yet, I tell you, even Solomon in all his splendour was not attired like one of these.

"But if that is how God clothes the grass in the fields, which is there today, and tomorrow is thrown on the stove, will he not all the more clothe you? How little faith you have! No, do not ask anxiously, 'What are we to eat? What are we to drink? What shall we wear?' All these are things for the heathen to run after, not for you, because your heavenly Father knows that you need them all. Set your mind on God's kingdom and his justice before everything else, and all the rest will come to you as well. So do not be anxious about tomorrow; tomorrow will look after itself. Each day has troubles enough of its own."

Neighbours   *(first verse only)*

The man that is open of heart to his neighbour,

And stops to consider his likes and dislikes,

His blood shall be wholesome whatever his labour,

His luck shall be with him whatever he strikes.

The Splendour of Morning shall duly possess him,

That he may not be sad at the falling of eve.

And, when he has done with mere living—God bless him!—

A many shall sigh, and one Woman shall grieve!

Rudyard Kipling
(1865–1936)

BE THOU MY VISION

A vision is something we see; vision is the means by which we see it. I think 'vision' in that opening line can have both meanings, if we see it as a request to be shown what we need to see.

This is not a sermon; it is just a short chat. Kevin said before our first hymn service that he didn't think there was time for an address, and I didn't press the point as we needed an introduction that would take a little while. We filled the slot by splitting a long second reading. But, since then, Kevin has invited David Hammond and Sally Levett to speak at other services, so I saw no reason why I should be prevented from having a go myself this time.

Had I made any comment in November, I might have drawn attention to "How blest are those who hunger and thirst to see right prevail" in the first reading and its possible relevance to the hymn, *Onward Christian Soldiers,* and the prayer, "Teach us, good Lord, to serve thee as thou deservest"—but I expect most people there would have guessed that anyway. This time, using hymns selected from those you have requested, it is harder to find a common theme.

But I can at least link the first reading with my claim that Christianity should be a simple religion to state and understand: the Sermon on the Mount puts it all very clearly. "You cannot serve God and Money" is quite explicit— a good example of something that is much easier to state than it is to put into practice. "Riches I heed not" might be a parallel. The second reading—Kipling once more, but very short this time—was included to suggest that concern for our neighbour will usually be less exciting than exemplified by the parable of the Good Samaritan: it could be no more than stopping to consider another person's preferences; thinking of his or her problems or difficulties rather than our own; seeing things from that other person's point of view.

I also hope that you will see a link between the first reading and the next hymn. After telling his listeners not to worry themselves about material things, Jesus requests them to "Set your mind on God's kingdom and his justice before everything else," continuing, "and *all the rest will come to you as well.*" I reckon that's a pretty good promise.

I don't think it is always sufficiently stressed that religion is not so much a set of abstract principles as *something that works*. Christians down the centuries — and, quite probably, people of other faiths as well — will have discovered that for themselves. And so the next hymn exhorts us, "O make but trial of his love: experience will decide . . ." Or, to put it rather more colloquially, we trust in a God who says to us, "You scratch my back, and I'll scratch yours!" A theme to which one might profitably return. Thank you.

Prayers

O Lord God, when thou givest to thy servants to endeavour any great matter, grant us also to know that it is not the beginning, but the continuing of the same until it be thoroughly finished, which yieldeth the true glory; through him who for the finishing of thy work laid down his life, our Redeemer, Jesus Christ.   *Amen.*

O God, our heavenly Father, help us always to be of a good courage. Let us not be disheartened by our difficulties, never doubting thy love nor any of thy promises. Give us grace that we may encourage others and always do our best to make life easier for those who need a friendly word or helping hand; for the sake of Jesus Christ our Lord.   *Amen.*

Save us, O Lord, waking, guard us sleeping, that awake we may watch with Christ, and asleep we may rest in peace.   *Amen.*

A few moments' silence for your own prayers.

The Lord's Prayer.

O Lord, forgive what we have been, sanctify what we are, and order what we shall be.   *Amen.*

The power of the Father, the wisdom of the Son, the love of the Holy Spirit, keep, teach, and guide us for ever.   *Amen.*

SING SOME MORE HYMNS

30th May 2004

Order of Service

Welcome & Notices (Kevin)

    Hymn 236 (Tune: *Carlisle*)
                Breathe on me, Breath of God

Brief introduction (David)

    Hymn 230 (Tune: *St. Cuthbert*)
        Our blest Redeemer, ere he breathed his tender last farewell

First reading (Robert)   Luke, Chapter 4, Verses 1–2 and 14–15;
        Luke, Chapter 10, Verses 17–24; Chapter 12, Verses 8–12;
        John, Chapter 3, Verse 8 *(NEB)*

    Hymn 344 (Tune: *St. Bees*)
                Hark my soul! It is the Lord

Second reading (Robert) "How do you Live Your Dash?" *by Linda*
                                              Ellis

    Hymn 233 (Tune: *Charity*)
                Gracious Spirit, Holy Ghost

Brief chat (David)

    Hymn 298 (Tune: *Lux benigna*)
            Lead, kindly Light, amid the encircling gloom

Prayers (Kevin)

    Hymn 182 (Tune: *Sussex*)
              Father, hear the prayer we offer

The service will proceed without announcements. All the hymns are in *Hymns Ancient & Modern Revised.*

Thank you for coming. Please use the adjacent voting form to list your own favourite hymns for a subsequent service.

This is our third hymns service; and we much appreciate the support you have been giving us. Peter Evans can't be here today, as he is with his family in the Isle of Wight, but he helped a lot with the planning. My brother, Robert, has agreed to do the readings, and Kevin the prayers we have chosen.

So far these services have all coincided with major events in the Church's year: Advent Sunday, the first Sunday of Lent, and now Pentecost, so we have selected hymns for these occasions as well as more general ones. There would be no Christianity without the Holy Spirit, so the festival of Pentecost is as important as any.

In looking for suitable readings, I searched through all the Gospels for references to the Holy Spirit, and was surprised to find that there were not all that many of them. We have chosen a selection of shorter extracts rather than just a single passage, so the first reading may seem a little fragmented. All are from Luke except one well-known verse from John at the end. This has a footnote, by the way, to say that 'wind' and 'spirit' are translated from a single Greek word which has both meanings.

As previously, we shall proceed without announcements. The next hymn is new to me, but it is the first one to be used on account of its having been requested by more than one person. Don't forget to let us know your favourite hymns; we hope that rather fewer of you have done so than expected indicates that you like the selection we make each time.

Luke 4, 1–2, 14–15

Full of the Holy Spirit, Jesus returned from the Jordan, and for forty days was led by the Spirit up and down the wilderness and tempted by the devil.

– – – – –

Then Jesus, armed with the power of the Spirit, returned to Galilee; and reports about him spread through the whole countryside. He taught in their synagogues and all men sang his praises.

Luke 10, 17–24

The seventy-two came back jubilant. "In your name, Lord," they said, "even the devils submit to us." He replied, "I watched how Satan fell, like lightning, out of the sky. And now you see that I have given you the power to tread underfoot snakes and scorpions and all the forces of the enemy, and nothing will ever harm you. Nevertheless, what you should rejoice over is not that the spirits submit to you, but that your names are enrolled in heaven."

At that moment Jesus exulted in the Holy Spirit and said, "I thank thee, Father, Lord of heaven and earth, for hiding these things from the learned and wise, and revealing them to the simple. Yes, Father, such was thy choice." Then turning to his disciples he said, "Everything is entrusted to me by my Father; and no one knows who the Son is but the Father, or who the Father is but the Son, and those to whom the Son may choose to reveal him."

Turning to his disciples in private he said, "Happy the eyes that see what you are seeing! I tell you, many prophets and kings wished to see what you now see, yet never saw it; to hear what you hear, yet never heard it."

Luke 12, 8–12

"I tell you this: everyone who acknowledges me before men, the Son of Man will acknowledge before the angels of God; but he who disowns me before men will be disowned before the angels of God.

"Anyone who speaks a word against the Son of Man will receive forgiveness; but for him who slanders the Holy Spirit there will be no forgiveness.

"When you are brought before synagogues and state authorities, do not begin worrying about how you will conduct your defence or what you will say. For when the time comes the Holy Spirit will instruct you in what to say."

John 3, 8

"The wind blows where it wills; you hear the sound of it, but you do not know where it comes from, or where it is going. So with everyone who is born from spirit."

How do you Live Your Dash?

David Ellis writes:–

My research in March 2019 revealed that this reading turned out to be a very slightly modified version of a poem, *The Dash*, by Linda Ellis, written in 1996, which became immensely popular the world over.

It was a fictional account of someone speaking at a friend's funeral who drew attention to the dates that might have been inscribed on her tombstone, recording when she was born and when she died, with a dash between them; hence the title of the poem.

It was copyright by Southwestern Inspire Kindness, Inc. of Nashville, Tennessee, and you can read it on their website, thedashpoem.com, and also purchase various souvenir items on which it is printed, but when I contacted them for permission to include the poem in our book they thanked me for recognizing their copyright, but said "Sorry, not any more" as they had now granted *exclusive* rights to another book publisher.

ON BEING 'LED'

As I started to work out what I could say to you this time I found myself having to make a compromise between the humility expected of a very ordinary church member and a desire to say something useful.

Having being born into a Christian home and therefore exposed to the Bible and Christian teaching at home and school from an early age, I have at least the experience of trying—admittedly harder at some times than others—to live as one of God's people for over half a century. If that has given me nothing to pass on, something would be seriously wrong.

Some years ago, a good friend agreed to go and see someone on my behalf. "I don't know what I'll say," he said to me, "but I shall be led." " 'I shall be led'?" I thought to myself, "I wonder what he means." But as I knew him to be a sincere Christian, there was really only one answer. And, later, only one deduction: "If Alan can be led, then so can I".

In my university days and after, I was often exhorted in Evangelical sermons, as I am sure you have been, to 'let God rule your life', 'give your life to Jesus' or some such. I must say that I have felt more than a little reluctant to do so, as it seemed to imply going into the religious equivalent of a hypnotic trance and somehow giving up personal control over my actions. As we shall sing in our next hymn, "I was not ever thus, nor prayed that Thou shouldst lead me on". Perhaps you have thought so too. If so, I can assure you that, if I have any personal experience of being 'led', and on occasions I think I may have, *it is not like that at all*.

You are always in the driving seat; you are always the one who makes the decisions, who decides to do this or not to do that. The prime mover in what you choose to do remains your own conscience. Perhaps that's why the prayer says of God, "whose service is perfect freedom". But I think there is more to it than that. You can feel at peace with God or you can be aware of having strayed, 'perverse and foolish', and at the same time confident of the promise inherent in "but yet in love He sought me". Just one tiny step back, one seemingly minor and insignificant decision for God, one step by the lost sheep *towards* the seeking good shepherd, can sometimes make a very big difference. Well, it has for me.

And when feeling at peace with God, and trying to go on making the right choices, you can get a glimpse of having been led to participate in some wider process. Life's a bit like rowing a boat; it's hard to see where you are going, as you're not actually looking in that direction, but you can see where you have been, as the water ripples in the boat's wake, and see how far you have come. You decide to do something, either because you want to or think you ought to, and realize its full implications only afterwards. You try something, not knowing how it will work out, but confident that whatever does happen will be for the best, even if the reason why is not immediately clear. For example, I have sometimes thought that I ought to visit someone, "but if God doesn't want me to see him, he'll be out"! Then you meet someone else quite by chance . . . There can be times when the interplay of events works out so happily and fortuitously that it is hard to believe you are living in the real, rational world. It seems so much more that you are part of a four-dimensional story with an Author.

On this summer evening, we shall have to take the opening line of our next hymn [*Lead, kindly Light, amid the encircling gloom*] in its metaphorical sense, in which it could seem all too true.

Prayers

God who didst give thy Holy Spirit to guide and strengthen thy faithful people, and to bind them into one fellowship; fill us now with the same Spirit, that our hearts may be all on fire to love thee: and loving thee, to love one another. Through Jesus Christ our Lord. *Amen.*

† O God, who art the author of peace and lover of concord, in knowledge of whom standeth our eternal life, whose service is perfect freedom; Defend us thy humble servants in all assaults of our enemies; that we, surely trusting in thy defence, may not fear the power of any adversaries, through the might of Jesus Christ our Lord. *Amen.*

Remember, O Lord, what thou hast wrought in us, and not what we deserve, and as thou hast called us to thy service, make us worthy of our calling; through Jesus Christ our Lord. *Amen.*

A few moments' silence for your own prayers.

The Lord's Prayer.

Save us, O Lord, waking, guard us sleeping, that awake we may watch with Christ, and asleep we may rest in peace. *Amen.*

The power of the Father, the wisdom of the Son, the love of the Holy Spirit, keep, teach, and guide us for ever. *Amen.*

SING SOME MORE HYMNS

31st October 2004

Order of Service

Welcome & Notices (David Hammond)

    Hymn 77 (Tune: *Was lebet*)
        O worship the Lord in the beauty of holiness

Brief introduction (David)

    Hymn 279 (Tune: *Regent Square*)
        Light's abode, celestial Salem

First reading (Peter) Matthew, Chapter 13, Verses 10–23 *(NEB)*

    Hymn 300 (Tune: *Abridge*)
        Be Thou my guardian and my guide

Second reading (Peter) Hebrews, Chapter 11, Verses 1–2, 8–10, 13–16, 23–25, 32–40 *(NEB)*

    Hymn 371 (Tune: *Darwall's 148th*)
        Ye holy angels bright

Brief chat (David)

    Hymn 527 (Tune: *Sine Nomine*)
        For all the saints who from their labours rest

Prayers (Peter)

    Hymn 735 (*Mission Praise;* words on page 25. Tune: *Finlandia*)
        We rest on Thee

The service will proceed without announcements. All the hymns except one (words opposite) are in *Hymns Ancient & Modern Revised.*

Thank you for coming. Please use the voting form overleaf to list your own favourite hymns for a subsequent service.

Kevin has left us to our own devices this time as he wanted to take the opportunity of attending a function he is not usually free for. We thank David Hammond for welcoming everyone and giving out the notices.

This is our fourth hymns service, and it is nearly a year since the first one. For the 'Songs of Praise' to support the Millennium Project people were asked to choose just one hymn. I thought we might get a better consensus by allowing everyone to select up to eight, but so far only a couple of hymns have been asked for by more than one person.

The main reason for this is that only a few of you have been returning the choice forms. We hope this means you like the hymns we have been having, and not that you don't intend to come again! We are quite happy to make the choice ourselves, but do feel free to ask for what you want, or to make any general comments.

Matthew 13, 10–23

The disciples went up to him and asked, "Why do you speak to them in parables?"

He replied, "It has been granted to you to know the secrets of the kingdom of Heaven; but to those others it has not been granted. For the man who has will be given more, till he has enough and to spare; and the man who has not will forfeit even what he has. That is why I speak to them in parables; for they look without seeing, and listen without hearing or understanding. There is a prophecy of Isaiah which is being fulfilled for them: 'You will hear and hear, but never understand; you will look and look, but never see. For this people has grown gross at heart; their ears are dull, and their eyes are closed. Otherwise, their eyes might see, their ears hear, and their heart understand, and then they might turn again, and I would heal them.'

"But happy are your eyes because they see, and your ears because they hear! Many prophets and saints, I tell you, desired to see what you now see, yet never saw it; to hear what you hear, yet never heard it.

"You, then, may hear the parable of the sower. When a man hears the word that tells of the Kingdom but fails to understand it, the evil one comes and carries off what has been sown in his heart. There you have the seed sown along the footpath. The seed sown on rocky ground stands for the man who, on hearing the word, accepts it at once with joy; but as it strikes no root in him he has no staying-power, and when there is trouble or persecution on account of the word he falls away at once. The seed sown among thistles represents the man who hears the word, but worldly cares and the false glamour of wealth choke it, and it proves barren. But the seed that fell into good soil is the man who hears the word and understands it, who accordingly bears fruit, and yields a hundredfold or, it may be, sixtyfold or thirtyfold."

Hebrews 11, 1–2, 8–10, 13–16, 23–25, 32–40

And what is faith? Faith gives substance to our hopes, and makes us certain of realities we do not see.

It is for their faith that the men of old stand on record.

By faith Abraham obeyed the call to go out to a land destined for himself and his heirs, and left home without knowing where he was to go. By faith he settled as an alien in the land promised him, living in tents, as did Isaac and Jacob, who were heirs to the same promise. For he was looking forward to the city with firm foundations, whose architect and builder is God.

All these persons died in faith. They were not yet in possession of the things promised, but had seen them far ahead and hailed them, and confessed themselves no more than strangers or passing travellers on earth. Those who use such language show plainly that they are looking for a country of their own. If their hearts had been in the country they had left, they could have found opportunity to return. Instead, we find them longing for a better country—I mean, the heavenly one. That is why God is not ashamed to be called their God; for he has a city ready for them.

By faith, when Moses was born, his parents hid him for three months, because they saw what a fine child he was; they were not afraid of the king's edict. By faith Moses, when he grew up, refused to be called the son of Pharaoh's daughter, preferring to suffer hardship with the people of God rather than enjoy the transient pleasures of sin.

Need I say more? Time is too short for me to tell the stories of Gideon, Barak, Samson, and Jephthah, of David and Samuel and the prophets. Through faith they overthrew kingdoms, established justice, saw God's promises fulfilled. They muzzled ravening lions, quenched the fury of fire, escaped death by the sword. Their weakness was turned to strength, they grew powerful in war, they put foreign armies to rout. Women received back their dead raised to life. Others were tortured to death, disdaining release, to win a better resurrection. Others, again, had to face jeers and flogging, even fetters and prison bars. They were stoned, they were sawn in two, they were put to the sword, they went about dressed in skins of sheep or goats, in poverty, distress, and misery. They were too good for this world. They were refugees in deserts and on the hills, hiding in caves and holes in the ground. These also, one and all, are commemorated for their faith; and yet they did not enter upon the promised inheritance, because, with us in mind, God had made a better plan, that only in company with us should they reach their perfection.

WHAT ARE SAINTS ?

Tomorrow, being All Saints' Day, has given us yet another theme for our hymns and readings. What can we say about Saints? Are they a special class of people, or are they just at the 'top end' of a continuous scale of God's servants, coming down to ordinary Christians — if any Christian can be ordinary—at the other end?

One thing we might note is that Jesus *chose* his disciples. He asked each one to follow him, but not everyone he asked did so. No one is actually recorded as replying, "No thanks, I'd rather not," but some had things they wanted to do first, and the rich young man who had kept all the Commandments since he was a boy went away with a heavy heart when Jesus suggested he sell all he had, give the money to the poor, and come and follow him. There is a need to respond as well as to be chosen.

We can also note from the Gospel accounts and the conversion of St Paul that people seem to have *become* saints rather than starting life as such. So there is hope for all of us, young or old. As a student I was impressed and inspired to learn from a sermon in chapel that our own College had produced a saint; I wonder how many undergraduates have thought to themselves, if it can produce one, it can produce another? One must have done, for I was told many years later that in fact *two* saints have been members of the College during its 650-year history.[1]

In the first reading Jesus tells his disciples that it has been granted to them to know the secrets of the kingdom of Heaven, before giving them the meaning of his Parable of the Sower. As we can read the Gospels for ourselves, with some at least of Jesus' explanations, we might say that this knowledge has been granted to us as well.

The second reading is about faith, and what has been achieved by some of the people from Old Testament times onwards whose faith has led them on. Faith in this sense is not a matter of accepting intellectual or theological propositions, but of getting on and doing, and if necessary fighting for, what we believe to be right, and trusting God to take care of the consequences.

There have been many saints through the ages, and the Catholic Church continues to name people of our own and recent times. Some have died for the causes they stood for; others have devoted long lives to the service of other people. Some have worked miracles. There must be many more whose deeds have gone unrecognized and unsung, but whose faith has been strong and their devotion to God's work unstinting.

"Thou wast their rock, their fortress, and their might," we shall be singing

---

[1] More information about these saints can be found in the top paragraph on page 206.

in the next hymn. Without that rock, that divine inspiration and encouragement, would there have been any saints? The Gospel for All Saints' Day includes the verse, "How blest are those whose hearts are pure; they shall see God". Are saints those people whose hearts are pure enough at least for the occasional glimpse, or, as St Paul put it, "Now we see only puzzling reflections in a mirror"?

Prayers

Father, we thank Thee for all Thy servants who have bravely followed Thee, and the light of Thy truth, even in the lonely ways. Give us, we beseech Thee, courage and endurance that we also may serve Thee as truly all our lives, through Jesus Christ our Lord. *Amen.*

‡ And here we give thee most high praise and hearty thanks for all thy saints, who have been the chosen vessels of thy grace, and lights of the world in their several generations; and we pray that, rejoicing in their fellowship and following their good examples, we may be partakers with them of thy heavenly kingdom. *Amen.*

A few moments' silence for your own prayers.

The Lord's Prayer.

O God Who is heroic love, keep alive in our hearts that adventurous spirit which makes men scorn the way of safety, so that Your Will can be done. For only so, Lord, may we be worthy of those courageous souls who in every age have ventured all things in obedience to Your call, and for whom the trumpets have sounded on the other side; through Jesus Christ our Lord. *Amen.*

May the Lord lead us when we go, and keep us when we sleep, and talk with us when we wake; may the Lord make His face to shine upon us and be gracious to us; the Lord lift up the light of His countenance upon us and give us peace, this day and for evermore. *Amen.*

We rest on Thee

We rest on Thee, our shield and our defender!
We go not forth alone against the foe;
Strong in Thy strength, safe in Thy keeping tender,
We rest on Thee, and in Thy name we go.
Strong in Thy strength, safe in Thy keeping tender,
We rest on Thee, and in Thy name we go.

Yes, in Thy name, O Captain of salvation!
In Thy dear name, all other names above;
Jesus our righteousness, our sure foundation,
Our Prince of glory and our King of love.
Jesus our righteousness, our sure foundation,
Our Prince of glory and our King of love.

We go in faith, our own great weakness feeling,
And needing more each day Thy grace to know:
Yet from our hearts a song of triumph pealing,
"We rest on Thee, and in Thy name we go."
Yet from our hearts a song of triumph pealing,
"We rest on Thee, and in Thy name we go."

We rest on Thee, our shield and our defender!
Thine is the battle, Thine shall be the praise;
When passing through the gates of pearly splendour,
Victors, we rest with Thee, through endless days.
When passing through the gates of pearly splendour,
Victors, we rest with Thee, through endless days.

Words by Edith Gilling Cherry (1872–97)
Music: Jean Sibelius (1865–1957)

SING SOME MORE HYMNS

30th January 2005

Order of Service

Welcome & Notices (David Hammond)

   Hymn 311 (Tune: *Mannheim*)
           Lead us, heavenly Father, lead us

Brief introduction (David)

   Hymn 166 (Tune: *Old Hundredth*)
           All people that on earth do dwell

First reading (Peter) Luke, Chapter 10, Verses 38–42 *(NEB)*

   Hymn 255 (Tune: *Aurelia*)
           The Church's one foundation

Second reading (Peter) "The Sons of Martha" *by Rudyard Kipling*

   Hymn 372 (Tune: *St. Denio*)
           Immortal, invisible, God only wise

Brief chat (David)

   Hymn 296 (Tune: *Cwm Rhondda*)
           Guide me, O thou great Redeemer

Prayers (Peter)

   Hymn 4 (Tune: *Melcombe*)
           New every morning is the love

The service will proceed without announcements. All the hymns are in *Hymns Ancient & Modern Revised.*

Thank you for coming. Please use the adjacent voting form to list your own favourite hymns for a subsequent service.

Once again Kevin has another function to go to: last time it was the Deanery Youth Service and today it's Derek Spencer's ordination. So we thank David Hammond for his welcoming remarks and for giving out the notices. We are also grateful, as always, to Peter Knowles and the choir for their support.

We were pleased to receive a good batch of choice forms after our October service; a number of very well known hymns were listed and of the six selected for today we were able to pick five that more than one of you had asked for. Please keep them coming in, and if you have any other comments or suggestions, don't forget that these are welcome too. Should we have more hymns, or fewer? Should we change the format of what we have between the hymns? Is four times a year about the right frequency? What should we do about bank holiday weekends, which usually coincide with fifth Sundays?

One of the hymns requested this time is a morning hymn, so as this is an evening service we have put it at the end and hope that when singing it you can think forward to tomorrow—Monday—morning!

Luke 10, 38–42

While they were on their way Jesus came to a village where a woman named Martha made him welcome in her home. She had a sister, Mary, who seated herself at the Lord's feet and stayed there listening to his words. Now Martha was distracted by her many tasks, so she came to him and said, "Lord, do you not care that my sister has left me to get on with the work by myself? Tell her to come and lend a hand." But the Lord answered, "Martha, Martha, you are fretting and fussing about so many things; but one thing is necessary. The part that Mary has chosen is best; and it shall not be taken away from her."

The Sons of Martha

The Sons of Mary seldom bother, for they have inherited that good part;
But the Sons of Martha favour their Mother of the careful soul and the
    troubled heart.
And because she lost her temper once, and because she was rude to the Lord
    her Guest,
Her Sons must wait upon Mary's Sons, world without end, reprieve, or rest.

It is their care in all the ages to take the buffet and cushion the shock.
It is their care that the gear engages; it is their care that the switches lock.
It is their care that the wheels run truly; it is their care to embark and entrain,
Tally, transport, and deliver duly the Sons of Mary by land and main.

They say to mountains, "Be ye removèd." They say to the lesser floods, "Be
   dry."
Under their rods are the rocks reprovèd—they are not afraid of that which is
   high.
Then do the hill-tops shake to the summit—then is the bed of the deep laid
   bare,
That the Sons of Mary may overcome it, pleasantly sleeping and unaware.

They finger death at their gloves' end where they piece and repiece the living
   wires.
He rears against the gates they tend: they feed him hungry behind their fires.
Early at dawn, ere men see clear, they stumble into his terrible stall,
And hale him forth like a haltered steer, and goad and turn him till evenfall.

To these from birth is Belief forbidden; from these till death is Relief afar.
They are concerned with matters hidden—under the earth-line their altars are:
The secret fountains to follow up, waters withdrawn to restore to the mouth,
And gather the floods as in a cup, and pour them again at a city's drouth.

They do not preach that their God will rouse them a little before the nuts work
   loose.
They do not teach that His Pity allows them to drop their job when they dam'-
   well choose.
As in the thronged and the lighted ways, so in the dark and the desert they
   stand,
Wary and watchful all their days that their brethren's days may be long in the
   land.

Raise ye the stone or cleave the wood to make a path more fair or flat—
Lo, it is black already with blood some Son of Martha spilled for that!
Not as a ladder from earth to Heaven, not as a witness to any creed,
But simple service simply given to his own kind in their common need.

And the Sons of Mary smile and are blessèd—they know the Angels are on
   their side.
They know in them is the Grace confessèd, and for them are the Mercies
   multiplied.
They sit at the Feet—they hear the Word—they see how truly the Promise
   runs:
They have cast their burden upon the Lord, and—the Lord He lays it on
   Martha's Sons!

Rudyard Kipling

(1865–1936)

CHRISTIAN WORSHIP IN SCHOOLS

As I have said before, this is only a brief chat, not a sermon, and it will be especially brief today as we have had a longish second reading. For those who haven't guessed, this was another poem by Kipling, giving an original slant to a familiar bible story. Kipling had indeed a detailed knowledge of the Bible and a love of it as literature, and it is said that he often wrote his verses to some hymn tune or other that happened to be running in his head. He also had a strong family link to the Church, as both his grandfathers were Methodist ministers and a great-grandfather on his mother's side was converted to that faith by John Wesley himself.[1]

This is our first hymn service not to coincide with a significant date in the Church calendar, so there is nothing to mark in our choice of hymns. Those selected have two main themes, worship and God's guidance, and there is no need to add any comments of mine to their majestic verses.

What I would like to express, however, is my personal regret and concern that this rich heritage of hymns, both words and music, is in danger of being lost to future generations by its no longer being passed on to children at school in the way that it was when most of us were young. Our school assembly would include a hymn, a reading and some prayers, and this made a good start to the day. I really missed this when I left school. Although the 1988 Education Reform Act provided for a daily non-denominational Christian act of worship, this has been phased out from many schools. In pursuit of multiculturalism and in deference to other faiths, we have allowed our own faith to be sidelined. Let us hope that this process can be reversed before it is too late.

---

[1] For this information I am indebted to M. M. Kaye's Foreword to *Rudyard Kipling: The Complete Verse* (Kyle Cathie, London, 1996), p. xviii.

Prayers

As the quiet splendour of the day dies away, we wait for the shining of the light that never fades. Call us from all that distracts; gather us into the quiet of thy love. Meet with us, O Father, for we seek thy face. *Amen.*

Loving Father, we thank thee for our homes and for all who love and care for us. May we ever be grateful for the good things we enjoy, not taking them for granted, but remembering always to give thanks. For the sake of him who was always thankful in all things, thy Son, our Lord Jesus Christ. *Amen.*

O God, Father and Friend of all: teach us how to be good friends. Help us to be loyal and true to those who love and trust us. Make us the kind of people on whom our friends may depend at all times. For Jesus' sake. *Amen.*

A few moments' silence for your own prayers.

The Lord's Prayer

Be thou, O Lord, within us to strengthen us, above us to protect us, beneath us to uphold us, before us to guide us, behind us to recall us, round us to fortify us. *Amen.*

The power of the Father, the wisdom of the Son, the love of the Holy Spirit, keep, teach, and guide us for ever. *Amen.*

SING SOME MORE HYMNS
29th May 2005

Order of Service

Welcome & Notices (Kevin)
Hymn 373 (Tune: *Richmond*)
Fill thou my life, O Lord my God
Brief introduction (David)
Hymn 160 (Tune: *Nicaea*)
Holy, Holy, Holy! Lord God Almighty!
First reading (Peter) Ephesians, Chapter 1, Verses 11–19 *(NEB)*
Hymn 73 (*M. Praise;* words overleaf. Tune: *Westminster Abbey*)
Christ is made the sure foundation
Second reading (Peter) Revelation, Chapter 21, Verses 1–7 *(NEB)*
Hymn 506 (*M. Praise;* words on p.104. Tune: *How Great Thou Art*)
O Lord my God! When I in awesome wonder
Third reading (David) A quote and an anecdote
Hymn 192 (Tune: *St Peter*)
How sweet the name of Jesus sounds
Prayers (Peter)
Hymn 184 (Tune: *Repton*)
Dear Lord and Father of mankind

The service will proceed without announcements. All the hymns except two (words opposite and overleaf) are in *Hymns Ancient & Modern Revised.*

Thank you for coming. Please use the separate voting form to list your own favourite hymns for a subsequent service.

Christ is made the sure foundation

Christ is made the sure foundation,
Christ the head and corner-stone
Chosen of the Lord and precious,
Binding all the Church in one;
Holy Zion's help for ever,
And her confidence alone.

All within that holy city
Dearly loved of God on high,
In exultant jubilation
Sing, in perfect harmony;
God the One-in-Three adoring
In glad hymns eternally.

We as living stones invoke you:
Come among us, Lord, today!
With Your gracious loving-kindness
Hear Your children as we pray;
And the fulness of Your blessing
In our fellowship display.

Here entrust to all Your servants
What we long from You to gain –
That on earth and in the heavens
We one people shall remain.
Till united in Your glory
Evermore with You we reign.

Praise and honour to the Father,
Praise and honour to the Son,
Praise and honour to the Spirit,
Ever Three and ever One:
One in power and one in glory
While eternal ages run.

Words from the Latin, John Mason Neale
(1818–66)

We welcome Kevin back for this service, and thank David Hammond for his help with the previous two hymns services. We are also grateful, as always, to Peter Knowles and the choir for their support.

It is four months since our service in January, but the next fifth Sunday is only two months away, in July. At least we shall avoid the August bank holiday this year. As I said last time, please keep the choice forms coming in, and don't forget that other comments or suggestions are welcome too. More hymns, or fewer? Should we change the format in any way? And is four times a year about the right frequency?

Ephesians 1, 11–19

In Christ indeed we have been given our share in the heritage, as was decreed in his design whose purpose is everywhere at work. For it was his will that we, who were the first to set our hope on Christ, should cause his glory to be praised. And you too, when you had heard the message of the truth, the good news of your salvation, and had believed it, became incorporate in Christ and received the seal of the promised Holy Spirit; and that Spirit is the pledge that we shall enter upon our heritage, when God has redeemed what is his own, to his praise and glory.

Because of all this, now that I have heard of the faith you have in the Lord Jesus and of the love you bear towards all God's people, I never cease to give thanks for you when I mention you in my prayers. I pray that the God of our Lord Jesus Christ, the all-glorious Father, may give you the spiritual powers of wisdom and vision, by which there comes the knowledge of him. I pray that your inward eyes may be illumined, so that you may know what is the hope to which he calls you, what the wealth and glory of the share he offers you among his people in their heritage, and how vast the resources of his power open to us who trust in him.

Revelation 21, 1–7

Then I saw a new heaven and a new earth, for the first heaven and the first earth had vanished, and there was no longer any sea. I saw the holy city, new Jerusalem, coming down out of heaven from God, made ready like a bride adorned for her husband. I heard a loud voice proclaiming from the throne: "Now at last God has his dwelling among men! He will dwell among them and they shall be his people, and God himself will be with them. He will wipe every tear from their eyes; there shall be an end to death, and to mourning and crying and pain; for the old order has passed away!"

Then he who sat on the throne said, "Behold! I am making all things new!" And he said to me, "Write this down; for these words are trustworthy and true. Indeed", he said, "they are already fulfilled. For I am the Alpha and the Omega, the beginning and the end. A draught from the water-springs of life will be my free gift to the thirsty. All this is the victor's heritage; and I will be his God and he shall be my son."

I decided this time to spare you my 'brief chat', and to fill in a few moments between hymns with a quote and an anecdote, taken from a little book I have of some five hundred of them.[1]

The quote is from Dr William Barclay, who was a well-known writer and evangelist at about the time when I was an undergraduate. 451

Worry refuses to learn the lesson of life. We are still alive and our heads are still above water; and yet if someone had told us what we would have to go through and what we have actually gone through, we would have said it was impossible. The lesson of life is that somehow we have been enabled to bear the unbearable and to do the undoable and to pass the breaking point and not to break. The lesson of life is that worry is unnecessary.

The anecdote is one with a local flavour. 371

A former Duke of Norfolk happened to be at his local railway station when a young Irish girl got off a train. She had come to be a maidservant at the Duke's castle, which was a mile from the station. Having a very heavy bag she tried to persuade the porter to carry it for her and offered him what little money she had.

The porter contemptuously refused, so the Duke, shabbily dressed, offered to take the bag. The two of them walked to the castle, chatting as they went along, and the Duke gratefully accepted the money she gave him. It was not until the following day when the girl was introduced to her employer that she realised who it was who had carried her bag.

---

[1] *Another 500 Quotes & Anecdotes* Compiled by John D. Beasley. Published by South Riding Press, London, 1996 (Numbered in the book as appended.)

Prayers   29th May 2005

Grant, we beseech thee, merciful Lord, to thy faithful people pardon and peace, that we may be cleansed from all our sins, and serve thee with a quiet mind, through Jesus Christ our Lord.   *Amen.*

Almighty God, creator of all, we thank thee for the beauty of the earth and sea and sky, for the happiness of our lives, for peaceful homes and healthful days, for our powers of mind and body, for faithful friends, for the joy of loving and being loved, and above all, for thy care for us made known in Jesus Christ our Lord.   *Amen.*

Grant us, we beseech thee, O Lord, the aid of thy Holy Spirit, that, whatever by his teaching we know to be our duty, we may by his grace be enabled to perform; through Jesus Christ our Lord.   *Amen.*

A few moments' silence for your own prayers.

The Lord's Prayer.

May the Lord lead us when we go, and keep us when we sleep, and talk with us when we wake; and may the peace of God, which passes all understanding, keep our hearts and minds in Jesus Christ our Lord.   *Amen.*

SING SOME MORE HYMNS

31st July 2005

Order of Service

Welcome & Notices (Kevin)

Hymn 365 (Tune: *Praise, my soul*)
Praise, my soul, the King of heaven

Brief introduction (David)

Hymn 361 (Tune: *Nottingham*)
Take my life, and let it be

First reading (Peter) Luke, Chapter 10, Verses 25–37 *(NEB)*

Hymn 281 (*Mission Praise;* words opposite)
I lift my eyes to the quiet hills

Second reading (Peter) "A Little Carved Horse"

Hymn 31 (*Mission Praise;* words overleaf. Tune: *Amazing Grace*)
Amazing grace – how sweet the sound

Brief chat (David)

Hymn 225 (Tune: *Evelyns*)
At the name of Jesus

Prayers (Peter)

Hymn 27 (Tune: *Eventide*)
Abide with me; fast falls the eventide

The service will proceed without announcements. All the hymns except two (words opposite and overleaf) are in *Hymns Ancient & Modern Revised.*

Thank you for coming. Please use the separate voting form to list your own favourite hymns for a subsequent service.

I lift my eyes

I lift my eyes
To the quiet hills,
In the press of a busy day;
As green hills stand
In a dusty land,
So God is my strength and stay.

I lift my eyes
To the quiet hills,
To a calm that is mine to share;
Secure and still
In the Father's will
And kept by the Father's care.

I lift my eyes
To the quiet hills,
With a prayer as I turn to sleep;
By day, by night,
Through the dark and light
My Shepherd will guard His sheep.

I lift my eyes
To the quiet hills,
And my heart to the Father's throne;
In all my ways,
To the end of days
The Lord will preserve His own.

Words from Psalm 121   *Timothy Dudley-Smith (b.1926)*

Amazing grace

Amazing grace – how sweet the sound –
That saved a wretch like me!
I once was lost, but now am found,
Was blind, but now I see.

'Twas grace that taught my heart to fear,
And grace my fears relieved;
How precious did that grace appear
The hour I first believed.

Through many dangers, toils and snares,
I have already come;
'Tis grace hath brought me safe thus far,
And grace will lead me home.

When we've been there ten thousand years
Bright shining as the sun,
We've no less days to sing God's praise
Than when we've first begun.

John Newton   (1725–1807)

We thank Kevin for welcoming you to this service, and Peter Knowles and the choir for their support. We are still getting back a relatively small proportion of the hymn choice forms. This means, of course, that if you do complete one there is a very good chance of one of your hymns being selected. Do be sure to come along and sing it! The hymns for each service are listed in advance in the parish magazine, so don't forget to look.

Luke 10, 25–37

On one occasion a lawyer came forward to put this test question to him: "Master, what must I do to inherit eternal life?" Jesus said, "What is written in the Law? What is your reading of it?" He replied, "Love the Lord your God with all your heart, with all your soul, with all your strength, and with all your mind; and your neighbour as yourself." "That is the right answer," said Jesus; "do that and you will live."

But he wanted to vindicate himself, so he said to Jesus, "And who is my neighbour?" Jesus replied, "A man was on his way from Jerusalem down to Jericho when he fell in with robbers, who stripped him, beat him, and went off leaving him half dead. It so happened that a priest was going down by the same road; but when he saw him, he went past on the other side. So too a Levite came to the place, and when he saw him went past on the other side. But a Samaritan who was making the journey came upon him, and when he saw him was moved to pity. He went up and bandaged his wounds, bathing them with oil and wine. Then he lifted him on to his own beast, brought him to an inn, and looked after him there. Next day he produced two silver pieces and gave them to the inn-keeper, and said, 'Look after him; and if you spend any more, I will repay you on my way back.' Which of these three do you think was neighbour to the man who fell into the hands of the robbers?" He answered, "The one who showed him kindness." Jesus said, "Go and do as he did."

A Little Carved Horse

One day, an old woman was standing outside a big shop on a busy street. She was waiting for a friend. The buses and cars rushed up and down the street. The people pushed past her looking very cross and the old woman felt very tired.

All at once, she saw a man looking at her. She thought that he must be lonely or that she reminded him of someone else. So she gave him a nice smile. At that he smiled too and came over to her. He opened a brown paper bag that he had in his hand. "I would like to give you a present," he said and put into her hand a little carved horse.

He was going to turn away without saying anything more, but the old woman said, "Why have you given me this?"

"I work at night as a watchman," said the man, "and I carve these little things out of bits of scrap wood that I pick up from the floor where I work. When I have carved a few, I walk along the street until I see someone that I think would like a present."

"Where did you learn to carve?" asked the old woman.

"No one ever showed me," he smiled. "Where I come from everyone carves."

Just then, the old woman's friend came out of the shop and saw the little carved horse. "Why," she cried, "This is quite beautiful! My sister has a gift shop and if you bring some more of them to her I'm sure that she could sell them for you."

But the man shook his head. "If I sold them, it would be just another job. I like to give them away." He gave her a nice smile and walked away into the crowd.

The old woman never saw the man again, but she always kept the little wooden horse and it became one of her treasures. It made her happy when she looked at it and she liked to think of the man who carved the little horses out of scrap wood and went up and down streets giving them away. And she thought of all the people in the busy city who had a little carved horse to make them happy.

WHAT DOES BEING A CHRISTIAN MEAN TO US ?

When we started these services just over eighteen months ago, I thought it would not be too difficult to think of something to say for a couple of minutes on each occasion, to fill one of the gaps between the hymns. However, inspiration is not always something that can be commanded and even though my aim has been a brief chat and not a sermon it hasn't seemed quite so easy this year as last. That's one reason why in May you had a quote and an anecdote instead.

When I started work in the Harlow area in the mid-sixties, I went along to evening service in the local church. Harlow being a new town, this was a light, airy, modern building. One thing they did that impressed me was to replace the sermon, over a period of several weeks, with a series of short talks by members of the congregation (one was someone I knew at work) on what being a Christian meant to each of them. Maybe we could do the same, which would give you the chance to hear someone else's ideas, or even to hold forth yourself! Just to think what one might say could well be a useful exercise.

For myself, I have tried to convey the conviction that Christianity is a simple religion, to state even if not necessarily to carry out. It was stated very clearly in our first reading, in the lawyer's initial reply to Jesus. Our two readings have exemplified large and small ways of doing things for other people: the traveller caring for the man who had been beaten and robbed and the nightwatchman giving away his little carved horses just to bring a little cheer to people he met in the street.

The Christian message itself must surely bring us all a lot of cheer: that this world we live in, in many ways beautiful but sometimes hostile and dangerous, is presided over by the God that Jesus taught us about, who is concerned for each one of us and has a purpose for His creation.

Christianity is not a set of abstract principles, but an attitude to life and a way of living *that has to be tried*. It may seem dauntingly difficult to put it into practice, but when we try to do so we often find that help is forthcoming, sometimes in unexpected ways.[1] So the encouragement that we can get from our religion is that it does actually seem to work.

I look forward to hearing what someone else has to say in October!

---

[1] Even the Good Samaritan had some help. He found an innkeeper who was willing to look after the injured man, on credit if need be.

Prayers

O God, our Father, give to the nations of the world a new heart of comradeship, that every people may bring its tribute of excellence to the common treasury, and all the world may go forward in the way which Christ has consecrated for us, until we come to that perfect kingdom into which all the nations shall bring their glory; through Jesus Christ.   *Amen.*

We praise thy name, O Father, for the beauty of the summer, the glory of the sky by day and night, the healthful wind and quickening rain. We thank thee for the bloom and fragrance of the flowers, the songs of the birds, and the joyousness of every living thing. In all that thou hast made we see the wonder of thy wisdom and care. Help us to trust thy never-failing goodness, the love which is beyond understanding, and surrounds our lives with blessing, for thy name's sake.   *Amen.*

Forgive, O Lord, all our sins today. Take away from us all weakness in resisting the wrong, and give us courage to stand for all that is true, pure, loyal, and unselfish. Forgive what we have been, sanctify what we are, and direct what we shall be. Grant this, O Father, for Jesus Christ's sake.   *Amen.*

A few moments' silence for your own prayers.

The Lord's Prayer.

May the blessing of almighty God rest upon us and upon all our work; may he give us light to guide us, courage to support us, and love to unite us, now and evermore.   *Amen.*

SING SOME MORE HYMNS

30th October 2005

Order of Service

Welcome & Notices (Kevin)

Hymn 50 (*Mission Praise;* words overleaf)
Be still, for the presence of the Lord

Brief introduction (David)

Hymn 163 (Tune: *Capetown*)
Three in One, and One in Three

First reading (Peter) Luke, Chapter 6, Verses 46–49 *(NEB)*

Hymn 304 (Tune: *Duke Street*)
Fight the good fight with all thy might

Second reading (David) Luke, Chapter 6, Verses 27–38 *(NEB)*

Hymn 197 (Tune: *Dominus regit me*)
The King of love my Shepherd is

Brief chat (Clive Seeley)

Hymn 33 (Tune: *St. Clement*)
The day thou gavest, Lord, is ended

Prayers (Peter)

Hymn 278 (Tune: *Ewing*)
Jerusalem the golden

The service will proceed without announcements. All the hymns except one (words opposite) are in *Hymns Ancient & Modern Revised.*

Thank you for coming. Please use the separate voting form to list your own favourite hymns for a subsequent service.

Be still, for the presence of the Lord

Be still,
    for the presence of the Lord,
      the Holy One, is here;
Come bow before Him now
With reverence and fear:
In Him no sin is found –
We stand on holy ground.
Be still,
    for the presence of the Lord,
      the Holy One, is here.

Be still,
    for the glory of the Lord
      is shining all around;
He burns with holy fire,
With splendour He is crowned:
How awesome is the sight –
Our radiant King of light!
Be still,
    for the glory of the Lord
      is shining all around.

Be still,
    for the power of the Lord
      is moving in this place:
He comes to cleanse and heal,
To minister His grace –
No work too hard for Him.
In faith receive from Him.
Be still,
    for the power of the Lord
      is moving in this place.

David J.Evans

Once again I thank Kevin for welcoming you to this service, and the choir for their support. Peter Knowles is on holiday today, so my brother, Robert, will be accompanying us on the piano instead, and we thank him for his assistance with this.

Thanks also to those who returned completed hymn choice forms. I hope we have selected hymns you all like.

And finally my especial thanks to Clive, who has taken up my challenge to tackle the 'brief chat' this evening. I am much looking forward to hearing what he has to say. I am also pleased to report that Philip has been preparing something for January.

Next year there will be five fifth Sundays, but whether we take them all up and have a service on New Year's Eve has yet to be decided!

Luke 6, 46–49

"Why do you keep calling me 'Lord, Lord'—and never do what I tell you? Everyone who comes to me and hears what I say, and acts upon it—I will show you what he is like. He is like a man who, in building his house, dug deep and laid the foundations on rock. When the flood came, the river burst upon that house, but could not shift it, because it had been soundly built. But he who hears and does not act is like a man who built his house on the soil without foundations. As soon as the river burst upon it, the house collapsed, and fell with a great crash."

Luke 6, 27–38

"But to you who hear me I say:–

"Love your enemies; do good to those who hate you; bless those who curse you; pray for those who treat you spitefully. When a man hits you on the cheek, offer him the other cheek too; when a man takes your coat, let him have your shirt as well. Give to everyone who asks you; when a man takes what is yours, do not demand it back. Treat others as you would like them to treat you.

"If you love only those who love you, what credit is that to you? Even sinners love those who love them. Again, if you do good only to those who do good to you, what credit is that to you? Even sinners do as much. And if you lend only where you expect to be repaid, what credit is that to you? Even sinners lend to each other if they are to be repaid in full. But you must love your enemies and do good; and lend without expecting any return; and you will have a rich reward: you will be sons of the Most High, because he himself is kind to the ungrateful and wicked. Be compassionate as your Father is compassionate.

46

"Pass no judgement, and you will not be judged; do not condemn, and you will not be condemned; acquit, and you will be acquitted; give, and gifts will be given you. Good measure, pressed down, shaken together, and running over, will be poured into your lap; for whatever measure you deal out to others will be dealt to you in return."

Regrettably, we do not have a record of what Clive Seeley had to say, as he spoke without notes or a pre-printed text. [Clive died in September 2013.]

Prayers

Grant, we beseech thee, merciful Lord, to thy faithful people pardon and peace, that we may be cleansed from all our sins, and serve thee with a quiet mind; through Jesus Christ our Lord. *Amen.*

O merciful Father, whose will it is that we should love one another, give us grace that we may fulfil it. Make us gentle, courteous and forbearing. Direct our lives so that we may each look to the good of the other in word and deed; and hallow all our friendships by the blessing of thy Spirit, for his sake who loved us and gave himself for us, Jesus Christ our Lord. *Amen.*

Blessed are thy Saints, O God and King, who have crossed the stormy seas of this mortal life, and have reached the harbour of peace and joy. Watch over us who are still on our dangerous voyage, and remember those who are exposed to the rough storms of trouble and temptations. Frail is our vessel, and the ocean is wide; but as in thy mercy thou hast set our course, so pilot the vessel of our life toward the everlasting shore of peace, and bring us at length to the quiet haven of our hearts' desire, where thou, O our God, art blessed and reignest in glory for ever and ever. *Amen.*

A few moments' silence for your own prayers.

The Lord's Prayer.

As the quiet splendour of the day dies away, we wait for the shining of the light that never fades. Call us from all that distracts; gather us into the quiet of thy love. Meet with us O Father, for we seek thy face. *Amen.*

May the love and friendship of Jesus go with us now and his Spirit abide with us for ever. *Amen.*

SING SOME MORE HYMNS

29th January 2006

Order of Service

Welcome & Notices (Kevin)

  Hymn 221 (Tune: *Nativity*)

        Come, let us join our cheerful songs

Brief introduction (David)

  Hymn 216 (Tune: *Gopsal*)

        Rejoice! The Lord is King!

First reading (Peter) Psalm 128 *(NEB)*

  Hymn 167 (Tune: *Hanover*)

        O worship the King all glorious above

Second reading (David) Luke, Chapter 2, Verses 39–52 *(NEB)*

  Hymn 382 (Tune: *Praxis pietatis*)

        Praise to the Lord, the Almighty, the King of creation

Brief chat (Philip Newman)

  Hymn 220 (Tune: *Truro*)

        Jesus shall reign where'er the sun

Prayers (Peter)

  Hymn 631 (*Mission Praise;* words overleaf. Tune: *Woodlands*)

        Tell out, my soul

The service will proceed without announcements. All the hymns except one (words opposite) are in *Hymns Ancient & Modern Revised.*

Thank you for coming. Please use the separate voting form to list your own favourite hymns for a subsequent service.

Tell out, my soul

Tell out, my soul, the greatness of the Lord!
Unnumbered blessings give my spirit voice;
Tender to me the promise of His word;
In God my Saviour shall my heart rejoice.

Tell out, my soul, the greatness of His name!
Make known His might, the deeds His arm has done;
His mercy sure, from age to age the same;
His holy name, the Lord, the Mighty One.

Tell out, my soul, the greatness of His might!
Powers and dominions lay their glory by.
Proud hearts and stubborn wills are put to flight,
The hungry fed, the humble lifted high.

Tell out, my soul, the glories of His word!
Firm is His promise, and His mercy sure.
Tell out, my soul, the greatness of the Lord
To children's children and for evermore!

Words from Luke 1   *Timothy Dudley-Smith (b.1926)*

Thank you all for coming, and this time especially to Philip, who has taken on the 'brief chat', and to Clive, for his sterling work on this last time. Any offers for next time will of course be welcomed.

As Peter Knowles is away again we are grateful once more to Robert for accompanying us on the piano, and, as usual, to the choir for their support. And thanks to Kevin for welcoming you and getting the service started.

We didn't have many hymn choice forms back this time, which is one reason why Peter and I chose the first hymn ourselves. (The other reason is that we were finding it a little difficult to select one that went well with the other five hymns you've chosen.) Maybe some of you have already told us all your favourite hymns. If you are not sure where to drop your completed forms in, Nightingales is a turning off Haglands Lane just past the shops.

This is our ninth hymn service, and so far we have not repeated any hymn, which means we have had fifty-four well-known or well-liked hymns. And there are still plenty of good ones we haven't had.

Psalm 128

Happy are all who fear the LORD,
> who live according to his will.
You shall eat the fruit of your own labours,
> you shall be happy and you shall prosper.
Your wife shall be like a fruitful vine
> in the heart of your house;
your sons shall be like olive-shoots
> round about your table.
This is the blessing in store for the man
> who fears the LORD.
May the LORD bless you from Zion;
> may you share the prosperity of Jerusalem
all the days of your life,
> and live to see your children's children!

Peace be upon Israel!

Luke 2, 39–52

When they had done everything prescribed in the law of the Lord, they returned to Galilee to their own town of Nazareth. The child grew big and strong and full of wisdom; and God's favour was upon him.

Now it was the practice of his parents to go to Jerusalem every year for the Passover festival; and when he was twelve, they made the pilgrimage as usual. When the festive season was over and they started for home, the boy Jesus stayed behind in Jerusalem. His parents did not know of this; but thinking that he was with the party they journeyed on for a whole day, and only then did they begin looking for him among their friends and relations. As they could not find him they returned to Jerusalem to look for him; and after three days they found him sitting in the temple surrounded by the teachers, listening to them and putting questions; and all who heard him were amazed at his intelligence and the answers he gave.

His parents were astonished to see him there, and his mother said to him, "My son, why have you treated us like this? Your father and I have been searching for you in great anxiety."

"What made you search?" he said. "Did you not know that I was bound to be in my Father's house?"

But they did not understand what he meant. Then he went back with them to Nazareth, and continued to be under their authority; his mother treasured up all these things in her heart. As Jesus grew up he advanced in wisdom and in favour with God and men.

Philip sent me a note before the service to say that he felt his talk should be styled as a Brief Homily rather than a Brief Chat, but we do not seem to have a record of what he said. DJE

Prayers

Help us, O Father, always to trust in thy goodness, and to cast all our cares upon thee; that walking with thee and following thee in all simplicity, we may possess quiet and contented minds; through Jesus Christ our Lord.   *Amen.*

We praise and bless thy holy name, O Lord, for all those who have laboured to serve the cause of freedom and good government in this land, and for all who have striven to uphold the sanctity of the home and family; for all who have sought to bless mankind by their sacrifice and service, and for all who have given their lives to enlarge the bounds of thy Kingdom on earth. For all the prophets, patriarchs and martyrs, and for all obscure and humble saints, we bless and praise thy holy name, through Jesus Christ our Lord.   *Amen.*

Most gracious God, who hast been merciful unto us not only in the year past but through all the years of our life, pardon our sins, fashion in us those virtues which are acceptable to thee, and grant that in sincerity we may serve thee more faithfully in the year that is to come, for Jesus Christ's sake. *Amen.*

Almighty God, who rulest the changing seasons, we bless thee that beneath all that now seems cold and dead, thou art keeping safe the hidden germs of life. Still thou dost clothe all things around us with beauty, sending forth thy frost and snow, filling the brief day with sunshine, and making the night glorious with countless stars. We thank thee for the shelter and comfort of our homes, and pray for those in poverty or sickness who shrink from the cold. Through Jesus Christ our Lord.   *Amen.*

A few moments' silence for your own prayers.

The Lord's Prayer.

† May the Lord bless us and keep us; the Lord make his face to shine upon us and be gracious to us; the Lord lift up the light of his countenance upon us and give us peace, this night and for evermore.   *Amen.*

SING SOME MORE HYMNS
30th April 2006

Order of Service

Welcome & Notices (Kevin)

Hymn 171 (Tune: *England's Lane*)
For the beauty of the earth

Brief introduction (David)

Hymn 99 (Tune: *Winchester New*)
Ride on! Ride on in majesty!

First reading (Peter) Mark, Chapter 11, Verses 1–11 *(NEB)*

Hymn 108 (Tune: *Rockingham*)
When I survey the wondrous Cross

Second reading (Peter) Luke, Chapter 23, Verses 32–48 *(NEB)*

Hymn 140 (Tune: *St. Albinus*)
Jesus lives! Thy terrors now

Third reading (David) Luke, Chapter 24, Verses 13–53 *(NEB)*

Hymn 157 (Tune: *Veni, creator Spiritus*)
Come, Holy Ghost, our souls inspire

Prayers (Peter)

Hymn 224 (Tune: *Diademata*)
Crown him with many crowns

The service will proceed without announcements. All the hymns are in *Hymns Ancient & Modern Revised.*

Thank you for coming. Please use the voting form opposite to list your own favourite hymns for a subsequent service.

As this service is quite close to Easter, we thought we would do it slightly differently this time. From the hymns people had asked for, we chose a sequence running from Palm Sunday to Pentecost, with readings to go with them, which has resulted in three readings instead of two, and no need for anyone to provide the 'brief chat'.

Once again I thank Kevin for welcoming you to this service, and my brother, Robert, for accompanying us on the piano.

Don't forget the hymn choice forms, which are on the service sheets this time. Now we have had sixty different hymns we could perhaps start having some of the more popular ones again.

The next hymn service will be in July.

Mark 11, 1–11

They were now approaching Jerusalem, and when they reached Bethphage and Bethany, at the Mount of Olives, he sent two of his disciples with these instructions: "Go to the village opposite, and, just as you enter, you will find tethered there a colt which no one has yet ridden. Untie it and bring it here. If anyone asks, 'Why are you doing that?', say, 'Our Master needs it, and will send it back here without delay.'"

So they went off, and found the colt tethered to a door outside in the street. They were untying it when some of the bystanders asked, "What are you doing, untying that colt?" They answered as Jesus had told them, and were then allowed to take it. So they brought the colt to Jesus and spread their cloaks on it, and he mounted.

And people carpeted the road with their cloaks, while others spread brushwood which they had cut in the fields; and those who went ahead and the others who came behind shouted, "Hosanna! Blessings on him who comes in the name of the Lord! Blessings on the coming kingdom of our father David! Hosanna in the heavens!"

He entered Jerusalem and went into the temple, where he looked at the whole scene; but, as it was now late, he went out to Bethany with the Twelve.

Luke 23, 32–48

There were two others with him, criminals who were being led away to execution; and when they reached the place called The Skull, they crucified him there, and the criminals with him, one on his right and the other on his left. Jesus said, "Father, forgive them; they do not know what they are doing."

54

They divided his clothes among them by casting lots. The people stood looking on, and their rulers jeered at him: "He saved others: now let him save himself, if this is God's Anointed, his Chosen." The soldiers joined in the mockery and came forward offering him their sour wine. "If you are the king of the Jews," they said, "save yourself." There was an inscription above his head which ran: "This is the king of the Jews."

One of the criminals who hung there with him taunted him: "Are not you the Messiah? Save yourself, and us." But the other answered sharply, "Have you no fear of God? You are under the same sentence as he. For us it is plain justice; we are paying the price for our misdeeds; but this man has done nothing wrong." And he said, "Jesus, remember me when you come to your throne." "He answered, "I tell you this: today you shall be with me in Paradise."

By now it was about midday and there came a darkness over the whole land, which lasted until three in the afternoon; the sun was in eclipse. And the curtain of the temple was torn in two. Then Jesus gave a loud cry and said, "Father, into thy hands I commit my spirit"; and with these words he died. The centurion saw it all, and gave praise to God. "Beyond all doubt," he said, "this man was innocent."

The crowd who had assembled for the spectacle, when they saw what had happened, went home beating their breasts.

Luke 24, 13–53

That same day two of them were on their way to a village called Emmaus, which lay about seven miles from Jerusalem, and they were talking together about all these happenings. As they talked and discussed it with one another, Jesus himself came up and walked along with them; but something held their eyes from seeing who it was. He asked them, "What is it you are debating as you walk?" They halted, their faces full of gloom, and one, called Cleopas, answered, "Are you the only person staying in Jerusalem not to know what has happened there in the last few days?" "What do you mean?" he said.

"All this about Jesus of Nazareth," they replied, "a prophet powerful in speech and action before God and the whole people; how our chief priests and rulers handed him over to be sentenced to death, and crucified him. But we had been hoping that he was the man to liberate Israel. What is more, this is the third day since it happened, and now some women of our company have astounded us: they went early to the tomb, but failed to find his body, and returned with a story that they had seen a vision of angels who told them he was alive. So some of our people went to the tomb and found things just as the women had said; but him they did not see."

"How dull you are!" he answered. "How slow to believe all that the prophets said! Was the Messiah not bound to suffer thus before entering upon his glory?" Then he began with Moses and all the prophets, and explained to them the passages which referred to himself in every part of the scriptures.

By this time they had reached the village to which they were going, and he made as if to continue his journey, but they pressed him: "Stay with us, for evening draws on, and the day is almost over." So he went in to stay with them. And when he had sat down with them at table, he took bread and said the blessing; he broke the bread, and offered it to them. Then their eyes were opened, and they recognized him; and he vanished from their sight. They said to one another, "Did we not feel our hearts on fire as he talked with us on the road and explained the scriptures to us?"

Without a moment's delay they set out and returned to Jerusalem. There they found that the Eleven and the rest of the company had assembled, and were saying, "It is true: the Lord has risen; he has appeared to Simon." Then they gave their account of the events of their journey and told how he had been recognized by them at the breaking of the bread.

As they were talking about all this, there he was, standing among them. Startled and terrified, they thought they were seeing a ghost. But he said, "Why are you so perturbed? Why do questionings arise in your minds? Look at my hands and feet. It is I myself. Touch me and see; no ghost has flesh and bones as you can see that I have." They were still unconvinced, still wondering, for it seemed too good to be true. So he asked them, "Have you anything here to eat?" They offered him a piece of fish they had cooked, which he took and ate before their eyes.

And he said to them, "This is what I meant by saying, while I was still with you, that everything written about me in the Law of Moses and in the prophets and psalms was bound to be fulfilled." Then he opened their minds to understand the scriptures. "This," he said, "is what is written: that the Messiah is to suffer death and to rise from the dead on the third day, and that in his name repentance bringing the forgiveness of sins is to be proclaimed to all nations. Begin from Jerusalem: it is you who are the witnesses to all this. And mark this: I am sending upon you my Father's promised gift; so stay here in this city until you are armed with the power from above."

Then he led them out as far as Bethany, and blessed them with uplifted hands; and in the act of blessing he parted from them. And they returned to Jerusalem with great joy, and spent all their time in the temple praising God.

Prayers

Almighty God, our creator and preserver, we thank thee for the springtime, in which thou art renewing the face of the earth and quickening all things. Thou who carest for the trees and flowers, revive and renew our life, that we may bring forth the fruit of good works, as disciples of him who came to quicken in human hearts the seed of eternal life; through Jesus Christ our Lord.
Amen.

O God, who hast made the heaven and the earth and all that is good and lovely therein, and hast shown us through Jesus, our Lord, that the secret of joy is a heart set free from selfish desires; help us to find delight in simple things and ever to rejoice in the richness of thy bounty; through the same Jesus Christ our Lord.
Amen.

O almighty God, the Father of all mankind, we pray thee to turn to thyself the hearts of all peoples and their rulers, that by the power of thy Holy Spirit peace may be established on the foundation of justice, righteousness, and truth; through him who was lifted up on the Cross to draw all men unto himself, even thy Son Jesus Christ our Lord.
Amen.

Almighty God, grant to us, we beseech thee, strength to do what is right, courage to do what is difficult, and grace to deny ourselves for the sake of others. May we be more willing to follow in the steps of Jesus Christ, our Lord, who steadfastly endured the Cross, giving his life for the world, who now liveth and reigneth with thee and the Holy Spirit, one God, world without end.
Amen.

A few moments' silence for your own prayers.

The Lord's Prayer.

O Lord, we beseech thee mercifully to receive our prayers; and grant that we may both perceive and know what things we ought to do, and also may have grace and power faithfully to fulfil the same; through Jesus Christ our Lord.
Amen.

May the love and friendship of Jesus go with us now and his Spirit abide with us for ever.
Amen.

SING SOME MORE HYMNS

30th July 2006

Order of Service

Welcome & Notices (David)

Hymn 205 (Tune: *Love Divine*)
  Love divine, all loves excelling

Brief introduction (David)

Hymn 483 (Tune: *Wir pflügen*)
  We plough the fields, and scatter the good seed on the land

First reading (Peter) Mark, Chapter 4, Verses 1–9 *(NEB)*

Hymn 271 (Tune: *Benson*)
  God is working his purpose out as year succeeds to year

Second reading (Peter) Mark, Chapter 4, Verses 10–20 *(NEB)*

Hymn 224 (*Mission Praise;* words overleaf. Tune: *Monks Gate*)
  He who would valiant be

Third reading (David) Matthew, Chapter 22, Verses 15–22 *(NEB)*

Hymn 182 (Tune: *Gott will's machen*)
  Father, hear the prayer we offer

Prayers (Peter)

Hymn 23 (Tune: *Canon*)
  Glory to thee, my God, this night

The service will proceed without announcements. All the hymns are in *Hymns Ancient & Modern Revised,* but for *He who would valiant be* we are using the version in *Mission Praise.*

Thank you for coming. Please use the separate voting form to list your own favourite hymns for a subsequent service.

He who would valiant be

He who would valiant be
'gainst all disaster,
Let him in constancy
Follow the Master.
There's no discouragement
Shall make him once relent,
His first avowed intent
To be a pilgrim.

Who so beset him round
With dismal stories,
Do but themselves confound –
His strength the more is.
No foes shall stay his might,
Though he with giants fight:
He will make good his right
To be a pilgrim.

Since, Lord, Thou dost defend
Us with Thy Spirit,
We know we at the end
Shall life inherit.
Then fancies flee away!
I'll fear not what men say,
I'll labour night and day
To be a pilgrim.

After John Bunyan (1628–88)
Percy Dearmer (1867–1936)

Apart from the first one, this service is the first for which no one returned any hymn choice forms. So we thought that as we had had ten of these services so far, all with different hymns, making sixty hymns in all, we would select some that we had already had, especially when they had been asked for several times. We hope you will like them, and also that you will let us have your preferences for next time. In order to print the selection in advance in the parish magazine, we need to have them early in the previous month.

For today's service, in the absence of a volunteer or some inspiration on my part, we have avoided the 'brief chat' by having three readings instead of two. However, with the hymns, readings and prayers, familiar as they may be, seeming to convey a clearer message than usual, perhaps the need for any further comment is that much the less.

Once again I thank my brother, Robert, for accompanying us on the piano, and also for the recital before the service.

The next hymn service will be in October. Please think between now and then about whether you would be willing to come to another service on New Year's Eve.

Mark 4, 1–9

On another occasion he began to teach by the lake-side. The crowd that gathered round him was so large that he had to get into a boat on the lake, and there he sat, with the whole crowd on the beach right down to the water's edge. And he taught them many things by parables.

As he taught he said:–

"Listen! A sower went out to sow. And it happened that as he sowed, some seed fell along the footpath; and the birds came and ate it up. Some seed fell on rocky ground, where it had little soil, and it sprouted quickly because it had no depth of earth; but when the sun rose the young corn was scorched, and as it had no proper root it withered away. Some seed fell among thistles; but the thistles shot up and choked the corn, and it yielded no crop. And some of the seed fell into good soil, where it came up and grew, and bore fruit; and the yield was thirtyfold, sixtyfold, even a hundredfold." He added, "If you have ears to hear, then hear."

Mark 4, 10–20

When he was alone, the Twelve and others who were round him questioned him about the parables. He replied, "To you the secret of the kingdom of God has been given; but to those who are outside everything comes by way of parables, so that (as Scripture says) they may look and look, but see nothing; they may hear and hear, but understand nothing; otherwise they might turn to God and be forgiven."

So he said, "You do not understand this parable? How then are you to understand any parable? The sower sows the word. Those along the footpath are people in whom the word is sown, but no sooner have they heard it than Satan comes and carries off the word which has been sown in them. It is the same with those who receive the seed on rocky ground; as soon as they hear the word, they accept it with joy, but it strikes no root in them; they have no staying-power; then, when there is trouble or persecution on account of the word, they fall away at once. Others again receive the seed among thistles; they hear the word, but worldly cares and the false glamour of wealth and all kinds of evil desire come in and choke the word, and it proves barren. And there are those who receive the seed in good soil; they hear the word and welcome it; and they bear fruit thirtyfold, sixtyfold, or a hundredfold."

Matthew 22, 15–22

Then the Pharisees went and agreed on a plan to trap him in his own words. Some of their followers were sent to him in company with men of Herod's party. They said, "Master, you are an honest man, we know; you teach in all honesty the way of life that God requires, truckling to no man, whoever he may be. Give us your ruling on this: are we or are we not permitted to pay taxes to the Roman Emperor?"

Jesus was aware of their malicious intention and said to them, "You hypocrites! Why are you trying to catch me out? Show me the money in which the tax is paid."

They handed him a silver piece. Jesus asked, "Whose head is this, and whose inscription?" "Caesar's," they replied. He said to them, "Then pay Caesar what is due to Caesar, and pay God what is due to God." This answer took them by surprise, and they went away and left him alone.

Prayers

Almighty God, grant to us, we beseech thee, strength to do what is right, courage to do what is difficult, and grace to deny ourselves for the sake of others. May we be more willing to follow in the steps of Jesus Christ, our Lord, who steadfastly endured the Cross, giving his life for the world, who now liveth and reigneth with thee and the Holy Spirit, one God, world without end. *Amen.*

We praise thy name, O Father, for the beauty of the summer, the glory of the sky by day and night, the healthful wind and quickening rain. We thank thee for the bloom and fragrance of the flowers, the songs of the birds, and the joyousness of every living thing. In all that thou has made we see the wonder of thy wisdom and care. Help us to trust thy never-failing goodness, the love which is beyond understanding, and surrounds our lives with blessing, for thy name's sake. *Amen.*

O almighty God, who makest the clouds thy chariots, and walkest upon the wings of the wind; we beseech thee for all who travel by air to their several duties and destinations; that thy presence may ever be with them, to pilot, and to protect; through Jesus Christ our Lord. *Amen.*

A few moments' silence for your own prayers.

The Lord's Prayer.

O Lord, we beseech thee mercifully to receive our prayers; and grant that we may both perceive and know what things we ought to do, and also may have grace and power faithfully to fulfil the same; through Jesus Christ our Lord. *Amen.*

Unto the King, eternal, immortal, invisible, the only wise God, be honour and glory for ever and ever. *Amen.*

SING SOME MORE HYMNS

29th October 2006

Order of Service

Welcome & Notices (Kevin)

Hymn 367 (Tune: *Gwalchmai*)
King of glory, King of peace

Brief introduction (David)

Hymn 278 (Tune: *Ewing*)
Jerusalem the golden

First reading (Peter) Luke, Chapter 19, Verses 1–10 *(NEB)*

Hymn 351 (Tune: *Vox dilecti*)
I heard the voice of Jesus say

Second reading (Peter) Luke, Chapter 15, Verses 1–10 *(NEB)*

Hymn 193 (Tune: *Aberystwyth*)
Jesu, lover of my soul

Third reading (Philip) "The Story of a Nail"

Hymn 303 (Tune: *St. Ethelwald*)
Soldiers of Christ, arise

Prayers (Peter)

Hymn 527 (Tune: *Sine Nomine*)
For all the saints who from their labours rest

The service will proceed without announcements. All the hymns are in *Hymns Ancient & Modern Revised.*

Thank you for coming. Please use the voting form opposite to list your own favourite hymns for a subsequent service.

Once again may I thank you all for coming. We had two choice forms back this time, so we have chosen some hymns from them and a couple more well-known ones to go with them.

You will see from the service sheets that Philip has found a piece for our third reading today, and we thank him for that, and also my brother, Robert, for accompanying us on the piano, and his recital before the service.

As I mentioned in July, the next fifth Sunday after this one will be on New Year's Eve. After that there is not another one until April. So can I ask for a show of hands: how many of you would be willing to come on 31st December?

Luke 19, 1–10

Entering Jericho he made his way through the city. There was a man there named Zacchaeus; he was superintendent of taxes and very rich. He was eager to see what Jesus looked like; but, being a little man, he could not see him for the crowd. So he ran on ahead and climbed a sycamore tree in order to see him, for he was to pass that way.

When Jesus came to the place, he looked up and said, "Zacchaeus, be quick and come down; I must come and stay with you today." He climbed down as fast as he could and welcomed him gladly. At this there was a general murmur of disapproval. "He has gone in," they said, "to be the guest of a sinner."

But Zacchaeus stood there and said to the Lord, "Here and now, sir, I give half my possessions to charity; and if I have cheated anyone, I am ready to repay him four times over." Jesus said to him, "Salvation has come to this house today!—for this man too is a son of Abraham, and the Son of Man has come to seek and save what is lost."

Luke 15, 1–10

Another time, the tax-gatherers and other bad characters were all crowding in to listen to him; and the Pharisees and the doctors of the law began grumbling among themselves: "This fellow," they said, "welcomes sinners and eats with them."

He answered them with this parable: "If one of you has a hundred sheep and loses one of them, does he not leave the ninety-nine in the open pasture and go after the missing one until he has found it? How delighted he is then! He lifts it onto his shoulders, and home he goes to call his friends and neighbours together. 'Rejoice with me!' he cries. 'I have found my lost sheep.' In the same way, I tell you, there will be greater joy in heaven over one sinner who repents than over ninety-nine righteous people who do not need to repent.

"Or again, if a woman has ten silver pieces and loses one of them, does she not light the lamp, sweep out the house, and look in every corner till she has found it? And when she has, she calls her friends and neighbours together, and says, 'Rejoice with me! I have found the piece that I lost.' In the same way, I tell you, there is joy among the angels of God over one sinner who repents."

THE STORY OF A NAIL

Off the coast of Malaya lies Sumatra. Nowhere in the world is the tropical jungle more dense than on this island, and yet it is populated by an estimated eight million people.

Hubert Mitchell, a missionary, had been called by God to take the gospel to the wild Kubu tribesmen of the interior. As Mitchell and his native workers fought their way into the jungle, the tropical sun beat mercilessly on their backs. The dense undergrowth resisted their every step; but to Hubert Mitchell, the big problem connected with the journey was not how to get to the Kubu tribesmen. Over and over again he asked himself, "How can I explain the reality of God's love to these illiterate, stone-age people? How can 1 make their darkened minds and hearts comprehend the great purpose of the sacrifice that was made on Calvary?"

Slowly they advanced to the middle of a clearing — then suddenly found themselves surrounded by an entire village which had moved out of hiding as one man. Flanked by warriors who needed but a single word for action, the chieftain of the tribe stood silently, watching with narrowed eyes the men who had dared to violate the privacy of his jungle home. At that moment, Hubert Mitchell became aware of sounds of normal life. Now there were barking dogs and crying children . . . and the missionary smiled. As the chieftain and the villagers watched, they seemed intrigued by that warm smile that found its way across Hubert's face.

The missionary was quick to sense their interest; and, instead of following the usual practice of presenting them with beads, buttons, and fish-hooks, he lost no time in telling them about the love of God. Hubert began by telling the story of Jesus Christ. He related from the Bible the account of Christ's sufferings and trials before His crucifixion. As the missionary told about the cross and the part that it played in the death of God's Son, the chief frowned and looked as though he wanted to speak. The missionary paused.

"What is a cross?" the chief asked. A look of surprise crossed Hubert's face. He wondered for a moment how he might describe a cross to those people who had never seen or heard of one. Turning to his native workers, Hubert told them to cut down a small tree and strip it of its branches. Then he fastened two of the larger pieces in the shape of a cross and placed the object before the chief. The native leader looked at the cross with interest, but wanted to know more.

"How was Christ fastened to the cross?" That was the next question asked of the missionary, and to better illustrate what happened, Hubert laid the cross on the ground and stretched himself upon it. Lying there with his arms outstretched, he told how the soldiers had driven nails into Christ's hands and feet. But the chief had still another question he wanted answered. He asked "What is nail?"

So! The people of the village had never seen a nail! Well, that would be easy to explain. "A nail is . . . "—but Hubert stopped. How did one describe a nail? He looked around for something that might resemble the object. But there was nothing in the entire village that even looked like a nail. The villagers stood by and watched. The chief waited, the question in his eyes unanswered. Hubert searched his own gear. Couldn't he find a nail somewhere? Just a small nail? A pin? But there was nothing. He gave up his search, admitted to the chief that he could find no nail. The chief had no further questions. Hubert was filled with frustration and deep concern. "For want of a nail, the shoe was lost . . . " The line from the nursery rhyme nudged his consciousness.

Quite dejected, Hubert began his evening meal of rice and fish. Usually for dessert he had fruit or a piece of native sugar cane. But on this night he idly picked up a can of Japanese oranges from his supplies and absentmindedly began to open it. He poured the oranges into a dish and started to toss the tin to a group of curious children nearby; but before the tin left Hubert's hand he heard a rattling sound inside it. Curiously he looked inside. He looked more closely. His eyes opened wide in amazement. There in the bottom of the tin was a nail! His mind was flooded with wonderment, almost unbelief—but the fact remained, there was a nail!

Taking the nail in his hand, Hubert rushed to the chief. The village quickly gathered. Then the missionary showed how the point of the nail was pounded into the hands and feet of the Saviour. The chief held the nail in his own hand, pressed it into his own flesh. He could see how strong it was, how sharp. Now the story of Christ was real to them; the cross and the nails were tangible things. The chief and many more that night were brought by grace to know Jesus Christ as their Saviour.

The chief was so moved that he left his village and acted as guide on a two-week's trek through the jungle in order that Hubert Mitchell might preach the Gospel to all the tribesmen of the area. And throughout the entire trip, clutched tightly in the chief's hand, was the nail . . . a never to be forgotten symbol of the suffering and death of the Saviour who had become his Lord and Master.

from *Cheering Words,* August 2001, p.122

included by permission of David Oldham, Publisher of *Cheering Words*

Prayers

O God, our Father, who hast made us in thine own image, with a mind to understand thy works, a heart to love thee, and a will to serve thee; increase in us that knowledge, love and obedience that we may grow daily in thy likeness; through Jesus Christ our Lord. *Amen.*

We bless thy holy Name, O God, for all thy servants who have finished their lives in thy faith and fear, and now rest from their labours. Give us grace, we beseech thee, to follow the example of their steadfastness and faithfulness, to thy honour and glory; through Jesus Christ our Lord. *Amen.*

O God, our heavenly Father, help us always to be of a good courage. Let us not be disheartened by our difficulties, never doubting thy love nor any of thy promises. Give us grace that we may encourage others and always do our best to make life easier for those who need a friendly word or helping hand; for the sake of Jesus Christ our Lord. *Amen.*

Almighty and everlasting God, who hast graciously given to us the fruits of the earth in their season, we yield thee humble and hearty thanks for these thy bounties, beseeching thee to give us grace rightly to use them, to thy glory and the relief of those in need. Through Jesus Christ our Lord. *Amen.*

Almighty God, the Giver of all good gifts, grant unto us a courteous spirit, a forgiving temper and an unselfish heart. Bestow upon us the spirit of self-sacrifice and cheerfulness, of hope and endurance. Increase in us the love of truth, of candour and of honour. Grant us courage to do what is right and, rejoicing in thee, to persevere unto the end; through Jesus Christ our Lord. *Amen.*

A few moments' silence for your own prayers.

The Lord's Prayer.

May the blessing of almighty God rest upon us and upon all our work; may he give us light to guide us, courage to support us, and love to unite us, now and evermore. *Amen.*

SING SOME MORE HYMNS

31st December 2006

Order of Service

Welcome & Notices (Kevin)

Hymn 75 (Tune: *Epiphany Hymn, Mission Praise 65*)
    Brightest and best of the sons of the morning
    (first verse repeated at the end)

Brief introduction (David)

Hymn 749 (*Mission Praise;* words overleaf. Tune: *Greensleeves*)
    What child is this

First reading (Peter) Matthew, Chapter 2, Verses 7–15, 19–23 *(NEB)*

Hymn 79 (Tune: *Dix*)
    As with gladness men of old

Second reading (Peter) Luke, Chapter 2, Verses 22–35 *(NEB)*

Hymn 631 (*Mission Praise;* words on page 48. Tune: *Woodlands*)
    Tell out, my soul

Third reading (Richard Holliday) "The Tablecloth"

Hymn 298 (Tune: *Lux benigna*)
    Lead, kindly Light, amid the encircling gloom

Prayers (Peter)

Hymn 72 (Tune: *Father, let me dedicate*)
    *Father, let me dedicate all **next** year to thee*

The service will proceed without announcements. Four of the hymns are in *Hymns Ancient & Modern Revised* and the other two in *Mission Praise.*

Thank you for coming. Please use the separate voting form to list your own favourite hymns for a subsequent service.

What child is this

What child is this, who, laid to rest,
On Mary's lap is sleeping?
Whom angels greet with anthems sweet,
While shepherds watch are keeping?
This, this is Christ the King,
Whom shepherds guard and angels sing:
Haste, haste to bring Him praise,
The babe, the Son of Mary.

Why lies He in such mean estate,
Where ox and ass are feeding?
Good Christian fear: for sinners here
The silent Word is pleading.
This, this is Christ the King,
Whom shepherds guard and angels sing:
Haste, haste to bring Him praise,
The babe, the Son of Mary.

So bring Him incense, gold, and myrrh,
Come, peasant, king, to own Him.
The King of kings salvation brings,
Let loving hearts enthrone Him.
This, this is Christ the King,
Whom shepherds guard and angels sing:
Haste, haste to bring Him praise,
The babe, the Son of Mary.

William Chatterton Dix
(1837–98)

Once again may I thank you all for coming, especially this evening being New Year's Eve. We had three choice forms back—one more than last time—so we have chosen some hymns from them and one more to go with them. We have tried to make our selection appropriate to mid-way between Christmas and Epiphany, while avoiding any we may have sung at the Carol Service two weeks ago. Robert will play the whole verse through first for any tunes that may not be not familiar. He has asked me to point out, with respect to our final hymn, that as there is not a lot left of *this* year, we should sing, "Father, let me dedicate all *next* year to thee."

As only two Gospels, Matthew and Luke, mention the birth of Jesus, it was even harder than with the hymns to pick passages that were not read during the Carol Service, but we have done what we could.

Philip lent me the book from which he read October's "Story of a Nail", and I found another story in it, this one with a Christmas theme, and Richard is kindly reading it for us. We thank him, and Robert again for his work on the piano.

The next fifth Sunday will be in April, followed by July, September and December again. We hope to see you all again then.

Matthew 2, 7–15, 19–23

Herod next called the astrologers to meet him in private, and ascertained from them the time when the star had appeared. He then sent them on to Bethlehem, and said, "Go and make a careful inquiry for the child. When you have found him, report to me, so that I may go myself and pay him homage."

They set out at the king's bidding; and the star which they had seen at its rising went ahead of them until it stopped above the place where the child lay. At the sight of the star they were overjoyed. Entering the house, they saw the child with Mary his mother, and bowed to the ground in homage to him; then they opened their treasures and offered him gifts: gold, frankincense, and myrrh. And being warned in a dream not to go back to Herod, they returned home another way.

After they had gone, an angel of the Lord appeared to Joseph in a dream, and said to him, "Rise up, take the child and his mother and escape with them to Egypt, and stay there until I tell you; for Herod is going to search for the child to do away with him." So Joseph rose from sleep, and taking mother and child by night he went away with them to Egypt, and there he stayed till Herod's death. This was to fulfil what the Lord had declared through the prophet: "I called my son out of Egypt."

The time came that Herod died; and an angel of the Lord appeared in a dream to Joseph in Egypt and said to him, "Rise up, take the child and his mother, and go with them to the land of Israel, for the men who threatened the child's life are dead." So he rose, took mother and child with him, and came to the land of Israel. Hearing, however, that Archelaus had succeeded his father Herod as king of Judaea, he was afraid to go there. And being warned by a dream, he withdrew to the region of Galilee; there he settled in a town called Nazareth. This was to fulfil the words spoken through the prophets: "He shall be called a Nazarene."

Luke 2, 22–35

Then, after their purification had been completed in accordance with the Law of Moses, they brought him up to Jerusalem to present him to the Lord (as prescribed in the law of the Lord: "Every first-born male shall be deemed to belong to the Lord"), and also to make the offering as stated in the law of the Lord: "A pair of turtle doves or two young pigeons."

There was at that time in Jerusalem a man called Simeon. This man was upright and devout, one who watched and waited for the restoration of Israel, and the Holy Spirit was upon him. It had been disclosed to him by the Holy Spirit that he would not see death until he had seen the Lord's Messiah. Guided by the Spirit he came into the temple; and when the parents brought in the child Jesus to do for him what was customary under the Law, he took him in his arms, praised God, and said:

"This day, Master, thou givest thy servant his discharge in peace; now thy promise is fulfilled.

"For I have seen with my own eyes the deliverance which thou hast made ready in full view of all the nations:

"A light that will be a relation to the heathen, and glory to thy people Israel."

The child's father and mother were full of wonder at what was being said about him. Simeon blessed them and said to Mary his mother, "This child is destined to be a sign which men reject; and you too shall be pierced to the heart. Many in Israel will stand or fall because of him, and thus the secret thoughts of many will be laid bare."

THE TABLECLOTH

The pastor and his wife, newly assigned to their first ministry to re-open a church in urban Brooklyn, arrived in early October excited about their opportunities. When they saw their church it was very run down and needed much work. They set a goal to have everything done in time to hold their first service on Christmas Eve. They worked hard, repairing pews, plastering walls, painting, etc., and on December 18th were ahead of schedule and just about finished. On December 19th a terrible tempest—a driving rainstorm—hit the area and lasted for two days.

On December 21st the pastor went over to the church. His heart sank when he saw that the roof had leaked, causing a large area of plaster about 6 feet by 8 feet to fall off the front wall of the sanctuary just behind the pulpit. The pastor cleaned up the mess on the floor and, not knowing what else to do but postpone the Christmas Eve service, headed home. On the way he noticed that a local business was having a flea-market-type sale for charity, so he stepped in. One of the items was a beautiful, hand-made, ivory-coloured crochet tablecloth with exquisite work, fine colours and a design embroidered right in the centre. It was just the right size to cover up the hole in the front wall. He bought it and headed back to the church. By this time it had started to snow. An older woman running from the opposite direction was trying to catch a bus. She missed it. The pastor invited her to wait in the warm church for the next bus 45 minutes later. She sat in a pew and paid no attention to the pastor while he got a ladder, hangers, etc., to put up the table cloth as a wall tapestry. He could hardly believe how beautiful it looked and it covered up the entire problem area.

Then he noticed the woman walking down the centre aisle. Her face was like a sheet. "Pastor," she asked, "Where did you get that tablecloth?" The pastor explained. The woman asked him to check the lower right corner to see if the initials EBG were crocheted into there. They were. These were her own initials, and she had made this tablecloth 35 years before, in Austria.

The woman could hardly believe it as the pastor told how he had just got the tablecloth. She explained that before the war she and her husband were well-to-do people in Austria. When the Nazis came she was forced to leave. Her husband was going to follow her the next week. She was captured, sent to prison and never saw her husband or her home again. The pastor wanted to give her the tablecloth, but she made the pastor keep it for the church. The pastor insisted on driving her home. That was the least he could do. She lived on the other side of Staten Island and was only in Brooklyn for the day for a house-cleaning job.

What a wonderful service they had on Christmas Eve! The church was almost full. At the end of the service the pastor and his wife greeted everyone at the door and many said they would return. One older man, whom the pastor recognized from the neighbourhood, continued to sit in one of the pews and stare, and the pastor wondered why he wasn't leaving.

The man asked him where he got the tablecloth on the front wall, because it was identical to one that his wife made years ago when they lived in Austria before the war. He told the pastor how the Nazis came, how he forced his wife to flee for her safety, and he was supposed to follow her. But he was arrested and put in a concentration camp. He never saw his wife or his home again for all the 35 years in between. The pastor asked him if he would allow him to take him for a little ride. They drove to Staten Island and to the house where the pastor had taken the woman three days earlier. He helped the man climb the three flights of stairs to the woman's apartment, knocked on the door, and he saw the greatest Christmas reunion he could ever imagine.

from *Cheering Words,* December 2001, p.182

included by permission of David Oldham, Publisher of *Cheering Words* [1]

---

[1] I wish to record my thanks to Pauline Johns, Secretary of the Strict Baptist Historical Society, who put me in touch with Andrew Toms, the Editor of *Cheering Words*, and David Oldham, its Publisher and former Editor, after I had contacted her through the SBHS website, to which I had discovered a link when in search of information about this magazine, which has been going strong since the mid nineteenth century. *DJE*

Prayers

We praise thee, O God, for the healthful delights of this season; for mirth quickening the blood, uniting us with others and refreshing us for work; for joy that heightens all our life and doubles our powers. Help us, we beseech thee, to share these blessings with others, kindling their hearts by our gladness; through Jesus, the Christ Child, our King. *Amen.*

Almighty God, whom once the nations worshipped under names of fear, but who hast revealed the glory of thy love in the birth of Jesus Christ; fill our hearts, as we remember his nativity, with the gladness of this great redemption. May we join in the heavenly song of glory to God in the highest, on earth peace, and goodwill towards men. Breathe into our hearts the spirit of Jesus, so that we may be led to thee in trust and obedience; through Jesus Christ our Lord. *Amen.*

O Lord Jesus Christ, to whom the wise men from the East brought gifts at Bethlehem, hasten the time, we beseech thee, when the wisdom of the East shall seek after thee and find thee. Grant that the peoples of Asia and Africa may offer to thee their treasures, their love, and their service, and bow before thee in worship, who livest and reignest with the Father and the Holy Spirit, one God for evermore. *Amen.*

Almighty God, who rulest the changing seasons, we bless thee that beneath all that now seems cold and dead, thou art keeping safe the hidden germs of life. Still thou dost clothe all things around us with beauty, sending forth thy frost and snow, filling the brief day with sunshine, and making the night glorious with countless stars. We thank thee for the shelter and comfort of our homes, and pray for those in poverty or sickness who shrink from the cold. Through Jesus Christ our Lord. *Amen.*

Most gracious God, who hast been merciful unto us not only in the year past but through all the years of our life, pardon our sins, fashion in us those virtues which are acceptable to thee, and grant that in sincerity we may serve thee more faithfully in the year that is to come, for Jesus Christ's sake. *Amen.*

A few moments' silence for your own prayers.

The Lord's Prayer.

Go forth into the world in peace; be of good courage; hold fast that which is good; render to no man evil for evil; strengthen the faint-hearted; support the weak; help the afflicted; honour all men; love and serve the Lord; rejoicing in the power of the Holy Spirit.

And the blessing of God Almighty, the Father, the Son, and the Holy Spirit, be upon us, and remain with us for ever. *Amen.*

SING SOME MORE HYMNS
29th April 2007

Order of Service

Welcome & Notices (Philip)

Hymn 246 (Tune: *Angel voices*)
Angel-voices ever singing

Introduction (David)

Hymn 368 (Tune: *Austria*)
Praise the Lord! Ye heavens, adore him

First reading (Peter) Ecclesiasticus, Chapter 2, Verses 1–6 *(NEB)*

Hymn 335 (Tune: *Franconia*)
Blest are the pure in heart

Second reading (Peter) Ecclesiasticus, Chapter 6, Verses 32–37;
Chapter 2, Verses 10–11 *(NEB)*

Hymn 377 (*Songs of Praise;* words opposite. Tune: *Stowey*)
When a knight won his spurs

Address for St George's Day (David)

Hymn 331 (Tune: *Thornbury*)
O Jesus I have promised

Prayers (Peter)

Hymn 487 (Tune: *Melita*)
Eternal Father, strong to save

The service will proceed without announcements. All the hymns except one (words opposite) are in *Hymns Ancient & Modern Revised.*

Thank you for coming. Please use the separate voting form to list your own favourite hymns for a subsequent service.

When a knight won his spurs

When a knight won his spurs, in the stories of old,
He was gentle and brave, he was gallant and bold;
With a shield on his arm and a lance in his hand
For God and for valour he rode through the land.

No charger have I, and no sword by my side,
Yet still to adventure and battle I ride,
Though back into storyland giants have fled,
And the knights are no more and the dragons are dead.

Let faith be my shield and let joy be my steed
'Gainst the dragons of anger, the ogres of greed;
And let me set free, with the sword of my youth,
From the castle of darkness the power of the truth.

Jan Struther (1901–53)

from *Enlarged Songs of Praise 1931*

Our hymn services have often come near some Christian festival or other, which has given us a theme. I noticed this time that we are as near as we can ever be to St George's Day, which set me thinking back many years to a service in Pulborough church, when the local Group were hosts to all the Scouts of Petworth & Pulborough District. It was planned by a small committee of the Rector, Revd Basil Maltin, and the organist, Ivan Thompson, who had both been Scouts themselves, two of the older boys who were also servers at the church, and myself.

With a bit of persuasion Sean, a 16-year-old Venture Scout, agreed to do the reading. I gave him half a dozen possible passages to choose from, and the one he picked was my first choice as well. I could hardly expect a boy to tackle something difficult if I wasn't prepared to take on anything myself, so I volunteered to give the address! "Good!" said Basil, "That'll save me doing it." I had a couple of months to think what to say, and to make sure before the service that he was happy with the text.

Concerned that I have got out of giving my 'brief chat' since July 2005, I thought first of selecting a few extracts for this evening, but on looking through it to find some I wasn't sure this was feasible. Some of what I said is in fact quite topical, as people are thinking now about the Falklands campaign 25 years on while then it was only the previous year. So with some trepidation I have decided to let you have all of it, and you will therefore need to imagine that you are all Scouts or Guides, and that there are something over four hundred of you, standing room only at the back of the church. So it was quite daunting for Sean to do the reading. I told him not to start until everyone had settled down: "If you wait for silence," I told him, "you will get it." No microphones in those days, so one had to speak up, and probably those at the back still couldn't hear.

Two things I should explain: firstly that 1982, 75 years on from when the Movement was founded, had been designated as "The Year of the Scout", and secondly the Scout Promise was something every boy had to make to become a Scout. For those not familiar with it, the UK version (for the later part of my time as a Scouter) runs: *"On my honour, I promise that I will do my best to do my duty to God and to the Queen, to help other people and to keep the Scout Law."* [see after the Prayers for the Scout Law]

We have split Sean's reading into two parts for our readings today, and then, just as between our contributions in 1983, the hymn that was ringing in my ears as I exchanged a wry smile with Sean and made my way to the pulpit. I apologise for the chat being over my usual maximum of five minutes; a fellow Scouter timed it at ten.

And what better hymn to sing after we had all renewed our Promise in the next part of the service than *O Jesus I have promised*?

Ecclesiasticus 2, 1–6

My son, if you aspire to be a servant of the Lord,
  prepare yourself for testing.
Set a straight course, be resolute,
  and do not lose your head in time of disaster.
Hold fast to him, never desert him,
  if you would end your days in prosperity.
Bear every hardship that is sent you;
  be patient under humiliation, whatever the cost.
For gold is assayed by fire,
  and the Lord proves men in the furnace of humiliation.
Trust him and he will help you;
  steer a straight course and set your hope on him.

Ecclesiasticus 6, 32–37

If it is your wish, my son, you can be trained;
  if you give your mind to it, you can become clever;
if you enjoy listening, you will learn;
  if you are attentive, you will grow wise.
When you stand among your elders,
  decide who is wise and join him.
Listen gladly to every godly argument
  and see that no wise proverb escapes you.
If you discover a wise man, rise early to visit him;
  let your feet wear out his doorstep.
Ponder the decrees of the Lord
  and study his commandments at all times.
He will strengthen your mind
  and grant your desire for wisdom.

Ecclesiasticus 2, 10–11

Consider the past generations and see:
  was anyone who trusted the Lord ever disappointed?
  was anyone who stood firm in the fear of him ever deserted?
  did he ever neglect anyone who prayed to him?
For the Lord is compassionate and merciful;
  he forgives sins and comes to the rescue in time of trouble.

ADDRESS FOR ST GEORGE'S DAY
PETWORTH & PULBOROUGH SCOUT DISTRICT
ST MARY'S CHURCH, PULBOROUGH   APRIL 1983

Well, this is the part you've all been waiting for—when you can sit down, relax and not have to do anything, while some bloke chats to you for ten minutes or so. You hope he won't be boring and you hope he won't go on too long. Well, I'll try. Before I start I'd like to say a prayer; you don't have to stand up again for it, but if I can hear you say 'Amen' at the end it will help to make me feel less nervous. . . . "May what I say—the words of my mouth—and the thoughts of all our hearts, be now and always acceptable in Your sight, O Lord my strength and my redeemer. Amen." . . . . Thank you.

The Year of the Scout. It's the Year of the Scout this year as it was the Year of the Scout last year, because it's really the 18 months of the Scout and it doesn't finish until after the Jamboree in July. It's an honour for Pulborough to be host to the whole District for the Year of the Scout St George's Day Parade. Thank you all for coming to our church.

A year ago half of us were marching in sunshine down a country lane to the church at Bury. And what was happening? Britain was going to war. It seemed incredible that in 1982 Britain would be at war with a hitherto quite friendly country in South America. I remember coming out of the shop with the paper on a Saturday morning and seeing that Argentina had invaded the Falklands. I thought, Oh, dear, what a pity. It never occurred to me that the Army and the Navy, with help from the Air Force, would go out there and get them back. I remember thinking when the Task Force set sail, will they really sink Argentine ships, with people on them? But they did. We all know the story and I'm not going to tell it again. The Year of the Scout: the year that Britain sent her forces 8000 miles to free British soil and British citizens from a foreign invader.

Much later in the year I read what the Archbishop of Canterbury said at the Falklands service. He said that we should try to build bridges of friendship with the Argentines, as we had both lost loved ones in the war. He said that no country should claim that God was on their side in a war. Too many wars have been fought with both sides claiming God's blessing for their actions. But it must be very hard to go to battle if you are not convinced that it is the right thing to do. And I think it is not wrong to believe that God is on your side . . . to believe that when you have good luck, the weather helps you or a bomb lands on your ship and doesn't go off, and so on, that God has been helping you. To be worthy of God's help we must behave as He would wish us to — and I am sure we were all encouraged by the many tales of selfless heroism, of men risking their own safety for the sake of rescuing other men from blazing ships, for example. I think the Bishop to the Forces spoke for many when he said at the recent memorial service, "We come with pride, not the pride of the victor over the vanquished, for there is no more magnanimous person in victory than the British soldier, sailor and airman."

The Year of the Scout has been quite a year. Today we are marking St George's Day, so let's remember him too. Who was St George? This is what our founder, Robert Baden-Powell, says in his book, *Scouting for Boys*.[1]

He was the patron saint of the knights of old, because he was the only one of all the saints who was a horseman. He is the Patron Saint of cavalry, from which the word, 'chivalry', is derived, and the special saint of England.

He is also the Patron Saint of Scouts everywhere. Therefore, all Scouts should know his story. St George was born in Cappadocia in the year AD 303. He enlisted as a cavalry soldier when he was seventeen, and soon became renowned for his bravery.

One one occasion he came to a city named Selem, near which lived a dragon who had to be fed daily with one of the citizens, drawn by lot.

The day St George came there, the lot had fallen upon the king's daughter, Cleolinda. St George resolved that she should not die, and so he went out and attacked the dragon, who lived in a swamp close by, and killed him.

St George was typical of what a Scout should be.

When he was faced by a difficulty or danger, however great it appeared—even in the shape of a dragon—he did not avoid it or fear it, but went at it with all the power he could put into himself and his horse. Although inadequately armed for such an encounter, having merely a spear, he charged in, did his best, and finally succeeded in overcoming a difficulty which nobody had dared to tackle.

That is exactly the way in which a Scout should face a difficulty or danger, no matter how great or terrifying it may appear to him or how ill-equipped he may be for the struggle. He should go in boldly and confidently, using every power that he can to try to overcome it, and the probability is that he will succeed.

I also looked up St George in an encyclopaedia, and this is what it said.

St George, who lived about 300 years after the birth of Christ, was a heroic soldier who gave up his life rather than deny his faith at the bidding of a Roman emperor. Edward III adopted his name as a war-cry for England, and the beautiful red cross of St George on a white ground became the English flag. [*Volume 4*, p.2333; full reference is on p.226]

---

[1] *Scouts' Edition*. C. Arthur Pearson, 1963, pp.152–153.

The Falklands, St George, Scouts, religion. What connects all these? One thing, I suggest, is courage. Courage to face danger, courage to tell the truth, courage to admit to belonging to a persecuted church. And "A Scout has courage in all difficulties," as we are reminded in the Scout Law.

What is courage? Courage is being frightened and putting up with it. Courage is saying, I know there is danger but I am not going to let it stop me doing what I know I ought to do. Courage is not giving up when life gets tough. Courage is feeling your hands shaking or your knees trembling but staying to face up to something and not running away. Courage is pretending to yourself that you are brave when you know too well you are not.

It may take a lot of courage to tell the truth sometimes. Perhaps we must admit to something we have done and face punishment or risk someone's anger. It may not cost us our life, as it did St George, but may still cost us dear in the short term. But the long-term result may be different. St George had to die, but he would be dead anyway by now. Today, sixteen hundred years later, we all honour St George. But who now remembers that Roman emperor?

So where does God come in? Well, I always like to think of our Duty to God as having two sides: the first is the one that most people think of—we serve Him by doing our best to help other people, by trying to keep the Scout Law and Promise, and so on. The second a lot of people seem to forget—it is quite simply stated: we should trust Him to look after us. Listen to what Jesus said in his Sermon on the Mount.

How little faith you have! No, do not ask anxiously, "What are we to eat? What are we to drink? What shall we wear?" All these are things for the heathen to run after, not for you, because your heavenly Father knows that you need them all. Set your minds on God's kingdom and His justice before everything else, and all the rest will come to you as well. So do not be anxious about tomorrow; tomorrow will look after itself. Each day has troubles enough of its own.

Then again, the sentence from our reading: "Was anyone who trusted the Lord ever disappointed? " And although it also says, "If you aspire to be a servant of the Lord, prepare yourself for testing", St Paul, I think, said, "You will not be tested above what you are able to withstand." In fact, time and again, throughout the Bible, comes the message, Don't worry, let God look after you; you do what you think is right and let God take care of the consequences. He won't let you down.

This is what I understand by having faith—it's not a matter of accepting a set of intellectual propositions. People do talk loosely about 'the Christian faith', but often they are really talking about the acceptance of Christian dogma, which someone has unkindly described as "believing a whole lot of things which you know aren't true". Clearly, to come to God we must believe something — that He exists and that He rewards those who search for Him [Hebrews 11, v,6]. But when it comes to the various 'extra' things that some religious people seem to believe in, I would say to you, by all means believe what you feel to be true. For the rest, don't worry, put them in a mental drawer marked 'Pending' and carry on without them for the time being. I often wonder about the people who don't believe in God at all, yet spend their lives helping other people. I like to think that when they die they'll be in for a big surprise — not only will they discover that God exists after all but, far from being angry at them for not believing in Him, He is instead quite pleased with what they have done with their lives. I feel sure that what counts is not how much you believe in God, but how much He believes in you. And faith is letting God direct our lives and trusting Him to look after us.

If we need faith to have courage, where do we get faith? We get it by trying. Not just by talking or thinking about religion, but by trying it for ourselves. Like St George, trying to help people who need our help. Taking a stand against injustice. Sticking up for our friends. Look back on your life and see how much God has done for you already, how much He has taught you. If you go on trying, you will find, as I have, that God goes on helping, teaching — and testing — you, and giving you opportunities to help other people and make them happy. Yet He always leaves to you the choice to take or reject those opportunities.

There is a hymn which starts, [The full hymn is on page 133.]

> Once to every man and nation,
> Comes the moment to decide:
> In the strife of truth with falsehood,
> For the good or evil side.

The second verse ends with the lines,

> Then it is the brave man chooses,
> While the coward stands aside.
> Till the multitude make virtue
> Of the faith they had denied.

Now that's where we can all count ourselves lucky. Lucky to be Scouts. Because as Scouts — and Cub Scouts — we have all been brave men and chosen; we have all said, Yes, I will make that Promise, on my honour. And I believe that God will help us all to keep it. A lady I know once said to me, "I have never met a bad Scout." She was 75 then, so she'd had time to look for one. She's 82 now; she says she still hasn't. We are all God's men (or women) already.

82

"The Lord's my Shepherd," we sing in that beautiful 23rd Psalm. I wonder, do you like to think of yourself as a sheep? I don't think I do. *Baa!* (I'd rather be a goat!) But you know, you don't have to be a sheep, and the Lord can still be your Shepherd. How? Quite easy, you can be one of his sheep*dogs*. As Scouts we are already a little bit special; if we want to, we can all be His sheepdogs. Just like parsons (of course, you know, that's why they wear dog collars). In the same way as the sheepdogs look after the sheep and keep them from wandering off and getting lost, you can take an interest in the others in your Six or Patrol. I have long thought that the most important part of being a Patrol Leader is the concern you show for the members of your Patrol; when you get a bit older, the most important part of being a Scouter will be the trouble you go to to make a personal friend of every member of your Pack, Troop or Unit. So if now your Scout Leader barks at you occasionally, you'll know why!

But I have had more than my ten minutes, which means that we have come to the time when we all renew our Promise and confirm that we have indeed made that choice and that we know what it means.

A Pulborough Scouter

Prayers   29th April 2007

We praise thy name, O Father, for the beauty of the summer, the glory of the sky by day and night, the healthful wind and quickening rain. We thank thee for the bloom and fragrance of the flowers, the songs of the birds, and the joyousness of every living thing. In all that thou has made we see the wonder of thy wisdom and care. Help us to trust thy never-failing goodness, the love which is beyond understanding, and surrounds our lives with blessing, for thy name's sake.   *Amen.*

O Lord God of Hosts, who didst give grace to thy servant George to lay aside the fear of man, and to confess thee even unto death, grant that we, too, may think lightly of earthly place and honour, and seek rather to please the Captain of our salvation, who has chosen us to be his soldiers; to whom with thee and the Holy Spirit be thanks and praise for all thy saints, now and for evermore.   *Amen.*

O God, the King of righteousness, lead us, we pray thee, in the ways of justice and of peace; inspire us to break down all tyranny and oppression, to gain for every man his due reward and from every man his due service; that each may live for all, and all may care for each, in the Name of Jesus Christ.   *Amen.*

A few moments' silence for your own prayers.

The Lord's Prayer

(Paraphrase used at St George's Day Service in 1983)

Heavenly Father, You alone are God.
May Your Kingdom come, and Your Will be done on earth as it
is in heaven.
Please give us today what You think we need:
Forgive us the wrong things that we do, and may we be ready to
forgive others.
Spare us from the testing which is beyond our strength; and
break evil's hold upon us.
For Yours is the kingdom whose days are not numbered,
Yours the power which shall not end,
Yours the glory which shall never fade.

O God Who is heroic love, keep alive in our hearts that adventurous spirit which makes men scorn the way of safety, so that Your Will can be done. For only so, Lord, may we be worthy of those courageous souls who in every age have ventured all things in obedience to Your call, and for whom the trumpets have sounded on the other side; through Jesus Christ our Lord. *Amen.*

May the Lord lead us when we go, and keep us when we sleep, and talk with us when we wake; may the Lord make His face to shine upon us and be gracious to us; the Lord lift up the light of His countenance upon us and give us peace, this day and for evermore. *Amen.*

Appendix The Scout Law as in the 1980s

1. A Scout is to be trusted
2. A Scout is loyal
3. A Scout is friendly and considerate
4. A Scout belongs to the world-wide family of Scouts
5. A Scout has courage in all difficulties
6. A Scout makes good use of his time and is careful of possessions and
property
7. A Scout has self-respect and respect for others

SING SOME MORE HYMNS

29th July 2007

Order of Service

Welcome & Notices (David)

Hymn 160 (Tune: *Nicaea*)
Holy, Holy, Holy! Lord God Almighty!

Brief introduction (David)

Hymn 255 (Tune: *Aurelia*)
The Church's one foundation

First reading (Tony) Psalm 15 *(1662 BCP)*

Hymn 184 (Tune: *Repton*)
Dear Lord and Father of mankind

Second reading (Philip) "A Guide at Warwick Castle"

Hymn 349 (Tune: *Misericordia*)
Just as I am, without one plea

Third reading (David) "The Threshold" *by Rudyard Kipling*

Hymn 197 (Tune: *dominus regit me*)
The King of love my Shepherd is

Prayers (Stuart)

Hymn 379 (Tune: *Nun danket*)
Now thank we all our God

The service will proceed without announcements. All the hymns are in *Hymns Ancient & Modern Revised.*

Thank you for coming. Please use the voting form opposite to list your own favourite hymns for a subsequent service.

Once again may I thank you all for coming. No Kevin today, as he has gone off to another Conference, and no Peter, as this is the day he comes back from his holiday (by train, he told me). Tony and Philip are doing the readings, and if Stuart can make it he will do the prayers; he was expecting a visitor this afternoon, so he may not be available.

We thank them for that, and for helping choose the hymns, readings and prayers; and also my brother, Robert, for accompanying us on the piano, and his recital before the service.

I have thought for some while over the past week or more about what I could say today, but in the end time has run out on me and you are getting a third reading instead, which I hope might provide some food for thought.

The next fifth Sunday is just two months away, on 30th September.

Psalm 15 (*1662 BCP*)

Lord, who shall dwell in thy tabernacle: or who shall rest upon thy holy hill?

Even he, that leadeth an uncorrupt life: and doeth the thing which is right, and speaketh the truth from his heart.

He that hath used no deceit in his tongue, nor done evil to his neighbour: and hath not slandered his neighbour.

He that setteth not by himself, but is lowly in his own eyes: and maketh much of them that fear the Lord.

He that sweareth unto his neighbour, and disappointeth him not: though it were to his own hindrance.[1]

He that hath not given his money upon usury: nor taken reward against the innocent.

Whoso doeth these things: shall never fall.

A Guide at Warwick Castle

During a recent holiday, two friends of mine visited Warwick Castle.

As they were led through lofty rooms and wide halls, they saw much to admire. At last they came to the castle chapel, and their guide paused. "Someone else will show you round here," he said. As they stepped inside the chapel they found to their amazement that their new guide was blind.

His name is Edward Miller. During the war he suffered terrible injuries, and, worse still, lost his sight. He spent a long time in hospital, and when he

---

[1] *Note from DE*: We had just selected this reading when my bridge partner called to enquire when he was going to get the cards that I had agreed to print for him. *Touché!*

86

left it seemed there was little he'd ever be able to do. Then he was given the chance of becoming a guide at Warwick Castle.

To learn all its history, and tiny details that visitors were sure to want to know, would have been a challenge for any man. To George, who had never seen any of the loveliness around him, it must have seemed impossible.

Yet learn it he did, and if you follow him round the chapel today he will point out glimpses of beauty that might otherwise escape you—the wonderful light on the face of Jesus in an old painting; the magnificent colours that have stayed unfaded for 700 years; an intricate carving, half- hidden in the darkness; and much more.

So, blind as he is, George is opening the eyes of others to the secrets of the chapel—and in doing so he has turned his tragedy into a triumph.

Entry for Monday August 2 from *The Friendship Book of Francis Gay, 1971*
London: D. C. Thomson & Co., 1970. Used by kind permission of D.C.Thomson & Co Ltd

The Threshold

In their deepest caverns of limestone
They pictured the Gods of Food—
The Horse, the Elk, and the Bison
That the hunting might be good;
With the Gods of Death and Terror—
The Mammoth, Tiger, and Bear.
And the pictures moved in the torchlight
To show that the Gods were there!
But that was before Ionia—
(Or the Seven Holy Islands of Ionia)
Any of the Mountains of Ionia,
Had bared their peaks to the air.

The close years packed behind them,
As the glaciers bite and grind,
Filling the new-gouged valleys
With Gods of every kind.
Gods of all-reaching power—
Gods of all-searching eyes—
But each to be wooed by worship
And won by sacrifice.
Till, after many winters, rose Ionia—
(Strange men brooding in Ionia)
Crystal-eyed Sages of Ionia
Who said, "These tales are lies.

"We dream one Breath in all things,
  "That blows all things between.
"We dream one Matter in all things—
  "Eternal, changeless, unseen.
"That the heart of the Matter is single
  "Till the Breath shall bid it bring forth—
"By choosing or losing its neighbour—
  "All things made upon Earth."
    But Earth was wiser than Ionia
    (Babylon and Egypt than Ionia)
    And they overlaid the teaching of Ionia
    And the Truth was choked at birth.

It died at the Gate of Knowledge—
  The Key to the Gate in its hand—
And the anxious priests and wizards
  Re-blinded the wakening land;
For they showed, by answering echoes,
  And chasing clouds as they rose,
How shadows should stand for bulwarks
  Between mankind and its woes.
    It was then that men bethought them of Ionia
    (The few that had not allforgot Ionia)
    Or the Word that was whispered in Ionia;
    And they turned from the shadows and the shows.

They found one Breath in all things,
  That moves all things between.
They proved one Matter in all things—
  Eternal, changeless, unseen;
That the heart of the Matter was single
  Till the Breath should bid it bring forth—
    Even as men whispered in Ionia,
    (Resolute, unsatisfied Ionia)
    Ere the Word was stifled in Ionia—
  All things known upon earth!

Rudyard Kipling

(1865–1936)

Prayers

A PRAYER OF ST FRANCIS OF ASSISSI

Lord, make us instruments of thy peace. Where there is hatred, let us give love; where there is injury, pardon; where there is discord, union; where there is doubt, faith; where there is despair, hope; where there is darkness, light; where there is sadness, joy; for thy mercy and for thy truth's sake. *Amen.*

Our Father, as we turn to the comfort of our rest, we remember those who must wake that we may sleep; bless those who watch over us at night, the firemen and police, and all who carry on through the hours of darkness the restless commerce of men on land and sea. We thank thee for their faithfulness and sense of duty; we pray thee for pardon, if our selfishness or luxury adds to their nightly toil. Grant that we may realise how dependent the safety of our loved ones and the comforts of life are on these our brothers, so that we may think of them with love and gratitude, and help to make their burden lighter; for the sake of Jesus Christ our Lord. *Amen.*

A PRAYER OF ST RICHARD OF CHICHESTER

Thanks be to thee, our Lord Jesus Christ, for all the benefits which thou hast won for us, for all the pains and insults thou hast borne for us. O most merciful Redeemer, Friend and Brother, may we know thee more clearly, love thee more dearly, follow thee more nearly, day by day. *Amen.*

A few moments' silence for your own prayers.

The Lord's Prayer

The power of the Father, the wisdom of the Son, the love of the Holy Spirit, be with us all evermore. *Amen.*

SIMPLE SERVICE, WITH HYMNS
30th September 2007

Order of Service

Welcome & Notices (Kevin)

Hymn 481 (Tune: *Monkland*)
Praise, O praise our God and King

Brief introduction (David)

Hymn 257 (Tune: *Abbots Leigh*)
Glorious things of thee are spoken

First reading (Christine) Genesis 18, 16–33; 19, 1–3, 12–30 *(NEB)*

Hymn 256 (Tune: *Thornbury*)
Thy hand, O God, has guided

Second reading (selected by Philip) "Precious Things"

Hymn 631 (Tune: *Leonie*)
The God of Abraham praise

Brief chat (Tony)

Hymn 266 (Tune: *Moscow*)
Thou, whose almighty word

Prayers (Peter)

Hymn 27 (Tune: *Eventide*)
Abide with me; fast falls the eventide

The service will proceed without announcements. All the hymns are in *Hymns Ancient & Modern Revised.*

Thank you for coming. Please use the voting form opposite to list your own favourite hymns for a subsequent service.

Once again may I thank you all for coming, and Robert for his musical work. It's nice to have Kevin back with us, after his having to miss the April and July services.

You will have noticed that we have got in first on next week's Harvest theme with our opening hymn, and there's a prayer or two on this theme as well.

Philip is unable to be with us this evening as he has a skin problem on his face called, I think, a solar kelatosis, requiring treatment which makes it come up in blisters. We wish him a speedy return to full health, and meanwhile thank Ena for stepping in and reading the piece that he had chosen for us.

As explained in the September magazine, we are changing our title with this service, and we hope you will agree that the new one is suitable, and more in line with what we do each time.

It is very heartening to have more people helping with the service. Christine said last time that she would be willing to do a reading, so we hope we haven't taken too much advantage of her by selecting quite a long one for her. Nothing, I assure you, to do with her having chosen a long hymn for us. You may not all know *The God of Abraham praise*, but as it has ten verses we are confident that you will be fully acquainted with it by the time we've finished singing it.

Last time I hadn't quite got round to working out something to say by way of a brief chat, so I had to read you a poem instead. I am pleased to say that I have been relieved of the task this time as well, and I am sure you will appreciate Tony's discourse.

The next fifth Sunday this year is the day before New Year's Eve, which should be a little more convenient than New Year's Eve itself.

The tune for the next hymn may not be quite the most familiar one for it, but it is a fine tune and a well-known one.

Genesis 18, 16–33; 19, 1–3, 12–30

The men set out and looked down towards Sodom, and Abraham went with them to start them on their way. The LORD thought to himself, "Shall I conceal from Abraham what I intend to do? He will become a great and powerful nation, and all nations on earth will pray to be blessed as he is blessed. I have taken care of him on purpose that he may charge his sons and family after him to conform to the way of the LORD and to do what is right and just; thus I shall fulfil all that I have promised for him." So the LORD said, "There is a great outcry over Sodom and Gomorrah; their sin is very grave. I must go down and see whether their deeds warrant the outcry which has reached me. I am resolved to know the truth."

When the men turned and went towards Sodom, Abraham remained standing before the LORD. Abraham drew near him and said, "Wilt thou really sweep away good and bad together? Suppose there are fifty good men in the city; wilt thou really sweep it away, and not pardon the place because of the fifty good men? Far be it from thee to do this—to kill good and bad together; for then the good would suffer with the bad. Far be it from thee. Shall not the judge of all the earth do what is just?" The LORD said, "If I find in the city of Sodom fifty good men, I will pardon the whole place for their sake." Abraham replied, "May I presume to speak to the Lord, dust and ashes that I am: suppose there are five short of the fifty good men? Wilt thou destroy the whole city for a mere five men?" He said, "If I find forty-five there I will not destroy it." Abraham spoke again, "Suppose forty can be found there?"; and he said, "For the sake of the forty I will not do it." Then Abraham said, "Please do not be angry, O Lord, if I speak again: suppose thirty can be found there?" He answered, "If I find thirty there I will not do it." Abraham continued, "May I presume to speak to the Lord: suppose twenty can be found there?" He replied, "For the sake of the twenty I will not destroy it." Abraham said, "I pray thee not to be angry, O Lord, if I speak just once more: suppose ten can be found there?" He said, "For the sake of the ten I will not destroy it." When the LORD had finished talking with Abraham, he left him, and Abraham returned home.

The two angels came to Sodom in the evening, and Lot was sitting in the gateway of the city. When he saw them he rose to meet them and bowed low with his face to the ground. He said, "I pray you, sirs, turn aside to my humble home, spend the night there and wash your feet; you can rise early and continue your journey." "No," they answered, "we will spend the night in the street." But Lot was so insistent that they did turn aside and enter his house. He prepared a meal for them, baking unleavened cakes, and they ate them.

The two men said to Lot, "Have you anyone else here, sons-in-law, sons, or daughters, or any who belong to you in the city? Get them out of this place, because we are going to destroy it. The outcry against it has been so great that the LORD has sent us to destroy it." So Lot went out and spoke to his intended sons-in-law. He said, "Be quick and leave this place; the LORD is going to destroy the city." But they did not take him seriously.

As soon as it was dawn, the angels urged Lot to go, saying, "Be quick, take your wife and your two daughters who are here, or you will be swept away when the city is punished." When he lingered, they took him by the hand, with his wife and his daughters, and, because the LORD had spared him, led him on until he was outside the city. When they had brought them out, they said, "Flee for your lives; do not look back and do not stop anywhere in the Plain. Flee to the hills or you will be swept away." Lot replied, "No, sirs. You have shown your servant favour and you have added to your unfailing care for me by saving my life, but I cannot escape to the hills; I shall be overtaken by the disaster, and die. Look, here is a town, only a small place, near enough for me to reach quickly. Let me escape to it—it is very small—and save my life." He said to him, "I grant your request: I will not overthrow this town you speak of. But flee there quickly, because I can do nothing until you are there." That is why the place was called Zoar.

The sun had risen over the land as Lot entered Zoar; and then the LORD rained down fire and brimstone from the skies on Sodom and Gomorrah. He overthrew those cities and destroyed all the Plain, with everyone living there and everything growing in the ground. But Lot's wife, behind him, looked back, and she turned into a pillar of salt.

Next morning Abraham rose early and went to the place where he had stood in the presence of the LORD. He looked down towards Sodom and Gomorrah and all the wide extent of the Plain, and there he saw thick smoke rising high from the earth like the smoke of a lime-kiln. Thus, when God destroyed the cities of the Plain, he thought of Abraham and rescued Lot from the disaster, the overthrow of the cities where he had been living. Lot went up from Zoar, and settled in the hill-country with his two daughters.

PRECIOUS THINGS

David Ellis writes:–

Philip selected this reading, which he had seen in a parish magazine. Its opening line read: "Imagine there is a bank that credits your account each morning with £86,400." An internet search for this line early in March 2019 indicated that it was quoted from a novel by a French author, Marc Levy, living in San Francisco, translated into English as *If Only It Were True,* and published in 2000 by Simon & Schuster, Inc. My application for permission to include it brought an automatic reply that this might take up to twelve weeks to obtain; no problem if we had applied last autumn, but too slow for our

publication deadline of 31st March. So Philip and I have decided to substitute
this very well-known poem by Kipling, which at least includes the reading's
theme of using time wisely, that daily bank credit of 86,400 seconds that must
be utilized during the day because it can never be allowed to accumulate.

IF—

If you can keep your head when all about you
    Are losing theirs and blaming it on you,
If you can trust yourself when all men doubt you,
    But make allowance for their doubting too;
If you can wait and not be tired by waiting,
    Or being lied about, don't deal in lies,
Or being hated, don't give way to hating,
    And yet don't look too good, nor talk too wise:

If you can dream—and not make dreams your master;
    If you can think—and not make thoughts your aim;
If you can meet with Triumph and Disaster
    And treat those two impostors just the same;
If you can bear to hear the truth you've spoken
    Twisted by knaves to make a trap for fools,
Or watch the things you gave your life to, broken,
    And stoop and build 'em up with worn-out tools:

If you can make one heap of all your winnings
    And risk it on one turn of pitch-and-toss,
And lose, and start again at your beginnings
    And never breathe a word about your loss;
If you can force your heart and nerve and sinew
    To serve your turn long after they are gone,
And so hold on when there is nothing in you
    Except the Will which says to them: "Hold on!"

If you can talk with crowds and keep your virtue,
    Or walk with Kings—nor lose the common touch,
If neither foes nor loving friends can hurt you,
    If all men count with you, but none too much;
If you can fill the unforgiving minute
    With sixty seconds' worth of distance run,
Yours is the Earth and everything that's in it,
    And—which is more—you'll be a Man, my son!

Rudyard Kipling
(1865–1936)

A brief note about Kipling's "If" on the previous page:–

First of all, it says "If you *can* . . ." and not "If you *always* . . .". And secondly, it was written long before the days of Political Correctness, at a time when the masculine gender implied also the feminine, put simply as "the male embraces the female". So those readers who wish to may read the concluding words as "you'll be a Woman, my daughter!" – *DJE*

PAIN, ILLNESS AND NATURAL CATASTROPHES

Many people are worried and confused by the number of natural catastrophes which appear to have been happening with increasing frequency in recent years: the Indonesian tsunami, hurricane Katrina and our own summer floods, to mention just a few. They have asked: what sins have these people committed to deserve such retribution, or, how can God exist if he allows such things to happen? Well, as far as sinning is concerned, I very much doubt if the people afflicted were any greater sinners than those who are lucky enough to live on higher and more stable ground, such as West Chiltington. Jesus pointed out that some Galileans who had been killed by Pilate, as well as eighteen men who had been killed when a tower at Siloam collapsed on them, were no more guilty that the rest, but he also pointed out that the rest needed to repent (Luke 13).

One bishop, I forget which one, was reported by the press as saying that Hull was flooded in response to the sins committed by its people! If he actually said that, I don't think he deserves to be a bishop, but knowing the rabble-rousing and inaccurate reporting capabilities of the press, I suspect that what he actually said was something along the lines of: "Well, if you mess around with the ecology of the Planet, don't be surprised if you get trouble." However, sinners and repenters both, all get swept up together in terrible events, natural and man-made.

Let me give you my thoughts on the matter.

First of all, I must stress that these are my thoughts alone and in no way are they officially approved, so if you think that I have got it wrong, please come and have a chat with me to show me the error of my ways.

It is a fact that our puny human bodies can only exist within certain quite close tolerances of pressure, temperature, gravity, etc. Satisfying these criteria for the Earth which God has given us to live on defines the size and position of the Earth relative to the Sun and results in our home having to be dynamic and active instead of dormant and passive. In the Universe as it is, there ain't no other way.

It works like this: the Earth has a solid core, that core is surrounded by a hot liquid mantle and floating on top of this is the thin crust on which we live.

This crust is rather like the skin that forms on top of a cup of hot chocolate as it cools. There are thin areas, which are full of water and form the oceans while thicker areas are the continents. The continents are a bit like floating islands which are pushed around by convection currents in the hot mantle. America, for example, is moving away from us by, I think, about 5 centimetres (2 inches) a year. This is not quite fast enough for some people, but they will just have to be patient. Where continents collide, the skin wrinkles and we have mountains like the Alps and the Himalayas. Where the continents are moving apart, the crust thins and even splits and we have volcanoes, like the Pacific 'Rim of Fire'. This process has been happening ever since the Earth cooled sufficiently for the crust to form, but of course to us it appears to be happening very slowly and we don't normally notice it. The rocks which form the crust do not like being pushed around and resist the motion for as long as they can but in the end they have to yield and an earthquake occurs. If this earthquake is under the sea, a tsunami can develop!

It's very similar with the weather: the summer causes the air to heat up and absorb large amounts of water from the oceans which swirls like the water going down the plughole in a bath, and results in storms of very high winds and eventually very heavy rainfalls (hurricanes in the Atlantic and typhoons in the Pacific). These things have to be, as an offshoot of the process which makes the Earth inhabitable for us; it's the way it works.

The same approach can be thought about illness and pain. When the body gets damaged, either by accident or illness, pain is the warning signal that things are not as they should be, and we need it to teach us not to do silly things such as putting a hand into boiling water—we only do that once and we don't leave it there for very long!

Now we come to the personal bit. It all depends how one interprets God. I think most people, at least those who do think about Him, think of Him as a father figure in the manner that Jesus taught, and it would sadden any father to know that his children were suffering for no reason of their own making. I suppose we could be blamed for living in places known to be dangerous but most of the world has little choice as to where they live. I think that we just have to accept that life is a risky business and that's the way it is, not that God has deliberately pointed his finger.

There is if course another side to the coin and that is that disasters do give us the opportunity to give help to our fellow men, but we don't often seem to make a very good job of it. However, the fact that we usually try does give us hope.

Tony Hills

Prayers

O God, who art the Father of us all, we pray thee to have pity on all who are cold or hungry or ill-clothed, and upon those who have no home. Show us what we can do to help them, and may we never rest until poverty and want are driven from every land; through Jesus Christ our Lord.   *Amen.*

We bless thy holy Name, O God, for all thy servants who have finished their lives in thy faith and fear, and now rest from their labours. Give us grace, we beseech thee, to follow the example of their steadfastness and faithfulness, to thy honour and glory; through Jesus Christ our Lord.   *Amen.*

Almighty and everlasting God, who hast graciously given to us the fruits of the earth in their season, we yield thee humble and hearty thanks for these thy bounties, beseeching thee to give us grace rightly to use them, to thy glory and the relief of those that need. Through Jesus Christ our Lord.   *Amen.*

Give, O Lord, to all who till the ground the wisdom to understand thy laws, and to co-operate with thy wise ordering of the world. Give to farmers and labourers the desire to work together in the spirit of justice and goodwill. Give to men of science the power to discover the secrets of nature. Give to our statesmen the will to make just laws. And grant that the fruits of thy bountiful earth may not be hoarded by selfish men or squandered by foolish men, but that all who work may share abundantly in the harvest of thy soil, according to thy will, revealed to us in Jesus Christ our Lord.   *Amen.*

A few moments' silence for your own prayers.

The Lord's Prayer

Be thou, O Lord, within us to strengthen us, above us to protect us, beneath us to uphold us, before us to guide us, behind us to recall us, round us to fortify us.   *Amen.*

SIMPLE SERVICE, WITH HYMNS
30th December 2007

Order of Service

Welcome & Notices (Kevin)

Hymn 77 (Tune: *Was lebet*)
O worship the Lord in the beauty of holiness

Brief introduction (David)

Hymn 192 (Tune: *St Peter*)
How sweet the name of Jesus sounds

First reading (Richard) 2 Corinthians 9, 6–15 *(NEB)*

Hymn 236 (Tune: *Carlisle*)
Breathe on me, Breath of God

Second reading (Peter) Romans 8, 26–30 *(NEB)*

Hymn 361 (Tune: *Nottingham*)
Take my life, and let it be

Brief chat (David)

Hymn 298 (Tune: *Lux benigna*)
Lead, kindly light, amid the encircling gloom

Prayers (Peter)

Hymn 296 (Tune: *Cwm Rhondda*)
Guide me, O thou great Redeemer

The service will proceed without announcements. All the hymns are in *Hymns Ancient & Modern Revised*.

Thank you for coming. Please use the voting form opposite to list your own favourite hymns for a subsequent service.

Once again may I thank you all for coming, and Robert for his invaluable musical work.

We are indebted to Viv for the hymns this time, so please note that as we haven't had many forms back over the last year or more there is a very good chance that if you do put in a form some or even all of your hymns may be used. You are welcome to return a form even if you have done so on previous occasions, and we are not averse to using again the occasional hymn that we have already had.

The next fifth Sunday is 30th March, which is a week after Easter and the day we put the clocks forward for Summer Time—a nice thought for us now in the middle of winter.[1]

2 Corinthians 9, 6–15

Remember: sparse sowing, sparse reaping; sow bountifully, and you will reap bountifully. Each person should give as he has decided for himself; there should be no reluctance, no sense of compulsion; God loves a cheerful giver. And it is in God's power to provide you richly with every good gift; thus you will have ample means in yourselves to meet each and every situation, with enough and to spare for every good cause. Scripture says of such a man: "He has lavished his gifts on the needy, his benevolence stands fast for ever."

Now he who provides seed for sowing and bread for food will provide the seed for you to sow; he will multiply it and swell the harvest of your benevolence, and you will always be rich enough to be generous.

Through our action such generosity will issue in thanksgiving to God, for as a piece of willing service this is not only a contribution towards the needs of God's people; more than that, it overflows in a flood of thanksgiving to God. For through the proof which this affords, many will give honour to God when they see how humbly you obey him and how faithfully you confess the gospel of Christ; and will thank him for your liberal contribution to their need and to the general good. And as they join in prayer on your behalf, their hearts will go out to you because of the richness of the grace which God has imparted to you. Thanks be to God for his gift beyond words!

---

[1] A rash prediction! Easter turned out to be colder than Christmas had been, and it snowed the weekend before our March service and the weekend afterwards!

Romans 8, 26–30

In the same way the Spirit comes to the aid of our weakness. We do not even know what it is right to pray for, but through our inarticulate groans the Spirit himself is pleading for us, and God who searches our inmost being knows what the Spirit means, because he pleads for God's own people in God's own way; and in everything, as we know, all things work together for good for those who love God and are called according to his purpose.

For God knew his own before ever they were, and also ordained that they should be shaped to the likeness of his Son, that he might be the eldest among a large family of brothers; and it is these, so fore-ordained, whom he has also called. And those whom he called he has justified, and to those whom he justified he has also given his splendour.

HOW THESE HYMNS SERVICES STARTED[1]

As we move into our fifth year of these services it might be of interest to think back to how they actually started. The inspiration was a *'SONGS of PRAISE' of your chosen hymns* held on 13th February 2000 in aid of the Millennium Fund, as I see from the service sheet I kept. We had been invited to request a single hymn, and I thought at the time that if you were to ask, say, a hundred people each to choose a hymn you would be liable to end up with a hundred hymns. I thought it would be a nice idea to repeat the venture, but to let people choose more hymns each, so that some at least might be asked for by several people. One day in the spring of 2003 I spoke to a friend who had also enjoyed this service, and he agreed that I should ask Kevin if we could try it again.

It was my friend's encouragement that had got the venture started, but eventually he told me that he had no time to help follow it through. In order to put a notice in the parish magazine in time for the first one, I had to find someone else in rather a hurry. So, having thought of some hymns we might use, I telephoned Peter Evans that Wednesday afternoon and to my amazement he was at home. And not only did he like the idea, but he was happy with all my suggested hymns. I printed out my notice, took it round to Kevin for his approval, handed it in and we were under way.

I suspect that I didn't actually look at the service sheet from 2000, or I should have noticed that we got through no less than fifteen hymns, one after the other, with a prayer after the first one and closing prayers and blessing

---

[1] For how they ended, see page 369.

before the last. That is probably why what we have actually done has been completely different. Because, if you are not going to sing lots of hymns in succession, you need something in between, such as some readings. Thus arose the simple format we have kept to throughout.

I had chatted to Peter enough times as we cleared up the hall after our Breakfast meetings to know that he shared my view of Christianity being a simple religion; and that is the theme I want to come back to today.

First I should just explain why we chose the first reading. We thought its theme of giving might also apply to Christmas giving. I had heard it long ago at a Harvest Festival service at Pulborough, and nine words, their context long forgotten, had stood out and proved encouraging ever since: "You will always be rich enough to be generous".

WHAT WE NEED TO BELIEVE, ON A POSTAGE STAMP ?

Thinking about the Christian religion being a simple one, one cannot but observe that while many massive tomes can and have been written on matters of theology, what one actually needs to believe could well be written on a single postage stamp. But like the hundred people choosing a hymn each, no doubt each and every one of us would write something different on his or her postage stamp. What would you write on yours? It might be an interesting exercise to consider this, if you haven't already.

Those of an Evangelical bent might select something like "Jesus died for me", which could be interpreted in different ways, the most mundane being that if Jesus had not died the way he did there could have been no resurrection and Christianity as a faith might never have taken off.

I have been thinking recently that you could do worse than "All things work together for good for those who love God". I find this reassuring for two reasons, the first of course being its message if it is really true—the assurance that however bleak the present may seem, something good can come from it if we have the patience and fortitude not to despair.

The second reason is that when we see it working in the trivial affairs of our own life, in little things that matter to us but not greatly to anyone else, we have that much more confidence that it will work for the bigger things as well. I had to take my car to Worthing a few weeks ago for some work to be done on it, coming home on the bus, and I have often had to stand at the bus stop for ten minutes or more before it arrived. On this particular morning I carefully calculated when I had to get up, but everything took longer than expected, and on the way in I passed the bus coming back. With nearly an hour to wait for the next one, I was thinking after booking in the car that "something good will come from this". To while away some of the time I thought I would walk round and pay a social visit to the printers who do work for me over there, as they were not far away. And as it happened, they had just completed the Christmas cards they had been doing for my customer and myself, so I took them home then, instead of four days later when the car was ready to collect.

That was a deliberately trivial example, but other, less trivial, sequels to sad or frustrating events are of course that much more encouraging in confirming the truth of the original saying, from our second reading.

A PLAN FOR EVERYONE'S LIFE ?

Although all our scriptures date from two thousand years ago, and the doctrine derived from them is correspondingly ancient, we would not say prayers if we didn't believe in a here-and-now to religion, if we didn't believe that these prayers could be answered in the form of future events.

We can all believe that the Good Lord has a plan for the life of each and every one of us; the only problem is that he doesn't actually tell us what it is! We may have hunches or premonitions, and sometimes these are borne out by future events, but in general we do not know the future; and that is just as well, for we might be overwhelmed at the prospect of bad or painful things to come, and not bother to work for the good ones.

The Old Testament records Abraham given very definite instructions concerning the quite unusual things he had to do, but at this distance in time we can't be sure that he actually found life any easier in this respect than we do, and that these divine commandments weren't written into his story afterwards. We can only attempt what we believe to be right for us, with the thought that if we are doing something for someone else we are probably not completely wasting our time. Speaking personally, I have put my energy into this or that organization for a longish period, but then have been abruptly stopped.[1] I can only conclude that it was right for me to work for them at the time, but not for ever. Looking back, one can see how far one has been led, but was this according to God's original plan, or did that plan have to be revised continually to take our actions and choices into account? Or both, perhaps? Anyway, we have two splendid hymns on the theme of guidance, next and after the prayers.[2]

---

[1] For yet another instance of this, see page 369!

[2] For convenience, this talk has been divided into three sections, each with a title. The text is just as printed on Boxing Day for Peter to see, but its final section turned out to be remarkably relevant to Kevin's announcement on the day of our service that he would be leaving our Parish to join the Catholics. Even the "two splendid hymns on the theme of guidance" could hardly have been more appropriate to the occasion!

Prayers   30th December 2007

O Father, who hast declared thy love to men by the birth of the holy Child at Bethlehem; help us to welcome him with gladness and to make room for him in our common days; so that we may live at peace with one another, and in goodwill with all thy family; through the same, thy Son Jesus Christ our Lord. *Amen.*

Almighty God, whom once the nations worshipped under names of fear, but who hast revealed the glory of thy love in the birth of Jesus Christ; fill our hearts, as we remember his nativity, with the gladness of this great redemption. May we join in the heavenly song of glory to God in the highest, on earth peace, and goodwill towards men. Breathe into our hearts the spirit of Jesus, so that we may be led to thee in trust and obedience; through Jesus Christ our Lord. *Amen.*

O Lord Jesus Christ, to whom the wise men from the East brought gifts at Bethlehem, hasten the time, we beseech thee, when the wisdom of the East shall seek after thee and find thee. Grant that the peoples of Asia and Africa may offer to thee their treasures, their love, and their service, and bow before thee in worship, who livest and reignest with the Father and the Holy Spirit, one God for evermore. *Amen.*

A few moments' silence for your own prayers.

The Lord's Prayer

May the blessing of almighty God rest upon us and upon all our work; may he give us light to guide us, courage to support us, and love to unite us, now and evermore. *Amen.*

SIMPLE SERVICE, WITH HYMNS

30th March 2008

Order of Service

Welcome & Notices (Diane)

Hymn 185 (Tune: *Richmond*)
Praise to the Holiest in the height

Brief introduction (David)

Hymn 134 (Tune: *Easter Hymn*)
Jesus Christ is risen today

First reading (Philip) John, Chapter 13, Verses 1–17 *(NEB)*

Hymn 372 (Tune: *St Denio*)
Immortal, invisible, God only wise

Second reading (Tony) John, Chapter 21, Verses 1–14 *(NEB)*

Hymn 271 (Tune: *Benson*)
God is working his purpose out

Third reading (Lyn) "The Daffodil Principle" *by Jaroldeen Edwards*

Hymn 506 (*M. Praise;* words overleaf. Tune: *How Great Thou Art*)
O Lord my God! When I in awesome wonder

Prayers (*chosen by* Peter and *read by* David)

Hymn 300 (Tune: *Abridge*)
Be thou my guardian and my guide

The service will proceed without announcements. All the hymns except one (words opposite) are in *Hymns Ancient & Modern Revised.*

Thank you for coming. Please use the separate voting form to list your own favourite hymns for a subsequent service.

O Lord my God! (How great Thou art)

O Lord my God! When I in awesome wonder
Consider all the works Thy hand hath made,
I see the stars, I hear the mighty thunder,
The power throughout the universe displayed;

Then sings my soul, my Saviour God, to Thee,
How great Thou art, how great Thou art!
Then sings my soul, my Saviour God, to Thee,
How great Thou art, how great Thou art!

When through the woods and forest glades I wander
And hear the birds sing sweetly in the trees;
When I look down from lofty mountain grandeur,
And hear the brook, and feel the gentle breeze;

Then sings my soul . . .

And when I think that God His Son not sparing,
Sent Him to die – I scarce can take it in,
That on the cross my burden gladly bearing,
He bled and died to take away my sin:

Then sings my soul . . .

When Christ shall come with shout of acclamation
And take me home – what joy shall fill my heart!
Then shall I bow in humble adoration
And there proclaim, my God, how great Thou art!

Then sings my soul . . .

Stuart Wesley Keene Hine
(1899–1989)

Once again may I thank you all for coming, Diane for coming along to take over Kevin's role in lending us some official support and giving out the notices, and Robert for his invaluable musical work.

Last time I concluded my introduction by saying that "the next fifth Sunday is 30th March, which is a week after Easter and the day we put the clocks forward for Summer Time—a nice thought for us now in the middle of winter." So here we are, just a week after an Easter colder than Christmas was, and still hoping that summer will be along soon.

Today's service has been overshadowed by Peter Evans's illness; his heart attack came on 10th February, just two days before he was due to come round to me to help select the hymns. It is comforting to know that in such circumstances we are still 'looked after', and that he was taken ill during the evening when he was with his family, who could take rapid action to get medical help to him.

Although he cannot be with us this evening, we were able to work out details of this service together during my visits to Worthing Hospital. I am grateful to Philip, now at last on the mend from his long attack of shingles, Tony and Lyn for their help with the readings today.

John 13, 1–17

It was before the Passover festival. Jesus knew that his hour had come and he must leave this world and go to the Father. He had always loved his own who were in the world, and now he was to show the full extent of his love.

The devil had already put it into the mind of Judas, son of Simon Iscariot, to betray him. During supper, Jesus, well aware that the Father had entrusted everything to him, and that he had come from God and was going back to God, rose from table, laid aside his garments, and taking a towel, tied it round him. Then he poured water into a basin, and began to wash his disciples' feet and to wipe them with the towel.

When it was Simon Peter's turn, Peter said to him, "You, Lord, washing my feet?"

Jesus replied, "You do not understand now what I am doing, but one day you will." Peter said, "I will never let you wash my feet."

"If I do not wash you," Jesus replied, "you are not in fellowship with me."

"Then, Lord," said Simon Peter, "not my feet only; wash my hands and head as well!"

Jesus said, "A man who has bathed needs only to wash his feet; he is altogether clean; and you are clean, though not every one of you." He added the words "not every one of you" because he knew who was going to betray him.

After washing their feet and taking his garments again, he sat down. "Do you understand," he asked, "what I have done for you? You call me 'Master' and 'Lord', and rightly so, for that is what I am. Then if I, your Lord and Master, have washed your feet, you also ought to wash one another's feet. I have set you an example: you are to do as I have done for you. In very truth I tell you, a servant is not greater than his master, nor a messenger than the one who sent him. If you know this, happy are you if you act upon it."

John 21, 1–14

Some time later, Jesus showed himself to his disciples once again, by the Sea of Tiberias; and in this way. Simon Peter and Thomas 'the Twin' were together with Nathanael of Cana-in-Galilee. The sons of Zebedee and two other disciples were also there. Simon Peter said, "I am going out fishing."

"We will go with you", said the others. So they started and got into the boat. But that night they caught nothing.

Morning came, and there stood Jesus on the beach, but the disciples did not know that it was Jesus. He called out to them, "Friends, have you caught anything?"

They answered "No."

He said, "Shoot the net to starboard, and you will make a catch."

They did so, and found they could not haul the net aboard, there were so many fish in it. Then the disciple whom Jesus loved said to Peter, "It is the Lord!"

When Simon Peter heard that, he wrapped his coat about him (for he had stripped) and plunged into the sea. The rest of them came on in the boat, towing the net full of fish; for they were not far from land, only about a hundred yards.

When they came ashore, they saw a charcoal fire there, with fish laid on it, and some bread. Jesus said, "Bring some of your catch."

Simon Peter went aboard and dragged the net to land, full of big fish, a hundred and fifty-three of them; and yet, many as they were, the net was not torn. Jesus said, "Come and have breakfast."

None of the disciples dared to ask "Who are you?" They knew it was the Lord. Jesus now came up, took the bread, and gave it to them, and the fish in the same way.

This makes the third time that Jesus appeared to his disciples after his resurrection from the dead.

The Daffodil Principle

Several times my daughter telephoned, "Mother, you must come and see the daffodils before they are over." I wanted to go but it was a two-hour drive from Laguna to Lake Arrowhead. "I will come next Tuesday," I promised, a little reluctantly, on her third call.

Next Tuesday dawned cold and rainy. Still, I had promised, so I drove there. When I finally walked into Carolyn's house and hugged and greeted my grandchildren, I exclaimed, "Forget about the daffodils, Carolyn! The road is invisible in the clouds and fog, and there is nothing in this world except you and these children that I want to see bad enough to drive another inch!"

My daughter smiled calmly and said, "We drive in this all the time, Mother."

"Well, you won't get me back on the road until it clears, then I'm heading for home," I assured her.

"I was hoping you'd take me over to the garage to pick up my car."

"How far will we have to drive?"

"Just a few blocks," said Carolyn. "I'll drive; I'm used to this."

After several minutes, I had to ask, "Where are we going? This isn't the way to the garage!"

"We are going to the garage the long way," Carolyn smiled. "By way of the daffodils!"

"Carolyn," I said sternly, "Please turn around."

"It's all right Mother, I promise. You'll never forgive yourself if you miss this experience."

After about 20 minutes, we turned on a small gravel road and I saw a small church. On the far side of the church, I saw a hand-lettered sign that said, "Daffodil Garden".

We got out of the car, and each took a child's hand, and I followed Carolyn down the path. Then, as we turned the corner of the path, I looked up and gasped. There before me lay the most glorious sight. It looked as if someone had taken a vat of gold and poured it down over the mountain peak and slopes. The flowers were planted in majestic swirling patterns, great ribbons and swathes of deep orange, white, lemon yellow, salmon pink, saffron and butter yellow. Each different-coloured variety was planted as a group so that it swirled and flowed like its own river with its own unique hue. There were five acres of flowers.

"But who has done this?" I asked Carolyn.

"It's just one woman", Carolyn answered. "She lives on the property — that's her home." Carolyn pointed to a well-kept 'A'-frame house that looked small and modest in the midst of all that glory. We went up to the house and on the patio we saw a poster. "Answers to the questions I know you are asking" was the headline.

The first answer was a simple one. "50,000 bulbs," it read. The second answer was, "One at a time, by one woman, two hands, two feet, and very little brain."

The third answer was, "Begun in 1958."

There it was — The Daffodil Principle. For me that moment was a life-changing experience. I thought of this woman whom I had never met, who, more than 40 years before, had begun, one bulb at a time, to bring this vision of beauty and joy to an obscure mountain-top. Still, just planting one bulb at a time, year after year, had changed the world.

This unknown woman had forever changed the world in which she lived. She had created something magnificent, beautiful and inspiring. The principle her daffodil garden taught is one of the greatest principles of celebration. This is that, learning to move towards our goals and desires one step at a time with small increments of daily effort, we, too, will find we can accomplish magnificent things. We can change the world.

It makes me sad in a way," I admitted to Carolyn. "What might I have accomplished if I had thought of a wonderful goal 35 or 40 years ago and had worked away at it 'one bulb at a time' through all those years? Just think what I might have achieved".

My daughter summed up the message of the day in her usual direct way. "Start tomorrow," she said.

It's pointless to think of the lost hours of yesterdays. The way to make 'learning' a lesson of celebration instead of a cause for regret is only to ask, "How can I put this to use today?" [1]

---

[1] Included as a reading for the Cambridge University Scout and Guide Club Gold Reunion *Scout and Guide's Own* (simple service, entitled "Flowers of Gold"), held Sunday 3rd August 2003. No source was indicated, but an internet search in January 2019 has revealed that this story was a chapter from *Celebration! Ten Principles of More Joyous Living* by Jaroldeen Asplund Edwards (Deseret Book, 1995), issued as a separate, illustrated, book in 2004. The bulbs were planted by Gene Bauer. Sadly, the Willow Fire of 1999 destroyed the Bauers' home, with its shady trees and garden. Miraculously, the daffodil bulbs below the ground survived and the garden remained open to visitors for three weeks every spring until 2009, when Gene Bauer was 83. She had been the Native Flora Chairwoman for California Garden Clubs, Inc. and to educate other members she had produced drawings and text of one plant each month, 56 of these hand-crafted in limited editions, from 1972 (later published as *Botanical Seriographs : the Gene Bauer Collection*, ESRI Press). She loved anything beautiful.

Prayers

O risen Lord, who after thy passion didst show thyself alive unto thine Apostles by many infallible proofs, and didst speak unto them the things that concern the kingdom of God: speak unto us also who wait upon thee, and fill us with joy and peace in believing; that we may abound in hope, and knowing thy will may faithfully perform it, even unto the end; through thy grace, who livest and reignest, Lord of the dead and of the living.   *Amen.*

O God, our heavenly Father, we thank thee for the beauty of the world around us. We thank thee for the love of parents, children and friends, for work and play, for food and clothing, and for all the happiness of life. Most of all we thank thee for the birth of Jesus Christ thy Son, for the example of his life and for the love which made him die for us. And we pray that we may ever serve him faithfully and fight his battles, through the same Jesus Christ our Lord.   *Amen.*

O God, our Father, we thank thee for all thy love has given us today. Forgive us everything we have thought, or said, or done, that has made thee sad or hurt others. May the lessons we have learnt and all the fun and joy we have had help us to please thee more, and may we take happiness into our homes and wherever we go. Bless and keep us all safe through the coming night, for Jesus Christ's sake.   *Amen.*

Be present, O merciful God, and protect us through the silent hours of this night, so that we who are fatigued by the changes and chances of this fleeting world may repose upon thy eternal changelessness: through Jesus Christ our Lord.   *Amen.*

A few moments' silence for your own prayers.

The Lord's Prayer

Irish Blessing

May the silence of the hills,
The joy of the wind,
The music of the birds,
The fire of the sun,
And the strength of the trees
Be in our hearts now and evermore —

May the road rise up to meet you.
May the wind be always at your back.
May the sun shine warm upon your face,
The rain fall soft upon your fields,
And until we meet again,
May your God hold you in the palm of His hand.

SIMPLE SERVICE, WITH HYMNS
29th June 2008

Order of Service

Welcome & Notices (Graham)

Hymn 365 (Tune: *Praise, my soul*)
Praise, my soul, the King of heaven

Brief introduction (David)

Hymn 50 (*Mission Praise;* words on page 44)
Be still, for the presence of the Lord

First reading (Tony) Ephesians, Chapter 6, Verses 10–18 *(NEB)*

Hymn 169 (Tune: *Westminster*)
My God, how wonderful thou art

Second reading (Tony) Luke, Chapter 7, Verses 1–10 *(NEB)*

Hymn 456 (*Mission Praise;* words opposite. Tune: *St Francis*)
Make me a channel of your peace

Brief chat (David)

Hymn 184 (Tune: *Repton*)
Dear Lord and Father of mankind

Prayers (David)

Hymn 265 (Tune: *Aurelia*) [Words are on page 368]
From Greenland's icy mountains

The service will proceed without announcements. All the hymns except two (words opposite and overleaf) are in *Hymns Ancient & Modern Revised.*

Thank you for coming. Please use the separate voting form to list your own favourite hymns for a subsequent service.

Make me a channel of your peace

Make me a channel of your peace.
Where there is hatred, let me bring your love.
Where there is injury, your pardon, Lord,
And where there's doubt, true faith in you.

Make me a channel of your peace.
Where there's despair in life, let me bring hope.
Where there is darkness only light,
And where there's sadness ever joy.

O Master, grant that I may never seek
So much to be consoled, as to console,
To be understood, as to understand,
To be loved, as to love, with all my soul.

Make me a channel of your peace.
It is in pardoning that we are pardoned,
In giving of ourselves that we receive,
And in dying that we're born to eternal life.

Words and Music: Sebastian Temple

Dedicated to Mrs Frances Tracy
© 1967, OCP, 5536 NE Hassalo, Portland, OR 97213.

---

[1] OCP is Oregon Catholic Press.

As always, may I thank you all for coming, especially anyone who has not come to one of these services before; I hope you find it useful, meaningful or whatever a service should be, and will want to come again. Thanks to Graham for coming along and giving out the notices, and to Robert for his invaluable musical work.

Well, after snow the week before and the week after our last service, despite our having put the clocks forward for Summer Time, we really are having some summer now. Our next service will also be a summer one, just two months away at the end of August.

Although Peter Evans cannot be with us this evening, he has been as hard-working as usual in sorting out details of the service. I am also grateful to Tony for his assistance with choosing the hymns and for doing the readings today.

Ephesians 6, 10–18

Finally then, find your strength in the Lord, in his mighty power. Put on all the armour which God provides, so that you may be able to stand firm against the devices of the devil. For our fight is not against human foes, but against cosmic powers, against the authorities and potentates of this dark world, against the superhuman forces of evil in the heavens. Therefore, take up God's armour; then you will be able to stand your ground when things are at their worst, to complete every task and still to stand. Stand firm, I say. Buckle on the belt of truth; for coat of mail put on integrity; let the shoes on your feet be the gospel of peace, to give you firm footing; and, with all these, take up the great shield of faith, with which you will be able to quench all the flaming arrows of the evil one. Take salvation for helmet; for sword, take that which the Spirit gives you—the words that come from God. Give yourselves wholly to prayer and entreaty; pray on every occasion in the power of the Spirit.

Luke 7, 1–10

When he had finished addressing the people, he went to Capernaum. A centurion there had a servant whom he valued highly; this servant was ill and near to death. Hearing about Jesus, he sent some Jewish elders with the request that he would come and save his servant's life. They approached Jesus and pressed their petition earnestly: "He deserves this favour from you," they said, "for he is a friend of our nation and it is he who built us our synagogue." Jesus went with them; but when he was not far from the house, the centurion sent friends with this message: "Do not trouble further, sir; it is not for me to have you under my roof, and that is why I did not presume to approach you in person. But say the word and my servant will be cured. I know, for in my position I am myself under orders, with soldiers under me. I say to one, 'Go', and he goes; to another, 'Come here', and he comes; and to my servant, 'Do this', and he does it." When Jesus heard this, he admired the man, and, turning to the crowd that was following him, he said, "I tell you, nowhere, even in Israel, have I found faith like this." And the messengers returned to the house and found the servant in good health.

WHY DO SO FEW PEOPLE COME TO CHURCH ?

I call this part of the service a 'brief chat', as it is not meant to be a sermon. I hope it provides an interlude between the hymns and makes a change from readings.

Last year we heard about a parish whose population was ten times ours, but the same number came to their church each Sunday as attend here. By that comparison we are doing well, but eighty in over three thousand is still not a lot, so why do so few people come to church?

One reason may be that they think that religion makes demands on them that they would rather not have to fulfil. Herod objected to John the Baptist, not because of his preaching but because he pointed out that he should not have married his brother's wife. Another may be that we do not have the strong Christian tradition in schools today that pertained a few decades ago. When I was at school, with our simple service at each morning assembly, I imagined that all my fellow pupils were basically Christian, and someone who called himself an atheist was quite unusual.

On the other hand, I have friends familiar with church services on account of being choirboys in their youth, who have drifted away since then. Something must have put them off.

The general excuse is the march of science, which has claimed that we are all random products of chance-driven processes, that what we are and what we do are determined by our genes, and that evolution supersedes the creation story in Genesis. To that one can say that at least Genesis got the basic order of things correct, even if its time-scale was a bit out.

People outside the Church may be under the impression that much of Christian doctrine is just not credible. They feel that we require them, like the White Queen, to be able to believe as many as six impossible things before breakfast. But those of us who do come to church must be of the opinion that the least believable aspects are also the least fundamental, and that more than enough *is* credible to provide a faith by which to live.

I was taught that we learn about our faith from three sources: the Bible, the teaching of the Church and our own personal experience. People outside the church may well be familiar with the Gospel story and have some idea of the Church's teaching, but they may not have the experience that Christians have of prayers being answered or of trying to do what is right and finding that help and guidance are given to them when they need it. "All we can do is nothing worth, unless God blesses the deed." But if He *does* bless the deed, that can be very encouraging.

So it's more constructive to believe, not in a God who set the world in motion and then went away and left it, but in one who is still actively concerned with it, and has a purpose for it that we may be able to help fulfil. And while it would be good to have our churches full, we don't want people to come simply for social reasons and because they find the services entertaining, but in the spirit of that post-Communion prayer, "Send us out into the world, to live and work to Thy praise and glory."

Prayers

Eternal God, in whose perfect kingdom no sword is drawn but the sword of righteousness, and no strength known but the strength of love; we pray thee so mightily to shed and spread abroad thy spirit that all peoples and ranks may be gathered under one banner of the Prince of peace; as children of one Father, Lord of love; to whom alone be dominion and glory now and for ever. *Amen.*

We praise thy name, O Father, for the beauty of the summer, the glory of the sky by day and night, the healthful wind and quickening rain. We thank thee for the bloom and fragrance of the flowers, the songs of the birds, and the joyousness of every living thing. In all that thou hast made we see the wonder of thy wisdom and care. Help us to trust thy never-failing goodness, the love which is beyond understanding, and surrounds our lives with blessing, for thy name's sake. *Amen.*

O Lord, from whom all good things do come, grant to us thy humble servants that by thy holy inspiration we may think those things that be good, and by thy merciful guiding may perform the same; through Jesus Christ our Lord. *Amen.*

A few moments' silence for your own prayers.

The Lord's Prayer

May the Lord bless us and keep us; the Lord make his face to shine upon us and be gracious to us; the Lord lift up the light of his countenance upon us and give us peace, this day and for evermore. *Amen.*

SIMPLE SERVICE, WITH HYMNS
31st August 2008

Order of Service

Welcome & Notices (Graham)

Hymn 246 (Tune: *Angel voices*)
Angel-voices ever singing

Brief introduction (David)

Hymn 344 (Tune: *St Bees*)
Hark, my soul! It is the Lord

First reading (Philip) Luke 15, 11–24 *(NEB)*

Hymn 17 (Tune: *Strength and Stay*)
O strength and stay upholding all creation

Second reading (Tony) Mark 2, 1–12 *(NEB)*

Hymn 250 (Tune: *Ravenshaw*)
Lord, thy word abideth

Brief chat (David)

Hymn 300 (Tune: *Abridge*)
Be thou my guardian and my guide

Prayers (Peter)

Hymn 382 (Tune: *Praxis pietatis*)
Praise to the Lord, the Almighty, the King of creation

The service will proceed without announcements. All the hymns are in *Hymns Ancient & Modern Revised*.

Thank you for coming. Please use the voting form opposite to list your own favourite hymns for a subsequent service.

As always, may I thank you all for coming, especially anyone who has not experienced one of these services before; I hope you will come again. Thanks to Graham for giving out the notices, and to Robert for his invaluable musical work.

We are of course very pleased to have Peter Evans back with us this evening. Though he was available to help plan the two previous services, this is the first one he has been able to come to this year, so now he can read the prayers as well as choose them. And we are both grateful to Philip and Tony for doing the readings today.

This is our second summer service of the year (well, it was a splendid day yesterday). But it will be winter again for our next one, at the end of November, and this will be our twenty-first, and five years to the day since we started these services in 2003.

Luke 15, 11–24

Again he said: "There was once a man who had two sons; and the younger said to his father, 'Father, give me my share of the property.' So he divided his estate between them. A few days later the younger son turned the whole of his share into cash and left home for a distant country, where he squandered it in reckless living. He had spent it all, when a severe famine fell upon that country and he began to feel the pinch. So he went and attached himself to one of the local landowners, who sent him on to his farm to mind the pigs. He would have been glad to fill his belly with the pods that the pigs were eating; and no one gave him anything.

"Then he came to his senses and said, 'How many of my father's paid servants have more food than they can eat, and here am I, starving to death! I will set off and go to my father, and say to him, Father, I have sinned, against God and against you; I am no longer fit to be called your son; treat me as one of your paid servants.' So he set out for his father's house.

"But while he was still a long way off his father saw him, and his heart went out to him. He ran to meet him, flung his arms round him, and kissed him. The son said, 'Father, I have sinned, against God and against you; I am no longer fit to be called your son.' But the father said to his servants, 'Quick! Fetch a robe, my best one, and put it on him; put a ring on his finger and shoes on his feet. Bring the fatted calf and kill it, and let us have a feast to celebrate the day. For this son of mine was dead and has come back to life; he was lost and is found.' And the festivities began."

Mark 2, 1–12

When after some days he returned to Capernaum, the news went round that he was at home; and such a crowd collected that the space in front of the door was not big enough to hold them. And while he was proclaiming the message to them, a man was brought who was paralysed. Four men were carrying him, but because of the crowd they could not get him near. So they opened up the roof over the place where Jesus was, and when they had broken through they lowered the stretcher on which the paralysed man was lying. When Jesus saw their faith, he said to the paralysed man, "My son, your sins are forgiven."

Now there were some lawyers sitting there and they thought to themselves, "Why does the fellow talk like that? This is blasphemy! Who but God alone can forgive sins?" Jesus knew in his own mind that this was what they were thinking, and said to them: "Why do you harbour thoughts like these? Is it easier to say to this paralysed man, 'Your sins are forgiven', or to say, 'Stand up, take your bed, and walk'? But to convince you that the Son of Man has the right on earth to forgive sins"—he turned to the paralysed man—"I say to you, stand up, take your bed, and go home." And he got up, took his stretcher at once, and went out in full view of them all, so that they were astounded and praised God. "Never before," they said, "have we seen the like."

VISITS FROM THE JWs

How many of us get that sinking feeling when we answer the door to find two people outside, clutching books and leaflets? Yes, it's the JWs, and no protest that we are already regular churchgoers is going to stop them offering us their magazines and asking to share some passage from the Bible with us.

While I respect their dedication in going round in this way (even just calling on people to collect money for charity is more than most of us are willing to undertake), it's not so much that their beliefs differ somewhat from ours that bothers me, as my not being in the mood to discuss such things when I may be trying to catch the post, or immersed in some task that I would prefer not to have interrupted. I did have a very interesting conversation with one some years ago, when he called unaccompanied on a Sunday morning and I was in the front garden sweeping up leaves.

Though we may not allow thoughts of a spiritual nature to disrupt our daily round, we do give them precedence in church, and even in a simple service such as this we can share a passage or two from scripture.

JESUS AND FORGIVENESS

Peter and I usually choose our readings because they are well known, without all that much regard for their themes. So it is something of a coincidence that both our readings today are related to forgiveness, though in rather different ways. There is one similarity, however, in that in both cases the forgiveness was freely given. One gets the impression that the prodigal's father was so ready to welcome him home that he was hardly listening to his prepared speech; and Jesus announced that the paralysed man's sins were forgiven without his making any request for absolution, and no doubt as much to his surprise as to everyone else's.

Not that either of them was forgiven without having made any effort of his own. The prodigal son had to come to his senses and realize that even his father's servants were better off than he was; he had to take the decision to set out on the long trek back home not knowing what sort of reception he would get, and work out what to say when he got there. The paralysed man had to get his friends to bring him to Jesus to heal his affliction, and these friends had to go to some lengths to get him near Jesus, even dismantling the roof of the house where he was. (I have often wondered how long it took to reinstate this afterwards.)

It has been suggested that Jesus' forgiveness of this man was essential to the healing process; that the paralysis was a psychosomatic result of the man's intense feelings of guilt, but we are not told what he had done; apart, that is, from letting his friends dismantle someone's roof. (Some people of course blame themselves unduly over trivial things, while others commit serious crimes and show no remorse at all.)

The story of the prodigal son comes after illustrations Jesus gave of people rejoicing at finding something that they had lost, and follows immediately his statement that "there is joy among the angels of God over one sinner who repents." So it is the turning back that counts. No sacrifices are asked for, nor even a willingness to forgive others, which of course Jesus deals with in other parables.

Prayers

Show thy loving kindness tonight, O Lord, to all who stand in need of thy help. Be with the weak to make them strong and with the strong to make them gentle. Cheer the lonely with thy presence and the distracted with thy peace. Prosper thy Church in the fulfilment of her mighty task, and grant thy blessing to all who have toiled today in Christ's name.   *Amen.*

O Lord, who ever rememberest all thy creatures, forgive us for our forgetfulness of them and of thee. Make us more able and willing to keep in mind the true purpose of our life, to work and pray for our brethren in all parts of the world, and to devote ourselves more and more in complete obedience to seek and to do thy holy will in all ways at all times; for Jesus Christ's sake.
Amen.

Praise be to thee, O God, who, through thy Son Jesus Christ, hast revealed thyself to the world. Praise be to thee, O God, that the light of the glorious Gospel of Christ, who is the image of God, has shined upon them that believe. Blessed be the Lord our God, for he has visited and redeemed his people, to give light to them that sit in darkness and in the shadow of death, and to guide our feet into the way of peace.   *Amen.*

Stretch forth, O Lord, the right hand of thy mercy upon all our relations and friends both near and far, that seeking thee with their whole heart, they may find their needs supplied both in body and soul; through Jesus Christ our Lord.
Amen.

A few moments' silence for your own prayers.

The Lord's Prayer

May the Lord lead us when we go, and keep us when we sleep, and talk with us when we wake; and may the peace of God, which passeth all understanding, keep our hearts and minds in Jesus Christ our Lord.   *Amen.*

SIMPLE SERVICE, WITH HYMNS

30th November 2008

Order of Service

Welcome & Notices (Graham)

Hymn 54 (Tune: *Cross of Jesus*)
Come, thou long-expected Jesus

Brief introduction (David)

Hymn 269 (Tune: *Little Cornard*)
Hills of the north, rejoice

First reading (Richard) Matthew 4, 18–25 *(NEB)*

Hymn 533 (Tune: *St. Andrew*)
Jesus calls us! O'er the tumult

Second reading (Philip) Luke 1, 26–38 *(NEB)*

Hymn 307 (Tune: *Morning Light*)
Stand up, stand up for Jesus

Brief chat (Tony)

Hymn 296 (Tune: *Cwm Rhondda*)
Guide me, O thou great Redeemer

Prayers (Peter)

Hymn 51 (Tune: *Helmsley*)
Lo, he comes with clouds descending

The service will proceed without announcements. All the hymns are in *Hymns Ancient & Modern Revised.*

Thank you for coming. Please use the voting form opposite to list your own favourite hymns for a subsequent service.

As most of you will have realized, I must start this introduction with an apology. Peter came round in November and we picked the hymns, and I duly prepared our usual piece for the magazine, but then somehow managed to e-mail David Burnett the August notice again instead of the November one. And it wasn't until I looked in the magazine and then checked what I had sent him that I discovered what had happened. For the record, he has put the correct notice in the December magazine.

As mentioned last time, this is our twenty-first 'hymns service', and five years to the day since we started in 2003. The next one will be at the end of March, when the weather should be getting warmer again (so long as we don't get the snow we had at that time this year), and after that the two summer ones, in May and August.

As always, may I thank you all for coming, especially anyone who has not experienced one of these services before; I hope you will come again. Thanks to Graham for giving out the notices, Richard and Philip for doing the readings, Tony for taking on the 'brief chat', and to Robert for his invaluable musical work.

Matthew 4, 18–25

Jesus was walking by the Sea of Galilee when he saw two brothers, Simon called Peter and his brother Andrew, casting a net into the lake; for they were fishermen. Jesus said to them, "Come with me, and I will make you fishers of men." They left their nets at once and followed him.

He went on, and saw another pair of brothers, James son of Zebedee and his brother John; they were in the boat with their father Zebedee, overhauling their nets. He called them, and at once they left the boat and their father, and followed him.

He went round the whole of Galilee, teaching in the synagogues, preaching the gospel of the Kingdom, and curing whatever illness or infirmity there was among the people. His fame reached the whole of Syria; and sufferers from every kind of illness, racked with pain, possessed by devils, epileptic, or paralysed, were all brought to him, and he cured them. Great crowds also followed him, from Galilee and the Ten Towns, from Jerusalem and Judaea, and from Transjordan.

Luke 1, 26–38

In the sixth month the angel Gabriel was sent from God to a town in Galilee called Nazareth, with a message for a girl betrothed to a man named Joseph, a descendant of David; the girl's name was Mary. The angel went in and said to her, "Greetings, most favoured one! The Lord is with you."

But she was deeply troubled by what he said and wondered what this greeting might mean. Then the angel said to her, "Do not be afraid, Mary, for

God has been gracious to you; you shall conceive and bear a son, and you shall give him the name Jesus. He will be great; he will bear the title 'Son of the Most High'; the Lord God will give him the throne of his ancestor David, and he will be king over Israel for ever; his reign shall never end."

"How can this be," said Mary, "when I have no husband?"

The angel answered, "The Holy Spirit will come upon you, and the power of the Most High will overshadow you; and for that reason the holy child to be born will be called 'Son of God'. Moreover your kinswoman Elizabeth has herself conceived a son in her old age; and she who is reputed barren is now in her sixth month, for God's promises can never fail."

"Here am I," said Mary; "I am the Lord's servant; as you have spoken, so be it."

Then the angel left her.

CONCERNING TIME

Tony summarized his November talk (from memory) as follows:–

I chose the subject because Francesca[1] had written a piece in the Parish Magazine in which she noted that God must be outside both space and time.

I started with the comment that before the advent of Einstein, everyone thought they knew that time was quite simple and constant for everyone. Einstein showed that time was relative to the speeds that observers were travelling. I noted that this had been confirmed experimentally by flying aircraft carrying atomic clocks both with and against the rotation of the Earth. I pointed out that this really did mean that when the crews caught up with each other on the ground, one crew really had aged less, albeit by a very small amount, than the other. (I may not have used these actual words but that was the gist of it.)

I then picked up Francesca's thoughts on God eternal having to be outside Space and Time and that any concept of Heaven must also be outside space and time. I suggested that it was just possible that our personality (rather than our physical bodies) could be accelerated to the speed of light. It is not possible to go faster than light in the physical universe, and so at this point, time would stop. Isn't that another way of describing 'eternity'?

---

[1] Revd Francesca Dixon (local Honorary Assistant Priest). Born on 8th August 1952, she was ten when she moved to Arundale School in Pulborough, an academically excellent private first school, where she was photographed by David as the 'fourth narrator' in *Hiawatha* in late 1963. Norman Wisdom saw the show as a parent and predicted "That Fourth Narrator will go far." She graduated from Cambridge in English and was ordained as one of the first women priests. She died from cancer on 29th June 2014 (a fifth Sunday) and is remembered with much affection by us all.

Prayers

† Almighty God, who didst give such grace unto thy holy Apostle Saint Andrew, that he readily obeyed the calling of thy Son Jesus Christ, and followed him without delay; grant unto us all, that we, being called by thy holy word, may forthwith give up ourselves obediently to fulfil thy holy commandments; through the same Jesus Christ our Lord.   *Amen.*

Show thy loving kindness tonight, O Lord, to all who stand in need of thy help. Be with the weak to make them strong and with the strong to make them gentle. Cheer the lonely with thy presence and the distracted with thy peace. Prosper thy Church in the fulfilment of her mighty task, and grant thy blessing to all who have toiled today in Christ's name.   *Amen.*

O Father, who hast declared thy love to men by the birth of the holy Child at Bethlehem; help us to welcome him with gladness and to make room for him in our common days; so that we may live at peace with one another, and in goodwill with all thy family; through the same, thy Son Jesus Christ our Lord.   *Amen.*

O God, our Father, give to the nations of the world a new heart of comradeship, that every people may bring its tribute of excellence to the common treasury, and all the world may go forward in the way which Christ has consecrated for us, until we come to that perfect kingdom into which all the nations shall bring their glory; through Jesus Christ.   *Amen.*

A few moments' silence for your own prayers.

The Lord's Prayer

Accept, O God, our offerings of praise and thanksgiving. Forgive, we pray thee, all that is imperfect in our worship, and help us to glorify and enjoy thee for ever; through Jesus Christ our Lord.   *Amen.*

124

SIMPLE SERVICE, WITH HYMNS
29th March 2009

Order of Service

Welcome & Notices (David Beal)

Hymn 92 (Tune: *Heinlein*)
Forty days and forty nights

Brief introduction (David Ellis)

Hymn 91 (Tune: *St. Andrew of Crete*)
Christian, dost thou see them

First reading (Christine) Matthew 3, 13–17; 4, 1–17 *(NEB)*

Hymn 197 (Tune: *Dominus regit me*)
The King of love my Shepherd is

Second reading (Tony) "The Gods of the Copybook Headings" *by Rudyard Kipling*

Hymn 160 (Tune: *Nicaea*)
Holy, Holy, Holy! Lord God Almighty!

Brief chat (David E.)

Hymn 365 (Tune: *Praise, my soul*)
Praise, my soul, the King of heaven

Prayers (Peter)

Hymn 33 (Tune: *St. Clement*)
The day thou gavest, Lord, is ended

The service will proceed without announcements. All the hymns are in *Hymns Ancient & Modern Revised*.

Thank you for coming. Please use the voting form opposite to list your own favourite hymns for a subsequent service.

Once again we have a 'hymns service' at the end of March, on the day the clocks go forward and, as suggested last November, when the weather should be getting warmer again. Next come the two summer ones, just two months ahead in May and then one in August.

As always, may I thank you all for coming, especially anyone who has not experienced one of these services before. There wasn't anyone in that category last time, but today is the first time for our new Rector; and we appreciate the encouragement he has already given us. I hope we live up to any expectations he may have of us. Do all come again, perhaps bringing a friend with you. Thanks to David for giving out the notices, to Christine and Tony for doing the readings, and Robert for his invaluable musical work.

As we are limited datewise by the occurrence of fifth Sundays, we have little control over the timing and can come near the start of Lent only if there are five Sundays in February, which happens just once in twenty-eight years; and when it did in 2004 we had only just started and were still thinking of well-known and fundamental passages of the Bible and had a second selection from the Sermon on the Mount. So this time, rather than go strictly by Passion Sunday, our first reading takes us back to the Temptations. I noticed the other day that this passage immediately precedes the one we had in November to remember St Andrew.

We said when we started these services that we would be having two readings, not necessarily both biblical. So for the second reading we are returning to Kipling, whose writings often bring a different slant. For those of you of a younger generation who may wonder what copybook headings are, I should explain that as youngsters, at school in Peter's case and at home in mine, we had these to teach us good handwriting. At the top and centre of every page were various well-known phrases or sayings in beautiful copper-plate script that we had to copy out as faithfully as we could several times. Thus we learnt not only to form our letters well, but also, for example, that the better part of valour is discretion.

Matthew 3, 13–17; 4, 1–17

Then Jesus arrived at the Jordan from Galilee, and came to John to be baptized by him. John tried to dissuade him. "Do you come to me?" he said; "I need rather to be baptized by you."

Jesus replied, "Let it be so for the present; we do well to conform in this way with all that God requires."

John then allowed him to come. After baptism Jesus came up out of the water at once, and at that moment heaven opened; he saw the Spirit of God descending like a dove to alight upon him; and a voice from heaven was heard saying, "This is my Son, my Beloved, on whom my favour rests."

Jesus was then led away by the Spirit into the wilderness, to be tempted by the devil.

For forty days and nights he fasted, and at the end of them he was famished. The tempter approached him and said, "If you are the Son of God, tell these stones to become bread." Jesus answered, "Scripture says, 'Man cannot live on bread alone; he lives on every word that God utters.'"

The devil then took him to the Holy City and set him on the parapet of the temple. "If you are the Son of God," he said, "throw yourself down; for Scripture says, 'He will put his angels in charge of you, and they will support you in their arms, for fear you should strike your foot against a stone.'" Jesus answered him, "Scripture says again, 'You are not to put the Lord your God to the test.'"

Once again, the devil took him to a very high mountain, and showed him all the kingdoms of the world in their glory. "All these," he said, "I will give you, if you will only fall down and do me homage." But Jesus said, "Begone, Satan; Scripture says, 'You shall do homage to the Lord your God and worship him alone.'"

Then the devil left him, and angels appeared and waited on him.

When he heard that John had been arrested, Jesus withdrew to Galilee; and leaving Nazareth he went and settled at Capernaum on the Sea of Galilee, in the district of Zebulun and Naphtali. This was in fulfilment of the passage in the prophet Isaiah which tells of "the land of Zebulun, the land of Naphtali, the road by the sea, the land beyond Jordan, heathen Galilee," and says:–

The people that lived in darkness saw a great light;
Light dawned on the dwellers in the land of death's dark shadow.

From that day Jesus began to proclaim the message: "Repent; for the kingdom of Heaven is upon you."

The Gods of the Copybook Headings

As I pass through my incarnations in every age and race,
I make my proper prostrations to the Gods of the Market-Place.
Peering through reverent fingers I watch them flourish and fall,
And the Gods of the Copybook Headings, I notice, outlast them all.

We were living in trees when they met us. They showed us each in turn
That Water would certainly wet us, as Fire would certainly burn:
But we found them lacking in Uplift, Vision and Breadth of Mind,
So we left them to teach the Gorillas while we followed the March of
    Mankind.

We moved as the Spirit listed. *They* never altered their pace,
Being neither cloud nor wind-borne like the Gods of the Market-Place;
But they always caught up with our progress, and presently word would come
That a tribe had been wiped off its icefield, or the lights had gone out in Rome.

With the Hopes that our World is built on they were utterly out of touch,
They denied that the Moon was Stilton; they denied she was even Dutch.
They denied that Wishes were Horses; they denied that a Pig had Wings.
So we worshipped the Gods of the Market Who promised these beautiful
    things.

When the Cambrian measures were forming, They promised perpetual peace.
They swore, if we gave them our weapons, that the wars of the tribes would
    cease.
But when we disarmed They sold us and delivered us bound to our foe,
And the Gods of the Copybook Headings said: *"Stick to the Devil you know."*

On the first Feminian Sandstones we were promised the Fuller Life
(Which started by loving our neighbour and ended by loving his wife)
Till our women had no more children and the men lost reason and faith,
And the Gods of the Copybook Headings said: *"The Wages of Sin is Death."*

In the Carboniferous Epoch we were promised abundance for all,
By robbing selected Peter to pay for collective Paul;
But, though we had plenty of money, there was nothing our money could buy,
And the Gods of the Copybook Headings said: *"If you don't work you die."*

Then the Gods of the Market tumbled, and their smooth-tongued wizards
    withdrew,
And the hearts of the meanest were humbled and began to believe it was true
That All is not Gold that Glitters, and Two and Two make Four—
And the Gods of the Copybook Headings limped up to explain it once more.

   .   .   .   .   .   .

As it will be in the future, it was at the birth of Man—
There are only four things certain since Social Progress began:–
That the Dog returns to his Vomit and the Sow returns to her Mire,
And the burnt Fool's bandaged finger goes wabbling back to the Fire;

And that after this is accomplished, and the brave new world begins
When all men are paid for existing and no man must pay for his sins,
As surely as Water will wet us, as surely as Fire will burn,
The Gods of the Copybook Headings with terror and slaughter return!

Rudyard Kipling

(1865–1936)

128

IS CHRISTIAN DOCTRINE FUNDAMENTALLY CREDIBLE ?

I call this part of the service a 'brief chat', in order to make quite clear that it is not meant to be a sermon. I hope it provides a little interlude between the hymns and makes a change from readings. At this service a year ago we had a third reading instead, and that was because I realized that I would not be able to complete what I was working on soon enough.

What I forgot this time was that I did complete that talk for June (see page 113), so the duplicated opening paragraphs are here very briefly summarized.

Kevin had told us about East Grinstead, whose parish population was ten times ours, but the same number came to their church each Sunday as attend here. By that comparison we are doing well, but eighty in over three thousand is still not a lot; so why do so few people come to church?

One reason may be that they think that religion makes demands on them that they would rather not have to fulfil, another that we do not have the strong Christian tradition in schools today that pertained a few decades ago. Even so, friends familiar with church services on account of being choirboys in their youth have drifted away, so something must have put them off. A further excuse is the march of science, which has claimed that evolution supersedes the creation story in Genesis.

On that basis one might suppose that churchgoers were uncritical and silly people, and that anyone with any sense would know that religious observance was a complete waste of time. I started thinking about this when I found myself taking issue with something in David's very first Sunday sermon. Not a main point, I hasten to add; just an aside. He said we were all quite ordinary people, and I thought, "Just a minute!" Of course, we should all *describe ourselves* as quite ordinary people, but most of our baker's dozen that morning were really quite distinguished, either in their careers or in what they did for the Church, or both. In other words, rather special people—and this set me thinking that perhaps it's the *special* people who come to church, and the proportion in West Chiltington may be higher because you need to be a bit special to afford to live here, unless, like my brother and me, you inherited your home from distinguished and hard-working parents. I leave that simply as a provocative comment and return to my theme of people outside the Church.

Who may be under the impression that much of Christian doctrine is just not credible. They feel we require them, like the White Queen, to be able to believe as many as six impossible things before breakfast. But can we reply to that charge by reminding the scientists that Genesis does recount correctly the order of how life on Earth developed, even if its time-scale was a bit out, and adding that the least believable aspects are not absolutely fundamental, and that it is possible to put together enough that *is* credible to provide a sound faith by which to live? For those who do come to church, the answer, whether or not we have consciously undertaken this exercise, must surely be yes.

I was taught that we learn about our faith from three sources: the Bible, the teaching of the Church and our own personal experience. Yet the Bible can be contradictory in places, our various churches teach different things, and everyone has his or her unique personal experience.

Put the three together, though, and the whole is more than the sum of its individual parts. Having our Bible we are more fortunate than Jesus was, for he had only the Old Testament writings from which to develop his spiritual insights, whereas we have the New as well, and of course many of those insights are recorded as his sayings and parables. The Church keeps us familiar with these by including them in the readings we listen to. Personal experience comes in when something from such a passage moves us to action; when we not only come to realize that we ought to do something but actually get round to doing it.

"First make your peace with your brother, and then leave your gift before the altar."

Oh.

I *am* having a difference of opinion with someone I have hitherto thought of as a friend. I *have* allowed myself some rude comments. If I get up early I might just have time to write a letter to say that I regret the situation and apologize if I have offended her, and that I still regard her as a friend. And you do.

Well, *I* did. It was a month or so ago and a cold morning when the roads were so treacherous that not everyone could get to the Breakfast Group. Having changed my route to drop that letter in the pillar box, I met someone who needed a brief helping hand, as I discovered as we both made our way down the same path. It wasn't the helping her that made me feel at one with the world, but the thought that I had been at the right place at the right time to do so. Trivial, yes, and probably the conviction that heaven and earth somehow seem to be the same place has a simple psychological explanation, but this does not detract from the personal experience that makes our faith at times so self-reinforcing.

Such experience makes me wonder what sort of a God Richard Dawkins does *not* believe in, with his advertisement proclaiming that we can get on and enjoy life as "there probably isn't a God". I prefer to believe in a God who makes life *more* enjoyable![1]

---

[1] Or, in other circumstances, less *un*enjoyable, for example, when we are comforted in times of distress.

Prayers

Almighty God, long-suffering and of great goodness, we confess to thee with our whole heart our neglect and forgetfulness of thy commandments, our wrong-doing, speaking and thinking, the harm we have done to others, and the good we have left undone. O God, forgive thy people who have sinned against thee, and raise us to newness of life; through Jesus Christ our Lord. *Amen.*

Father, we thank thee for all the benefits that we have received from thy goodness. To thy blessing we owe every success, every opportunity for doing good, every impulse in the right way, every victory we have gained over ourselves, every thought of thy presence—all are alike thy gifts to us. Give us strength and wisdom to walk faithfully and joyfully in the way of willing obedience to thy law, and cheerful trust in thy love. The best thanksgiving we can offer to thee is to live according to thy will; grant us every day to offer it more perfectly, and to grow in the knowledge of thy will and the love thereof evermore. *Amen.*

Almighty God, our creator and preserver, we thank thee for the springtime, in which thou art renewing the face of the earth and quickening all things. Thou who carest for the trees and flowers, revive and renew our life, that we may bring forth the fruit of good works, as disciples of him who came to quicken in human hearts the seed of eternal life; through Jesus Christ our Lord. *Amen.*

Show thy loving kindness tonight, O Lord, to all who stand in need of thy help. Be with the weak to make them strong and with the strong to make them gentle. Cheer the lonely with thy presence and the distracted with thy peace. Prosper thy Church in the fulfilment of her mighty task, and grant thy blessing to all who have toiled today in Christ's name. *Amen.*

A few moments' silence for your own prayers.

The Lord's Prayer

Go forth into the world in peace; be of good courage; hold fast that which is good; render to no man evil for evil; strengthen the faint-hearted; support the weak; help the afflicted; honour all men; love and serve the Lord; rejoicing in the power of the Holy Spirit.

And the blessing of God Almighty, the Father, the Son, and the Holy Spirit, be upon us, and remain with us for ever. *Amen.*

SIMPLE SERVICE, WITH HYMNS

31st May 2009

Order of Service

Welcome & Notices (David Beal)

Hymn 578 (*Songs of Praise;* words overleaf)
Mine eyes have seen the glory

Brief introduction (David Ellis)

Hymn 61 (*Hymns for Today.* Tune: *Slane*)
Lord of all hopefulness

First reading (Philip) Matthew, Chapter 7, Verses 1–5, 7–14, 24–29
(NEB)

Hymn 309 (*Songs of Praise;* words on page 133. Tune: *Ebenezer*)
Once to every man and nation

Second reading (Tony) Mark, Chapter 4, Verses 1–9, 35–41 *(NEB)*

Hymn 313 (*Hymns Ancient & Modern Revised.* Tune: *St Aëlred*)
Fierce raged the tempest o'er the deep

Brief chat (David E.)

Hymn 281 (*Mission Praise;* words on page 37)
I lift my eyes to the quiet hills
Prayers (Peter)

Hymn 735 (*Mission Praise; words on page 25.* Tune: *Finlandia*)
We rest on Thee, our shield and our defender

The service will proceed without announcements. Only one hymn this time is in *Hymns Ancient & Modern Revised.* Two are in *Mission Praise,* one is in *Hymns for Today* and the other two are in *Songs of Praise* (words opposite and overleaf).

Thank you for coming. Please use the separate voting form to list your own favourite hymns for a subsequent service.

Mine eyes have seen the glory

Mine eyes have seen the glory of the coming of the Lord;
He is trampling out the vintage where the grapes of wrath are stored;
He hath loosed the fateful lightning of his terrible swift sword:
His Truth is marching on.
Glory, glory, Hallelujah! Glory, glory, Hallelujah!
Glory, glory, Hallelujah! His Truth is marching on.

I have seen him in the watch-fires of a hundred circling camps;
They have builded him an altar in the evening dews and damps;
I have read his righteous sentence by the dim and flaring lamps:
His Day is marching on.
Glory, glory, Hallelujah! Glory, glory, Hallelujah!
Glory, glory, Hallelujah! His Day is marching on.

I have read a fiery gospel, writ in burnished rows of steel:
"As ye deal with my contemners, so with you my grace shall deal";
Let the Hero born of woman crush the serpent with his heel,
Since God is marching on.
Glory, glory, Hallelujah! Glory, glory, Hallelujah!
Glory, glory, Hallelujah! Since God is marching on.

He has sounded forth the trumpet that shall never call retreat;
He is sifting out the hearts of men before his judgment-seat;
O be swift, my soul, to answer him; be jubilant, my feet!
Our God is marching on.
Glory, glory, Hallelujah! Glory, glory, Hallelujah!
Glory, glory, Hallelujah! Our God is marching on.

In the beauty of the lilies Christ was born across the sea,
With a glory in his bosom that transfigures you and me;
As he died to make men holy, let us die to make men free,
While God is marching on.
Glory, glory, Hallelujah! Glory, glory, Hallelujah!
Glory, glory, Hallelujah! While God is marching on.

He is coming like the glory of the morning on the wave;
He is wisdom to the mighty, he is succour to the brave;
So the world shall be his foot-stool, and the soul of time his slave:
Our God is marching on.   *Mrs Julia Ward Howe*
Glory, glory, Hallelujah! Glory, glory, Hallelujah!   *(1819–1910)*
Glory, glory, Hallelujah! Our God is marching on.

Once to every man and nation

Once to every man and nation
Comes the moment to decide,
In the strife of truth with falsehood,
For the good or evil side:
Some great cause, God's new Messiah,
Offering each the bloom or blight;
And the choice goes by for ever
'Twixt that darkness and that light.

Then to side with truth is noble,
When we share her wretched crust,
Ere her cause bring fame and profit,
And 'tis prosperous to be just;
Then it is the brave man chooses,
While the coward stands aside,
Till the multitude make virtue
Of the faith they had denied.

By the light of burning martyrs,
Christ, thy bleeding feet we track,
Toiling up new Calvaries ever
With the cross that turns not back.
New occasions teach new duties;
Time makes ancient good uncouth;
They must upward still and onward
Who would keep abreast of truth.

Though the cause of evil prosper,
Yet 'tis truth alone is strong;
Though her portion be the scaffold,
And upon the throne be wrong,
Yet that scaffold sways the future,
And, behind the dim unknown,
Standeth God within the shadow,
Keeping watch above his own.

J. Russell Lowell (1819–1891)

This is our first summer 'hymns service' of the year, the other one being due in August; and, as always, Peter and I are most grateful to you all for coming, to David for being with us to see fair play, to Philip and Tony for doing the readings, and to Robert for his work on the piano.

This is not the first time our service has coincided with Pentecost; the other time was in 2004, and having had twenty at our first service and thirty at our second we had hopes of something like forty for that third one. However, we had forgotten the bank holiday weekend, which may have been the main factor in bringing numbers down to a select seven. Of course it may be that a number of those who came in February didn't like my saying, before the very first of my 'brief chats', that since Kevin had "let David Hammond and Sally Levett loose at other services" I saw no reason why I shouldn't have a go myself. And some people at our first two services had thought they were coming to Evensong.

So my initial thought for this time was that I might repeat what I had put together for 2004, as only half a dozen people would have heard it then, and most of these would have forgotten it, but you may be glad to know that it hasn't worked out like that at all. Instead, my theme is linked to one of the hymns, and one we picked simply because we hadn't had it before . . . It was easy enough to fit our second reading to this hymn, but rather harder to find a reading to go with "Once to every man and nation comes the moment to decide . . ." We finally settled on a selection which ends with the parable that Mr P. A. Tharp, our truly Christian headmaster (when I was at Collyer's School, Horsham – motto *Honor Deo* – in the mid-Fifties) always made sure was read in Assembly on the last day of term; and coincidentally our second reading begins with the parable with which he had us start each term.

The hymns this time are quite unusual, because only one can be found in our customary hymn book; we have had to give you all three hymn books and still print the words of two more hymns on the service sheet. I have included the authors' names not only to give them due recognition but also to show that both hymns are out of copyright.

Matthew 7, 1–5, 7–14, 24–29

[Jesus said:] "Pass no judgement, and you will not be judged. For as you judge others, so you will yourselves be judged, and whatever measure you deal out to others will be dealt back to you. Why do you look at the speck of sawdust in your brother's eye, with never a thought for the great plank in your own? Or how can you say to your brother, 'Let me take the speck out of your eye', when all the time there is that plank in your own? You hypocrite! First take the plank out of your own eye, and then you will see clearly to take the speck out of your brother's."

"Ask, and you will receive; seek, and you will find; knock, and the door will be opened. For everyone who asks receives, he who seeks finds, and to him who knocks, the door will be opened.

"Is there a man among you who will offer his son a stone when he asks for bread, or a snake when he asks for fish? If you, then, bad as you are, know how to give your children what is good for them, how much more will your heavenly Father give good things to those who ask him!

"Always treat others as you would like them to treat you: that is the Law and the prophets.

"Enter by the narrow gate. The gate is wide that leads to perdition, there is plenty of room on the road, and many go that way; but the gate that leads to life is small and the road is narrow, and those who find it are few."

"What then of the man who hears these words of mine and acts upon them? He is like a man who had the sense to build his house on rock. The rain came down, the floods rose, the wind blew, and beat upon that house; but it did not fall, because its foundations were on rock. But what of the man who hears these words of mine and does not act upon them? He is like a man who was foolish enough to build his house on sand. The rain came down, the floods rose, the wind blew, and beat upon that house; down it fell with a great crash."

When Jesus had finished this discourse the people were astounded at his teaching; unlike their own teachers he taught with a note of authority.

Mark 4, 1–9, 35–41

On another occasion he began to teach by the lake-side. The crowd that gathered round him was so large that he had to get into a boat on the lake, and there he sat, with the whole crowd on the beach right down to the water's edge. And he taught them many things by parables.

As he taught he said:–

"Listen! A sower went out to sow. And it happened that as he sowed, some seed fell along the footpath; and the birds came and ate it up. Some seed fell on rocky ground, where it had little soil, and it sprouted quickly because it had no depth of earth; but when the sun rose the young corn was scorched, and as it had no proper root it withered away. Some seed fell among thistles; but the thistles shot up and choked the corn, and it yielded no crop. And some of the seed fell into good soil, where it came up and grew, and bore fruit; and the yield was thirtyfold, sixtyfold, even a hundredfold."

He added, "If you have ears to hear, then hear."

That day, in the evening, he said to them, "Let us cross over to the other side of the lake."

So they left the crowd and took him with them in the boat where he had been sitting; and there were other boats accompanying him. A heavy squall came on and the waves broke over the boat until it was all but swamped. Now he was in the stern asleep on a cushion; they roused him and said, "Master, we are sinking! Do you not care?"

He stood up, rebuked the wind, and said to the sea, "Hush! Be still!"

The wind dropped and there was a dead calm. He said to them, "Why are you such cowards? Have you no faith even now?"

They were awestruck and said to one another, "Who can this be whom even the wind and the sea obey?"

METEOROLOGY AND BIBLICAL MIRACLES

Before we decided that Saturday's *Daily Telegraph* was just too bulky and changed to Friday's, I always used to enjoy Philip Eden's pieces on the back page about the weather. On 9th December 2000 he opened by saying that the Bible rarely featured in the lists of references normally appended to learned papers in meteorological journals, but recently he had come across an article with 22 of them. This was written by the scholar H. W. Sansom and entitled "Meteorology in the Bible".[1] Philip Eden commented that attempts to explain some of the miraculous events in the New Testament, such as the Transfiguration and the Ascension, in terms of atmospheric physics and chemistry were "never completely persuasive. Many readers will insist that such attempts are unnecessary and some may even find them objectionable. Others will regard them as perfectly legitimate subjects for scientific investigation.

"One New Testament miracle that falls within the purview of meteorologists is the calming of the storm on the Sea of Galilee. . . . Sansom offers a convincing explanation. The Sea of Galilee . . . is a small inland sea, roughly ten miles long by five miles wide, located in the deeply incised valley of the River Jordan. The hills to the east and west rise 2,500 feet above the lake, while some distance to the north is the 9,200 ft Mount Hermon.

"Mountainous regions provide a perfect setting for anabatic (up-slope) and katabatic (down-slope) winds, and these are particularly strong in sunny climates where large temperature contrasts can develop between sunlit slopes and shaded ones. Downslope winds are very common during the evenings and set in very abruptly. Nor is there any warning of them, as they normally occur under clear skies. They provide a mechanism to transfer cold air from the

---

[1] Published by the Royal Meteorological Society in their journal, *Weather, Volume 6, Issue 2 (February 1951)*, pp.51–54. The Society kindly sent me a PDF of Sansom's paper, from which I noted that Dr Sansom was not as convinced as Philip Eden was that the waves on the lake would have died down very rapidly when the wind stopped.

higher slopes towards the valley bottom: cold air is heavier than warm air. Once that transfer has been completed the katabatic wind will stop blowing as suddenly as it sprang up, and on a relatively small lake the waves would die down very quickly."[1]

Now it could be that Jesus was more familiar with katabatic winds than his disciples appear to have been, and that he had calmly gone off to sleep at the back of the boat because he knew there was nothing to worry about; but he might just have been very tired from a long day's teaching. Suddenly woken up and implored to do something about the storm, what else could he have said but what was clearly expected of him? Followed, as Mark notes, by a rather petulant "Why are you such cowards?"

I personally see no reason why we should not look for non-magical explanations for apparently miraculous events, and I am certain that such explanations should not weaken our faith. This is because I feel that the actual mechanism is secondary to the effect of such events on the people who witnessed them. The result of this incident was that Jesus' status in the eyes of his disciples was considerably enhanced—"Who can this be whom even the wind and the sea obey?" Another reason for welcoming some natural mechanism is that this makes it that much more likely that the event in question actually happened.

On the other hand, I would not suggest that Jesus stage-managed this incident specifically to achieve that outcome, for example by refusing to wake up until he was pretty sure that the storm was about to end anyway. He criticized his companions for their lack of faith, which was something he himself had in ample measure. On this interpretation it would have just so happened that the storm came to its end at precisely the moment that he "rebuked the wind" and told the sea to be still. People describe the facility that some people have for being blessed with unexpectedly happy turns of events as 'serendipity'. Another way of looking at it would be to acknowledge it simply as God's programme for that particular day. Only He knew when the squall would blow itself out and when the people in the boat would finally become so concerned that they woke Jesus in desperation.

Where does this leave us with respect to the last verse of our hymn, "So when our life is clouded o'er, and storm-winds drift us from the shore, say, lest we sink to rise no more, 'Peace, be still'." ?

I suggest we turn to what Jesus said in the Sermon on the Mount, reported by Matthew, some of which was included in our first reading: "Set your mind on God's kingdom and his justice before everything else, and all the rest will come to you as well. So do not be anxious about tomorrow; tomorrow will

---

[1] Extracts from Philip Eden's article included by permission of *The Daily Telegraph*.

138

look after itself." The fact that we ask for help from Jesus in difficult times, in the words of this hymn or in other ways, rather than fretting anxiously that we shall not be able to cope, parallels the disciples' asking Jesus to help them in the storm (that is, assuming that they wanted him to do more than just assist with the bailing), and means that we are trusting God to look after us as Jesus exhorted us to.

Again, when the storm-winds of our lives drift us from the shore, we can take comfort in the final lines of the preceding hymn, " . . . standeth God within the shadow, keeping watch above His own" and take strength from this evening's final hymn, "We rest on Thee, our shield and our defender".

Prayers

O God, our heavenly Father, help us always to be of a good courage. Let us not be disheartened by our difficulties, never doubting thy love nor any of thy promises. Give us grace that we may encourage others and always do our best to make life easier for those who need a friendly word or helping hand; for the sake of Jesus Christ our Lord. *Amen.*

O God, of unchanging faithfulness and truth, give to each of us, we pray thee, thy Holy Spirit; and make us so steadfast in right endeavour and so faithful to the trust placed in us, that we may be a firm foundation upon which this community may be built up in righteousness, to the praise of thy holy Name, through Jesus Christ our Lord. *Amen.*

We praise thy name, O Father, for the beauty of the summer, the glory of the sky by day and night, the healthful wind and quickening rain. We thank thee for the bloom and fragrance of the flowers, the songs of the birds, and the joyousness of every living thing. In all that thou has made we see the wonder of thy wisdom and care. Help us to trust thy never-failing goodness, the love which is beyond understanding, and surrounds our lives with blessing, for thy name's sake. *Amen.*

Remember, O Lord, what thou hast wrought in us, and not what we deserve, and as thou hast called us to thy service, make us worthy of our calling; through Jesus Christ our Lord. *Amen.*

A few moments' silence for your own prayers. And as we think ahead to the words of the Lord's Prayer let us call to mind those who have wronged us, and ask ourselves how far we have gone towards forgiving them.

The Lord's Prayer.

Save us, O Lord, waking, guard us sleeping, that awake we may watch with Christ, and asleep we may rest in peace. *Amen.*

The power of the Father, the wisdom of the Son, the love of the Holy Spirit, keep, teach, and guide us for ever. *Amen.*

SIMPLE SERVICE, WITH HYMNS

30th August 2009

Order of Service

Welcome & Notices (David Beal)

Hymn 50 (*Words and music by David J. Evans; see page 44*)
Be still, for the presence of the Lord

Brief introduction (David Ellis)

Hymn 640 (Tune: *Aurelia*)
The Church's one foundation

First reading (Tony) "The Glory of the Garden" *by Rudyard Kipling*

Hymn 132 (Tune: *Sussex*)
Father, hear the prayer we offer

Second reading (Philip) Exodus Chapter 2, Verses 23–25;
Chapter 3, Verses 1–12 *(NEB)*

Hymn 435 (Tune: *Living Lord*)
Lord Jesus Christ, You have come to us

Brief chat (Richard Holliday)

Hymn 16 (Tune: *Michael*)
All my hope on God is founded

Prayers (Peter)

Hymn 224 (Tune: *Monks Gate; words on page 58*)
He who would valiant be

The service will proceed without announcements. All the hymns are in *Mission Praise.*

Thank you for coming. Please use the voting form opposite to list your own favourite hymns for a subsequent service.

This is our second summer 'hymns service' of the year, the other one having been in May; and, as always, Peter and I are most grateful to you all for coming, to David for being with us to see fair play, to Tony and Philip for doing the readings, and to Robert for his work on the piano.

And I am especially grateful this time to Richard, for taking on the 'brief chat' and making this a holiday weekend in more ways than one.

The hymns today are not so unusual as last time, but this is the first of all our services for which we are not using *Hymns Ancient & Modern Revised* at all, because all of them can be found in *Mission Praise*.

Our next service would be due on 29th November, but David is planning to hold a special *Advent Hymn Service*, which will be extra to the customary *Nine Lessons and Carols* in December. He suggested this morning that we could move our hymns service forward to the third Sunday, 15th, which is all right with Peter, Tony, Philip and me, but Robert will be away that weekend.

The Glory of the Garden

Our England is a garden that is full of stately views,
Of borders, beds and shrubberies and lawns and avenues,
With statues on the terraces and peacocks strutting by;
But the Glory of the Garden lies in more than meets the eye.

For where the old thick laurels grow, along the thin red wall,
You find the tool- and potting-sheds which are the heart of all;
The cold-frames and the hot-houses, the dungpits and the tanks,
The rollers, carts and drain-pipes, with the barrows and the planks.

And there you'll see the gardeners, the men and 'prentice boys
Told off to do as they are bid and do it without noise;
For, except when seeds are planted and we shout to scare the birds,
The Glory of the Garden it abideth not in words.

And some can pot begonias and some can bud a rose,
And some are hardly fit to trust with anything that grows;
But they can roll and trim the lawns and sift the sand and loam,
For the Glory of the Garden occupieth all who come.

Our England is a garden, and such gardens are not made
By singing:— "Oh, how beautiful!"—and sitting in the shade,
While better men than we go out and start their working lives
At grubbing weeds from gravel-paths with broken dinner-knives.

There's not a pair of legs so thin, there's not a head so thick,
There's not a hand so weak and white, nor yet a heart so sick,
But it can find some needful job that's crying to be done,
For the Glory of the Garden glorifieth every one.

Then seek your job with thankfulness and work till further orders,
If it's only netting strawberries or killing slugs on borders;
And when your back stops aching and your hands begin to harden,
You will find yourself a partner in the Glory of the Garden.

Oh, Adam was a gardener, and God who made him sees
That half a proper gardener's work is done upon his knees,
So when your work is finished, you can wash your hands and pray
For the Glory of the Garden, that it may not pass away!
And the Glory of the Garden it shall never pass away!

Rudyard Kipling

(1865–1936)

Exodus 2, 23–25; 3, 1–12

Years passed, and the king of Egypt died, but the Israelites still groaned in slavery. They cried out, and their appeal for rescue from their slavery rose up to God. He heard their groaning, and remembered his covenant with Abraham, Isaac and Jacob; he saw the plight of Israel, and he took heed of it.

Moses was minding the flock of his father-in-law Jethro, priest of Midian. He led the flock along the side of the wilderness and came to Horeb, the mountain of God. There the angel of the Lord appeared to him in the flame of a burning bush. Moses noticed that, although the bush was on fire, it was not being burnt up; so he said to himself, "I must go across to see this wonderful sight. Why does not the bush burn away?"

When the Lord saw that Moses had turned aside to look, he called to him out of the bush, "Moses, Moses."

And Moses answered, "Yes, I am here."

God said, "Come no nearer; take off your sandals; the place where you are standing is holy ground." Then he said, "I am the God of your forefathers, the God of Abraham, the God of Isaac, the God of Jacob." Moses covered his face, for he was afraid to gaze on God.

The Lord said, "I have indeed seen the misery of my people in Egypt. I have heard their outcry against their slave-masters. I have taken heed of their sufferings, and have come down to rescue them from the power of Egypt, and to bring them up out of that country into a fine, broad land; it is a land flowing with milk and honey, the home of Canaanites, Hittites, Amorites, Perizzites, Hivites, and Jebusites. The outcry of the Israelites has now reached me; yes, I have seen the brutality of the Egyptians towards them. Come now; I will send you to Pharaoh and you shall bring my people Israel out of Egypt."

"But who am I," Moses said to God, "that I should go to Pharaoh, and that I should bring the Israelites out of Egypt?"

God answered, "I am with you. This shall be the proof that it is I who have sent you: when you have brought the people out of Egypt, you shall all worship God here on this mountain."

Richard Holliday's talk was very short, and we do not have a record of it.

Prayers

We shall start with a short one:–

O Lord, let us not live to be useless; for Christ's sake.   *Amen.*

O God of our life, there are days when the burdens we carry chafe our shoulders and weigh us down; when the road seems dreary and endless, the skies grey and threatening, when our lives have no music in them and our hearts are lonely, and our souls have lost their courage. Flood the path with light, we beseech thee; turn our eyes to where the skies are full of promise; tune our hearts to brave music; give us the sense of comradeship with heroes and saints of every age; and so quicken our spirits that we may be able to encourage the souls of all who journey with us on the road of life; to thy honour and glory.   *Amen.*

Loving Father, we thank thee for our homes and for all who love and care for us. May we ever be grateful for the good things we enjoy, not taking them for granted, but remembering always to give thanks. For the sake of him who was always thankful in all things, thy Son, our Lord Jesus Christ.   *Amen.*

O God of all goodness and grace, who art worthy of a greater love than we can either give or understand, fill our hearts, we beseech thee, with such love towards thee that nothing may seem too hard for us to do or to suffer in obedience to thy will; and grant that thus we may become daily more like unto thee, and dwell more and more in the light of thy presence; through Jesus Christ our Lord.   *Amen.*

A few moments' silence for your own prayers. And as we think ahead to the words of the Lord's Prayer let us call to mind those times when other people have wronged us, and ask ourselves how far we have gone towards forgiving them.

The Lord's Prayer.

May the Lord lead us when we go, and keep us when we sleep, and talk with us when we wake; and may the peace of God, which passeth all understanding, keep our hearts and minds in Jesus Christ our Lord.   *Amen.*

SIMPLE SERVICE, WITH HYMNS

15th November 2009

Order of Service

Welcome & Notices (David B.)

Hymn 375 (Tune: *Luckington*)
Let all the world in every corner sing

Brief introduction (David E.)

Hymn 442 (Tune: *Royal Oak*)
All things bright and beautiful

First reading (Philip) St Luke, Chapter 7, Verses 36–50 *(NEB)*

Hymn 164 (Tune: *Rivaulx*)
Father of heaven, whose love profound

Second reading (Tony) St Matthew, Chapter 18, Verses 19–35 *(NEB)*

Hymn 278 (Tune: *Ewing*)
Jerusalem the golden

Brief chat (David E.)

Hymn 51 (*Mission Praise;* words on page 10. Tune: *Slane*)
Be thou my vision, O Lord of my heart

Prayers (Peter)

Hymn 311 (Tune: *Mannheim*)
Lead us, heavenly Father, lead us

The service will proceed without announcements. All the hymns except one (words opposite) are in *Hymns Ancient & Modern Revised.*

Thank you for coming. Please use the voting form overleaf to list your own favourite hymns for a subsequent service.

144

Welcome to the first of our winter 'hymns services'; the next one will be at the end of January. As always, Peter and I thank David and all of you for coming, Tony and Philip for the readings, and Robert especially this time for rescheduling his weekend away in order to be here to do his usual sterling work on the piano.

This time we are back to *Hymns Ancient & Modern Revised*, except for just one from *Mission Praise.*

Don't forget to let us have your choice of hymns for future services; having given us one is the past doesn't disqualify you from submitting another one. Just make sure you come to sing the hymns you've chosen!

Luke 7, 36–50

One of the Pharisees invited him to dinner; he went to the Pharisee's house and took his place at table. A woman who was living an immoral life in the town had learned that Jesus was dining in the Pharisee's house and had brought oil of myrrh in a small flask. She took her place behind him, by his feet, weeping. His feet were wetted with her tears and she wiped them with her hair, kissing them and anointing them with the myrrh. When his host the Pharisee saw this he said to himself, "If this fellow were a real prophet, he would know who this woman is that touches him, and what sort of woman she is, a sinner."

Jesus took him up and said, "Simon, I have something to say to you." "Speak on, Master", said he. "Two men were in debt to a money-lender: one owed him five hundred silver pieces, the other fifty. As neither had anything to pay with he let them both off. Now, which will love him most?"

Simon replied, "I should think the one that was let off most."

"You are right", said Jesus. Then turning to the woman, he said to Simon, "You see this woman? I came to your house: you provided no water for my feet; but this woman has made my feet wet with her tears and wiped them with her hair. You gave me no kiss; but she has been kissing my feet ever since I came in. You did not anoint my head with oil; but she has anointed my feet with myrrh. And so, I tell you, her great love proves that her many sins have been forgiven; where little has been forgiven, little love is shown."

Then he said to her, "Your sins are forgiven." The other guests began to ask themselves, "Who is this, that he can forgive sins?" But he said to the woman, "Your faith has saved you; go in peace."

Matthew 18, 19–35

Jesus said, "Again I tell you this: if two of you agree on earth about any request you have to make, that request will be granted by my heavenly Father. For where two or three have met together in my name, I am there among them."

Then Peter came up and asked him, "Lord, how often am I to forgive my brother if he goes on wronging me? As many as seven times?" Jesus replied, "I do not say seven times; I say seventy times seven.

"The kingdom of heaven, therefore, should be thought of in this way: There was once a king who decided to settle accounts with the men who served him. At the outset there appeared before him a man whose debt ran into millions. Since he had no means of paying, his master ordered him to be sold to meet the debt, with his wife, his children, and everything he had. The man fell prostrate at his master's feet.

" 'Be patient with me,' he said, 'and I will pay in full'; and the master was so moved with pity that he let the man go and remitted the debt. But no sooner had the man gone out than he met a fellow-servant who owed him a few pounds; and catching hold of him he gripped him by the throat and said, 'Pay me what you owe.'

"The man fell at his fellow-servant's feet, and begged him, 'Be patient with me, and I will pay you'; but he refused, and had him jailed until he should pay the debt. The other servants were deeply distressed when they saw what had happened, and they went to their master and told him the whole story. He accordingly sent for the man.

" 'You scoundrel!' he said to him; 'I remitted the whole of your debt when you appealed to me; were you not bound to show your fellow-servant the same pity as I showed to you?' And so angry was the master that he condemned the man to torture until he should pay the debt in full.

"And that is how my heavenly Father will deal with you, unless you each forgive your brother from your hearts."

WHY *DO* SOME PEOPLE COME TO CHURCH?

Forgive, O Lord, what we have been, sanctify what we are, and direct what we shall be, for Jesus Christ's sake.

In my brief chat during our March service, I tried to think of reasons why many people didn't come to church nowadays: were they under the impression that much of Christian doctrine was just not credible?

146

To complement that, it might be useful to ask why there are still some people who *do* come to our church. As it seems that everyone who lives more than a few hundred yards away arrives by car, there can't be many like me who enjoy the walk to church and back. A more general reason could be because it is 'what we do on Sundays'.

Then, of course, we might come to see our friends. There is no doubt that those we meet at church are exceptionally nice; being a Christian does have some real and positive effect on the sort of person you are. And this leads to another need to attend: we come to support the other people who do, as well as those who take the trouble to officiate at our services, for we all know that it is more cheering for everyone to be part of a thriving congregation rather than a sparse one. Fortunately, we have a church which is small enough never to seem empty, and it's quite nice for the dozen or more who come at 8 o'clock to have a pew each, room for our service books on the pew in front, and quiet before the service.

Continuing the social theme, we always get a good crowd at services that are followed by refreshments; mulled wine and mince pies after the Nine Lessons & Carols, or a Harvest Lunch, for example. That might be said to go right back to the Feeding of the Five Thousand, though as in that case the refreshments must have been somewhat unexpected they could not have been a reason for coming.

Some people like the beautiful language of the services, especially the Prayer Book services. They have listened to it, week in, week out, for decades, and it must be admitted that Cranmer had a splendid turn of phrase; he also did his best to make it intelligible to everyone, whatever their linguistic background, so he would 'double up' by linking a word of Latinate origin with one from Anglo-Saxon, as when we are exhorted to "acknowledge and confess" our "sins and wickedness", and not "dissemble nor cloke them". But, given that the best-attended services are those in modern language, and that these services were introduced when I was in my twenties, while I am now receiving a pension, any people who come for this reason may well grow fewer as the years go on.

Aside from the language, old or new, what would an outsider make of our services? If we believe in the validity of prayer; if we take Jesus' "ask and you will receive"[1] to heart or his "if two of you agree on earth about any request you have to make, that request will be granted by my heavenly Father",[2] who could doubt the value of praying for the sick of our parish, or the peace of the world and wisdom for its leaders?

[1] Luke 11, 9
[2] Matthew 18, 19–20

But the bulk of the service is more about ourselves. The new version, and the old Mattins, seem logical in that we have the Commandments near the start and follow immediately with the Confession, in which we admit to not having kept these too well, and that's fair enough. We are none of us perfect, and so we can all willingly assent to the mild form of the modern confession. Calling to mind one's shortcomings, however, is not as easy as it might sound, even if one tries to do this when saying a prayer before the service. We may be well aware of them at the time, but have forgotten them by Sunday, or we might not even have been aware of them unless someone else has happened to be bold enough to tell us.

'Repentance' is one of those words that has changed its meaning over the years. In biblical terms it implied, not so much being "heartily sorry for these our misdoings", but a turning round, a change of life away from selfishness and towards "walking from henceforth in His holy ways".

John the Baptist called for repentance, and Jesus stressed the need for certain townships of his day to repent. But I don't think he asked his own disciples to repent, although he told them how he expected them to behave and he was critical of their wrong attitudes and instances of their lack of faith. And when they were accused of breaking the Sabbath he spoke up in their defence. What he did tell them about their wrongdoing was that it would be forgiven them in proportion to their readiness to forgive other people, and this principle is enshrined in the Lord's Prayer, which we include in all our services.

So I just wonder if people really do come to church because of a guilt complex that is not alleviated by regret for their failings, and by trying to do better another time—after all, living the Christian life needs constant practice and can never be perfect—nor by their being forgiving towards other people, but must somehow be cleansed by means of a Sacrament that invokes the Jewish concept of atoning sacrifice to claim that Jesus' death somehow absolves everyone from their sins for all time? Or do we perhaps feel, when we take part in a rite whose usage has stood the test of time for nearly two millennia, that when we come to the altar rail and we take the Communion Elements we are somehow closer to God than we can be at other times?

Why do *you* come to church? Not to listen to me, I suspect. Far better, to be reminded of the words of scripture through readings from the Bible. And to worship God, as we can do when we sing some of these hymns, or to ask for guidance and to receive inspiration when we sing others. And I hope we can indeed enjoy singing them!

Prayers

Grant, we beseech thee, merciful Lord, to thy faithful people pardon and peace, that we may be cleansed from all our sins, and serve thee with a quiet mind; through Jesus Christ our Lord.   *Amen.*

O Almighty and everlasting God, we praise thy holy Name for all the blessings, known and unknown, which we have this day received from thy bounty, beseeching thee still to continue thy fatherly care over us, and to give us such a sense of thy mercies that we may show forth our thankfulness by a humble, holy and devout life, in Jesus Christ our Lord.   *Amen.*

† Almighty God, who hast given us grace at this time with one accord to make our common supplications unto thee; and dost promise that when two or three are gathered together in thy name thou wilt grant their requests: fulfil now, O Lord, the desires and petitions of thy servants, as may be most expedient for them; granting us in this world knowledge of thy truth, and in the world to come life everlasting.   *Amen.*

A few moments' silence for your own prayers. And as we think ahead to the words of the Lord's Prayer let us call to mind those times when other people have wronged us, and ask ourselves how far we have gone towards forgiving them.

The Lord's Prayer.

Go forth into the world in peace; be of good courage; hold fast that which is good; render to no man evil for evil; strengthen the faint-hearted; support the weak; help the afflicted; honour all men; love and serve the Lord; rejoicing in the power of the Holy Spirit.

And the blessing of God Almighty, the Father, the Son, and the Holy Spirit, be upon us, and remain with us for ever.   *Amen.*

SIMPLE SERVICE, WITH HYMNS

31st January 2010

Order of Service

Welcome & Notices (David Beal)

Hymn 4 (Tune: *Melcombe*)
New every morning is the love

Brief introduction (David Ellis)

Hymn 444 (Tune: *Buckland*)
Loving Shepherd of thy sheep

First reading (David E.) Matthew Chapter 6, Verses 19–34 *(NEB)*

Hymn 290 (Tune: *Wiltshire*)
Through all the changing scenes of life

Second reading (Clive Cole) 1 Timothy Chapter 6, Verses 3–12 *(NEB)*

Hymn 166 (Tune: *Old Hundredth*)
All people that on Earth do dwell

Brief chat (Philip)

Hymn 256 (Tune: *Thornbury*)
Thy hand, O God, has guided

Prayers (Peter)

Hymn 629 (Tune: *St. Gertrude*)
Onward, Christian soldiers

The service will proceed without announcements. All the hymns are in *Hymns Ancient & Modern Revised.*

Thank you for coming. Please use the voting form opposite to list your own favourite hymns for a subsequent service.

Welcome to the second of our winter 'hymns services'; next time we should be in summer, at the end of May. As always, Peter and I thank David and all of you for coming, and Robert for his usual sterling work on the piano. I am especially grateful to Philip this time, for taking on the 'brief chat'; we have chosen readings to complement what he is going to say. I had to print the service sheets yesterday without being completely sure who would be doing these, as the people I asked had engagements earlier in the day that could delay their getting here, so the names shown may not be the right ones. Our thanks to the readers nonetheless.

We are always glad to receive people's choice of hymns for future services; we don't seem to be getting many these days, so do think now about what you would like for the service in May. We need to know by about the end of March. And we hope you'll be available to come and sing the hymns you ask for!

Matthew 6, 19–34

"Do not store up for yourselves treasure on earth, where it grows rusty and moth-eaten, and thieves break in to steal it. Store up treasure in heaven, where there is no moth and no rust to spoil it, no thieves to break in and steal. For where your wealth is, there will your heart be also.

"The lamp of the body is the eye. If your eyes are sound, you will have light for your whole body; if the eyes are bad, your whole body will be in darkness. If then the only light you have is darkness, the darkness is doubly dark.

"No servant can be slave to two masters; for either he will hate the first and love the second, or he will be devoted to the first and think nothing of the second. You cannot serve God and Money.

"Therefore I bid you put away anxious thoughts about food and drink to keep you alive, and clothes to cover your body. Surely life is more than food, the body more than clothes. Look at the birds of the air; they do not sow and reap and store in barns, yet your heavenly Father feeds them. You are worth more than the birds! Is there a man of you who by anxious thought can add a foot to his height? And why be anxious about clothes? Consider how the lilies grow in the fields; they do not work, they do not spin; and yet, I tell you, even Solomon in all his splendour was not attired like one of these. But if that is how God clothes the grass in the fields, which is there today, and tomorrow is thrown on the stove, will he not all the more clothe you? How little faith you have! No, do not ask anxiously, 'What are we to eat? What are we to drink? What shall we wear?' All these are things for the heathen to run after, not for you, because your heavenly Father knows that you need them all. Set your mind on God's kingdom and his justice before everything else, and all the rest will come to you as well. So do not be anxious about tomorrow; tomorrow will look after itself. Each day has troubles enough of its own."

1 Timothy 6, 3–12

This is what you are to teach and preach. If anyone is teaching otherwise, and will not give his mind to wholesome precepts—I mean those of our Lord Jesus Christ—and to good religious teaching, I call him a pompous ignoramus. He is morbidly keen on mere verbal questions and quibbles, which give rise to jealousy, quarrelling, slander, base suspicions, and endless wrangles: all typical of men who have let their reasoning powers become atrophied and have lost grip of the truth. They think religion should yield dividends; and of course religion does yield high dividends, but only to the man whose resources are within him. We brought nothing into the world, because when we leave it we cannot take anything with us either, but if we have food and covering we may rest content. Those who want to be rich fall into temptations and snares and many foolish harmful desires which plunge men into ruin and perdition. The love of money is the root of all evil things, and there are some who in reaching for it have wandered from the faith and spiked themselves on many thorny griefs.

But you, man of God, must shun all this, and pursue justice, piety, fidelity, love, fortitude, and gentleness. Run the great race of faith and take hold of eternal life. For to this you were called; and you confessed your faith nobly before many witnesses.

WORSHIP OF MONEY AS A PLAGUE ON SOCIETY

Brief Chat . . . it says on your programme—well, this one could well be styled, "Something to say".

Perhaps what follows carries a strong message in the current climate of despicable examples of greed and blatant materialism displayed by those in positions of authority and responsibility. This abuse of privilege is best exemplified under two now well-known media clichés: "Bankers' bonuses" and "M.P.s' expenses".

Of course, *not all* senior bankers and *not all* M.P.s have so succumbed to their opportunities for greed, but *any at all* are far too many.

On the other hand, God has exposed the frailties of mankind with the recent havoc wreaked by the Central American earthquake . . . but this colossal tragedy is quite another matter and in a context all its own.

The greed for (and consequent worship of) money is, I suspect, present in all of us to a certain degree . . . that's human nature. So, perhaps, we shouldn't feel smug and even self-righteous. To feel contrite is one of the reasons for Church attendance!

But it *would* seem that our Church affinity and consequent grasp of Scripture has strengthened our resolve to tread the proverbial "straight and narrow" of practising right or wrong?

Trawling through some of my archival papers I came across a most profound Letter-to-the-Editor of a provincial daily newspaper that I had espied around a decade ago.

This, and by sheer coincidence due to quite another matter, prompted me to a recent re-reading of 1 Timothy Chapter 6 (specifically in the *New English Bible*), at around the same time.

Consequently I have brought the basics of both sets of these texts together in a form that will do no harm for your absorption right now.

It is relevant, hereabouts, to quote from 1 Timothy Chapter 6 and in particular Verses 9 & 10 (from the *N.E.B.*) "Those who want to be rich fall into temptations and snares and many foolish harmful desires which plunge men into ruin and perdition. The love of money is the root of all evil things, and there are some who in reaching for it have wandered from the faith and spiked themselves on many thorny griefs."

And here I add: "*Purveyors of Bankers' Bonuses please take note*"!!

So, to parts of that newspaper piece:–

"If some of our ancestors came back they might brand some aspects of life today as a plague brought about by the Devil. Traditional religion is in steady decline. That might be all very well if it was replaced by values that made for a sane, caring society but the manipulators of our lives seem determined that in place of old-time religion we are to be brainwashed into thinking that all that matters is making money, and spending it."

To which I add: "Owners of top-level Premiership football clubs, for instance"!!

"For all too many people, the modern equivalent of the Ten Commandments involves belief in the false gods of supermarkets, theme parks, fast cars, pop stars and others who want to be millionaires. This has become such a priority that television is now swamped with zany advertising and frenetic trailers about programmes that all too often consist of mindless drivel.

"If present trends continue, it may not be long before significant numbers of people demonstrate their desire for a return to a saner life, with values that help them to withstand the tough times that, apparently, lie ahead.

"A visit to a village church might help to put things into perspective. Regardless of the beliefs that led to the construction of such buildings and their continuance over many centuries, such places often exude an atmosphere of peace *and reassurance* that enables even the casual visitor to accept that there are many more important things in life than the worship *of money!!*"

Now, in my opinion Verses 17–19 from this particular Chapter from 1 Timothy round this whole subject off rather well . . . I do hope that most of you will agree?

Hence (again from the *N.E.B.*):–

"Instruct those who are rich in this world's goods not to be proud, and not to fix their hopes on so uncertain a thing as money, but upon God, who endows us richly with all things to enjoy. Tell them to do good and to grow rich in noble actions, to be ready to give away and to share, and so acquire a treasure which will form a good foundation for the future. Thus they will grasp the life which is life indeed."

Finally, Verse 21:–

"Grace be with you all!"

Amen

Philip Newman

154

Prayers

O Lord, who never failest both to hear and to answer the prayer that is sincere; let not our minds be set on worldly things when we pray, nor our prayers end upon our lips, but send us forth with power to work thy will in the world; through Jesus Christ our Lord. *Amen.*

Father, we thank thee for all the benefits that we have received from thy goodness. To thy blessing we owe every success, every opportunity for doing good, every impulse in the right way, every victory we have gained over ourselves, every thought of thy presence—all are alike thy gifts to us. Give us strength and wisdom to walk faithfully and joyfully in the way of willing obedience to thy law, and cheerful trust in thy love. The best thanksgiving we can offer to thee is to live according to thy will; grant us every day to offer it more perfectly, and to grow in the knowledge of thy will and the love thereof evermore. *Amen.*

O Lord, our heavenly Father, be with us in our homes. Make us to be loving and patient in our own families, forgiving others, as we remember how much we ourselves need to be forgiven. Keep us from all hastiness of temper, and all want of thoughtfulness for others in little things. Make us more ready to give than to receive; and grant that in our homes the holy law of love may reign, bringing to us a foretaste of thy Kingdom, where thy love shall be the everlasting joy of thy people for ever. Through Jesus Christ our Lord. *Amen.*

A few moments' silence for your own prayers. And as we think ahead to the words of the Lord's Prayer let us also call to mind those times when other people have wronged us, and ask ourselves how far we have gone towards forgiving them.

The Lord's Prayer.

O God, our Father, who hast made us in thine own image, with a mind to understand thy works, a heart to love thee, and a will to serve thee; increase in us that knowledge, love and obedience that we may grow daily in thy likeness; through Jesus Christ our Lord. *Amen.*

O Lord, forgive what we have been, sanctify what we are, and order what we shall be. *Amen.*

SIMPLE SERVICE, WITH HYMNS
30th May 2010

Order of Service

Welcome & Notices (David B.)

Hymn 161 (Tune: *Laus Deo*)
Bright the vision that delighted

Brief introduction (David E.)

Hymn 375 (Tune: *Luckington*)
Let all the world in every corner sing

First reading (Tony) from "Spectator ab Extra" *by Arthur H. Clough*

Hymn 164 (Tune: *Rivaulx*)
Father of heaven, whose love profound

Second reading (Estelle) St Matthew, Chapter 26, Verses 6–13 *(NEB)*

Hymn 160 (Tune: *Nicaea*)
Holy, Holy, Holy! Lord God Almighty

Brief chat (David E.)

Hymn 395 (*Mission Praise;* words overleaf. Tune: *Rhuddlan*)
Judge eternal, throned in splendour

Prayers (Peter)

Hymn 293 (Tune: *Monks Gate*)
Who would true valour see

The service will proceed without announcements. All the hymns except one (words opposite) are in *Hymns Ancient & Modern Revised.*

Thank you for coming. Please use the voting form overleaf to list your own favourite hymns for a subsequent service.

Judge Eternal

Judge eternal, throned in splendour,
Lord of lords and King of kings,
with Your living fire of judgement
purge this realm of bitter things;
solace all its wide dominion
with the healing of Your wings.

Still the weary folk are pining
for the hour that brings release;
and the city's crowded clangour
cries aloud for sin to cease;
and the homesteads and the woodlands
plead in silence for their peace.

Crown, O God, Your own endeavour;
cleave our darkness with Your sword;
feed the faithless and the hungry
with the richness of Your word;
cleanse the body of this nation
through the glory of the Lord.

Henry Scott-Holland, 1847–1918

Welcome to the first of our summer 'hymns services'. As always, thank you all for coming, and 'the team' for all your efforts, including of course Robert for his sterling work on the piano. I am especially grateful to Estelle, for joining us by taking on the second reading.

We are missing Philip this evening; perhaps you can all send him some healing thoughts as he recovers from surgery of less than a week ago to remove a melanoma from his cheek below the eye. He told me last night that he still looks as though he has been in a fight.

Please bear with us in that our first reading is somewhat light-hearted.

Spectator Ab Extra

A S I sat at the café, I said to myself,
They may talk as they please about what they call pelf,
They may sneer as they like about eating and drinking,
But help it I cannot, I cannot help thinking,
How pleasant it is to have money, heigh ho!
How pleasant it is to have money.

I sit at my table *en grand seigneur,*
And when I have done, throw a crust to the poor;
Not only the pleasure, one's self, of good living,
But also the pleasure of now and then giving.
So pleasant it is to have money, heigh ho!
So pleasant it is to have money.

I drive through the streets, and I care not a damn;
The people they stare, and they ask who I am;
And if I should chance to run over a cad.
I can pay for the damage if ever so bad.
So pleasant it is to have money, heigh ho!
So pleasant it is to have money.

We stroll to our box and look down on the pit,
And if it weren't low should be tempted to spit;
We loll and we talk until people look up,
And when it's half over we go out and sup.
So pleasant it is to have money, heigh ho!
So pleasant it is to have money.

The best of the tables and best of the fare—
And as for the others, the devil may care;

It isn't our fault if they dare not afford
To sup like a prince and be drunk as a lord.
  So pleasant it is to have money, heigh ho!
  So pleasant it is to have money.

We sit at our tables and tipple champagne;
Ere one bottle goes, comes another again;
The waiters they skip and they scuttle about,
And the landlord attends us so civilly out.
  So pleasant it is to have money, heigh ho!
  So pleasant it is to have money.

It was but last winter I came up to Town,
But already I'm getting a little renown;
I get to good houses without much ado,
Am beginning to see the nobility too.
  So pleasant it is to have money, heigh ho!
  So pleasant it is to have money.

O dear! What a pity they ever should lose it!
For they are the gentry that know how to use it;
So grand and so graceful, such manners, such dinners,
But yet, after all, it is we are the winners.
  So pleasant it is to have money, heigh ho!
  So pleasant it is to have money.

Thus I sat at my table *en grand seigneur,*
And when I had done threw a crust to the poor;
Not only the pleasure, one's self, of good eating,
But also the pleasure of now and then treating.
  So pleasant it is to have money, heigh ho!
  So pleasant it is to have money.

They may talk as they please about what they call pelf,
And how one ought never to think of one's self,
And how pleasures of thought surpass eating and drinking—
My pleasure of thought is the pleasure of thinking
  How pleasant it is to have money, heigh ho!
  How pleasant it is to have money.

Arthur Hugh Clough
(1819–1861)

Matthew 26, 6–13

Jesus was at Bethany in the house of Simon the leper, when a woman came to him with a small bottle of fragrant oil, very costly; and as he sat at table she began to pour it over his head.

The disciples were indignant when they saw it. "Why this waste?" they said; "it could have been sold for a good sum and the money given to the poor."

Jesus was aware of this, and said to them, "Why must you make trouble for the woman? It is a fine thing she has done for me. You have the poor among you always; but you will not always have me. When she poured this oil on my body it was her way of preparing me for burial. I tell you this: wherever in all the world this gospel is proclaimed, what she has done will be told as her memorial."

SOCIETY NEEDS WEALTHY PEOPLE !

Philip Newman made some trenchant comments on financial matters in our January brief chat, as printed in the March magazine. I thought at the time that there might be some further mileage in the same subject, but as I did not start putting my ideas together until a few hours before this May service I have subsequently revised them a little.

Philip quoted the well-known words from Chapter 6 of 1 Timothy, that "the love of money is at the root of all evil things" and the less familar continuation, "and there are some who on reaching for it have wandered from the faith and spiked themselves on many thorny griefs". Jesus' teaching from the Sermon on the Mount in also quite explicit—"no man can serve two masters: you cannot worship God and Money".

Yet we cannot manage without it, and it is a truism to say that, like fire, it is a good servant but a bad master.

That some people should have more than others is inevitable in a society where how much we have is dependent not only on how hard we work but also on what we do and how effective our labours are. It is no bad thing that in a place such as West Chiltington many people can pay for assistance in looking after their homes and gardens; this keeps other residents in work. I have been reading a book by Boris Johnson,[1] and in a piece originally published in *The Daily Telegraph* on 27th February 1995, with the title, "Riches have become the bad dreams of Avarice", dealing with people's resentment against high-salaried executives he comments that:–

---

[1] *Have I Got Views For You* (Harper Perennial, 2006, updated edition, 2008)

160

Middle-income Britain has fallen for an absurd redistributive fallacy, as if lopping a few noughts off Lord Alexander's bonus could make a difference to NatWest's customers. We seem to have forgotten that society needs rich people, even sickeningly rich people, and not just to provide jobs for those who clean swimming pools and resurface tennis courts. If British history had not allowed outrageous financial rewards for a few top people, there would be no Chatsworth, no Longleat. The stately homes of England would never have been built, nor much great art commissioned. There would be no Nuffield Trust. Yes! Had a certain Quaker family not profited enormously from making chocolate there would be no Rowntree Foundation . . . The point, surely, needs no labouring.[1]

Colleges and universities were founded and endowed by people who could afford to. My own College recently put up a building to house all its first-year students. Some 2000 former students had donated a total of ten million pounds to make it possible.

On the other hand, it must be admitted that, supply and demand being what they are, prices of houses, for example, will rise and may go out of reach of poorer folk when too many other people can afford to buy them.

Another downside of people having plentiful spending money is that it can make them wasteful. Why bother to put on an extra pullover in the winter, for example, when it is easier just to turn the heating up?

In 1972 I had a young American fellow psychical researcher staying with me for a few days before we attended a conference in Amsterdam. We made the trip from my flat in Epping to visit a veteran researcher in Bath, and on the way we stopped at a petrol station. My friend told me that he could put into his own car twice the 7½ gallons I was putting into mine, and what's more, it was half the price I was having to pay. So I asked him how many miles his car did to the gallon and, yes, it was half what mine did. So filling up cost him a similar sum, and took him much the same distance; but it required twice as much fuel.

And, like Philip, I wonder about football clubs. We form clubs to play the game, and teams from the various clubs play each other to test their skills. Big business takes over and the pursuit of victory on the field drives up the prices for the 'star' players who are deemed necessary to achieve that victory. And we finish up with English clubs full of overseas players—and then wonder why we find it so hard to put together a team of English players that will do well in international competition.

On a personal level, the Dickensian formula, "Income a pound, expenditure nineteen and sixpence; result happiness; expenditure a pound and

---

[1] © Boris Johnson / Telegraph Media Group Limited

sixpence, result misery" still holds good. While people can make use of credit to sustain expenditure of even more than that pound and sixpence, the end result is still going to be misery. "How pleasant it is to have money" rings very true for those used to tiresome and time-consuming juggling of finances to find enough for the weekly shopping.

As a young lad I did very well at school and imagined that I would land a good job and earn lots of money, but having the good fortune to have been brought up in a Christian home, I was aware of how difficult it was said to be for a rich man to enter the kingdom of heaven, and knew I had to strive harder than most to be good. It didn't actually work out that way; for more than half my life I have been self-employed on a minimal income. But I have been extraordinarily fortunate in having a mother willing to let me live 'at home' for twenty years more or less for nothing. Though I think she was a bit surprised in 1994, when I bought myself a new car, after sixteen years of borrowing hers. Our late parents bought our home, and my brother and I live in it. And now, while I am still working, a State Pension has doubled my income. Result —I actually have some I can give away . . . Which of course is very pleasant!

Jesus said that "Whoever shall save his life shall lose it, and he who loses his life for my sake and the Gospel's, the same shall save it."

That may well apply in certain parts of the world even today, but in our comfortable country village it's really rather too melodramatic. So let's rephrase it a bit, taking the highwayman's choice to those he held up: "Your money or your life!" Thus, "whoever saves (hoards) his money shall lose it, and he who spends his money for my sake and the Gospel's, the same shall save it." Maybe that is something we can bear in mind in a more down-to-earth way for guidance in the Christian life.

And, as it is often said that "Time is Money", a parallel motif could apply to our time as well.

Prayers

God, who as at this time didst teach the hearts of thy faithful people by sending to them the light of thy Holy Spirit, grant us by the same Spirit to have a right judgement in all things, and evermore to rejoice in his holy comfort; through the merits of Christ Jesus our Saviour, who liveth and reigneth with thee in the unity of the same Spirit; one God, world without end. *Amen.*

We praise thy name, O Father, for the beauty of the summer, the glory of the sky by day and night, the healthful wind and quickening rain. We thank thee for the bloom and fragrance of the flowers, the songs of the birds, and the joyousness of every living thing. In all that thou has made we see the wonder of thy wisdom and care. Help us to trust thy never-failing goodness, the love which is beyond understanding, and surrounds our lives with blessing, for thy name's sake. *Amen.*

O Lord we pray thee to raise up leaders of the people who will fear thee and thee alone, whose delight shall be to do thy will and work thy work: that the heart of this people may be wise, its mind sound, and its will righteous; through Christ our Lord. *Amen.*

Almighty and everlasting God, we praise thee for all that thou hast done for our nation. Make us worthy of thy goodness, reverent in the use of freedom, just in the exercise of power, generous in the protection of weakness; and may our deepest trust ever be in thee, the Lord of nations and the King of kings. *Amen.*

O God, our Father, give to the nations of the world a new heart of comradeship, that every people may bring its tribute of excellence to the common treasury, and all the world may go forward in the way which Christ has consecrated for us, until we come to that perfect kingdom into which all the nations shall bring their glory; through Jesus Christ. *Amen.*

Show thy loving kindness tonight, O Lord, to all who stand in need of thy help. Be with the weak to make them strong and with the strong to make them gentle. Cheer the lonely with thy presence and the distracted with thy peace. Prosper thy Church in the fulfilment of her mighty task, and grant thy blessing to all who have toiled today in Christ's name. *Amen.*

A few moments' silence for your own prayers.

The Lord's Prayer.

May the blessing of almighty God rest upon us and upon all our work; may he give us light to guide us, courage to support us, and love to unite us, now and evermore. *Amen.*

SIMPLE SERVICE, WITH HYMNS
29th August 2010

Order of Service

Welcome & Notices (David B.)

Hymn 31 (*Mission Praise;* words on p.38. Tune: *Amazing Grace*)
Amazing grace – how sweet the sound

Brief introduction (David E.)

Hymn 181 (Tune: *London New*)
God moves in a mysterious way

First reading (Anne) Mark, Chapter 10, Verses 23–31 *(NEB)*

Hymn 428 (*Mission Praise;* words overleaf. Tune: *Lord of the Years*)
Lord, for the years Your love has kept and guided

Second reading (Estelle) James, Chapter 2, Verses 14–26 *(NEB)*

Hymn 506 (Tune: *Old 104th*)
Disposer supreme, and Judge of the earth

Brief chat (David E.)

Hymn 254 (Tune: *University*)
The Church of God a kingdom is

Prayers (Peter)

Hymn 660 (*Mission Praise;* words on page 165. Tune: *Crimond*)
The Lord's my shepherd, I'll not want

The service will proceed without announcements. Three hymns are in *Hymns Ancient & Modern Revised* and the other three are in *Mission Praise* (words opposite and overleaf).

Thank you for coming. Please use the separate voting form to list your own favourite hymns for a subsequent service.

Lord, for the Years Your love

Lord, for the years Your love has kept and guided,
urged and inspired us, cheered us on our way,
sought us and saved us, pardoned and provided:
Lord of the years, we bring our thanks today.

Lord, for that word, the word of life which fires us,
speaks to our hearts and sets our souls ablaze,
teaches and trains, rebukes us and inspires us:
Lord of the word, receive Your people's praise.

Lord, for our land in this our generation,
spirits oppressed by pleasure, wealth and care:
for young and old, for commonwealth and nation,
Lord of our land, be pleased to hear our prayer.

Lord, for our world where men disown and doubt You,
loveless in strength, and comfortless in pain,
hungry and helpless, lost indeed without You:
Lord of the world, we pray that Christ may reign.

Lord, for ourselves; in living power remake us –
self on the cross and Christ upon the throne,
past put behind us, for the future take us:
Lord of our lives, to live for Christ alone.

Timothy Dudley-Smith (b.1926)

The Lord's my Shepherd

The Lord's my shepherd, I'll not want;
He makes me down to lie
in pastures green; He leadeth me
the quiet waters by.

My soul He doth restore again,
and me to walk doth make
within the paths of righteousness,
e'en for His own name's sake.

Yea, though I walk through death's dark vale,
yet will I fear no ill;
for Thou art with me, and Thy rod
and staff me comfort still.

My table Thou hast furnishèd
in presence of my foes;
my head Thou dost with oil anoint,
and my cup overflows.

Goodness and mercy all my life
shall surely follow me;
and in God's house for evermore
my dwelling-place shall be.

Francis Rous (1579–1659)

Welcome to the second of our summer 'hymns services'. As always, thank you all for coming, and 'the team' for all your efforts, including of course Robert for his sterling work on the piano. I am especially grateful to Anne, for taking on the first reading, and to Estelle, for agreeing to do the second one again.

We welcome Philip back this evening; and we also welcome David and Mary back from their holiday, just in time to have us all back to the Rectory after this service, an invitation for which we are most grateful, and we hope everyone here will be able to join us in taking it up.

Finally, don't forget to let me have a note of any hymns you would like included in the next service. We don't get nearly as many of these back as we originally expected, so if you do let us have one there is a good chance of your selection being used. I seem to remember we have some from Anne and Graham this time.

Mark 10, 23–31

Jesus looked round at his disciples and said to them, "How hard it will be for the wealthy to enter the kingdom of God!" They were amazed that he should say this, but Jesus insisted, "Children, how hard it is for those who trust in riches to enter the kingdom of God! It is easier for a camel to pass through the eye of a needle than for a rich man to enter the kingdom of God."

They were more astonished than ever, and said to one another, "Then who can be saved?" Jesus looked them in the face and said, "For men it is impossible, but not for God; to God everything is possible."

At this Peter spoke. "We here," he said, "have left everything to become your followers." Jesus said, "I tell you this: there is no one who has given up home, brothers or sisters, mother, father or children, or land, for my sake and for the Gospel, who will not receive in this age a hundred times as much—houses, brothers and sisters, mothers and children, and land—and persecutions besides; and in the age to come eternal life. But many who are first will be last and the last first."

James 2, 14–26

My brothers, what use is it for a man to say he has faith when he does nothing to show it? Can that faith save him? Suppose a brother or a sister is in rags with not enough food for the day, and one of you says, "Good luck to you, keep yourselves warm, and have plenty to eat", but does nothing to supply their bodily needs, what is the good of that? So with faith; if it does not lead to action, it is in itself a lifeless thing.

But someone may object: "Here is one who claims to have faith and another who points to his deeds." To which I reply: "Prove to me that this faith you speak of is real though not accompanied by deeds, and by my deeds I will prove to you my faith." You have faith enough to believe that there is one God. Excellent! The devils have faith like that, and it makes them tremble.

But can you not see, you quibbler, that faith divorced from deeds is barren? Was it not by his action, in offering his son Isaac upon the altar, that our father Abraham was justified? Surely you can see that faith was at work in his actions, and that by these actions the integrity of his faith was fully proved. Here was fulfilment of the words of Scripture: "Abraham put his faith in God, and that faith was counted to him as righteousness"; and elsewhere he is called 'God's friend'.

You see then that a man is justified by deeds and not by faith in itself. The same is true of the prostitute Rahab also. Was not she justified by her action in welcoming the messengers into her house and sending them away by a different route? As the body is dead when there is no breath left in it, so faith divorced from deeds is lifeless as a corpse.

OLDER, BUT STILL ACTIVE AND CONSTRUCTIVE

"The time has come," the Walrus said, "to talk of many things" — and though his suggestion of subject-matter was somewhat bizarre I am sure he would otherwise have fitted in well with our Men's Breakfast Group.[1]

When I mentioned our existence to David at the reception after his Induction, Tony had already, tongue-in-cheek I hope, told him we were a lot of grumpy old men. Old? Some of us *are* the wrong side of three-score years and ten, but that's not old by West Chiltington standards. And rather than being grumpy, we can sometimes be quite constructive.

It was with the encouragement of a Breakfast Group member that I first had the idea of these services, and when he was unavailable it was my friendship with another member, Peter, that got them started seven years ago; and has kept them going ever since. Others have given talks. And the Editor of the Parish Magazine is one of our number.

We were reflecting a few weeks ago that we seem to have abandoned the younger generation—or perhaps they have abandoned us in retreating to their bedrooms and computers and their mobile phones, thereby exposing themselves to various influences, by no means all benign, that we have little or no control over, and which would seem to be driven by commercial interests (such as Facebook). At the same time, however, the young are 'wrapped in

---

[1] This group has been mentioned several times in the course of these services. It was started in January 2000 by Revd Kevin O'Donnell and Peter Evans, initially to make use of the New Vestry, an extension to the Church just opened, but soon moved to the Church Hall. We meet from 9 to 10 on Saturday mornings and partake of croissants or rolls with butter and marmalade, plus coffee or tea.

cotton wool' and surrounded by more and more rules and regulations, in the name of health and safety or for 'child protection', or perhaps on account of the prevailing 'compensation culture'. The *Daily Telegraph,* reporting on the 2007 Scout Jamboree,[1] noted that there would "be no cooking on open fires—health and safety regulations . . . must be upheld. Instead, the pots and pans will gently boil on gas rings, safely supervised by adults." And what would the Scouts do, but "learn about issues including slavery, women's rights, Aids and environmental problems." Rather different from the boating, rock climbing and motorcycling offered at a West Sussex international camp in 1980. I wonder what the hardier overseas Scouts of 2007 thought of their UK hosts.

Being a constructive group, as I said, we also considered the question of what we could do about this perceived generation gulf. Could we not invite articulate youngsters to breakfast with us on a Saturday morning, if they are willing to get up early enough and are not involved with paper rounds? Does anyone here have any children or grandchildren who might risk coming along and taking part in our sometimes erudite discussions?

Thinking about this double generation gap, I am reminded that forty years ago, when I decided to do something more interesting than working for an electronics firm, and take up psychical research, I was introduced to someone who knew about the topic I was planning to study, and he proved very helpful and became a good friend. His name was Victor Bearman. One day the date on a pot of his wife's home-made jam led to my finding out that I had been born on his *fiftieth* birthday. This is not quite a parallel to trying to bridge the gap from the Breakfast Group to those in their late teens, as I was nearly thirty when we met, but the age difference is much the same.

Not only was he interested in the psychic but he was an Elder of the Presbyterian Church and had a very honest and independent approach to religion, which he expounded in monthly addresses to a group of church members and 'enquirers', and later incorporated into booklets and books that I had the privilege of printing and publishing for him (most of which — commercial spot—are still in print). He had read widely and critically and was dismayed at the variance between what was taught in church and the findings of modern biblical scholarship. The first book I printed for him was entitled *Truth—Or Tradition? A Challenge to Christendom,*[2] but a few years earlier, in response to the Church of England setting up an enquiry, he penned a booklet setting out what he thought they should be thinking about, with the title, *Operation or Autopsy?*[3] Hugh Montefiore, a noted New Testament scholar,

---

[1] A century on, Scouts' campfires burn strong. *Daily Telegraph,* Saturday, 28th July, 2007, p.5.

[2] New Barnet: H. V. Bearman, 1976 (now distributed by D. J. Ellis).

[3] Gerrards Cross: Colin Smythe, 1972 (now distributed by D. J. Ellis).

was Dean of my College when I was an undergraduate. He was later Bishop of Birmingham. In 2000 and 2003, we met at Churches' Fellowship[1] conferences and subsequently exchanged some letters in the autumn of 2003. I sent him several of Victor's books. He commented that Victor in *Operation or Autopsy? had* made his points rather aggressively, *but he was in fact quite right.*

When my findings regarding that research topic proved opposite to the views that Victor had held about it, he was generous enough to write that he had found my arguments and experiments convincing. In return, as readers of the Parish Magazine may have noticed, I have taken up his penchant for controversial observations regarding current doctrine.

Anyone who might think that retirement represents cessation of useful activity would do well to reflect on this extract from the Foreword of a book[2] he wrote in an attempt to explain the Christian life to, say, an intelligent scientist with no religious background, which was published just after his death in 1986 but written seventeen years earlier:–

I retired in 1951, with visions of plenty of time to watch cricket at Lords, to see things I had had no time for previously, and of spending my few declining years in a relaxed frame of mind.

Not on your life! I've never been to Lords, etc., but I have spent eighteen years of 'retirement' so fully engaged in what seemed worthwhile activities, closely connected with the 'kingdom of the mind', that I have continually wondered how I ever found time for a business life of forty years!

It has not been the life I vaguely imagined and aspired to have—it has been immensely more rich and worthwhile than any such dreams. Some thinkers have declared that happiness was the object of life. Certainly mankind spends much of its energies seeking happiness and finding disillusion. Happiness is a by-product of the good life and the good life really consists in doing the will of God—in the last analysis. Some of my friends who share my general outlook laughingly agree with my general summing-up of life between our occasions of meeting together: 'Never a dull moment!'

His eighteen years of retirement finished as thirty-five, and he may well be remembered more for what he did in them (he also played bowls for a Hertfordshire team well into his eighties) than for his quite distinguished work as a Fire Surveyor. I am comforted by the thought that there are quite a number of people in West Chiltington who in their many different ways are equally active in their years of so-called retirement.

---

[1] See pages 306–307. Hugh Montefiore is also mentioned on pages 200 and 329.

[2] *Good News for Modern Man* by H. V. Bearman. Pulborough: D. J. Ellis, 1986.

Prayers   29th August 2010

Forgive, O Lord, all our sins today. Take away from us all weakness in resisting the wrong, and give us courage to stand for all that is true, pure, loyal, and unselfish. Forgive what we have been, sanctify what we are, and direct what we shall be. Grant this, O Father, for Jesus Christ's sake.   *Amen.*

Loving Father, we thank thee for our homes and for all who love and care for us. May we ever be grateful for the good things we enjoy, not taking them for granted, but remembering always to give thanks. For the sake of him who was always thankful in all things, thy Son, our Lord Jesus Christ.   *Amen.*

We praise and bless thy holy name, O Lord, for all those who have laboured to serve the cause of freedom and good government in this land, and for all who have striven to uphold the sanctity of the home and family; for all who have sought to bless mankind by their sacrifice and service, and for all who have given their lives to enlarge the bounds of thy Kingdom on earth. For all the prophets, patriarchs and martyrs, and for all obscure and humble saints, we bless and praise thy holy name, through Jesus Christ our Lord.   *Amen.*

Show thy loving kindness tonight, O Lord, to all who stand in need of thy help. Be with the weak to make them strong and with the strong to make them gentle. Cheer the lonely with thy presence and the distracted with thy peace. Prosper thy Church in the fulfilment of her mighty task, and grant thy blessing to all who have toiled today in Christ's name.   *Amen.*

A few moments' silence for your own prayers.

The Lord's Prayer.

Irish Blessing

May the silence of the hills,
The joy of the wind,
The music of the birds,
The fire of the sun,
And the strength of the trees
Be in our hearts now and evermore —

May the road rise up to meet you.
May the wind be always at your back.
May the sun shine warm upon your face,
The rain fall soft upon your fields,
And until we meet again,
May your God hold you in the palm of His hand.

SIMPLE SERVICE, WITH HYMNS

31st October 2010

Order of Service

Welcome & Notices

Hymn 482 (Tune: *St. George*)
Come, ye thankful people, come

Brief introduction (David E.)

Hymn 631 (*Mission Praise;* words on page 48. Tune: *Woodlands*)
Tell out, my soul

First reading (Clive) Luke, Chapter 10, Verses 1–9 *(NEB)*

Hymn 371 (Tune: *Darwall's 148th*)
Ye holy angels bright

Second reading (Tony) Hebrews, Chapter 13, Verses 1–9 *(NEB)*

Hymn 346 (Tune: *Nearer Home*)
For ever with the Lord!

Brief chat (David E.)

Hymn 35 (Tune: *Thuringia*)
Round me falls the night

Prayers (Peter)

Hymn 27 (Tune: *Eventide*)
Abide with me; fast falls the eventide

The service will proceed without announcements. All the hymns except one (words opposite) are in *Hymns Ancient & Modern Revised.*

Thank you for coming. Please use the voting form overleaf to list your own favourite hymns for a subsequent service.

Welcome to the first of what we might call our 'cooler-weather' hymn services. The next one will be at the end of January, and then it's warmer weather, we hope, in April again. As always, thank you all for coming, and 'the team' for your efforts, including of course Robert for his sterling work on the piano. I am especially grateful to Clive, who said he would be willing to take on a reading this time.

We are on All Saints Sunday, but have left the appropriate hymns to be sung earlier in the day, and start in fact with a harvest hymn from earlier in the month. As this is the day the clocks are changed, our final hymn, with its "fast falls the eventide", seems particularly appropriate!

Finally, may I remind you of our dependence on the hymns you ask for. We are happy to go along with your selections, unless we have only just had the hymn concerned, but equally happy to put in some of our own choice if not enough are requested . . .

Luke 10, 1–9

After this the Lord appointed a further seventy-two and sent them on ahead in pairs to every town and place he was going to visit himself. He said to them: "The crop is heavy, but labourers are scarce; you must therefore beg the owner to send labourers to harvest his crop. Be on your way. And look, I am sending you like lambs among wolves. Carry no purse or pack, and travel barefoot. Exchange no greetings on the road. When you go into a house, let your first words be, 'Peace to this house'. If there is a man of peace there, your peace will rest upon him; if not, it will return and rest upon you. Stay in that one house, sharing their food and drink; for the worker earns his pay. Do not move from house to house. When you come into a town and they make you welcome, eat the food provided for you; heal the sick there, and say, 'The kingdom of God has come close to you'."

Hebrews 13, 1–9

Never cease to love your fellow-Christians.

Remember to show hospitality. There are some who, by so doing, have entertained angels without knowing it.

Remember those in prison as if you were there with them; and those who are being maltreated, for you like them are still in the world.

Marriage is honourable; let us all keep it so, and the marriage-bond inviolate; for God's judgement will fall on adulterers.

Do not live for money; be content with what you have; for God himself has said, "I will never leave you or desert you"; and so we can take courage and say, "The Lord is my helper, I will not fear; what can man do to me?"

Remember your leaders, those who first spoke God's message to you; and reflecting upon the outcome of their life and work, follow the example of their faith.

Jesus Christ is the same yesterday, today, and for ever. So do not be swept off your course by all sorts of outlandish teachings; it is good that our souls should gain their strength from the grace of God, and not from scruples about what we eat, which have never done any good to those who were governed by them.

RESISTANCE TO TRADITIONAL CREEDS AND LITURGY

I mentioned in a piece in the August Parish Magazine that, while staying with a cousin in Yorkshire in June, I had purchased and had time to read Bishop John Robinson's *The New Reformation?*, published by SCM Press in 1965, two years after his *Honest to God*. One can't give even a summary of a book of over 140 pages in a brief chat, but there was one point I noted that might be relevant to our attempts to get people to come back to Church, as we have been doing each year about the end of September. When meeting groups of people who had written to him about that first book, he found himself being taken aback by "the vehemence with which almost everyone reacted against the traditional credal and liturgical formulae" (p.39). For example, someone had said to him, "All the Church seems to have to say to me is, 'Come to Evensong and stand up and say the Creed', and this I feel I neither want to nor can." He suggests that this attitude "represents a deep-seated resistance to start from given truths, to prescribe the definition in advance of the experience, the believing ahead of the seeing. For men today cannot see Jesus as the Son of God until they have seen him as the Son of Man. And this is apparently what the Church makes it impossible for them to do." (p.40). So I think that if we really want people to 'come back to Church' we should go a little distance to meet them, and offer a simpler service that includes nothing that they can't endorse. Later in this chapter John Robinson says (p.44):–

Let the historic creeds and confessions be there, in the way that title-deeds and constitutions are, but let us not constantly be straining men's loyalty, sincerity and understanding by asking them to take them upon their lips or to sign on the dotted line. I would gladly see subscription to the Thirty-Nine Articles abolished, as it has been in other parts of the Anglican Communion without disaster or loss of definition. When we need public affirmations of belief (and like confessions we can overdo them), let us have simple, untechnical ones. And let them begin with 'We' not 'I'. For this reflects much more accurately the status (and the confidence) of public proclamation as opposed to (the varying degrees of) private dedication.

It is very understandable that in earlier times the Church would have found it useful to set down a summary of what its members could believe as the main tenets of their faith—about God and about Jesus and how we relate to them. To have something coherent and straightforward to which everyone could subscribe is obviously better than letting people entertain all sorts of outlandish ideas. But the problem is that since then we have become more critical and ready to question what we are told. Certain statements in the Creeds and elsewhere in our services now strike us as quite clearly incapable of being substantiated. We may ask ourselves, why am I affirming this, or we may join in saying them because they are part of the service, probably thinking of them as not so much literally true, but metaphorically, symbolically and/or spiritually meaningful. While people outside the Church no doubt expect us to be convinced of their literal truth, and to want them to believe the same as well.

We were wondering at the Breakfast Group yesterday whether people outside the Church think we all still believe in the Genesis account of the world being created in six days. But as Church members we do not have to be unreceptive to advances in biology, geology and astronomy.

I don't know what John Robinson would have regarded as "simple, untechnical affirmations of belief". However, I am sure he would start with Jesus, and with the content of his teaching as well as the significance of his life. What Jesus said about our relationships with one another, and what he did to show his own concern for other people, stand alone as an unsurpassed ethical framework. "By their fruits you will know them," he is reported to have said, and by his teaching we know Jesus. So, given the self-evident validity of Jesus' teaching about personal relationships, we are on as good ground as any in giving credence to what he tells us about God. That God is not an abstract principle of justice, that needs to be appeased by ritual observances, but a caring father-figure, concerned even for the sparrows, who knows what we need even before we ask. We are not to worry about food and clothing, but to set our minds upon his kingdom, "and all the rest will come to you as well".

Taking this injunction into our lives can also be self-validating. Our conscience may urge us to do something, but having done it we can find ourselves in a position to be useful in some other way we had not thought of at the time. In trying to 'do the right thing' we find ourselves assisted in unexpected ways. I am sure this must be other people's experience and I regard it more as 'how the world works' than merely as coincidence. Put simply, it appears that heaven helps not only those who help themselves, but also those who help others. People who have achieved great things may well have started from something small and relatively insignificant.

Another thing we can believe in is the power of prayer. From Jesus' teaching about two or three being gathered together in his name and agreeing on what they should ask, to our own personal experience of prayers being answered; from remarkable healings resulting from prayer and/or the ministrations of people with an apparent healing gift. Again, we read in the New Testament of Jesus' gift of healing working with the faith of the people by whom it was requested, whether for themselves or for someone else.

In offering these brief comments my aim is to suggest that, whether or not we subscribe to an official formulation of our faith, we still have enough to believe in to form a sufficient basis for worthwhile action.

Prayers

Almighty God, who canst bring good out of evil, and makest even the wrath of man to turn to thy praise; teach thy children to live together in charity and peace, and grant that the nations of the world may be united in a firmer fellowship for the promotion of thy glory and the good of all mankind; through Jesus Christ our Lord. *Amen.*

O God, our heavenly Father, help us always to be of a good courage. Let us not be disheartened by our difficulties, never doubting thy love nor any of thy promises. Give us grace that we may encourage others and always do our best to make life easier for those who need a friendly word or helping hand; for the sake of Jesus Christ our Lord. *Amen.*

Almighty and everlasting God, in whom we live and move and have our being, who hast created us for thyself, so that we can find rest only in thee; grant unto us purity of heart and strength of purpose, so that no selfish passion may hinder us from knowing thy will, no weakness from doing it; but in thy light may we see light clearly, and in thy service find perfect freedom, for Jesus Christ's sake. *Amen.*

A few moments' silence for your own prayers.

The Lord's Prayer.

May the Lord lead us when we go, and keep us when we sleep, and talk with us when we wake; and may the peace of God, which passeth all understanding, keep our hearts and minds in Jesus Christ our Lord. *Amen.*

SIMPLE SERVICE, WITH HYMNS

30th January 2011

Order of Service

Welcome & Notices (David B.)

Hymn 184 (Tune: *Repton*)
Dear Lord and Father of mankind

Brief introduction (David E.)

Hymn 236 (Tune: *Carlisle*)
Breathe on me, Breath of God

First reading (David E.) I John, Chapter 4, Verses 7–12, 17–21 *(NEB)*

Hymn 359 (Tune: *St Margaret*)
O Love that wilt not let me go

Second reading (David E.) Psalm 53 *(NEB)*

Hymn 258 (Tune: *Richmond*)
City of God, how broad and far

Brief chat (Tony)

Hymn 45 (*Hymns for Today;* words opposite. Tune: *Quem pastores*)
Jesus, good above all other

Prayers (Peter)

Hymn 697 (*Mission Praise;* words overleaf. Tune: *Margaret*)
Thou didst leave thy throne and thy kingly crown

The service will proceed without announcements. Four hymns are in *Hymns Ancient & Modern Revised,* one is in *Hymns for Today* and the other is in *Mission Praise* (words opposite and overleaf).

Thank you for coming. Please use the separate voting form to list your own favourite hymns for a subsequent service.

Jesus, good above all other

Jesus, good above all other,
gentle child of gentle mother,
in a stable born our brother,
    give us grace to persevere.

Jesus, cradled in a manger,
for us facing every danger,
living as a homeless stranger,
    make we thee our King most dear.

Jesus, for thy people dying,
risen Master, death defying,
Lord in heaven, thy grace supplying,
    keep us to thy presence near.

Jesus, who our sorrows bearest,
all our thoughts and hopes thou sharest,
thou to man the truth declarest;
    help us all thy truth to hear.

Lord, in all our doings guide us;
pride and hate shall ne'er divide us;
we'll go on with thee beside us,
    and with joy we'll persevere.

Percy Dearmer (1867–1936)
partly based on J. M. Neale (1818–66)

Thou didst leave Thy throne and Thy kingly crown

Thou didst leave Thy throne
and Thy kingly crown,
when Thou camest to earth for me;
but in Bethlehem's home
was there found no room
for Thy holy nativity:
O come to my heart, Lord Jesus,
there is room in my heart for Thee.

Heaven's arches rang
when the angels sang,
proclaiming Thy royal degree;
but of lowly birth
cam'st Thou, Lord, on earth,
and in great humility:
O come to my heart, Lord Jesus,
there is room in my heart for Thee.

The foxes found rest,
and the birds their nest,
in the shade of the cedar-tree;
but Thy couch was the sod,
O Thou Son of God,
in the deserts of Galilee;
O come to my heart, Lord Jesus,
there is room in my heart for Thee.

Thou camest, O Lord,
with the living word
that should set thy people free;
but, with mocking scorn,
and with crown of thorn,
they bore Thee to Calvary:
O come to my heart, Lord Jesus,
Thy cross is my only plea.

When heaven's arches ring,
and her choirs shall sing,   *Emily*
at Thy coming to victory,   *Elizabeth*
let Thy voice call me home,   *Steele*
saying, "Yet there is room,   *Elliott*
there is room at my side for thee!"
And my heart shall rejoice, Lord Jesus,   *(1836–97)*
when Thou comest and callest for me.

Well, after three chilly months, we have our second winter hymns service, and our thirtieth in all. The next one will be at the end of May, when we hope it will be warm again. As always, thank you all for coming, and 'the team' for your efforts, including of course Robert for his sterling work on the piano. I am especially grateful to Tony, who, with a little persuasion, agreed to take on the brief chat this time. So that leaves me to do the readings.

Following my remark last time, reminding you of our dependence on the hymns you ask for, I am pleased to say that we had several forms returned, with enough hymns requested to account for this service and the next, if we use them all. But do please keep them coming.

Just a word of explanation about the hymns printed on the service sheet. You will see that *Jesus good above all other* is "partly based on" a hymn by J. M. Neale. This was *Jesus kind above all other*, which was the one we mistakenly announced in the Parish Magazine. But that one has only two verses, while this one has five. The one on the back is in fact in *Hymns Ancient and Modern Revised*, but Robert, who chose it, says he prefers the slightly different wording at the ends of the final two verses.

I John 4, 7–12, 17–21

Dear friends, let us love one another, because love is from God. Everyone who loves is a child of God and knows God, but the unloving know nothing of God. For God is love; and his love was disclosed to us in this, that he sent his only Son into the world to bring us life. The love I speak of is not our love for God, but the love he showed to us in sending his Son as the remedy for the defilement of our sins. If God thus loved us, dear friends, we in turn are bound to love one another. Though God has never been seen by any man, God himself dwells in us if we love one another; his love is brought to perfection within us.

God is love; he who dwells in love is dwelling in God, and God in him. This is for us the perfection of love, to have confidence on the day of judgement, and this we can have, because even in this world we are as he is. There is no room for fear in love; perfect love banishes fear. For fear brings with it the pains of judgement, and anyone who is afraid has not attained to love in its perfection. We love because he loved us first. But if a man says, 'I love God', while hating his brother, he is a liar. If he does not love the brother whom he has seen, it cannot be that he loves God whom he has not seen. And indeed this command comes to us from Christ himself: that he who loves God must also love his brother.

Psalm 53

The impious fool says in his heart,
  'There is no God.'
How vile men are, how depraved and loathsome;
  not one does anything good!
God looks down from heaven
  on all mankind
to see if any act wisely,
  if any seek out God.
But all are unfaithful, all are rotten to the core;
  not one does anything good,
  no, not even one.

Shall they not rue it,
these evildoers who devour my people
  as men devour bread,
  and never call upon God?

There they were in dire alarm
when God scattered them.
The crimes of the godless were frustrated;
  for God had rejected them.
If only Israel's deliverance might come out of Zion!
  When God restores his people's fortunes,
let Jacob rejoice, let Israel be glad.

HOW DIFFERENT PEOPLE THINK OF GOD TODAY

I came across this poem by Arthur Hugh Clough and used it as the basis:–

There is No God

'There is no God,' the wicked saith,
  'And truly it's a blessing,
For what he might have done with us
  It's better only guessing.'

'There is no God,' a youngster thinks,
  'Or really, if there may be,
He surely didn't mean a man
  Always to be a baby.'

'There is no God, or if there is,'
  The tradesman thinks, ' 'twere funny
If he should take it ill in me
  To make a little money.'

'Whether there be,' the rich man says,
  'It matters very little,
For I and mine, thank somebody,
  Are not in want of victual.'

Some others, also, to themselves
  Who scarce so much as doubt it,
Think there is none, when they are well,
  And do not think about it.

But country folks who live beneath
  The shadow of the steeple;
The parson and the parson's wife,
  And mostly married people;

Youths green and happy in first love,
  So thankful for illusion;
And men caught out in what the world
  Calls guilt, in first confusion;

And almost everyone when age,
  Disease, or sorrows strike him,
Inclines to think there is a God,
  Or something very like him.

Arthur Hugh Clough (1819–1861)

Although Clough lived in the mid 19th Century, I felt that his comments were as applicable to people today as they were to those of his own time.

The verse about the wicked made me think of Richard Dawkins, that charming and clever 'Anti Religionist', who notes the horrors and wars that have been carried out in the name of religion throughout the ages. I don't actually think that Dawkins is wicked, rather that he has misplaced the guilt for the atrocities on 'God' rather than on man's faulty interpretation of him.

Youngsters. This verse is very apt for the youth of today. Like their predecessors, they know everything, so God is obviously nonsense; besides, if he did exist, he would interfere with their love lives.

Tradesmen (bankers, etc.) would probably rather not know about God: he might not approve of some of their methods.

Rich people. These could well feel uncomfortable if they remember Jesus' answer to the questioner who asked how he could enter the Kingdom of Heaven —sell all your goods and give the money to the poor.

Fit and well people in their prime often find their lives full of 'earthly' things: families, careers, pastimes that leave no room (or energy) for God.

There are not very many 'country folk' around today and those few are kept busy just earning a living; albeit, being closer to Nature, they tend to think more positively.

As will young people who find love, though they often seem to discover later that love can be lost, more often than in yesteryear. Standards have changed, which give a lack of stability and this seems to everyone's disadvantage.

The last verse seems particularly applicable to me. Life's 'hiccoughs' strike and encourage deeper thoughts which, despite one having the same information as Dawkins, lead to an alternative solution, especially when we need his help, that: 'Perhaps there is a God—or something very like him.'

Tony Hills

Prayers

Father, we thank thee for all the benefits that we have received from thy goodness. To thy blessing we owe every success, every opportunity for doing good, every impulse in the right way, every victory we have gained over ourselves, every thought of thy presence—all are alike thy gifts to us. Give us strength and wisdom to walk faithfully and joyfully in the way of willing obedience to thy law, and cheerful trust in thy love. The best thanksgiving we can offer to thee is to live according to thy will; grant us every day to offer it more perfectly, and to grow in the knowledge of thy will and the love thereof evermore. *Amen.*

Almighty God, who rulest the changing seasons, we bless thee that beneath all that now seems cold and dead, thou art keeping safe the hidden germs of life. Still thou dost clothe all things around us with beauty, sending forth thy frost and snow, filling the brief day with sunshine, and making the night glorious with countless stars. We thank thee for the shelter and comfort of our homes, and pray for those in poverty or sickness who shrink from the cold. Through Jesus Christ our Lord. *Amen.*

O Lord we beseech thee to bless and prosper us, gathered together here this day. Make us quick to understand the needs and feelings of others and grant us sweet reasonableness in all our dealings with our fellow men. Make us large-hearted in helping and keep us from unkind words and unkind silences. And grant that, living always in the brightness of thy presence, we may reflect thy light in dark places. *Amen.*

We praise and bless thy holy name, O Lord, for all those who have laboured to serve the cause of freedom and good government in this land, and for all who have striven to uphold the sanctity of the home and family; for all who have sought to bless mankind by their sacrifice and service, and for all who have given their lives to enlarge the bounds of thy Kingdom on earth. For all the prophets, patriarchs and martyrs, and for all obscure and humble saints, we bless and praise thy holy name, through Jesus Christ our Lord. *Amen.*

A few moments' silence for your own prayers.

The Lord's Prayer.

The power of the Father, the wisdom of the Son, the love of the Holy Spirit, keep, teach, and guide us for ever. *Amen.*

SIMPLE SERVICE, WITH HYMNS

29th May 2011

Order of Service

Welcome & Notices (David Beal)

Hymn 365 (Tune: *Praise, my soul*)
Praise, my soul, the King of heaven

Introduction (David E.)

Hymn 31 (Tune: *Ellers*)
Saviour, again to thy dear name we raise

First reading (David E.) "The Female of the Species" *by Rudyard Kipling*

Hymn 399 (Tune: *Hyfrydol*)
Alleluia! Sing to Jesus

Second reading (Tony) Genesis, Chapter 3 *(NEB)*

Hymn 296 (Tune: *Cwm Rhondda*)
Guide me, O thou great Redeemer
Chat (David E.)

Hymn 205 (Tune: *Love divine*)
Love divine, all loves excelling

Prayers (Philip, if Peter unavailable)

Hymn 456 (*Mission Praise;* words on page 111. Tune: *St Francis*)
Make me a channel of Your peace

The service will proceed without announcements. All the hymns except one (words opposite) are in *Hymns Ancient & Modern Revised.*

Thank you for coming. **Please join us in the New Vestry after the service** *for a glass of wine, with the compliments of the 'hymns team', and something to eat, with the compliments of the Churchwardens.*

And please use the voting form overleaf to list your own favourite hymns for a subsequent service.

Here we are at our first summer hymns service, and I draft this in the hope that I shall be welcoming a fair number of you to it. My thanks to our Churchwardens for offering to supply you with eats after the service, to go with the glass of wine promised in the magazine by Peter and me.

And as always, my thanks for their efforts to 'the team', especially to Robert for providing our music. And thanks to Robert's friend, Peter, who comes up from Littlehampton whenever he can, so as to be with us.

For our service a year ago, I didn't start setting down a text for what I call my 'brief chat' until the afternoon of the day of the service; but I got going on today's a good month in advance, in case I might forget what I wanted to say. There are times in the year, most notably the spring and early summer, when I find writing easier than at other times, and I began to feel more 'creative' this year on 24th March, the day after Peter and Tony had called to check over my report for the APCM and I had taken the opportunity to get them to select the hymns for today. (As this was well before we knew what hymns would be used at the Royal Wedding service, our inclusion of two of these is completely coincidental.)

I am careful not to give David Beal any intimation of what I am planning, to absolve him from any blame for it, but I do share the text with at least one other member of our team, which this time has resulted in draft after draft coming back to me with passages marked with notes saying that this or that point needed to be explained more clearly, thus developing it from one version to another. So I hope you will forgive its consequent greater length than usual.

As what I was intending to say seemed likely to prove rather more controversial even than my remarks on other occasions, Peter and I thought it best to put *Guide me, O thou great Redeemer* immediately before it! I am not entirely sure what suggested our theme for this time, but it may well have been the current debate about women bishops.

If you have glanced down the service sheet you may have noticed that we have chosen for our (non-biblical) first reading something so un-PC that whoever even reads it out is probably risking prosecution under the Gender Relations Act or some such, which is why I thought I had better read it myself and not expose another member of our team to such risk. But please reserve your judgment on it until you have heard it through; for the author was not an MCP nor was he unsympathetic to the Christian faith. Both his grandfathers were Methodist ministers, as was a great grandfather on his mother's side, who had been converted to that faith by the great John Wesley himself. And in common with all great poets, he knew a bit about human nature.

We like to conclude with a hymn which will go on 'ringing in your ears' well beyond the end of the service; our choice this time is a quiet one, but with its essential message we think it fits the closing role well.

The Female of the Species

When the Himalayan peasant meets the he-bear in his pride,
He shouts to scare the monster, who will often turn aside,
But the she-bear thus accosted rends the peasant tooth and nail.
For the female of the species is more deadly than the male.

When Nag the basking cobra hears the careless foot of man,
He will sometimes wriggle sideways and avoid it if he can.
But his mate makes no such motion where she camps beside the
    trail.
For the female of the species is more deadly than the male.

When the early Jesuit fathers preached to Hurons and Choctaws,
They prayed to be delivered from the vengeance of the squaws.
'Twas the women, not the warriors, turned those stark enthusiasts
    pale.
For the female of the species is more deadly than the male.

Man's timid heart is bursting with the things he must not say,
For the Woman that God gave him isn't his to give away;
But when hunter meets with husband, each confirms the other's
    tale—
The female of the species is more deadly than the male.

Man, a bear in most relations—worm and savage otherwise,—
Man propounds negotiations, Man accepts the compromise.
Very rarely will he squarely push the logic of a fact
To its ultimate conclusion in unmitigated act.

Fear, or foolishness, impels him, ere he lay the wicked low,
To concede some form of trial even to his fiercest foe.
Mirth obscene diverts his anger! Doubt and Pity oft perplex
Him in dealing with an issue—to the scandal of The Sex!

But the Woman that God gave him, every fibre of her frame
Proves her launched for one sole issue, armed and engined for the
    same;
And to serve that single issue, lest the generations fail,
The female of the species must be deadlier than the male.

She who faces Death by torture for each life beneath her breast
May not deal in doubt or pity—must not swerve for fact or jest.

These be purely male diversions—not in these her honour dwells.
She the Other Law we live by, is that Law and nothing else.

She can bring no more to living than the powers that make her great
As the Mother of the Infant and the Mistress of the Mate.
And when Babe and Man are lacking and she strides unclaimed to
    claim
Her right as femme (and baron), her equipment is the same.

She is wedded to convictions—in default of grosser ties;
Her contentions are her children, Heaven help him who denies!—
He will meet no suave discussion, but the instant, white-hot, wild,
Wakened female of the species warring as for spouse and child.

Unprovoked and awful charges—even so the she-bear fights,
Speech that drips, corrodes and poisons—even so the cobra bites,
Scientific vivisection of one nerve till it is raw
And the victim writhes in anguish—like the Jesuit with the squaw!

So it comes that Man, the coward, when he gathers to confer
With his fellow-braves in council, dare not leave a place for her
Where, at war with Life and Conscience, he uplifts his erring hands
To some God of Abstract Justice—which no woman understands.

And Man knows it! Knows, moreover, that the Woman that God gave
    him
Must command but may not govern—shall enthral but not enslave
    him.
And *She* knows, because She warns him, and Her instincts never fail,
That the Female of Her Species is more deadly than the Male.

Rudyard Kipling
(1865–1936)

Genesis 3

The serpent was more crafty than any wild creature that the Lord God had made. He said to the woman, "Is it true that God has forbidden you to eat from any tree in the garden?"

The woman answered the serpent, "We may eat the fruit of any tree in the garden, except for the tree in the middle of the garden; God has forbidden us either to eat or to touch the fruit of that; if we do, we shall die."

The serpent said, "Of course you will not die. God knows that as soon as you eat it, your eyes will be opened and you will be like gods knowing both good and evil."

When the woman saw that the fruit of the tree was good to eat, and that it was pleasing to the eye and tempting to contemplate, she took some and ate it. She also gave her husband some and he ate it. Then the eyes of both of them were opened and they discovered that they were naked; so they stitched fig-leaves together and made themselves loincloths.

The man and his wife heard the sound of the Lord God walking in the garden at the time of the evening breeze and hid from the Lord God among the trees of the garden. But the Lord God called to the man and said to him, "Where are you?"

He replied, "I heard the sound as you were walking in the garden, and I was afraid because I was naked, and I hid myself."

God answered, "Who told you that you were naked? Have you eaten from the tree which I forbade you?"

The man said, "The woman you gave me for a companion, she gave me fruit from the tree and I ate it."

Then the Lord God said to the woman, "What is this that you have done?"

The woman said, "The serpent tricked me, and I ate."

Then the Lord God said to the serpent: "Because you have done this you are accursed more than all cattle and all wild creatures. On your belly you shall crawl, and dust you shall eat all the days of your life. I will put enmity between you and the woman, between your brood and hers. They shall strike at your head, and you shall strike at their heel."

To the woman he said: "I will increase your labour and your groaning, and in labour you shall bear children. You shall be eager for your husband, and he shall be your master."

And to the man he said: "Because you have listened to your wife and have eaten from the tree which I forbade you, accursed shall be the ground on your account. With labour you shall win your food from it all the days of your life. It will grow thorns and thistles for you, none but wild plants for you to eat. You shall gain your bread by the sweat of your brow until you return to the ground; for from it you were taken. Dust you are, to dust you shall return."

The man called his wife Eve because she was the mother of all who live. The Lord God made tunics of skins for Adam and his wife and clothed them. He said, "The man has become like one of us, knowing good and evil; what if he now reaches out his hand and takes fruit from the tree of life also, eats it and lives for ever?"

So the Lord God drove him out of the garden of Eden to till the ground from which he had been taken. He cast him out, and to the east of the garden of Eden he stationed the cherubim and a sword whirling and flashing to guard the way to the tree of life.

FOR WHOM DID JESUS DIE ?

A few years ago at a Breakfast Group meeting we looked out of the window of the Church Hall and saw a large pile of garden rubbish that was stacked high to make a bonfire. When David Burnett asked whether we had any heretics, I was careful to keep quiet.

More recently, in a piece that David as Editor kindly included in the May 2010 Parish Magazine, "Some Thoughts on Mission", I noted that "While the Church of England is very tolerant of its members' varying beliefs, this tolerance is founded on the premiss that the Church's current doctrine is totally correct, and therefore everyone who begs to differ, though kindly tolerated, is simply misguided (heretical in former times)."

Before I go any further, I shall have to introduce some apparently disparate strands, which I hope I shall be able to knit together.

Many years ago there was an article in the *Readers' Digest* entitled "Genius at Midnight", which related how people lying awake at night would occasionally think of something they felt was quite profound, only to find that in the morning they couldn't recall what it was. So someone kept a pencil and paper by his bed to solve this problem, and when he got up in the morning, convinced that he had thought of something that would win the war, he discovered that all he had written was "The skin is mightier than the banana"! The distinguished American psychologist, William James, under the influence of nitrous oxide, which can have the same effect when it is not strong enough to function as an anaesthetic, is said to have coined the immortal couplet, "Higamous, hogamous, woman is monogamous; hogamous, higamous, man is polygamous". Note that this doesn't mean that though man would like a lot of wives, woman only wants one husband. That would be monoandrous, not monogamous. The couplet says that woman wants man to have only one wife.

Then I am sure many of you know the saying, "I sought my God, but Him I could not see; I sought my soul, but my soul eluded me; I sought my brother, and I found all three." I think that is incomplete, and would modify it to read, ". . . I sought my brother *and my sister*, and I found *all four*." 'Brother' might imply 'sister', but 'I sought my sibling' doesn't sound right! In my mid-twenties, when I was involved with the Scouts, I was a tiny bit concerned that I liked boys so much, until I discovered that I liked girls even better. While it's frustrating as a normal red-blooded heterosexual male to be approaching three-score years and ten and still single—appreciating that if one still hopes to father any children one needs to marry someone perhaps half a century one's junior, raising the intriguing prospect of having a mother-in-law young enough to be one's daughter—it does, I suppose, have the compensation that one can devote time and effort to trying to bring some cheer or necessary comfort to a possibly distressed member of the opposite sex (the equivalent of "I sought my sister") without the risk of upsetting a monogamous wife by leaving her feeling jealous or neglected. But I digress.

One night, over thirty years ago, I got to thinking about this myth of Adam and Eve and the forbidden fruit in the Garden of Eden that we had for our second reading. I don't mean to regard the account unkindly by calling it a myth, if we define this as a story which can be metaphorically or symbolically or spiritually true while not necessarily being factually true. At any rate, it was recorded in the Hebrew or Jewish scriptures and thus it was engraved on the Jewish psyche.

What I could not help thinking was that St Paul, and the others who were desperately trying to come to terms with the significance of Jesus' life after he had gone from among them, hadn't got it quite right. In fact, they and our present-day Church had got it completely wrong. Making perhaps too much of the Crucifixion coinciding with the celebration of the Passover, the image of the sacrificial lamb from that feast has been applied to Jesus; the fact that Jesus had led a totally blameless life being matched to that lamb having to be one without blemish, and then whereas the blood of the lamb had served to mark out the Israelite homes so that they were spared the slaughter of the first-born to be visited on the homes of all the Egyptians, the Jewish concept of sacrifice to atone for sin has somehow been brought in as well, leading to the interpretation that Jesus' death on the Cross was the means whereby a vengeful God had been so appeased that he had been persuaded to forgive all the sins of the whole of mankind. Jesus is thus envisaged as having "taken away the sins of the world" despite the fact that everyone can see that sin and wrongdoing are still very much with us. While Jesus had indeed described himself as the Good Shepherd, who was prepared to lay down his life for his sheep, rather than flee when danger threatened, as a hireling might, that is rather different from allowing himself to be led to the sacrificial altar as if he were one of his own lambs. Just because this notion is suggested by a well-known passage from Isaiah does not, in my view, absolve the New Testament writers from what I see as muddled thinking not worthy of their intellect. So it seemed to me that some other form of symbolism might be appropriate.

Before we ask, who blamed whom for what, it might be useful to look at the symbolism of this 'knowledge of good and evil'. Adam did not hide from God because he felt guilty at having been disobedient in eating what he was told not to eat; he hid because he felt ashamed at being naked. This awareness of our own bodies, and the feeling that there are parts of them that we should rather other people did not look at, is what separates humankind from the whole of the rest of the animal kingdom. Some have fur or feathers, or long hair, to cover up the parts in question, but, with or without such clothing for their 'modesty', all other creatures go about in the nude without it apparently bothering them at all. This is such a basic fact that no one comments on it.

Returning to the story, while it was God who confronted Adam with his disobedience in eating of the fruit that he was commanded not to eat, Adam shifted the blame to "the woman you gave me for a companion" and Eve was quick to blame the serpent. The latter was allotted his punishment as related, but God *there and then exacted the penalty on both Adam and Eve*, by turning them out of the Garden, lest he, now knowing good and evil, "reaches out his hand and takes fruit from the tree of life also, eats it and lives for ever". So if we now ask, who needs to be forgiven by whom, the answer must surely be that Woman needs to be forgiven by Man.

Now, before all the feminine hackles in the congregation rise, and I am targeted for lynching after this service, I need to explain two things. First, that there is a difference between an actual wrong and a perceived wrong. Clearly, all wrongs that might require forgiveness have to have been perceived wrongs, but they need not have been actual. You would not consider forgiving someone you did not know had hurt you, but you would see possible forgiveness as relevant to some action which you thought had compromised you, even though in truth this was not the case. Secondly, the people of Jesus' day believed that the story of the Garden, as related in their scriptures, was historically accurate, while most of us today accept no more than its symbolic truth. I am saying that Woman needs to be forgiven by Man simply because in the story Adam laid on Eve the blame for his having eaten the forbidden fruit. And of course it was more a case of passing the buck than an actual wrong; it surely was Adam's decision that he would eat the fruit Eve gave him.

And so I developed the thesis that, if we need to attach some symbolic significance to Jesus' death on the Cross, it really makes much more sense to say that *he died on behalf of Man to redeem Woman*. What puzzled me in 1980, or whenever, was that although this seemed to be quite a logical inference, I had never come across the idea as being put forward by anyone else. No one seems to have remarked that the most loved of all our Good Friday hymns was written by a *woman* (Mrs C. F. Alexander) and gone on to suggest that "He died that we might be forgiven" was really "that we *women* might be forgiven". But by Man, not by "some God of Abstract Justice— which no woman understands" (as distinct from the God that we all profess to believe in, Who said, even through the Old Testament scriptures, "I will have obedience rather than sacrifice.").

The late C. S. Lewis, whose book, *Miracles* (Fontana, 1960), I read when I was an undergraduate, relates how before he became a Christian he looked for some symbolism in Jesus' life and death, but the myth of the 'corn king' dying and rising in a way analogous to seed dying in the ground and then rising to prolific life just did not fit (although there is a hymn writer who thinks it does: see J. M. C. Crum's *Like wheat that springeth green*). But he didn't discuss any other symbolism. He didn't connect the shedding of Jesus' blood on the Cross with "She who faces Death by torture for each life beneath her breast", to borrow another line from our first reading.

In a male-dominated society, Jesus championed women. "Neither do I condemn thee", "Her sins are forgiven because she loved much", to remind you of but two stories. Then the parable of the Sheep and the Goats, with its "For when I was hungry, you gave me food;" through to "anything you did for one of my brothers here, however humble, you did for me." struck me some fifty years ago as the perfect acknowledgement of what mothers do for their infants. Given the progress that women have made towards equality in the last couple of millennia, Jesus' mission towards women could really be described as having been pretty successful. Especially when you compare how women are treated under Christianity with their lot under, say, Islam. Given that in Genesis, Chapter 3, Eve was told that "your husband . . . shall be your master", Woman's recent rise towards equality might be seen as a move towards liberation from this age-old restriction placed on her freedom of action.

Other people I have talked to about this remain wedded to the more traditional interpretation and are sceptical of any re-evaluation such as mine, though one long-standing family friend did say, many years ago, that she thought I might be right. How the *serpent* could be redeemed will have to wait for another talk, if I am allowed to give one after what I have been saying this evening!

Where my thesis leaves women priests (or bishops) must be a subject of speculation, but it might be necessary to drop the notion that in the Eucharist the celebrant takes the place of Jesus.

Of course, you don't need to fit Jesus' death to any symbolism. Just ask yourself how Jesus, who is reported to have said "Greater love hath no man than this, that he lay down his life for his friend", and encouraged his followers to love also their enemies, could have lived with himself had the crowd called for him to go free and Barabbas had been crucified in his place. Or consider that if the Cross was part of the Divine plan, as indeed it must have been, so also was the Resurrection, which lit the torch of the Christian faith.

In conclusion, I apologize for expressing from this pulpit a view of what is known as the Doctrine of the Atonement so at variance with two thousand years of Christian teaching, but, God willing—permissively, as I trust is going to be the case; I dare not claim directively—I find myself unable to do otherwise, simply because I believe that obeying our Lord's Commandment to 'love God with all your mind' is incompatible with uncritical, unthinking acceptance of every tenet of orthodox dogma.

Prayers

We praise thy name, O Father, for the beauty of the summer, the glory of the sky by day and night, the healthful wind and quickening rain. We thank thee for the bloom and fragrance of the flowers, the songs of the birds, and the joyousness of every living thing. In all that thou has made we see the wonder of thy wisdom and care. Help us to trust thy never-failing goodness, the love which is beyond understanding, and surrounds our lives with blessing, for thy name's sake. *Amen.*

O God, who art the Father of us all, we pray thee to have pity on all who are cold or hungry or ill-clothed, and upon those who have no home. Show us what we can do to help them, and may we never rest until poverty and want are driven from every land; through Jesus Christ our Lord. *Amen.*

Almighty God, the Giver of all good gifts, grant unto us a courteous spirit, a forgiving temper and an unselfish heart. Bestow upon us the spirit of self-sacrifice and cheerfulness, of hope and endurance. Increase in us the love of truth, of candour and of honour. Grant us courage to do what is right and, rejoicing in thee, to persevere unto the end; through Jesus Christ our Lord. *Amen.*

O Lord God, whose will and joy it is that thy children love one another; bless our friendships, that they may be made happy and kept pure by thine unseen presence, now and at all times; through Jesus Christ our Lord. *Amen.*

Come, Holy Spirit, into our hearts;
Be thou within us to purify us;
Before us to lead us;
Behind us to restrain us;
Above us to lift us up;
Beneath us to sustain us;
Round us to protect us;
All the days of our life. *Amen.*

A few moments' silence for your own prayers.

The Lord's Prayer

† Almighty God, who hast given us grace at this time with one accord to make our common supplications unto thee; and dost promise that when two or three are gathered together in thy name thou wilt grant their requests: fulfil now, O Lord, the desires and petitions of thy servants, as may be most expedient for them; granting us in this world knowledge of thy truth, and in the world to come life everlasting. *Amen.*

May God the Father, the Son and the Holy Spirit be with us all this day and evermore. *Amen.*

194

SIMPLE SERVICE, WITH HYMNS
31st July 2011

Order of Service

Welcome & Notices (David Beal)

Hymn 311 (Tune: *Mannheim*)
Lead us, heavenly Father, lead us

Introduction (David E.)

Hymn 37 (*Mission Praise; Words and Music: Martin Nystrom*)
As the deer

First reading (Ena) 2 Peter, Chapter 1, Verses 2–11 *(NEB)*

Hymn 217 (Tune: *Miles Lane*)
All hail the power of Jesus' name

Second reading (Clive S.) Matthew, Chapter 21, Verses 23–46 *(NEB)*

Hymn 220 (Tune: *Truro*)
Jesus shall reign where'er the sun

Brief Chat (Tony)

Hymn 208 (Tune: *Bishopthorpe*)
Immortal love for ever full

Prayers (Philip)

Hymn 257 (Tune: *Austria*)
Glorious things of thee are spoken

The service will proceed without announcements. All the hymns except one (words opposite) are in *Hymns Ancient & Modern Revised.*

*Thank you for coming. **Please join us in the New Vestry after the service** for a glass of wine, with the compliments of the 'hymns team', and something to eat, with the compliments of the Churchwardens.*

And please use the voting form overleaf to list your own favourite hymns for a subsequent service.

Although we discovered that the hymn, *As the Deer*, with Martin Nystrom singing it, could be downloaded in a choice of formats for a modest fee, we were unsure how to obtain the necessary permission to reproduce its words.

To make use of the space we had reserved for it, we are including a story which fits well with one of the themes of our book, namely that it often seems that something has to go wrong for something else to go right (see p.249). It also allows us to feature the service our readers are supporting by purchasing copies of our book.

Saving Lives at Sea

Many readers will have seen the series of television programmes on BBC2 with the title printed above, brought to us with the use of today's recording technology, showing lifeboat work as it happened. It is announced that the crews are 'ordinary people'. Well, they may have been ordinary before they trained to become lifeboat crew, but in the work they do they are in my opinion no longer ordinary at all, but have become very special people. *DJE*

Below is the entry for Saturday November 6 from

The Friendship Book of Francis Gay, 1971

London: D. C. Thomson & Co., 1970.

Do all things really work together for good?

Sometimes it hardly seems so. Certainly, William Hillary would not have agreed when a stroke of ill-fortune lost him much of his estate in Essex, and he had to move to a more modest home in Douglas, Isle of Man.

But, for the first time he saw the terrible toll of the sea. Many vessels foundered in storms off the shores, and their crews perished. So in 1823 he appealed to the nation to make the waters round Britain safe, and announced his plan for a lifeboat service. A year later the Lifeboat Institution was born.

William himself gave four lifeboats to the Isle of Man, and whenever he could, went out as a member of their crew. Because of his heroism, scores of lives were saved, and he was one of the first men to be awarded the gold medal of the R.N.L.I. — the medal that, to this day, is given to lifeboatmen for outstanding courage.

When he died in 1847 there were 20 lifeboats. Today [1970] there are 249, and since the first was launched, nearly 100,000 lives have been saved — all because a man's bad luck took him to live at the seaside.

Even if no memorial had ever been raised to William Hillary, none would have been needed. For surely every lifeboat — and every life saved — is his memorial.

Well, after just two months, we have our second summer hymns service, and, sadly, the second in succession that Peter is unable to be with us. While last time he and Karen were very concerned about Sarah, who was in hospital in London, this time Karen has simply taken him away on holiday. But, as last time, he was involved in the planning, and, again as last time, Philip has kindly stepped in to do the prayers.

We are also repeating our offer to you all to join us for a glass of wine after the service; Peter, Tony and I shared the cost of this in May, and it worked out to such a modest sum each that we felt we could well afford a repetition. However, to make less work for Pam, we have told her that a few 'nibbles' to go with it will be quite sufficient.

Our next hymns service will be at the end of October, when we hope the weather will still be fairly pleasant. As always, thank you all for coming, and 'the team' for your efforts, including Robert for his sterling work on the piano, and Pam for providing refreshments. I am especially grateful to Tony, who is taking on the brief chat again; in fact, the team are letting me take a break this time, probably to make up for my having so much to say in May.

I also have Francesca to thank, for giving me a book on prayer which was compiled by my College friend, Revd Jim Cotter. We have chosen a prayer from it, and we rather liked this little passage that we found in it:–

We may try to ignore disturbing questions, but they do not go away. We may try to suppress them, but they cannot be forgotten. We may try to hide from them like naked Adam, but we cannot escape them. And it is a delusion to suppose that we shall get comforting answers. To live with our uncertainties . . . is the very truth of faith. To endure the sifting process of interrogation is the hallmark of discipleship.

2 Peter 1, 2–11

Grace and peace be yours in fullest measure, through the knowledge of God and Jesus our Lord.

His divine power has bestowed on us everything that makes for life and true religion, enabling us to know the One who called us by his own splendour and might. Through this might and splendour he has given us his promises, great beyond all price, and through them you may escape the corruption with which lust has infected the world, and come to share in the very being of God.

With all this in view, you should try your hardest to supplement your faith with virtue, virtue with knowledge, knowledge with self-control, self-control with fortitude, fortitude with piety, piety with brotherly kindness, and brotherly kindness with love.

These are gifts which, if you possess and foster them, will keep you from being either useless or barren in the knowledge of our Lord Jesus Christ. The man who lacks them is short-sighted and blind; he has forgotten how he was cleansed from his former sins. All the more then, my friends, exert yourselves to clinch God's choice and calling of you. If you behave so, you will never come to grief. Thus you will be afforded full and free admission into the eternal kingdom of our Lord and Saviour Jesus Christ.

Matthew 21, 23–46

Jesus entered the temple, and the chief priests and elders of the nation came to him with the question: "By what authority are you acting like this? Who gave you this authority?"

He replied, "I have a question to ask too; answer it, and I will tell you by what authority I act. The baptism of John: was it from God, or from men?"

This set them arguing among themselves: "If we say, 'from God', he will say, 'Then why did you not believe him?' But if we say, 'from men', we are afraid of the people, for they all take John for a prophet."

So they answered, "We do not know."

And Jesus said: "Then neither will I tell you by what authority I act.

"But what do you think about this? A man had two sons. He went to the first, and said, 'My boy, go and work today in the vineyard.' 'I will, sir,' the boy replied; but he never went.

"The father came to the second and said the same. 'I will not,' he replied, but afterwards he changed his mind and went. Which of these two did as his father wished?"

"The second," they said.

Then Jesus answered, "I tell you this: tax-gatherers and prostitutes are entering the kingdom of God ahead of you. For when John came to show you the right way to live, you did not believe him, but the tax-gatherers and prostitutes did; and when you had seen that, you did not change your minds and believe him.

"Listen to another parable. There was a landowner who planted a vineyard: he put a wall around it, hewed out a winepress, and built a watch-tower; then he let it out to vine-growers and went abroad. When the vintage season approached, he sent his servants to the tenants to collect the produce due to him. But they took his servants and thrashed one, murdered another, and stoned a third. Again, he sent other servants, this time a larger number; and they did the same to them. At last he sent to them his son. 'They will respect my son,' he said.

"But when they saw the son the tenants said to one another, 'This is the heir; come on, let us kill him, and get his inheritance.' And they took him, flung him out of the vineyard, and murdered him. When the owner of the vineyard comes, how do you think he will deal with those tenants?"

"He will bring those men to a bad end," they answered, "and hand the vineyard over to other tenants, who will let him have his share of the crop when the season comes."

Then Jesus said to them, "Have you never read the scriptures: 'The stone which the builders rejected has become the main corner-stone. This is the Lord's doing, and it is wonderful in our eyes'? Therefore, I tell you, the kingdom of God will be taken away from you, and given to a nation that yields the proper fruit."

When the chief priests and Pharisees heard his parables, they saw that he was referring to them; they wanted to arrest him, but they were afraid of the people, who looked on Jesus as a prophet.

SOME THOUGHTS ON THE NICENE CREED

At our May service, David put his neck on the line by proposing a novel, gender-related, way of linking the story of Adam and Eve to what is known as the Atonement, dismissing the traditional interpretation as "muddled thinking" on the part of the New Testament writers "not worthy of their intellect". I too have some contentious thoughts for you, this time regarding the Nicene Creed, which we know so well.

One of the main problems confronting the integration of Islam into the modern world has been the belief that the Koran is literally the final word of God, directly revealed to the Prophet Muhammad. This has fixed Islam in the mind-set and interpretation of the late seventh century, with its brutal public execution by stoning of adulterous women, heretics and other 'heinous criminals'.

However, it has recently dawned on me (things dawn on me very slowly) that we are in an even worse situation with the Nicene Creed, as we are locked in the mind-set and knowledge level of the end of the *third* century. The authors of this Creed would have had no knowledge of the world outside the Mediterranean, Europe and the Middle East, except for some hints of India and beyond. They would have had no knowledge of the Universe and its immense size, apart from the celestial dome they saw above them, with the Sun and Moon passing through it and the stars dancing in a repeatable pattern, except for the few that unreasonably wandered about (the planets), and for the next 1300 years they even thought that the Sun went round the Earth. Most of them believed that the world was flat, although people looking out over the sea must have seen the hulls of ships disappearing before their masts and sails did, sailors saw mountain tops appearing before the rest of the land, and a certain Greek mathematician, whose name escapes me [it was Eratosthenes—*DJE*], managed to make a remarkably accurate estimate of the diameter of the Earth.

Constantine the Great, so the story goes, had won his Empire through conflict and under the sign of the Cross. He apparently became a Christian, although he was not baptised until he was on his deathbed. Recognising the benefits of having a single religion throughout the Empire he decreed that Christianity would be that state religion. However, there were several versions of Christianity from which to choose, and there were many aspects, even the divinity of Jesus, on which they did not all agree.

Constantine therefore called a council of Church leaders to meet at Nicaea and to agree on a common theology, the final output of which was the Nicene Creed, by which we are still invited to "affirm our faith" at every Communion service today. In doing so, I sometimes wonder if other people experience the same feelings of uncertainty that I do.

It might well be thought that faith was something other than assenting to a series of dogmatic statements such as we find here. There is in fact a whole section on faith in Chapter 11 of the Epistle to the Hebrews, and it is put most simply in Verse 6: " . . . without faith it is impossible to please him; for anyone who comes to God must believe that He exists and that He rewards those who search for Him." (*NEB*).

Beyond that, we have what Jesus himself taught, which is surely more fundamental than what has been asserted about him. But of course it was the quality and authority of this teaching, the miraculous healings and other works that he had performed, coupled with the example of his life and, above all, the events subsequent to his being sent for execution by the Roman authorities, that marked him out as someone very special in God's interaction with the world.

His authority and indeed 'God-like' and miraculous behaviour needed to be explained by the Apostles, who were of course all good Jewish boys. Their Ten Commandments only allowed one God, but nobody had said a thing about the 'Son of God'. Jesus did tell a parable about the absent master of a vineyard sending "his son" to reason with his tenants—but, to be fair, Jesus did not claim that he was God's *only* son, as he also referred to "your father in heaven" as well as "my father in heaven", and when asked for advice on how to pray, he gave us that great prayer which begins: "Our father". If Jesus was God's Son, it was but a small step to asserting that he could not have had an earthly father, which introduces the notion of the 'Virgin Birth', a concept not apparently held by the Early Church (see St Paul in Romans 1, verse 4).

I must admit that I felt some considerable relief when I first noted that this

Creed does not actually state that Jesus died on the Cross, only that he suffered and was buried. The concept that someone who was really clinically dead, and had been so for about 36 hours, which would have allowed decomposition to become considerably advanced, at least within the brain, could subsequently become alive again is really very difficult to swallow, yet that is exactly what those around at the time (the Apostles) did. Not only did they believe it but they preached 'Christ crucified and resurrected' until the end of their lives, and very sticky that end was for nearly all of them! They certainly had a 'Resurrection Experience' unless the whole thing was pure fiction, and I don't believe that for one minute!

I have always thought that the concept of the Trinity was contrived and not really necessary. I have no problem with the 'Holy Spirit' as the spirit of God in action. We know that Jesus was a man but the concept that he was also God in human form can present real difficulties of comprehension. Bishop Hugh Montefiore in his paperback, *Beyond Reasonable Doubt* (London: Hodder & Stoughton, 1963), said that he believed in Jesus' divinity *because he did the work of God*, so if we can postulate that he was enabled to accomplish this because he was consistently 'led by the Holy Spirit', perhaps this may simplify things a bit.

I believe that the problems that I have outlined above are the very ones responsible for the majority of 'thinking' Europeans being unwilling to accept Christianity today. They were not taught the basics at school (unless it was a faith school) and it is not surprising that, when presented with the 'official' line, they cannot believe it, and become 'secularised'.

Nearly fifty years ago, Bishop John Robinson and several others tried to work out a re-interpretation, but they were eventually 'frozen out'.[1] Luckily for me, the Church of England is a broad church, and as I do not have to assent to the 39 Articles I am unlikely to be expelled, so long as I make sure people understand that I am only throwing out some ideas that may give them something to think about.

Tony Hills

---

[1] John Robinson's books, *Honest to God* and *The New Reformation?* are mentioned on pp.173–174. Bishop Hugh Montefiore's sympathetic comments on Victor Bearman's outspoken diagnosis of the 'Crisis of the Christian Faith' expressed in his *Operation or Autopsy?* are noted on pp.168–169, and David's disappointment at the reaction of our Church of England to *The Myth of God Incarnate* is on p.294.

Also very worth reading is *Objections to Christian Belief* by D. M. MacKinnon et al. London: Constable & Co., 1963. This is the record of a series of lectures given in Cambridge in February 1963 under the auspices of the Divinity Faculty, three of which David attended. MacKinnon dealt with Moral Objections, H. A. Williams with Psychological, A. R. Vidler with Historical and J. S. Bezzant with Intellectual ones.

Prayers

O Lord, our heavenly Father, be with us in our homes. Make us to be loving and patient in our own families, forgiving others, as we remember how much we ourselves need to be forgiven. Keep us from all hastiness of temper, and all want of thoughtfulness for others in little things. Make us more ready to give than to receive; and grant that in our homes the holy law of love may reign, bringing to us a foretaste of thy Kingdom, where thy love shall be the everlasting joy of thy people for ever. Through Jesus Christ our Lord. *Amen.*

Summer

GRATITUDE for the cosseting of the sun

for the play and sparkle of water

for the gentle rain

for the ripening of the grain

for the shade of the woodland

for the quiet sunsets

for the long and lingering twilight

for the nectar of night

O God, our Father, give to the nations of the world a new heart of comradeship, that every people may bring its tribute of excellence to the common treasury, and all the world may go forward in the way which Christ has consecrated for us, until we come to that perfect kingdom into which all the nations shall bring their glory; through Jesus Christ.   *Amen.*

A few moments' silence for your own prayers.

The Lord's Prayer.

Let us go forth into the world in peace; let us be of good courage; holding fast that which is good; rendering to no man evil for evil; strengthening the faint-hearted; supporting the weak; helping the afflicted; honouring all men; loving and serving the Lord; rejoicing in the power of the Holy Spirit.

And may the blessing of God Almighty, the Father, the Son, and the Holy Spirit, be upon us, and remain with us for ever.   *Amen.*

SIMPLE SERVICE, WITH HYMNS
30th October 2011

Order of Service

Welcome & Notices (Diane)

Hymn 219 (Tune: *Crüger*)
Hail to the Lord's Anointed

Brief introduction (David E.)

Hymn 281 (*Mission Praise;* words on page 37)
I lift my eyes to the quiet hills

First reading (Tony) Mark, Chapter 4, Verses 10–23 *(NEB)*

Hymn 288 (*Mission Praise;* words opposite. Tune: *I need Thee*)
I need Thee every hour

Second reading (Philip) John, Chapter 15, Verses 1–17 *(NEB)*

Hymn 361 (Tune: *Nottingham*)
Take my life, and let it be

Brief chat (David E.)

Hymn 349 (Tune: *Misericordia*)
Just as I am, without one plea

Prayers (Peter)

Hymn 289 (Tune: *Kocher*)
O happy band of pilgrims

The service will proceed without announcements. Four hymns are in *Hymns Ancient & Modern Revised,* and the others are in *Mission Praise* (words opposite and overleaf).

Thank you for coming. **Please join us in the New Vestry after the service** for a glass of wine (alternatives available).

Please use the separate voting form to list your own favourite hymns for a subsequent service.

I need Thee every hour

I need Thee every hour, most gracious Lord:
No tender voice like Thine can peace afford.
I need Thee, O I need Thee!
Every hour I need Thee;
O bless me now, my Saviour!
I come to Thee.

I need Thee every hour, stand Thou near by;
Temptations lose their power when Thou art nigh.
I need Thee, O I need Thee!
Every hour I need Thee;
O bless me now, my Saviour!
I come to Thee.

I need Thee every hour, in joy or pain;
Come quickly and abide, or life is vain.
I need Thee, O I need Thee!
Every hour I need Thee;
O bless me now, my Saviour!
I come to Thee.

I need Thee every hour, teach me thy will;
And Thy rich promises in me fulfil.
I need Thee, O I need Thee!
Every hour I need Thee;
O bless me now, my Saviour!
I come to Thee.

I need Thee every hour, most Holy One;
O make me Thine indeed, Thou blessèd Son!
I need Thee, O I need Thee!
Every hour I need Thee;
O bless me now, my Saviour!
I come to Thee.

Annie Sherwood Hawks
(1835–1918)

Well, we are now at the end of October, and as hoped the weather is still quite mild. As always, thank you all for coming, and 'the team' for your efforts, including Robert for his sterling work on the piano. I am especially pleased to be able to welcome Peter back, after his missing our two summer services for one reason or another. David Beal, however, has sent apologies as he is celebrating his niece's 18th birthday; we thank Diane for welcoming everyone.

We are again inviting you to join us for a glass of wine after the service; Peter has been helping to pay for this each time, so it's only fair that he should have a chance to enjoy it too. We thank Pam for providing refreshments; we did tell her not to trouble this month, but she said she would just bring a little.

Mark 4, 10–23

When he was alone, the Twelve and others who were round him questioned him about the parables. He replied, "To you the secret of the kingdom of God has been given; but to those who are outside everything comes by way of parables, so that (as Scripture says) they may look and look, but see nothing; they may hear and hear, but understand nothing; otherwise they might turn to God and be forgiven."

So he said, "You do not understand this parable? How then are you to understand any parable? The sower sows the word. Those along the footpath are people in whom the word is sown, but no sooner have they heard it than Satan comes and carries off the word which has been sown in them. It is the same with those who receive the seed on rocky ground; as soon as they hear the word they accept it with joy, but it strikes no root in them; they have no staying-power; then, when there is trouble or persecution on account of the word, they fall away at once. Others again receive the seed among thistles; they hear the word, but worldly cares and the false glamour of wealth and all kinds of evil desire come in and choke the word, and it proves barren. And there are those who receive the word in good soil; they hear the word and welcome it; and they bear fruit thirtyfold, sixtyfold, or a hundredfold."

He said to them, "Do you bring in the lamp to put it under the meal-tub, or under the bed? Surely it is brought in to be set on the lamp-stand? For nothing is hidden unless it is to be disclosed, and nothing put under cover unless it is to come into the open. If you have ears to hear, then hear."

John 15, 1–17

Jesus said, "I am the real vine, and my Father is the gardener. Every barren branch of mine he cuts away; and every fruiting branch he cleans, to make it more fruitful still. You have already been cleansed by the word that I spoke to you. Dwell in me, as I in you. No branch can bear fruit by itself, but only if it remains united with the vine; no more can you bear fruit, unless you remain united with me.

"I am the vine, and you are the branches. He who dwells in me, as I dwell in him, bears much fruit; for apart from me you can do nothing. He who does not dwell in me is thrown away like a withered branch. The withered branches are heaped together, thrown on the fire, and burnt.

"If you dwell in me, and my words dwell in you, ask what you will, and you shall have it. This is my Father's glory, that you may bear fruit in plenty and so be my disciples. As the Father has loved me, so I have loved you. Dwell in my love. If you heed my commands, you will dwell in my love, as I have heeded my Father's commands and dwell in his love.

"I have spoken thus to you, so that my joy may be in you, and your joy complete. This is my commandment: love one another, as I have loved you. There is no greater love than this, that a man should lay down his life for his friends. You are my friends, if you do what I command you. I call you servants no longer; a servant does not know what his master is about. I have called you friends, because I have disclosed to you everything that I heard from my Father. You did not choose me: I chose you. I appointed you to go on and bear fruit, fruit that shall last; so that the Father may give you all that you ask in my name. This is my commandment to you: love one another."

SAINTS AND AN EVOLVING CHURCH ?

Although a couple of days early, today is All Saints Sunday, and we have picked a reading that we had for All Saints in 2004, but one that might not normally be associated with this theme. It's not quite the same, as we had the version in Matthew then, and this time we have the one from Mark. The reading describes how Jesus tells his disciples that the secret of the kingdom of God has been given to them, before explaining the Parable of the Sower. In this we may feel ourselves included with the disciples, and hence in a small way at one with them as saints, as we too are granted this explanation. And of course there are many other similar instances in the Gospels. As Jesus taught them so also does he teach us.

206

Again thinking back to 2004, when I was talking about saints I noted that I had heard that my College had produced one, and later that there were two. These would have been among the martyrs the magazine told us about a few years ago: Catholics who maintained this faith in the time of Elizabeth I, when to do so was a treasonable offence.[1]

Whether they were or not, it is certainly true to say that saints are not necessarily pious people who spend their lives preaching and doing good but can also be rebels — people who defy authority for the sake of what they believe to be right, or to draw attention to what they see as wrong. Though I would hasten to add that such action is open to any of us, and by no means restricted to saints.

We are much more friendly these days towards the Catholics, and indeed to our fellow Christians of other denominations as well, but this does not mean that the Church of today doesn't need any rebels. We had John Robinson in the early Sixties with *Honest to God* and his later book, *The New Reformation?*, and there were others about that time who made some critical comments on cherished beliefs, but as Tony said in July they were eventually 'frozen out'. I was therefore much encouraged to read what Philip's friend Edward Moorland had to say in our October Parish Magazine.[2]

His first point was that the Church should not be unchanging, but "must be evolving all the time to serve society as it changes". As he said, you wouldn't go on using a horse and cart when lorries, trains and planes were available. You may say, What about *Onward Christian Soldiers*, with its "But the Church of Jesus constant will remain" ? Though as it says earlier, "Like a mighty army moves the Church of God" perhaps 'constant' in this context means faithful rather than immutable.

Moorland explains that "Our ancestors in the Middle Ages were obsessed by their sins and the consequent hell-fire promised them, so they were desperate to be forgiven the former in order to escape the latter. Our generation has little awareness of sin . . ." It took us four centuries, he notes, to move on from the Book of Common Prayer, and I would add that though we have updated the language for the services we have left the underlying theology more or less as it was. We start with the Commandments, and then continue logically to a confession that we have failed to keep them which no reasonable person could take issue with, but after the readings, sermon and

[1] On 1st October 2018, the College installed as Master Dr Pippa Rogerson, not only the first woman to be Master in the 670 years of the College's history, but also the first Catholic Master since its Third Founder, Dr John Caius, in 1559.
[2] Extracted from a booklet by Mr Moorland, a retired Anglican priest, entitled, *I can see clearly now—Christian Faith and the Church.*

prayers for the Church and the world the next and most significant part of the Communion service would seem to any outsider to represent a rather elaborate ritual for having our sins forgiven.

To get away from such a conception of this part of the service would require such a radical change as to keep the Church in theological debate for the next couple of centuries, but if we could somehow envisage the bread and the wine as distributed and accepted *in memory of* Jesus, and not as symbolic of the 'taking away of the sins of the world' perhaps the service would be more meaningful for those who find this doctrine of the implications of the Crucifixion somewhat difficult to assimilate. Even a minister of religion, such as the present Dean of my College, Revd Dr Cally Hammond, in her book, *Passionate Christianity* (London: SPCK, 2007), says she doesn't believe the 'penal substitution theory', that Jesus suffered as punishment for our sins (though what she does believe is admittedly rather complicated),[1] yet this idea is embedded in the service.

It would do no harm to replace the long prayers in this section with something more succinct, and this might render us less likely to be aligned with those who Jesus said thought they would be heard because of their much speaking. It might also help to get repentance back to its biblical meaning of turning away from wrong-doing and striving to do better in future, and to restore our being forgiven to its proportional relationship to our readiness to forgive others.

I suspect that other churchgoers, when they thought about it, if they really looked closely at the words of the prayers we affirm and those we join in, would find this aspect of our liturgy not entirely convincing, but probably the truth is that we come along to the services and accept and join in with them because this is what is laid down for us to do. Also we may come, not because we endorse every word of the service, but also to align ourselves with the 'good men, and women, and true' who also take the trouble to attend Church each week. But whether we adjourn for a cup of coffee afterwards or go straight home, do we think all that much about the implications of what we have taken part in? Or am I being very unfair?

---

[1] See further discussion on page 332.

Prayers

Almighty and everlasting God, who hast graciously given to us the fruits of the earth in their season, we yield thee humble and hearty thanks for these thy bounties, beseeching thee to give us grace rightly to use them, to thy glory and the relief of those that need. Through Jesus Christ our Lord.   *Amen.*

O God, who hast made the heaven and the earth and all that is good and lovely therein, and hast shown us through Jesus, our Lord, that the secret of joy is a heart set free from selfish desires; help us to find delight in simple things and ever to rejoice in the richness of thy bounty; through the same Jesus Christ our Lord.   *Amen.*

For people forced to travel . . .
refugees . . . homeless . . . wayfarers . . .
Be with them on the road:
Be present to them.

For people beset by danger . . .
living in war zones . . . victims of crime . . .
those working on front lines . . .
Be with them in their anxiety:
Be present to them.

For people lacking direction . . .
the confused . . . the listless . . . the despairing . . .
Show them the way:
Be present to them.

For people whose way is barred . . .
the hungry . . . the prisoners . . . the unemployed . . .
Set their feet on the road:
Be present to them.

For people who want to turn back . . .
the persecuted . . . the failed . . . the discouraged . . .
Encourage them and strengthen them:
Be present to them.

For people who refuse to move . . .
the smug . . . the contented . . . the satisfied . . .
Give them a hunger for righteousness:
Be present to them.

For people who wander in darkness . . .
the depressed . . . the bereaved . . .
the dying . . .
Shed your light upon them:
Be present to them.

For people who walk alone . . .
the isolated . . . the housebound . . .
the handicapped . . .
Be their companion:
Be present to them.

For people who are travelling . . .
by land . . . by sea . . . by air . . .
Be a pillar of fire for them:
Go ahead of them.

For people on pilgrimage . . .
walking to the ancient places . . .
facing the hazards of the road . . .
journeying deep within . . .
Be the cairns on their path:
Be the staff that supports them.

A few moments' silence for your own prayers.

The Lord's Prayer.

Accept, O God, our offerings of praise and thanksgiving. Forgive, we pray thee, all that is imperfect in our worship, and help us to glorify and enjoy thee for ever; through Jesus Christ our Lord.   *Amen.*

Unto the King, eternal, immortal, invisible, the only wise God, be honour and glory for ever and ever.   *Amen.*

SIMPLE SERVICE, WITH HYMNS

29th January 2012

Order of Service

Welcome & Notices (David Beal)

Hymn 506 (*M. Praise;* words on p.104. Tune: *How Great Thou Art*)
O Lord my God! When I in awesome wonder

Brief introduction (David E.)

Hymn 314 (Tune: *Martyrdom*)
As pants the hart for cooling streams

First reading (Philip) Genesis, Chapter 1, Verses 20–31 *(NEB)*

Hymn 171 (Tune: *England's Lane*)
For the beauty of the earth

Second reading (Clive C.) John, Chapter 1, Verses 1–14 *(NEB)*

Hymn 192 (Tune: *St Peter*)
How sweet the name of Jesus sounds

Brief Chat (Tony) "Science and the Bible"

Hymn 216 (Tune: *Gopsal*)
Rejoice! The Lord is King

Prayers (Peter)

Hymn 255 (Tune: *Aurelia*)
The Church's one foundation

The service will proceed without announcements. All the hymns except one (words opposite) are in *Hymns Ancient & Modern Revised.*

Thank you for coming. Please use the separate voting form to list your own favourite hymns for a subsequent service.

*I was involved with running the final of a bridge competition in Worthing
that afternoon, so I left my usual introduction with Peter to read if I wasn't
quite back in time. In the event I just made it with a couple of minutes to spare.*

This is our 'winter' service, but fortunately the weather is still quite mild.
Our next one will be at the end of April, when we hope it will be quite a bit
warmer. As always, thank you all for coming, and 'the team' for your efforts,
especially Tony for taking on the talk again, but also Clive and Philip for
doing the readings. I usually thank Robert for his sterling work on the piano,
but this time I must thank him for his work on the new digital keyboard.

I have to continue with an apology, as although Peter and I selected this
evening's hymns when intended I didn't send the list immediately to David
Burnett, and when the January Parish Magazine went to press a little earlier
than usual to allow for the Christmas break I found myself too late to get them
in. I have sent David the wrong file more than once, but I think this is the first
time I have missed the magazine altogether.

Rather than inviting you to join us for a glass of wine after the service, we
decided to let you all get home promptly, but we hope to resume this feature
on a subsequent occasion.

Genesis 1, 20–31

God said, "Let the waters teem with countless living creatures, and let
birds fly above the earth across the vault of heaven." God then created the
great sea-monsters and all living creatures that move and swarm in the waters,
according to their kind, and every kind of bird; and God saw that it was good.
So he blessed them and said, "Be fruitful and increase, fill the waters of the
seas; and let the birds increase on land." Evening came, and morning came, a
fifth day.

God said, "Let the earth bring forth living creatures, according to their
kind: cattle, reptiles, and wild animals, all according to their kind." So it was;
God made wild animals, cattle and all reptiles, each according to its kind; and
he saw that it was good. Then God said, "Let us make man in our image and
likeness to rule the fish in the sea, the birds of heaven, the cattle, all wild
animals on earth, and all reptiles that crawl upon the earth."

So God created man in his own image; in the image of God he created
him; male and female he created them. God blessed them and said to them,
"Be fruitful and increase, fill the earth and subdue it, rule over the fish in the
sea, the birds of heaven, and every living thing that moves upon the earth."
God also said, "I give you all plants that bear seed everywhere on earth, and
every tree bearing fruit which yields seed: they shall be yours for food. All

green plants I give for food to the wild animals, to all the birds of heaven, and to all reptiles on earth, every living creature." So it was; and God saw all that he had made, and it was very good. Evening came, and morning came, a sixth day.

John 1, 1–14

When all things began, the Word already was. The Word dwelt with God, and what God was, the Word was. The Word, then, was with God at the beginning, and through him all things came to be; no single thing was created without him. All that came to be was alive with his life, and that life was the light of men. The light shines on in the dark, and the darkness has never quenched it.

There appeared a man named John, sent from God; he came as a witness to testify to the light, that all might become believers through him. He was not himself the light; he came to bear witness to the light. The real light which enlightens every man was even then coming into the world.

He was in the world; but the world, though it owed its being to him, did not recognize him. He entered his own realm, and his own would not receive him. But to all who did receive him, to those who have yielded him their allegiance, he gave the right to become children of God, not born of any human stock, or by the fleshly desire of a human father, but the offspring of God himself. So the Word became flesh; he came to dwell among us, and we saw his glory, such glory as befits the Father's only Son, full of grace and truth.

SCIENCE AND THE BIBLE

I was appalled to learn recently that at least forty million Americans and no doubt many others around the world (Creationists) remain convinced that the Earth (and presumably the Universe) was created only about 6,000 years ago. This figure is arrived at from calculations made from Biblical information only.

I think that this does the cause of Christianity no good whatsoever, as much of the non-Christian world could well associate the majority of Christians with this concept, and regard them as absolute 'nutters' and therefore not to be taken seriously.

I have very few heroes in my life and none of them is a sportsman, singer, film star or other passing celebrity. However, Darwin, Samuel Pepys and Nelson are, and so is Stephen Hawking (and not only for the fact that, wheelchair-bound, he managed to run away with his nurse).

Darwin is a giant and cannot be ignored. He might have become a doctor but could not stand surgery before the age of anaesthetics and he seemed destined to become a country parson, but he joined the *Beagle* as 'personal companion' (a gentleman but not in the Navy) to the Captain, Fitzroy, and as Ship's Naturalist, and the rest, as they say, is history. However, with his work on *The Origin of Species*, Darwin eventually lost his Christian faith, which was especially painful for him with the death of his favourite daughter. Fitzroy, that brilliant cartographer and navigator and conventional Christian, ended up taking his own life.

Science tells us that 'mass' and 'energy' are interchangeable (Einstein defined it in his famous equation, $E = mc^2$, which was demonstrated at White Sands and Hiroshima). Mass (not the Eucharist) is easy to understand and we experience it on Earth as 'weight' because of the gravitational pull of the Earth. However, the same object doesn't weigh as much on the Moon, for instance, although its mass is the same, because the gravitational pull of the Moon is much less. That's why spacemen can jump much higher (and slower) on the Moon than they can on Earth.

Energy is not so simple. I don't really know what it is and I don't think anyone else does. The only definition I can find is the old engineer's one that energy is the property of being able to do 'work'. (Work is defined as moving a force through a distance, such as lifting up a weight to a certain height.) We cannot make energy, nor can we destroy it; however, we can change its form. We can change it from chemical energy to heat to make steam under pressure, to drive a turbine to generate electrical energy. Most of it goes into the atmosphere as heat and probably radiates eventually into space, or else it contributes to 'global warming'.

Science also tells us that all the mass in the Universe was created (or changed from energy) at one point (the Creation), about 13.9 billion years ago, and everything else comes from that point, with our solar system being born about 4.5 billion years ago. These figures are all based on measurements of such things as the 'red shift' in the light from stellar objects (which shows that the Universe is expanding) and radioactive decay of some elements to establish time scales. These figures may refined but I doubt if they will be changed significantly.

Now we come to the evolution of life from its beginning, through very primitive plants and animals to those we know today, including our own species. The first people whom we would recognize as modern human beings, *Homo sapiens*, appeared about 200,000 years ago.

So where does this lead us? Most thinking people accept this story as fact but of course there is the potential problem for Christians in that the scientific story is at some variance with the story as told in Genesis.

214

I have no problems with squaring the circle between science and the Bible and I'll try to explain why. We need to have a look at the origins of Genesis. I guess that it was probably written about 1200 BC, around the time of the Exodus. We don't know what its provenance was or who in fact wrote it. I know it is sometimes attributed to Moses but we don't really know who he was. I know the story and Moses is certainly an Egyptian name and some pharaohs even used it as part of their names (e.g. Tutmoses).

The story was probably around within the Hebrew tribes before then. The Hebrews seem to have been a group of nomadic desert herders who would have sat around their camp fires on starry desert nights and, like humans the world over, would have questioned where the world as they knew it came from and who controlled it. The story that we know today would have been completely impossible for them to deal with and I think we may assume that the Holy Spirit was clever enough to help them conceive a story they could identify with (and so could the rest of the world until the end of the 19th century).

What we can say is that our understanding of God today, and the only God I can believe in, has to be of a much greater and cleverer Deity than that understood by the early Hebrews over 3000 years ago. They weren't that wrong, but they couldn't go far enough in the detail. Watch this space, for we still have more to learn.

I think that if we compare the Genesis story of God creating Man from clay (or the earth) and breathing life into him with our current knowledge regarding the slow evolution of life and Man, it really is the same story, isn't it?

There is another problem which is nothing to do with evolution and which we might consider at some 'later' chat (if I'm allowed to), and that is the theology of 'The Fall of Man' and the Atonement.

Tony Hills

Prayers

Almighty God, who rulest the changing seasons, we bless thee that beneath all that now seems cold and dead, thou art keeping safe the hidden germs of life. Still thou dost clothe all things around us with beauty, sending forth thy frost and snow, filling the brief day with sunshine, and making the night glorious with countless stars. We thank thee for the shelter and comfort of our homes, and pray for those in poverty or sickness who shrink from the cold. Through Jesus Christ our Lord. *Amen.*

Almighty God, creator of all, we thank thee for the beauty of the earth and sea and sky, for the happiness of our lives, for peaceful homes and healthful days, for our powers of mind and body, for faithful friends, for the joy of loving and being loved, and above all, for thy care for us made known in Jesus Christ our Lord. *Amen.*

Almighty and everlasting God, in whom we live and move and have our being, who hast created us for thyself, so that we can find rest only in thee; grant unto us purity of heart and strength of purpose, so that no selfish passion may hinder us from knowing thy will, no weakness from doing it; but in thy light may we see light clearly, and in thy service find perfect freedom, for Jesus Christ's sake. *Amen.*

O Lord, let us not live to be useless; for Christ's sake. *Amen.*

A few moments' silence for your own prayers.

The Lord's Prayer.

ST PATRICK'S BREASTPLATE

May the strength of God pilot us.
May the power of God preserve us.
May the wisdom of God instruct us.
May the hand of God protect us.
May the way of God direct us.
May the shield of God defend us.
May the host of God guard us against the snares of evil and the
    temptations of the world.
May Christ be with us, Christ before us, Christ in us, Christ over us.
May thy salvation, O Lord, be always ours, this day and for evermore.
Amen.

SIMPLE SERVICE, WITH HYMNS
29th April 2012

Order of Service

Welcome & Notices (David Beal)

Hymn 140 (Tune: *St. Albinus*)
Jesus lives! Thy terrors now

Brief introduction (David E.)

Hymn 128 (Tune: *St. Fulbert*)
Ye choirs of new Jerusalem

First reading (Philip) John Chapter 21, Verses 1–14 *(NEB)*

Hymn 256 (Tune: *Thornbury*)
Thy hand, O God, has guided

Second reading (Tony) Matthew Chapter 22, Verses 15–33 *(NEB)*

Hymn 186 (Tune: *Halton Holgate*)
Firmly I believe and truly

Brief chat (David E.)

Hymn 335 (Tune: *Franconia*)
Blest are the pure in heart

Prayers (Peter)

Hymn 487 (Tune: *Melita*)
Eternal Father, strong to save

The service will proceed without announcements. All the hymns are in *Hymns Ancient & Modern Revised.*

Thank you for coming. **Please join us in the New Vestry after the service** *for a glass of wine (alternatives available).*

Please use the voting form opposite to list your own favourite hymns for a subsequent service.

Looking forward to this service at our January one, I expressed the hope that by now the weather would be "quite a bit warmer". I am not sure that it is, but at least we haven't had snow the previous week, as we did on another occasion when I predicted better weather. As always, may I thank you all for coming, and 'the team' for their efforts, Philip and Tony for doing the readings, and Robert on the new keyboard.

As on several occasions last year, we are inviting you to join us for a glass of wine after the service, for which our thanks to Diane for bringing the glasses and to Pam for kindly supplying refreshments.

Finally, may I draw your attention to the forms printed on the service sheets, and encourage at least some of you to choose some hymns and return the forms to me in due course with your lists.

John 21, 1–14

Some time later, Jesus showed himself to his disciples once again, by the Sea of Tiberias; and in this way. Simon Peter and Thomas 'the Twin' were together with Nathanael of Cana-in-Galilee. The sons of Zebedee and two other disciples were also there. Simon Peter said, "I am going out fishing."

"We will go with you", said the others. So they started and got into the boat. But that night they caught nothing.

Morning came, and there stood Jesus on the beach, but the disciples did not know that it was Jesus. He called out to them, "Friends, have you caught anything?"

They answered "No."

He said, "Shoot the net to starboard, and you will make a catch."

They did so, and found they could not haul the net aboard, there were so many fish in it. Then the disciple whom Jesus loved said to Peter, "It is the Lord!"

When Simon Peter heard that, he wrapped his coat about him (for he had stripped) and plunged into the sea. The rest of them came on in the boat, towing the net full of fish; for they were not far from the land, only about a hundred yards.

When they came ashore, they saw a charcoal fire there, with fish laid on it, and some bread. Jesus said, "Bring some of your catch."

Simon Peter went aboard and dragged the net to land, full of big fish, a hundred and fifty-three of them; and yet, many as they were, the net was not torn. Jesus said, "Come and have breakfast."

None of the disciples dared to ask "Who are you?" They knew it was the Lord. Jesus now came up, took the bread, and gave it to them, and the fish in the same way.

This makes the third time that Jesus appeared to his disciples after his resurrection from the dead.

Matthew 22, 15–33

Then the Pharisees went and agreed on a plan to trap him in his own words. Some of their followers were sent to him in company with men of Herod's party. They said, "Master, you are an honest man, we know; you teach in all honesty the way of life that God requires, truckling to no man, whoever he may be. Give us your ruling on this: are we or are we not permitted to pay taxes to the Roman Emperor?"

Jesus was aware of their malicious intention and said to them, "You hypocrites! Why are you trying to catch me out? Show me the money in which the tax is paid."

They handed him a silver piece. Jesus asked, "Whose head is this, and whose inscription?"

"Caesar's", they replied.

He said to them, "Then pay Caesar what is due to Caesar, and pay God what is due to God."

This answer took them by surprise, and they went away and left him alone.

The same day Sadducees came to him, maintaining that there is no resurrection. Their question was this: "Master, Moses said, 'If a man should die childless, his brother shall marry the widow and carry on his brother's family.' Now we knew of seven brothers. The first married and died, and as he was without issue his wife was left to his brother. The same thing happened with the second, and the third, and so on with all seven. Last of all the woman died. At the resurrection, then, whose wife will she be, for they had all married her?"

Jesus answered: "You are mistaken, because you know neither the scriptures nor the power of God. At the resurrection men and women do not marry, but are like angels in heaven.

"But about the resurrection of the dead, have you never read what God himself said to you: 'I am the God of Abraham, the God of Isaac, and the God of Jacob'? He is not God of the dead but of the living."

The people heard what he said, and were astounded at his teaching.

WHAT CAN WE OFFER THAT IS POSITIVE ?

It has always been my hope that our simple format might encourage the attendance of people who would not otherwise come to Church, but although we haven't been entirely unsuccessful in that aim we haven't yet had a large influx of non-Churchgoers. However, putting these talks in the Parish Magazine does give those outside the Church the chance to read them. What can we offer such people by way of something positive to believe in?

Cardinal Newman set out his own beliefs simply and succinctly in the words of the hymn we have just sung, but how does "God is Three and God is One" or "Manhood taken by the Son" strike someone outside the Church? At best, as a summary of the "teachings" of "Holy Church" in the form of a formula to express what cannot fully be comprehended?

I expect everyone's beliefs are personal to themselves, and different in varying degree from everyone else's. Belief, after all, might be defined as an attitude of mind concerning something we either don't know or are at least not sure of. Therefore, if we have knowledge of something, we don't need belief. How much of what we say we believe isn't actually a matter of belief at all, but of acquaintance with fact; in other words, of knowledge?

First of all, we can be certain that the man we know as Jesus lived on this Earth some two thousand years ago and that he exercised a ministry during which he healed the sick, and in his teaching, often using the stories we call parables, he did his best to convey to people his concept of what God is like and of how therefore they should live their lives. His call to love our neighbour 'as ourselves', our neighbour being anyone in need of our assistance at any given time, though much easier to state than to carry out, is strikingly simple; his injunction to love even our enemies no doubt struck his hearers as a novel and rather unwelcome idea!

We can be certain that Jesus healed the sick from the Gospel records of crowds continually following him and seeking his healing touch; if it had proved ineffective they would soon have given up. Also since other people have a healing gift and unexplained healing occurs even today.

Secondly, we can regard it as established fact that Jesus, apparently having got on the wrong side of the religious authorities of his day, was sentenced to execution by crucifixion, but that, as we celebrate each year at Easter, he was seen afterwards as alive by many of his followers. Had they not been convinced of his resurrection, Christianity as a religion might never have taken off, certainly not in the way that it did.

We started this service with that tremendous Easter hymn, *Jesus lives!* Stirring words and a splendid tune to sing them to. But from our second reading it is clear that Jesus was happy to confirm the truth of life after death in his teaching before then, and to stress that Abraham, Isaac and Jacob were even then among the living, so the words of the hymn that "*Henceforth* is death but the gate of life immortal" may be reading more into the interpretation of the resurrection than is strictly necessary.

What we can say of God must perforce be rather more tentative. But at least we are aware of living on this planet in a vast and constantly evolving universe. While recognizing that it is in our nature to try to puzzle out why anything happens, and where all we are conscious of came from, we are faced with the choice between supposing that it all just happened with the Big Bang, which took place some 13 billion years ago according to cosmologists, and that everything subsequent is merely a random cause-and-effect event, or postulating some overarching entity that not only created everything but also in some way sustains and directs it all. In either case there will always be unanswerable questions, such as What went Bang? and Who made God? that we being creatures of this universe are scarcely likely to be able to comprehend the answers to, but we can at least take the alternative of our choice as a working hypothesis.

I can see no point in adopting a 'God' theory that omits His function of sustaining and directing. If He set it all going and then left it to evolve by the chance processes postulated by the materialists, we are no better off in believing in Him than they are in not doing so. Religious people do believe in an active God, for they say prayers and trust that some at least of these will be answered, "as may be most expedient for them". We can look back at the great events of history and the relatively trivial ones of our own lives, and appreciate that "Thy hand, O God, has guided thy flock from age to age", and accept that when the 'pure in heart' are blest with 'seeing our God' they are afforded not an image of a personage but a glimpse of how He has acted to bring His kingdom that much nearer. The more we do see instances of the Divine acting in everyday life, the more we shall be inclined to feel that we no longer *believe*, we *know*.

Of course, there is a vast edifice of what religious people over the centuries have come to believe, and awareness of this could well deter others from joining us. Every week we are invited to "affirm our faith, in the words of the Creed", but perhaps I am not the only one to suspect that we are not so much affirming our faith, which has grounds other than the words which follow, but assenting to dogma, by no means all of which can be substantiated. The answer, surely, is to keep things simple, and to make a distinction between what we might think of as essential, which we believe, and the secondary, which we need not necessarily disbelieve. Jesus achieved a tremendous simplification when he declared that on the two Commandments, to love God and love our neighbour, hung all the Law and the Prophets.

This gives us a basis for action, as does Jesus' asking how we can say we love God, whom we have not seen, if we don't love our brother, whom we have seen. What might give us grounds for faith is receiving some unexpected assistance when we do try to help that brother, to encourage us to think that we might indeed be doing the right thing. A faith that can sometimes be self-reinforcing will feel sounder and more positive to us than merely subscribing to a formulation of doctrine, however venerable.

Prayers

Almighty God, our creator and preserver, we thank thee for the springtime, in which thou art renewing the face of the earth and quickening all things. Thou who carest for the trees and flowers, revive and renew our life, that we may bring forth the fruit of good works, as disciples of him who came to quicken in human hearts the seed of eternal life; through Jesus Christ our Lord.
Amen.

O Christ, the light of men, who on the third day didst arise from the grave and shed thy bright beams upon the darkness of the world; grant we beseech thee, that, enlightened by thy presence, we may walk as children of the day, to the glory of thy Name, who livest and reignest, world without end.   *Amen.*

O risen Lord, who after thy passion didst show thyself alive unto thine Apostles by many infallible proofs, and didst speak unto them the things that concern the kingdom of God: speak unto us also who wait upon thee, and fill us with joy and peace in believing; that we may abound in hope, and knowing thy will may faithfully perform it, even unto the end; through thy grace, who livest and reignest, Lord of the dead and of the living.   *Amen.*

A few moments' silence for your own prayers.

The Lord's Prayer.

As the quiet splendour of the day dies away, we wait for the shining of the light that never fades. Call us from all that distracts; gather us into the quiet of thy love. Meet with us O Father, for we seek thy face.   *Amen.*

The power of the Father, the wisdom of the Son, the love of the Holy Spirit, keep, teach, and guide us for ever.   *Amen.*

SIMPLE SERVICE, WITH HYMNS
29th July 2012

Order of Service

Welcome & Notices (David B.)

Hymn 379 (Tune: *Nun danket*)
Now thank we all our God

Brief introduction (David E.)

Hymn 242 (Tune: *Quam dilecta*)
We love the place, O God

First reading (Laura) Ephesians, Chapter 6, Verses 10–20 *(NEB)*

Hymn 307 (Tune: *Morning Light*)
Stand up, stand up for Jesus

Second reading (Christine) Matthew, Chapter 5, Verses 17–26 *(NEB)*

Hymn 291 (Tune: *University College*)
Oft in danger, oft in woe

Brief chat (David E.)

Hymn 43 (Tune: *Bishopthorpe*)
This is the day the Lord hath made

Prayers (Peter)

Hymn 660 (*Mission Praise;* words on page 165. Tune: *Crimond*)
The Lord's my shepherd, I'll not want

The service will proceed without announcements. All the hymns are in *Hymns Ancient & Modern Revised* except the last one, which is in *Mission Praise* (words opposite). *Thank you for coming.*
   Please join us in the New Vestry after the service for a glass of wine *(alternatives available) and some light refreshments.*
   Please use the voting form overleaf (or request a separate one) to list your own favourite hymns for a subsequent service.

Well, even if the weather in April wasn't "quite a bit warmer" than it was in January, it is certainly warmer now, if almost as wet. As always, it is my pleasant task to thank you all for coming, tearing yourselves away from the Olympics—and I must say I was glad the women's road race was finished by 3.35 p.m., which gave me time to recover from the excitement before coming this evening. Also 'the team' for their efforts, with Robert once again on the new keyboard. He'll play right through the whole verse of each of the two hymns that may be a little unfamiliar. This time we have two young ladies to do the readings for us, but Tony hasn't been idle, as he has already done a draft of a very interesting talk for September. He and Peter have also vetted my talk for this evening.

As there are but two months until our next service, we shall need your hymn choices back by about 6th August. We have had three successive services on 29th of the month, so next year the equivalent services will be in different months, with Easter Day a fifth Sunday! In fact, we are having five hymns services this year, with the fifth on 30th December, but I shall be ninety, and even my umbrella will have reached its three-score years and ten, by the time we also have a fifth Sunday in February, as we did in 2004.

As on several occasions since David and Mary kindly invited us all back to the Refectory—sorry, the Rectory—for refreshments after our August service in 2010, just after they had returned from their holiday, we are inviting you to join us for a glass of wine (or fruit juice) in the New Vestry after this service, for which our thanks to Diane and Malcolm for bringing the glasses, and Diane also for subsequently washing them, and to Pam for kindly supplying refreshments.

Ephesians 6, 10–20

Finally then, find your strength in the Lord, in his mighty power. Put on all the armour which God provides, so that you may be able to stand firm against the devices of the devil. For our fight is not against human foes, but against cosmic powers, against the authorities and potentates of this dark world, against the superhuman forces of evil in the heavens.

Therefore, take up God's armour; then you will be able to stand your ground when things are at their worst, to complete every task and still to stand. Stand firm, I say. Buckle on the belt of truth; for coat of mail put on integrity; let the shoes on your feet be the gospel of peace, to give you firm footing; and, with all these, take up the great shield of faith, with which you will be able to quench all the flaming arrows of the evil one. Take salvation for helmet; for sword, take that which the Spirit gives you—the words that come from God.

Give yourselves wholly to prayer and entreaty; pray on every occasion in the power of the Spirit. To this end keep watch and persevere, always interceding for all God's people; and pray for me, that I may be granted the right words when I open my mouth, and may boldly and freely make known his hidden purpose, for which I am an ambassador—in chains. Pray that I may speak of it boldly, as it is my duty to speak.

Matthew 5, 17–26

[Jesus continued,] "Do not suppose that I have come to abolish the Law and the prophets; I did not come to abolish, but to complete. I tell you this: so long as heaven and earth endure, not a letter, not a stroke, will disappear from the Law before all that it stands for is achieved. If any man therefore sets aside even the least of the Law's demands, and teaches others to do the same, he will have the lowest place in the kingdom of Heaven, whereas anyone who keeps the Law and teaches others so will stand high in the kingdom of Heaven. I tell you, unless you show yourselves far better men than the Pharisees and the doctors of the law, you can never enter the kingdom of Heaven.

"You have learned that our forefathers were told, 'Do not commit murder; anyone who commits murder must be brought to judgement.' But what I tell you is this: Anyone who nurses anger against his brother [without good cause][1] must be brought to judgement. If he abuses his brother he must answer for it to the court; if he sneers at him he will have to answer for it in the fires of hell.

"If, when you are bringing your gift to the altar, you suddenly remember that your brother has a grievance against you, leave your gift where it is before the altar. First go and make your peace with your brother, and only then come back and offer your gift.

"If someone sues you, come to terms with him promptly while you are both on your way to court; otherwise he may hand you over to the judge, and the judge to the constable, and you will be put in jail. I tell you, once you are there you will not be let out until you have paid the last farthing."

---

[1] Not in all 'witnesses'.

SOME THOUGHTS ON THE HISTORY OF CHRISTIANITY

She had sparkling blue eyes, very short brown hair and a merry sense of humour; she was slight and slim and said she was not very handy with a punt pole. I met her at my College in June 2010 because she was the student who had telephoned me in March to tell me about current College life and then encourage me to make a donation. We had interests in common, both having been concerned with darkrooms in the College, and we discovered that we had attended the same school. She gave me her home address and I looked out some things to send her that I hoped she'd be interested in. As she had been a Scout (not a Guide) I thought of the talk I gave to my Venture Scouts (aged 16–20) when we had started a Unit in High Wych in Hertfordshire in 1975. It took me a week to find it in my files from long ago, but I was glad I had taken the trouble, whether or not my young acquaintance found it of any interest. The requirement for the Scouts to be invested included that they should understand "What it means to be a Venture Scout" and I had decided to tell them. Just two sentences struck me recently as being relevant in a very different context: "The Unit as a Unit should act as a Scout should act as a Scout. Just as there are times when as individuals we must act in an unselfish manner, so there are times when the groups to which we belong must do the same." That is not always obvious to the people who serve their groups so loyally that they set those groups' interests before those of all others.

Also in my files from long ago are some notes made at the start of 1977, in which I suggested that "confessing our sins to God in private and then forgetting about them isn't exactly doing anything positive. Nor does it help much more to confess to a priest who is bound to secrecy. Is it not much better to tell our friends what we have done wrong, and trust them not to spread it around too much? After all, we are happy enough to tell them about what we think we have done right! Harder still is the problem of making amends to those we have wronged." I suggested that if we tried to do so, God would help us.

We have Jesus' words as recorded in our second reading (Matthew, Chapter 5, verses 23–24), "If, when you are bringing your gift to the altar, you suddenly remember that your brother has a grievance against you, leave your gift where it is before the altar. First go and make your peace with your brother, and only then come back and offer your gift." Again, this stresses the need to try to make amends in addition to coming to Church and having one's wrongdoings forgiven in the course of a service. Those verses used to bother me as I walked home from the eight o'clock, with respect to an incident when I had put down the phone on someone that I had liked and respected, and now saw occasionally at Church. Though over thirteen years had passed, a letter of apology was clearly indicated—a prompt reply to which assured me that I had been forgiven long ago and expressed sadness that the incident had troubled me for so long.

On a shorter time-scale, I owe an apology to St Paul for saying in my talk last May that the concept of Jesus as the Lamb of God taking away the sins of the world represented muddled thinking on his part. For I later noticed that it wasn't St Paul at all, but John the Baptist, as recorded in John's Gospel (Chapter 1, Verse 29) who had made such an assertion. As Jesus' ministry was then only just about to begin, this must surely be regarded as a theological statement by the writer of that Gospel. *[The text on p.190 has been amended.]*

There have been some good television programmes on religious topics in recent years. A four-part series on the life of Muhammad was very informative, and one part explained, among many other things, why Jerusalem is sacred to Muslims as well as to Christians. Earlier, the series on the history of Christianity was particularly thought-provoking, not least the one on the Crusades. In normal English usage, a crusade is a holy war, a fight, perhaps involving personal sacrifice, for some noble objective. But this is not how a Muslim would see it; for him to describe someone as a crusader would be to ascribe an epithet of the worst kind.

Some people have regarded two of our hymns today, and others, as too 'militaristic', but our first reading emphasizes that "our fight is not against human foes". It was not ever thus.

The programme showed the Crusades in a different light, asserting that the Pope of the time had decided that the best way to deal with the problem of warring barons was to give them something to do, so he sent them to the Middle East to 'free' Jerusalem from the Infidels. The way they treated their enemies would have had them prosecuted as war criminals in modern times. The atrocities committed in the name of the Church (apparently) were set down, not by some infidel as propaganda, but by one of their own party, a French priest who was travelling with them. And of course the perpetrators had no concern for the sacredness of Jerusalem to the people they were fighting.

For a second opinion I turned to our family set of encyclopaedias for children; beautiful books, written over a hundred years ago.[1] Would they paint a rosier picture? Well, yes and no. I quote:–

"To this day pilgrims make their way, often on foot, from all the countries round, to visit the sacred shrines of the Holy City, and it was the tales of the bad treatment of the pilgrims long ago that roused Europe to start the Crusades.

---

[1] *The Children's Encyclopaedia*, edited by Arthur Mee. *Volume Five*, pp.3154–3155. London: The Educational Book Co., 1909.

"The Fourth Crusade . . . fell very far short of the high aims with which these 'Holy Wars' began. Detained for a while at Venice waiting for ships to carry them eastwards, the Crusaders were persuaded to take up the private quarrels of the Venetians, and in the end they helped them to besiege Constantinople. The city was taken on the second attack, and the inhabitants were treated with terrible cruelty; their beautiful city was sacked, and the art treasures that Constantine and his successors had gathered together were ruined. To make paltry coins, the most beautiful bronze statues the world has ever seen were cast into the melting-pot. So 'Christians' of the West treated Constantinople of the East."

The caption under a painting on the facing page confirms the story:–

"Since the middle of the sixth century [Constantinople] has undergone no fewer than twenty-six sieges and has been captured eight times. But its most terrible experience was in 1204, when it was captured by the Crusaders . . . the so-called Christian warriors acted more barbarously than any Turkish invaders have ever done."

I was interested to note what it said under the other picture:–

"The capture of Constantinople by the Turks in 1453 was another terrible experience for the ill-fated city . . . But the fall of Constantinople was . . . not simply the triumph of Crescent over Cross; it had more far-reaching effects than any other event in modern history, for by driving scholars with their books into Italy from the East, it led to the great revival of learning, and this again led to the Reformation."

While it might be claimed that the Crusaders were so little under the control of the Church of the time that its leaders were not really to blame for what was done, that is not how the Muslims view their history.

So, if our Church of today, as a body of Christians, can view itself, collectively, as a Christian with a life extending from Jesus' Resurrection to the present day, and can acknowledge in that life a blemish for which Cranmer's immortal words, "the remembrance of them is grievous unto us; the burden of them is intolerable", are eminently suitable, can we therefore "leave our gift where it is before the altar, and first go and make our peace with our brothers", the Muslims?

Another of the programmes on the history of Christianity recorded that the Church of England had at least apologized to the Jews for the persecution they had suffered in our country in the eleventh century, but has the Western Church ever apologized to the Muslims for the atrocities committed in our name by the above-mentioned Crusaders? If God will help His Church to do this, might He not also help bring about a more peaceful relationship between the peoples of our faith and theirs?

228

The programme on the life of Muhammad showed him as remarkably forgiving towards his enemies, in a truly Christian spirit; the Koran, I am told, states in many places that Islam accepts that Moses and Jesus were true prophets of God and that Muslims should be courteous to Jews and Christians—the 'People of the Book'. But how much of that goodwill was forfeited in 1204?

Prayers

Almighty God, who gave a day of rest to your people, and through your Spirit has consecrated this day to be a perpetual memorial of your Son's resurrection, grant that we may so use your gift that, refreshed and strengthened in soul and body, we may serve you faithfully in the coming week, and throughout our lives, through Jesus Christ our Lord.   *Amen.*

Almighty God, from whom all thoughts of truth and peace proceed, we pray you to kindle in all hearts the true love of peace. Guide with your pure wisdom the politicians and governments of the world, that in tranquillity your kingdom may grow till the whole earth is filled with the knowledge of your perfect love. We ask this in Jesus' name.   *Amen.*

Lord, we beseech you to send us such seasonable weather that in due course we may harvest the fruits of the earth; and remembering that we are taught to pray for our daily bread, we pray also for those who have gone hungry today, who will be hungry tomorrow, and whom we could do so much to help: never let us become complacent, or forget our responsibilities to our brothers and sisters whose needs are greater than ours.   *Amen.*

Father, we ask you to look mercifully on all who are sick or suffering, remembering especially those known to us, near and dear to us. . . . We ask your blessing on them and on all who minister to them, that they may be restored in body and mind.   *Amen.*

A few moments' silence for your own prayers.

The Lord's Prayer.

May the blessing of almighty God rest upon us and upon all our work; may he give us light to guide us, courage to support us, and love to unite us, now and evermore.   *Amen.*

† And the grace of our Lord Jesus Christ, the love of God, and the fellowship of the Holy Spirit, be with us all, this night and always.   *Amen.*

SIMPLE SERVICE, WITH HYMNS

30th September 2012

Order of Service

Welcome & Notices (David B.)

Hymn 223 (Tune: *Laudes Domini*)
When morning gilds the skies

Brief introduction (Peter)

Hymn 483 (Tune: *Wir pflügen*)
We plough the fields, and scatter

First reading (Philip) Exodus, Chapter 9, v.22 to 10, v.2 edited *(NEB)*

Hymn 266 (Tune: *Moscow*)
Thou, whose almighty word

Second reading (David E.) Exodus, Chapter 13, v.17 to Chapt.14, v.31
edited *(NEB)*

Hymn 377 (*Songs of Praise;* words on page 75. Tune: *Stowey*)
When a knight won his spurs

Brief chat (Tony) "Moses and the Pharaohs"

Hymn 377 (Tune: *Monkland*)
Let us, with a gladsome mind

Prayers (Laura)

Hymn 27 (Tune: *Eventide*)
Abide with me; fast falls the eventide

The service will proceed without announcements. All the hymns are
in *Hymns Ancient & Modern Revised* except one, which is in *Songs of
Praise* (words opposite). *Thank you for coming.*

Please join us in the New Vestry after the service *for a glass of
wine (alternatives available) and some light refreshments.*

*Please use the voting form overleaf (or request a separate one) to list
your own favourite hymns for a subsequent service.*

Just for a change, which is of course as good as a rest, we are taking on different tasks from our usual ones this evening.

Tony has worked out a very interesting talk on an unusual topic; he had it ready for July, but David wanted to say something then in case he ran out of ideas for one in the autumn. We had a team of four, with Laura joining Tony, David and myself, to plan the service, selecting readings to go with Tony's talk, but then we inadvertently left David to decide on his own which order to have the hymns in. And, yes, we really do have two successive hymns with the same number (from different hymn books). We finish with the only one of four very well-known hymn tunes that was correctly identified by Oxbridge students on *University Challenge*.

Rather than do nothing more, David thought he'd like to take on the rather long second reading, with Philip for the first one, which recounts just a sample of some of the well-known events that Tony has put his scientific mind to explaining.

That left me to read his Introduction, so we have moved Laura to the Prayers, which is only fair as she supplied the first one, by Martin Luther. We stopped short of putting David Beal on the keyboard and getting Robert to give out the notices, as this would hardly be fair on either of them, given that Robert puts in the time beforehand to select and practise music for when people are arriving and departing, and we know that David enjoys this rare chance of taking it easy and letting us do the work.

One other constant is our invitation to you to join us for a glass of wine (or fruit juice) in the New Vestry after this service, for which our thanks go to Diane and Malcolm for everything involving the glasses, and to Pam for bringing the edible refreshments.

We are still almost in summer, albeit Indian, but our next service, on the fifth fifth Sunday of 2012, namely 30th December, will be very definitely a winter one. We look forward to seeing you all again then, and thank you as always for coming along this evening.

Exodus 9, 22–30, 34–35; 10, 1–2

The Lord said to Moses, "Stretch out your hand towards the sky to bring down hail on the whole land of Egypt, on man and beast and every growing thing throughout the land." Moses stretched out his staff towards the sky, and the Lord sent thunder and hail, with fire flashing down to the ground. The Lord rained down hail on the land of Egypt, hail and fiery flashes through the hail, so heavy that there had been nothing like it in all Egypt from the time that Egypt became a nation. Throughout Egypt the hail struck everything in the fields, both man and beast; it beat down every growing thing and shattered every tree. Only in the land of Goshen, where the Israelites lived, was there no hail.

Pharaoh sent and summoned Moses and Aaron. "This time I have sinned," he said; "the Lord is in the right; I and my people are in the wrong. Intercede with the Lord, for we can bear no more of this thunder and hail. I will let you go; you need wait no longer." Moses said, "When I leave the city I will spread out my hands in prayer to the Lord. The thunder shall cease, and there shall be no more hail, so that you may know that the earth is the Lord's. But you and your subjects—I know that you do not yet fear the Lord God."

When Pharaoh saw that the downpour, the hail, and the thunder had ceased, he sinned again, he and his courtiers, and became obdurate. So Pharaoh remained obstinate; as the Lord had foretold through Moses, he did not let the people go.

Then the Lord said to Moses, "Go into Pharaoh's presence. I have made him and his courtiers obdurate, so that I may show these my signs among them, and so that you can tell your children and grandchildren the story: how I made sport of the Egyptians, and what signs I showed among them. Thus you will know that I am the Lord."

Exodus 13, 17–18, 20–22; 14, 1–8, 10, 11, 13, 14, 19–26, 28, 31

Now when Pharaoh let the people go, God did not guide them by the road towards the Philistines, although that was the shortest; for he said, "The people may change their minds when they see war before them, and turn back to Egypt." So God made them go round by way of the wilderness towards the Red Sea; and the fifth generation of Israelites departed from Egypt.

They set out from Succoth and camped at Etham on the edge of the wilderness. And all the time the Lord went before them, by day a pillar of cloud to guide them on their journey, by night a pillar of fire to give them light, so that they could travel night and day. The pillar of cloud never left its place in front of the people by day, nor the pillar of fire by night.

The Lord spoke to Moses and said, "Speak to the Israelites: they are to turn back and encamp before Pi-hahiroth, between Migdol and the sea to the east of Baal-zephone; your camp shall be opposite, by the sea. Pharaoh will then think that the Israelites are finding themselves in difficult country, and are hemmed in by the wilderness. I will make Pharaoh obstinate, and he will pursue them, so that I may win glory for myself at the expense of Pharaoh and all his army; and the Egyptians shall know that I am the Lord." The Israelites did as they were bidden.

When the king of Egypt was told that the Israelites had slipped away, he and his courtiers changed their minds completely, and said, "What have we done? We have let our Israelite slaves go free!" So Pharaoh put horses to his chariot, and took his troops with him. He took six hundred picked chariots and all the other chariots of Egypt, with a commander in each. Then Pharaoh king of Egypt, made obstinate by the Lord, pursued the Israelites as they marched defiantly away. Pharaoh was almost upon them when the Israelites looked up and saw the Egyptians close behind. In their terror they clamoured to the Lord for help.

"Have no fear, Moses answered; "stand firm and see the deliverance that the Lord will bring you this day; for as sure as you see the Egyptians now, you will never see them again. The Lord will fight for you; so hold your peace."

The angel of God, who had kept in front of the Israelites, moved away to the rear. The pillar of cloud moved from the front and took its place behind them and so came between the Egyptians and the Israelites. And the cloud brought on darkness and early nightfall, so that contact was lost throughout the night.

Then Moses stretched out his hand over the sea, and the Lord drove the sea away all night with a strong east wind and turned the sea-bed into dry land, and the Israelites went through the sea on the dry ground. The Egyptians went in pursuit of them far into the sea, all Pharaoh's horse, his chariots, and his cavalry. In the morning watch the Lord looked down on the Egyptian army through the pillar of fire and cloud, and he threw them into a panic. He clogged their chariot wheels and made them lumber along heavily. Then the Lord said to Moses, "Stretch out your hand over the sea, and let the water flow back over the Egyptians, their chariots and their cavalry." The water flowed back and covered all Pharaoh's army, the chariots and the cavalry, which had pressed the pursuit into the sea. Not one man was left alive.

When Israel saw the great power which the Lord had put forth against Egypt, all the people feared the Lord, and they put their faith in him and in Moses his servant.

MOSES AND THE PHARAOHS

Unusually for me, I'm going to start off with a prayer:–

"May the good God live who delights in truth, Lord of Heaven and earth, the Great, illuminating the two lands. May the Father live, divine and royal, rejoicing in the horizon in his aspect of the light which is in the Sun, who lives for ever."

Now that's not a bad prayer and I don't think any Jew, Christian or even Muslim could have much objection to it.

However, it was engraved about 3,300 years ago on a stela, a sort of boundary marker to a city known to us as Amarna, which had been built in the desert on the opposite bank of the Nile to the Valley of the Kings, about half-way between Cairo and Luxor.

The man who had it engraved was a Pharaoh who came to the throne as Amunhotep IV but later changed his name to Akenaten. You may not be familiar with him but you will probably know of his beautiful Queen, Nefertiti, whose face is seen all around the world; also his second successor, Tutankhamun.

Akenaten was the most unusual and puzzling Pharaoh that we know of. All other Pharaohs are depicted as having perfect male bodies, and they are often shown killing their enemies. Not so Akenaten; his physique was quite strange: an elongated head and neck, thin spindly lower legs on fat thighs, a fattish tum and female breasts! He also had long thin hands and feet. Was he a hermaphrodite? Probably not, as he managed to sire six daughters with his Queen. He is often depicted playing with these children, obviously loving them dearly. Again, the only Pharaoh ever shown doing this!

The most astonishing thing he did, however, was to change the state religion. Egypt, in common with the rest of the ancient world and for over 2,000 years, had worshipped a multitude of Deities, the chief of which was Amun-Re, whose Temple was situated at Thebes, where the Pharaohs normally resided. As Amunhotep IV, he suddenly closed all the old temples and established his new city at Amarna, further north along the Nile. That was where he changed his name to Akenaten and proclaimed his new religion for the worship of the "One true God who could not be depicted by a graven image"! Where have I met that before?

Who do we know who was described as a "Prince of Egypt" and believed in one God only? Moses, of course. Working back from the known date of the fall of Jericho through forty years of wandering does put him in the right time frame.

Something very dramatic, perhaps cataclysmic, must have happened in Egypt! Akenaten's father (Amunhotep III) could not cope with it and Akenaten took over, although his father lived on for a further twelve years, perhaps as Co-Regent.

Now, is there anything that we are aware of which could account for the great changes made by Akenaten? There are no clues from the Egyptological record, but of course we have a devastating series of 'plagues' being inflicted on the Egyptians recounted in the story of the Exodus! There is darkness, the Nile is poisoned, fish die, there are plagues of frogs, maggots and flies, the death of cattle and horses and finally of the 'first-born'. Is it too much to suggest that Amunhotep III was the unnamed Pharaoh of the Exodus and that Akenaten tried to put things right with his understanding of the God of the Hebrews? I personally think this has a lot going for it!

But there is more. I kid myself that I am a rational being who looks for cause and effect. If daylight is blotted out, something opaque must have got between the Sun and the Earth. If the Nile is undrinkable and its fish die, something must have poisoned it.

Do we know of any 'natural' events which could result in 'plagues' like those recorded in Exodus? Violent large volcanic eruptions can! We probably all remember the Mount St Helens explosion in north-west America in 1980 and the chaos it caused. This was only a 'small' event, about equivalent to 50,000 tons of TNT (or 2½ times as much as the Nagasaki atomic bomb). The explosion at Krakatoa in the East Indies at the end of the 19th Century was calculated as a million tons of TNT (i.e. 50 atom bombs). It is recorded that the explosion was heard in north Australia and that there was no daylight for a week up to 800 kilometres downwind. It was also thought to have killed over 36,000 people!

Now the question is, was there a similar event in the right time frame, somewhere near Egypt? Surprise, surprise, yes there was! In the Aegean Sea, north of Crete, lie the remains of what was one island called Thira, which is now several small ones. In about the same period as the Exodus, it blew its top off in the great grandad of all explosions, with a force of about six million tons of TNT, or 300 atomic bombs! The fall-out cloud from this must have been enormous, with black darkness, hot cinders, poisonous dust and perhaps acid rain: just the thing to have caused all the plagues quoted in Exodus—red rain, rotting fish, poisoned rivers leading to plagues of insects and frogs and multiple deaths in the population. The only 'miracle' this doesn't cover is the turning of Aaron's staff into a snake, but this must have been a trick, as Pharaoh's magicians could do the same thing.

Such an eruption as the Thira one must have caused at least one tsunami, and this would have rolled up and down the Mediterranean like a wave in a bath tub. We all saw the effects of the Japanese tsunami on TV, so we know what they can do. The effects were also noted by the BBC on 12th August 2012, in the programme, *Ten Things You Didn't Know About Tsunamis*. I don't know where the idea of the Israelites crossing the Red Sea came from, but if, following a column of smoke during the day and one of fire at night, they went further north, through the Nile Delta towards the normally tide-less Mediterranean, we could have an explanation of the parting of the waters followed by the drowning of the pursuing Egyptian army.[1]

None of my thoughts denies the 'Hand of God' in this; they do no more than suggest how it may have worked. The downside of the liberation of the Israelites from Egypt is seen when the number of people who died as a result of the Thira eruption is contemplated. It certainly effectively put an end to the Minoan civilization on Crete!

When I started this exercise, I thought that to some extent I would end up 'debunking' the story of the Exodus, but the very reverse has happened. I had what was almost a moment of Epiphany when I realized that History did in fact open the very real possibility that all the 'plagues' described in Exodus really did happen!

Just to end the story, Akenaten and his city lasted about 17 years, Nefertiti died about six years before Akenaten, who was succeeded by a short-lived boy-king, Smenkhare. His younger brother, Tutankaten, followed for a few years and reinstated the old religion, changing his name to Tutankhamun, for which he appeared to have been given his fabulous tomb.

I didn't think of all this myself, but for many years I've been convinced that there must have been some connection between Moses and Akenaten.

Tony Hills

---

[1] A more recent programme on BBC4, again titled *Ten Things You Didn't Know About Tsunamis,* included the theory that the parting of the waters followed by the drowning of the pursuing Egyptian army could have been the result of a tsunami, as suggested by Tony in this talk in 2012.

Prayers

It is your will that we not only call you father, but that all of us together call you *our* Father, and thus offer our prayers with one accord for all. Grant us, therefore, brotherly love and unity, that we may know and think of one another as true brothers and sisters, and pray to you, our own common Father, for all people and for every person, even as one child prays for another to its father.

Let no one among us seek his own good or forget before you the good of others; but, all hatred, envy and dissension laid aside, may we love one another as good and true children of God, and thus say with one accord not 'my Father', but '*our* Father'.   *Amen.*

Make your ways known upon earth, Lord God, your saving power among all peoples. Renew your Church in holiness and help us to serve you with joy. Guide the leaders of all nations, that justice may prevail throughout the world. Let not the needy be forgotten, nor the hope of the poor be taken away. Make us instruments of your peace and let your glory be over all the earth. *Amen.*

Lord God, we live in disturbing days: across the world, prices rise, debts increase, markets are in turmoil, jobs are taken away, and fragile security is under threat. Loving God, meet us in our fear and hear our prayer: be a tower of strength amidst the shifting sands, and a light in the darkness; help us receive your gift of peace, and fix our hearts where true joys are to be found, in Jesus Christ our Lord.   *Amen.*

Merciful father, the strength of all who suffer, defender of all who trust in you, whose compassion never fails; look with mercy upon the stricken people of Syria, touch the hearts of all who oppress, that they may be open to the ways of justice and of peace; through Jesus Christ our Lord, who suffered and died for all and who lives with you and the Holy Spirit, now and for ever.
Amen.

A few moments' silence for your own prayers.

The Lord's Prayer.

May the Lord bless us and keep us; the Lord make his face to shine upon us and be gracious to us; the Lord lift up the light of his countenance upon us and give us peace, this night and for evermore.   *Amen.*

SIMPLE SERVICE, WITH HYMNS
30th December 2012

Order of Service

Welcome & Notices

Hymn 220 (Tune: *Truro*)
Jesus shall reign where'er the sun

Brief introduction (David E.)

Hymn 45 (*Hymns for Today;* words on p.177. Tune: *Quem pastores*)
Jesus, good above all other

First reading (Laura) "Eddi's Service" *by Rudyard Kipling*

Hymn 75 (Tune: *Epiphany Hymn, Mission Praise 65*)
Brightest and best of the sons of the morning

Second reading (Clive C.) Extract from *Morte d'Arthur* (*Tennyson*)

Hymn 279 (Tune: *Regent Square*)
Light's abode, celestial Salem

Chat (David E.)

Hymn 178 (Tune: *University*)
The God of love my Shepherd is

Prayers (Peter)

Hymn 735 (*Mission Praise;* words on page 25. Tune: *Finlandia*)
We rest on Thee, our shield and our defender

Closing blessing

The service will proceed without announcements. Four hymns are in *Hymns Ancient & Modern Revised,* one is in *Hymns for Today* and the other is in *Mission Praise* (words opposite and overleaf).

Please join us in the New Vestry after the service *for a glass of wine (alternatives available) and some light refreshments.*

Thank you for coming. Please use the separate voting form to list your own favourite hymns for a subsequent service.

238

Thank you all for coming, and my thanks as always to everyone in our team who has helped plan this service and will be taking part in it.

This introduction is shorter than usual because my 'chat' is rather less 'brief'. I thought the colleagues who checked that for me might suggest something I should leave out, but they didn't!

We have long felt that finishing as the strains of the final hymn die away is just a bit too sudden, so we are trying a slight change in our format by adding a 'closing blessing' to conclude with instead.

After that, do come back to the Vestry for a drink and a mince pie.

EDDI'S SERVICE

Eddi, priest of St. Wilfrid
  In the chapel at Manhood End,
Ordered a midnight service
  For such as cared to attend.

But the Saxons were keeping Christmas,
  And the night was stormy as well.
Nobody came to service,
  Though Eddi rang the bell.

"Wicked weather for walking,"
  Said Eddi of Manhood End.
"But I must go on with the service
  For such as care to attend."

The altar-lamps were lighted,—
  An old marsh-donkey came,
Bold as a guest invited,
  And stared at the guttering flame.

The storm beat on at the windows,
  The water splashed on the floor,
And a wet, yoke-weary bullock
  Pushed in through the open door.

"How do I know what is greatest,
How do I know what is least?
That is My Father's business,"
Said Eddi, Wilfrid's priest.

"But—three are gathered together
Listen to me and attend.
I bring good news, my brethren!"
Said Eddi of Manhood End.

And he told the Ox of a Manger
And a Stall in Bethlehem,
And he spoke to the Ass of a Rider
That rode to Jerusalem.

They steamed and dripped in the chancel,
They listened and never stirred,
While, just as though they were Bishops,
Eddi preached them The Word,

Till the gale blew off on the marshes
And the windows showed the day,
And the Ox and the Ass together
Wheeled and clattered away.

And when the Saxons mocked him,
Said Eddi of Manhood End,
"I dare not shut His chapel
On such as care to attend."

Rudyard Kipling

(1865–1936)

EXTRACT FROM MORTE D'ARTHUR

And slowly answered Arthur from the barge:
"The old order changeth, yielding place to new,
And God fulfils himself in many ways,
Lest one good custom should corrupt the world.
Comfort thyself: what comfort is in me?
I have lived my life, and that which I have done
May He within himself make pure! But thou,
If thou shouldst never see my face again,
Pray for my soul. More things are wrought by prayer
Than this world dreams of. Wherefore, let thy voice
Rise like a fountain for me night and day.
For what are men better than sheep or goats
That nourish a blind life within the brain,
If, knowing God, they lift not hands of prayer
Both for themselves and those who call them friend?
For so the whole round earth is every way
Bound by gold chains about the feet of God.
But now farewell. I am going a long way
With these thou seëst—if indeed I go—
(For all my mind is clouded with a doubt)
To the island-valley of Avilion;
Where falls not hail, or rain, or any snow,
Nor ever wind blows loudly; but it lies
Deep-meadow'd, happy, fair with orchard-lawns
And bowery hollows crown'd with summer sea,
Where I will heal me of my grievous wound."

So said he, and the barge with oar and sail
Moved from the brink, like some full-breasted swan
That, fluting a wild carol ere her death,
Ruffles her pure cold plume, and takes the flood
With swarthy webs. Long stood Sir Bedivere
Revolving many memories, till the hull
Look'd one black dot against the verge of dawn,
And on the mere the wailing died away.

Alfred Tennyson, D.C.L. (publ. 1863)

SOME THOUGHTS ABOUT PRAYER

Christmas is often said to be a time for children, and for children it is a time when they can make requests for what they want. So perhaps if I keep mainly to our asking God for help rather than expressing thanksgiving or penitence, I could try to say something this evening on the vast topic of prayer.

The late Revd Dr Martin Israel, then Chairman of the Churches' Fellowship for Psychical & Spiritual Studies, once declared that:–

Prayer is one of the easiest things in life and also the most difficult. It comes naturally to a child, is hardest for those who are intellectually poised, and is the ultimate answer to all the problems in life.

Well, as many of us could be described as 'intellectually poised', let's ponder not so much on how hard it is, but on what might make it useful.

Firstly, as David Beal pointed out recently with respect to James and John saying to Jesus that they would like him to do whatever they asked of him, we can't just tell God what to do. Thus the well-known prayer taking up Jesus' "promise that when two or three are gathered together in thy name thou wilt grant their requests" continues: "fulfil . . . the desires and petitions of thy servants, *as may be most expedient for them*". The biblical passage from Matthew says, "if two of you agree on earth about any request you have to make" and this indicates that the most important part of the process may well be the prior agreement about what to ask.

It is impracticable for larger congregations than we have at 8 o'clock to precede the communal prayers with a discussion about what to ask for, but we can indicate our assent with the *Amen* or another form of words.

As Christians our source of guidance, not only on prayer of course but on all aspects of how to live, must be the teaching of Jesus as reported in the Gospels, and these do provide plenty of helpful information.

However, it is clear from these Gospel writings that Jesus did not have an empty spiritual slate; he had all the Hebrew scriptures that we now call the Old Testament to draw his own inspiration from, under the guidance of the Holy Spirit; he knew these well and taught in the synagogues. So there is no reason why saints and others coming after Jesus, with the same guidance, and familiarity with his teachings, should not have insights too.

There are also other sources. The data of psychical research that ESP, or telepathy, is not exactly an efficient means of communication could be more than a little discouraging, if you consider the implication that when we 'say our prayers' we may not actually have a direct line to God (or even to some spirit intermediary), and thus may not be communing with anyone but ourselves. After my Confirmation, my mother passed on to me her copy of a tiny book called *Helps to Worship*, dated 1877, 4th edition 1881, reprinted 1929 (completing over two million copies). It had lots of good prayers and verses to fill any waiting before or after Communion, however many people there might be at the service. It also had a simple form for one's own prayers and I would make use of this at bedtime—until I knew it so well that I would get right through it from memory without even attending to a word of it myself. Prayer does need to be rather more intense than that.

But whether our private prayers are 'heard' or not, it can still be useful to frame them as if spoken to a greater, wiser being, while sorting out our thoughts and clarifying our motives. And if even just one or two of one's more heartfelt petitions are granted in the form of subsequent events, we are thereby assured that they were not said in vain.

All the lengthy prayers that make up our prescribed forms of church service can at least get us into the right mood, but I sometimes wonder what the Deity makes of the reasoned arguments put forward in some of them, such as "We appreciate that we have no right to claim anything for ourselves, but you are a God renowned for being merciful, so don't weigh our merits; just pardon our shortcomings, and then grant, etc." One can almost imagine the reply, "And have you been forgiving towards those who have wronged you?" "Well, actually, no. That's another of our shortcomings which we should like forgiven."

An interesting point regarding these prescribed prayers came up quite unexpectedly at the end of October. Unable to find anyone else to take the service at 8 o'clock the day after he was taking his family away on a half-term break, David Beal said that it would be quite all right for Peter and me to conduct the service instead. We couldn't include the Prayer of Consecration, which only a Priest is authorized to say (and now in this Diocese, only a priest who has been CRB-checked), but we would not need to: consecrated Elements were already in the Aumbry, and Peter has been licensed to distribute these (he chalice-assists on a regular basis). I am sure David would not have said that we could do this if it wasn't legitimate, but it does seem to me that the scheme reduces the Prayer of Consecration to the status of a magical incantation. I can see how it normally fits into the service, preparing us for Communion, but I am not convinced that it can be left out on account of its having been said *on a previous occasion* over those particular wafers and flagon of wine.

Prayer, surely, needs a link to action. *Laborare est orare* [to work is to pray], as the Romans said; Heaven helps them who help themselves, and, no doubt, even more so those who *try to help other people*. I have heard it said that it might be 'better to go upstairs and pray for someone than to call and visit' him or her, but isn't that visit (always assuming that it is not inconvenient or otherwise unwelcome to the person visited) a form of prayer?

A friend of ours is unwell. We can 'think' suitable words requesting healing for him to a visualized Deity, or we can arrange to take him some lunch. Which is the prayer? Does not the latter action convey to the Deity our concern for our friend, with the implied request that He grant him some healing?

"More things are wrought by prayer than this world dreams of". Craig Marsh, a New Zealander, was diagnosed with stomach cancer. He went to many healers over something like a decade, but his condition got worse; surgery was needed and most of his stomach had to be removed. With death from the cancer seemingly just a month or so ahead, he went to a Christian Conference in the United States, as 'one last function'. The people there knew of his illness and the six hundred Methodist ministers attending agreed that they would all 'pray for Craig'. He felt a rumbling inside him and then had a craving for Kentucky Fried Chicken, the last thing anyone with a digestive problem should try to eat, but eat it he did, without ill effect. Doctors found his stomach had come back. We heard his story at first hand in West Chiltington after Kevin had invited him.

How do we pray for something major in our own lives, some positive development that we really, perhaps desperately, want, but if need be could manage without, unlike relief from a life-threatening illness?

Putting words into any normal form of prayer just seems woefully inadequate, but if we can accept Jesus' promise that God knows what we want before we ask Him, the petition need remain no more than a deep longing, a hope, as it were, for something we dare not even ask for. I try to say to myself, 'If God wants it, He will arrange it (though that doesn't mean that I won't have to work for it); if He doesn't want it, then neither should I.' But that 'neither should I' is the hardest part!

The famous American evangelist, Billy Graham, came to England in 1966, and I went with a Christian friend from the laboratory where I then worked in Harlow, Essex, to hear him preach at the Albert Hall. Did I come away recognizing him as a great evangelist? Yes, but not because of the general drift of his sermon, which was not unlike many I had heard before at Christian Union meetings in my student days. Nor yet because of the number of people from all over the auditorium who came forward at his bidding at the end, and were dealt with very professionally by a team of people who put them in touch with their local churches; but, as often happens, because of one thing he said which seemed to speak to me. "God always answers prayer," he said, "but not everybody realizes that there are *three* answers. Sometimes He says, 'Yes'; sometimes He says, 'No' . . . and sometimes He says, 'Wait'." The implication, therefore, is that if one sees no apparent result, the answer might not be No. If He says, 'Wait for forty years', then one must wait for forty years (as indeed the Israelites had to[1])! But as I worked out much later, there is the slight drawback in that one can go on thinking that the answer might yet be Wait, when actually it was No all along . . .

How we try to make ourselves worthy of what we long for might be approached indirectly. "Set your mind on God's kingdom and his justice before everything else," said Jesus, "and all the rest will come to you as well." If I want God to help me, then surely I must take especial care to do my best for anyone that I come across who needs my help. A subtle distinction needs to be made here. Sure, we say with St Paul that we are unprofitable servants, and we pray, "Teach us, good Lord, . . . to labour and not to ask for any reward save that of knowing that we do Thy will", (and even that, though asked for, is not always granted); but if there is a reward that we long for, while we have no right to *expect* it as a result, the labour may well be a necessary factor even if not a sufficient one.

There is certainly comfort in "Ask and you will receive; seek and you will find; knock and the door will be opened" and in "If you, bad as you are, know how to give your children what is good for them, how much more will your heavenly Father give good things to those who ask Him!"

Will what I want help me to follow Jesus more closely; will it do good to someone else? On the other hand, am I perhaps actually being guided into longing for this particular outcome? Such questions need to be pondered over, but they can only be answered fully by future events (in other words, by God in His own good time).

A couple of thoughts to end with; first a quotation from a remarkable paperback, *The Cross and the Switchblade*, published nearly fifty years ago: "People who don't believe in miracles shouldn't pray for them."[2]

The second, my own on hearing of the vote regarding women bishops: We should not request the Holy Spirit to guide our deliberations if we are not prepared to be led in a direction in which we had not expected to be travelling.

Prayers

Almighty God, who rulest the changing seasons, we bless thee that beneath all that now seems cold and dead, thou art keeping safe the hidden germs of life. Still thou dost clothe all things around us with beauty, sending forth thy frost and snow, filling the brief day with sunshine, and making the night glorious with countless stars. We thank thee for the shelter and comfort of our homes, and pray for those in poverty or sickness who shrink from the cold. Through Jesus Christ our Lord.   *Amen.*

---

[1] With the result that when they besieged Jericho an earthquake demolished its walls!
[2] By David Wilkerson, Pyramid paperback edition, New York, 1964, p.61.

O Lord, we do not pray for tasks equal to our strength; we ask for strength equal to our tasks.

Teach us, good Lord, to serve thee as thou deservest; to give and not to count the cost; to fight and not to heed the wounds; to toil and not to seek for rest; to labour and not to ask for any reward save that of knowing that we do thy will. *Amen.*

As Jesus said, "How blest are the peacemakers; God shall call them his sons," we include this PRAYER OF ST FRANCIS OF ASSISSI :–

Lord, make us instruments of thy peace.
Where there is hatred, let us give love;
where there is injury, pardon;
where there is discord, union;
where there is doubt, faith;
where there is despair, hope;
where there is darkness, light;
where there is sadness, joy;
for thy mercy and for thy truth's sake. *Amen.*

† O God, forasmuch as without thee we are not able to please thee, grant that thy Holy Spirit may in this, and all things, direct and rule our hearts; through Jesus Christ our Lord. *Amen.*

† Almighty God, who hast given us grace at this time with one accord to make our common supplications unto thee; and dost promise that when two or three are gathered together in thy name thou wilt grant their requests: fulfil now, O Lord, the desires and petitions of thy servants, as may be most expedient for them; granting us in this world knowledge of thy truth, and in the world to come life everlasting. *Amen.*

A few moments' silence for your own prayers.

The Lord's Prayer.

May the Lord lead us when we go, and keep us when we sleep, and talk with us when we wake; and may the peace of God, which passeth all understanding, keep our hearts and minds in Jesus Christ our Lord. *Amen.*

Closing Blessing

Go forth into the world in peace; be of good courage; hold fast that which is good; render to no man evil for evil; strengthen the faint-hearted; support the weak; help the afflicted; honour all men; love and serve the Lord; rejoicing in the power of the Holy Spirit.

And the blessing of God Almighty, the Father, the Son, and the Holy Spirit, be upon us, and remain with us for ever. *Amen.*

SIMPLE SERVICE, WITH HYMNS
31st March 2013

Order of Service

Welcome & Notices (David Burnett)
Hymn 98 (Tune: *St Theodulph*)
All glory, laud and honour

Brief introduction (David Ellis)
Hymn 130 (Tune: *Victory*)
O sons and daughters, let us sing!

First reading (Laura) Luke, Chapter 23, Verses 32–34, 39–43 *(NEB)*
Hymn 140 (Tune: *St Albinus*)
Jesus lives! Thy terrors now

Second reading (Philip) Luke, Chapter 24, Verses 13–43 *(NEB)*
Hymn 224 (Tune: *Diademata*)
Crown him with many crowns

Brief chat (David E.)
Hymn 225 (Tune: *Evelyns*)
At the name of Jesus

Prayers (Peter)
Hymn 578 (*Songs of Praise;* on p.132. Tune: *John Brown's Body*)
Mine eyes have seen the glory
Closing Blessing

The service will proceed without announcements. All the hymns are in *Hymns Ancient & Modern Revised* except the last one, which is in *Songs of Praise* (words opposite). *Thank you for coming.* Voting sheet for your own choice of hymns for next time is on the back page.

Please join us in the New Vestry after the service for a glass of wine *(alternatives available).*

Thank you all for coming, and my thanks as always to everyone in our team who has helped plan this service and will be taking part in it.

We are grateful also to David Beal for having family commitments this afternoon, and so leaving to us the privilege of conducting a service on Easter Day.

Although most of our hymns have an Easter theme, we thought we would lead into this by starting with one from Palm Sunday.

I was hoping that our winter service was the one on 30th December, but we are still in winter today, even at the beginning of Summer Time. Let's hope it is warmer at the end of June.

Last time, to avoid ending abruptly as the strains of the final hymn die away, we tried concluding with a 'closing blessing' instead, and we shall have one again this evening.

After that, do come back to the Vestry for a glass of wine or fruit juice (we have brought apple juice this time instead of grapefruit, to allow for people on statins) and this time an Easter biscuit, which I made yesterday evening.

Luke 23, 32–34, 39–43

There were two others with him, criminals who were being led away to execution; and when they reached the place called 'The Skull', they crucified him there, and the criminals with him, one on his right and the other on his left. Jesus said, "Father, forgive them; they do not know what they are doing."

One of the criminals who hung there taunted him: "Are not you the Messiah? Save yourself, and us."

But the other answered sharply, "Have you no fear of God? You are under the same sentence as he. For us it is plain justice; we are paying the price for our misdeeds; but this man has done nothing wrong." And he said, "Jesus, remember me when you come to your throne."

He answered, "I tell you this: today you shall be with me in Paradise."

Luke 24, 13–43

That same day two of them were on their way to a village called Emmaus, which lay about seven miles from Jerusalem, and they were talking together about all these happenings. As they talked and discussed it with one another, Jesus himself came up and walked along with them; but something held their eyes from seeing who it was.

He asked them, "What is it that you are debating as you walk?"

They halted, their faces full of gloom, and one, called Cleopas, answered, "Are you the only person staying in Jerusalem not to know what has happened there in the last few days?"

"What do you mean?" he said.

"All this about Jesus of Nazareth," they replied, "a prophet powerful in speech and action before God and the whole people; how our chief priests and rulers handed him over to be sentenced to death, and crucified him. But we had been hoping that he was the man to liberate Israel. What is more, this is the third day since it happened, and now some women of our company have astounded us: they went early to the tomb, but failed to find his body, and returned with a story that they had seen a vision of angels who told them he was alive. So some of our people went to the tomb and found things just as the women had said; but him they did not see."

"How dull you are!" he answered. "How slow to believe all that the prophets said! Was the Messiah not bound to suffer thus before entering upon his glory?" Then he began with Moses and all the prophets, and explained to them the passages which referred to himself in every part of the scriptures.

By this time they had reached the village to which they were going, and he made as if to continue his journey, but they pressed him: "Stay with us, for evening draws on and the day is almost over."

So he went in to stay with them. And when he had sat down with them at the table, he took bread and said the blessing; he broke the bread, and offered it to them. Then their eyes were opened, and they recognized him; and he vanished from their sight. They said to one another, "Did we not feel our hearts on fire as he talked with us on the road and explained the scriptures to us?"

Without a moment's delay they set out and returned to Jerusalem. There they found that the Eleven and the rest of the company had assembled, and were saying, "It is true: the Lord has risen; he has appeared to Simon." Then they gave their account of the events of their journey and told how he had been recognized by them at the breaking of the bread.

As they were talking about all this, there he was, standing among them. Startled and terrified, they thought they were seeing a ghost. But he said, "Why are you so perturbed? Why do questionings arise in your minds? Look at my hands and feet. It is I myself. Touch me and see; no ghost has flesh and bones as you can see that I have."

They were still unconvinced, still wondering, for it seemed too good to be true. So he asked them, "Have you anything here to eat?"

They offered him a piece of fish they had cooked, which he took and ate before their eyes.

SOMETHING GOING WRONG FOR SOMETHING TO GO RIGHT

I was asking four years ago why many people do not come to Church, and wondering what it was that had put them off. Perhaps it was the idea that religious beliefs were incompatible with modern science.

To find out how this world we live in works, scientists have to make observations as well as devising and conducting experiments. We in turn can try to find patterns in life. In recent years I have noted how certain events in my own life have followed one another. Looking wider, I have found examples of what might actually be a quite general phenomenon.

To take a trivial instance: I do quarterly mailings for a customer, and so I buy lots of stamps. Paul was just about to count out those I had ordered when I found I had come without the card to pay for them. So I hurried home for it, and got there just in time to take a phone call I was glad not to have missed.

We are all at least vaguely familiar with the story of Job from the Old Testament, and his so-called comforters implying that he must somehow be to blame for his misfortunes. But as the story finally relates, Job's fault lay in *complaining* that they should have befallen him, as he had always done his best to be a pretty decent fellow. Once this had been explained to him by a younger adviser than the others, the way was open for him to repent, not of any former wrongdoing, but of his challenging God's wisdom in allowing them to happen. And his tale then has a very happy ending.

If we can take to heart those splendid words from Romans 8, 28, that "All things work together for good with those who love God" we can perhaps say to ourselves, if anything goes awry, "Something good will come from this: I wonder what?" Amazingly, I have found that it very often does! On the one hand, we live in a real, rational, mechanical world, in which events occur by the normal processes of cause and effect. On the other hand, as Christians, we must maintain a parallel belief in something almost magical; in prayers being answered and in somehow being looked after by a God who actually cares individually for us. One deduction might be that what happens by 'chance' is divinely directed.

The principle that I am trying to describe is that "Something has to go wrong for some other, perhaps more important, thing to go right."

During the evolution of our Solar System, an orbital interaction between the big planets, Jupiter and Saturn, apparently resulted in the Earth being bombarded with a lot of small asteroids and comets. Comets are composed mainly of ice, so the Earth, from being barren rock like Mars, gained enough water for the oceans to form, and from these oceans there eventually developed Life. We could perhaps see the orbital interaction and the bombardment as something that 'went wrong', but the formation of the seas and then the development of Life is undoubtedly something that 'went right'. We are more familiar with the theory of the asteroid that crashed on the Earth and put paid to the dinosaurs. The asteroid impact threw up so much dust that vegetation died and these big creatures starved, but the much smaller mammals were able to survive.

From the Old Testament we are familiar with the tale of King David having Uriah the Hittite sent to the front line of battle and thus certain death, so that he would be able to have his widow, Bathsheba, for his wife. That was most definitely wrong, as Nathan was bold enough to point out to him. David and Bathsheba had a son, who died in infancy, but their second son was Solomon, one of the greatest kings the nation ever had, famed for his wisdom and for building the Temple.

Tony told us in October about his research suggesting that a massive volcanic eruption in the Mediterranean had been the cause of the plagues that had come upon Egypt, with a tsunami whose incidence could well have enabled the Israelites to make their escape from bondage there.

From the New Testament it is clear that if St Paul had not been imprisoned we should not now have his Epistles.[1]

Of course, my theme is reflected in the saying that every cloud has a silver lining, and the song about April showers leading to May flowers.

But these seem trite on this glorious day in the Church's year when we celebrate something that went splendidly right because something else a few days earlier had gone so terribly wrong. Not long after riding into Jerusalem on a donkey to popular acclaim, Jesus had been arrested and led off to a cruel execution. Yet miraculously he was now alive again.

That this did happen is historically incontrovertible. And because it happened his disciples were revitalized and inspired to proclaim what has become known as the Christian faith. No resurrection, no Christianity.

That the whole sequence of events was the work of God we Christians do not doubt. The Gospel records, as we heard in our second reading, make it clear that the risen Jesus was not a ghost, or 'apparition'. How he had come back to life again will remain a mystery, but we can speculate and wonder if there is something simpler than the sort of celestial magic that we are expected to accept, whereby Jesus' body was dematerialized out of the tomb and that he then took on some new 'spiritual body' that had supernormal powers and could, for example, appear or disappear at will. Some more plausible mechanism might discourage rational people outside the Church from accusing us of believing in magic.

---

[1] And see pages 290–291 for a parallel example with reference to John Bunyan.

We have often seen how God works through people. Wrapped and laid in the tomb, Jesus, though unconscious, may still have been just alive. Unable to help himself, he might possibly have been assisted by a group of people quite separate from his Jewish followers, such as some Roman soldiers who had benefited from his healing work. They would have been strong enough to move the stone, and sensible enough to put the graveclothes back as if he had vanished out of them. Jesus' recovery from his ordeal would still have been miraculous; his returning from the dead no less the work of God. What "inspired his brethren to suffer and to die" was their *belief* that he had risen; their admiration of his courage in accepting his horrific treatment as essential to the Divine scheme.[1]

Prayers

Yesterday I was crucified with Christ;
today I am glorified with him.
Yesterday I was dead with Christ;
today I am sharing in his resurrection.
Yesterday I was buried with him;
today I am waking with him from the sleep of death.

Gregory of Nazianzus (389)

On this day that the Lord has made.
let us pray for the people he has redeemed.

That we may live as those who believe in the triumph of the cross:

That all people may receive the good news of his victory:

That those born to new life in the waters of baptism
may know the power of his resurrection:

That those who suffer pain and anguish
may find healing and peace in the wounds of Christ:

That in the undying love of Christ
we may be united with all who have died in the faith of Christ:

Let us commend the world, in which Christ rose from the dead,
to the mercy and protection of God.

Amen.

---

[1] This hypothesis is developed in detail in my article, "A Christian parapsychologist?" in the March 2002 issue of *The Christian Parapsychologist, Vol.15, No.1,* pp.14–17, published by the Churches' Fellowship for Psychical and Spiritual Studies, with related correspondence in the June and September 2002 and March 2003 issues. *DJE*

Heavenly Father,
in your Son Jesus Christ
you have given us a true faith and a sure hope.
Strengthen this faith and hope in us all our days,
that we may live as those who believe in
the communion of saints
the forgiveness of sins
and the resurrection to eternal life;
through Jesus Christ our Lord.

Amen.

We thank you, O God, for the pleasures you have given us through our senses; for the glory of thunder, for the mystery of music, the singing of birds and the laughter of children.

We thank you for the delights of colour, the awe of the sunset, the wild roses in the hedgerows, the smile of friendship.

We thank you for the sweetness of flowers and the scent of hay.

Truly, O Lord, the earth is full of your riches! *Amen.*

A few moments' silence for your own prayers.

The Lord's Prayer.

Unto the King, eternal, immortal, invisible, the only wise God, be honour and glory for ever and ever. *Amen.*

Closing Blessing

Irish Blessing

May the silence of the hills,
The joy of the wind,
The music of the birds,
The fire of the sun,
And the strength of the trees
Be in our hearts now and evermore —

May the road rise up to meet you.
May the wind be always at your back.
May the sun shine warm upon your face,
The rain fall soft upon your fields,
And until we meet again,
May your God hold you in the palm of His hand.

SIMPLE SERVICE, WITH HYMNS

30th June 2013

Order of Service

Welcome & Notices (David Foard)

Hymn 50 (*Mission Praise;* words on page 44)
Be still, for the presence of the Lord

Brief introduction (David)

Hymn 167 (Tune: *Hanover*)
O worship the King all glorious above

First reading (Laura) Genesis, Chapter 1, Verses 1–28, 31; Chapter 2,
Verses 1–4 *(NEB)*

Hymn 271 (Tune: *Benson*)
God is working his purpose out

Second reading (Tony) "St Mary's Church"

Hymn 269 (Tune: *Little Cornard*)
Hills of the north, rejoice

Brief chat (David)

Hymn 200 (*Mission Praise;* words overleaf. Tune: *Great is Thy Faithfulness*)
Great is Thy faithfulness

Prayers (Peter)

Hymn 23 (Tune: *Canon*)
Glory to thee, my God, this night

Closing blessing (Philip)

The service will proceed without announcements. All the hymns except two (words opposite and overleaf) are in *Hymns Ancient & Modern Revised.*

Please join us in the New Vestry after the service *for a glass of wine (alternatives available).*

Thank you for coming. Please use the separate voting form to list your own favourite hymns for a subsequent service.

Great is Thy faithfulness

Great is Thy faithfulness, O God my Father,
there is no shadow of turning with Thee;
Thou changest not, Thy compassions they fail not,
as Thou hast been Thou for ever will be.

Great is Thy faithfulness,
great is Thy faithfulness;
morning by morning new mercies I see;
all I have needed Thy hand hath provided –
great is Thy faithfulness, Lord, unto me!

Summer and winter, and spring-time and harvest,
sun, moon and stars in their courses above,
join with all nature in manifold witness
to Thy great faithfulness, mercy and love.

Great is Thy faithfulness,
great is Thy faithfulness;
morning by morning new mercies I see;
all I have needed Thy hand hath provided –
great is Thy faithfulness, Lord, unto me!

Pardon for sin, and a peace that endureth,
Thine own dear presence to cheer and to guide;
strength for today and bright hope for tomorrow,
blessings all mine, with ten thousand beside!

Great is Thy faithfulness,
Great is Thy faithfulness;
morning by morning new mercies I see;
all I have needed Thy hand hath provided –
Great is Thy faithfulness, Lord, unto me!

Words: Thomas O. Chisholm (1866–1960)

Thank you all for coming to this our fortieth 'hymns service', and my thanks as always to everyone who has helped with the planning and will be taking part, and indeed to all who contributed to the first thirty-nine.

We apologize to David Beal for not acceding to his suggestion that we have this service a week earlier, to avoid clashing with the Deanery Evensong at Storrington, but we appreciated his concern to be with us.

We are also without our Churchwardens, so we much appreciate David Foard's taking on the Welcome & Notices, and helping carry in the Keyboard.

After winter services, in December and March, we really have a summer one today. Let's hope that 29th September will be warm as well. We shall look forward to then; please let us have your hymn suggestions by early August.

Once again we are having a 'closing blessing' to give a less abrupt ending. After that, please come back to the Vestry for a glass of wine or fruit juice.

Genesis 1, 1–28, 31; 2, 1–4

In the beginning God created heaven and earth. The earth was without form and void, with darkness over the face of the abyss, and the spirit of God hovering over the surface of the waters. God said, "Let there be light," and there was light; and God saw that the light was good, and he separated light from darkness. He called the light day, and the darkness night. So evening came, and morning came, the first day.

God said, "Let there be a vault between the waters, to separate water from water." So God made the vault, and separated the water under the vault from the water above it, and so it was; and God called the vault heaven. Evening came, and morning came, a second day.

God said, "Let the waters under heaven be gathered into one place, so that dry land may appear;" and so it was. God called the dry land earth, and the gathering of the waters he called seas; and God saw that it was good. Then God said, "Let the earth produce fresh growth, let there be on the earth plants bearing seed, fruit-trees bearing fruit each with seed according to its kind." So it was; the earth yielded fresh growth, plants bearing seed according to their kind and trees bearing fruit each with seed according to its kind; and God saw that it was good. Evening came, and morning came, a third day.

God said, "Let there be lights in the vault of heaven to separate day from night, and let them serve as signs both for festivals and for seasons and years. Let them also shine in the vault of heaven to give light on earth." So it was; God made the two great lights, the greater to govern the day and the lesser to govern the night; and with them he made the stars. God put these lights in the vault of heaven to give light on earth, to govern day and night, and to separate light from darkness; and God saw that it was good. Evening came, and morning came, a fourth day.

God said, "Let the waters teem with countless living creatures, and let birds fly above the earth across the vault of heaven." God then created the great sea-monsters and all living creatures that move and swarm in the waters, according to their kind, and every kind of bird; and God saw that it was good. So he blessed them and said, "Be fruitful and increase, fill the waters of the seas; and let the birds increase on land." Evening came, and morning came, a fifth day.

God said, "Let the earth bring forth living creatures, according to their kind: cattle, reptiles, and wild animals, all according to their kind." So it was; God made wild animals, cattle, and all reptiles, each according to its kind; and he saw that it was good. Then God said, "Let us make man in our image and likeness to rule the fish in the sea, the birds of heaven, the cattle, all wild animals on earth, and all reptiles that crawl upon the earth." So God created man in his own image; in the image of God he created him; male and female he created them. God blessed them and said to them, "Be fruitful and increase, fill the earth and subdue it, rule over the fish in the sea, the birds of heaven, and every living thing that moves upon the earth."

So it was; and God saw all that he had made, and it was very good. Evening came, and morning came, a sixth day.

Thus heaven and earth were completed with all their mighty throng. On the sixth day God completed all the work he had been doing, and on the seventh day he ceased from all his work. God blessed the seventh day and made it holy, because on that day he ceased from all the work he had set himself to do.

This is the story of the making of heaven and earth when they were created.

St Mary's Church

There's a Village down in Sussex
   and it's on the River Chilt.
It's got a little old stone Church,
   you know, one the Normans built.

For nine hundred years she's stood there
   and opened up her door
to the people of the Village
   and their fathers long before.

Her ride was rather bumpy,
   when King Henry on Rome took.
She had to lose her 'Holy Mass'
   but gained Cranmer's beauteous book.

The altar stone must be destroyed,
   the Puritans decreed.
The parishioners were puzzled,
   and really did not see the need.

So they put it in the Sanctuary
   and hid it in the floor,
And there it slept quite peacefully
   four hundred years or more.

The Rector noticed something odd
   in the place he often kneeled.
It made him poke around a bit
   all was soon revealed!

The Village has grown bigger:
   four thousand souls or more.
The old Church still stands on her hill
   and opens up her door.

If you should peep around it
   and the Church seems rather tight,
You might count a hundred and fifty;
   from the Village, that's not bright.

If you ask them why they don't come in,
   they've excuses that stretch far:
"Johnny has got his football,
   and the wife will need the car."

The story they can't bring themselves
   to believe in any more.
They've all read Darwin and Dawkins
   and scholarly tomes by the score.

But if they read these carefully,
   they'll find that all they do
Is explain the way the work was done
   'Creation through and through'.

The time took far much longer
   than the Bible stories tell,
But Einstein proved 'Relativity'
   and sunk that one as well!

RAH

Introduce $E = mc^2$. Try to explain that nothing is really as it seems to be.

SOME THOUGHTS ABOUT THE CREATION

As some of the hymns selected for this evening, and then Tony's poem, had a common theme, the other members of our team suggested that we should have the beginning of Genesis as our first reading and that I should try to say something about the Creation.

While that passage from Genesis is quite simple to understand, how the account came to be recorded is not so simple. My copy of the Old Testament from the *New English Bible* has a ten-page introduction that explains what texts were available to the translators. This says that much of the story . . . "must have been handed down by word of mouth for many generations . . . no manuscripts have survived from the period before the destruction of Jerusalem and the deportation of the Jews into exile in 587/6 B.C." (p.xi). So as no one was there to witness the Creation, we can suppose either that God dictated it to Moses (who has been credited with compiling the first five books of the Bible) or that the story was passed down from Adam to Seth and descendants to Abraham, after God had recounted it to Adam. Or we can take the more straightforward view that what we have is a brave and commendable attempt by the Hebrew people to make sense of the world in which they found themselves.

I say commendable because, in contrast to other creation stories, the account of the development of life on this planet is remarkably consistent with scientific understanding in terms of the order in which it was all said to happen: plant life on land, living creatures first in the seas and later on the land, animals, and finally man. Certainly, we now understand that the Sun and other stars were around before the Earth was formed; and while it's puzzling that there were day and night on the first 'day' but the Sun, Moon and stars not until the fourth, even this discrepancy has inspired the very interesting conjecture that it wasn't the creation of these sources of illumination that occurred on the fourth 'day' but the development of creatures with the ability to see them.[1]

The Hebrew people didn't have telescopes, let alone radio telescopes, so they had no idea of how far away the stars were. Nor had the science of meteorology developed, so they supposed that as rain came down it must have come from above. Hence perhaps the idea of the waters on the earth and the waters above, separated by the vault of the heavens.

But what do we ourselves make nowadays of the most perplexing and unfathomable question of all, namely why does anything exist at all?

---

[1] As suggested in the chapter on Sight in Andrew Parker's book, *The Genesis Enigma,* London: Doubleday, 2009.

The astronomers tell us that the whole physical Universe came into being some thirteen billion years ago, with what they call the Big Bang. But they have yet to say what went bang, and why. Perhaps it was in response to the command, 'Let there be light'? The religious standpoint is that there was a Creator, whom we call God. Yet this, likewise, fails to answer the question of Who made God, except by asserting that God is outside Time and so has always existed and always will.

As Christians, we assert that Jesus, by his life and teaching, revealed more about what this 'eternal' Creator is like than anyone else has.

Now if God, having created everything and set it going, then left it (and us) to develop either deterministically or by the operation of pure chance, whether or not the universe had a Creator would seem now to be irrelevant. Why pray to a God who no longer interacts with His creation? Of course He may have built in some mechanism by which spiritual power is available to those who know where to seek it; some way that the right kind of prayer can result in a suitable answer—making God rather like the wife who goes out but leaves a message, 'Your supper is in the oven'. But this is not what Jesus teaches when he says that God is aware even of one sparrow falling to the ground, chiding his listeners for their lack of faith, and asking, "Are you not worth many sparrows?"

Yet experience of how God interacts with His world does not make Him like the genie of Aladdin's lamp. In general, He shows a healthy respect for the Laws of Nature (which it is not surprising, for it has been said that He *is* the Laws of Nature). What at first sight is miraculous can eventually turn out to be the result of a comprehensible process.

For us to be creative, we must use our imagination. By analogy, can we regard the physical universe as a product of the Divine imagination? Is Life a multi-dimensional 'book', of which God is the author?

Surely, as Tony's poem suggests, science and faith in God need not clash. If science is really seeking after truth it cannot be harmful to what should be a true religion. Does it matter that Creation may have taken longer than six rotations of our planet? If there is an understandable even if incompletely elucidated mechanism of how Life may have evolved, does that actually do any more than evoke our wonder at it all? And when we learn how one 'chance' event has led to another, can we escape pondering whether these were all 'just chance'?

The clashes of Science with Religion, from Galileo and Darwin to Dawkins, have shown that dogmatism, the insistence that one's tenets represent the truth and nothing but the truth, is not a constructive attitude. Is it not more objective to adopt a healthy agnosticism about the questions to which we should be honest enough to admit that we don't know the answers? The

260

scientists who make a religion out of their own philosophy of science are as guilty as the theologians who would not look through Galileo's telescope.

Dawkins' *The God Delusion* found an answer in Alister McGrath's *The Dawkins Delusion*.[1] Rupert Sheldrake in *The Science Delusion* has recently examined ten assertions of present-day scientific dogma and shown them to be unsubstantiated.[2]

Science and religion can reinforce each other if they stop arguing and turn to experimentation.[3] To take one example, people who are more forgiving have been shown to live longer and have fewer heart problems, simply because their forgiving nature makes their lives less stressful.

So the sensible way is to go lightly on theory and concentrate on the practice. McGrath draws attention to Dawkins' "failure to distinguish between 'belief in God' and 'religion'" (p.56) and reminds his readers of the great theme of the prophetic tradition of the Hebrew scriptures "that Israel's religion has become corrupted and detached from the faithful obedience to a God who loves justice, mercy and personal integrity. . . . Dawkins is right when he argues that it is necessary to criticize religion; yet he appears unaware that it possesses internal means of reform and renewal. This is especially evident in the ministry of Jesus of Nazareth . . . Jesus' mission was to challenge the religious forms of his day and, in the end, that was what led to him being crucified." (p.57).

Prayers

O praise the Lord.
How good it is to sing psalms to our God!
How pleasant to praise him!

Psalm 147, verse 1 (NEB)

"Thou art worthy, O Lord our God, to receive glory and honour and power, because thou didst create all things; by thy will they were created, and have their being!"

Revelation, Chapter 4, verse 11 (NEB)

---

[1] Dawkins' book: London: Bantam, 2006. McGrath's book: London: SPCK, 2007.

[2] London: Coronet (Hodder & Stoughton), 2013.

[3] In this talk I omitted to take up Tony's suggestion after his poem (p.257) to "try to explain that nothing is really as it seems to be." So perhaps I could add something about what is known as wave–particle dualism, that the elementary particles from which 'matter' is built up behave like waves as well as 'things'; and light, normally seen in terms of waves, also consists of particles (called photons). So particles have a time dimension to them, and therefore should be regarded as 'events' and not just as 'things'. Turning that round evokes the intriguing thought that events may be features of our created existence at least as fundamental as are the objects we find in it. *DJE*

O Lord, ruler of the world, even while the Earth was without form you were King, and you will still reign when all things are brought to an end. You are supreme and you will never be equalled. You are power and might: there is neither beginning nor end in you.

Jewish prayer

In peace, let us pray to Jesus our Lord,
Who ever lives to make intercession for us.

Saviour of the world,
be present in all places of suffering, violence and pain,
and bring hope even in the darkest night.
Inspire us to continue your work of reconciliation today.

Lord of the Church,
empower by your Spirit all Christian people,
and the work of your Church in every land.
Give us grace to proclaim the gospel joyfully in word and deed.

Shepherd and Guardian of our souls,
guide and enable all who lead and serve this community
and those on whom we depend for our daily needs.
Grant that we may seek the peace and welfare of this place.

Great Physician,
stretch out your hand to bring comfort, wholeness and peace
to all who suffer in body, mind or spirit.
Fill us with compassion, that we may be channels of
your healing love.

Conqueror of death,
remember for good those whom we love but see no longer.
Help us to live this day in the sure and certain hope of
your eternal victory.

Let us commend ourselves, and all for whom we pray,
to the mercy and protection of God.

A few moments' silence for your own prayers.

The Lord's Prayer.

Unto the King, eternal, immortal, invisible, the only wise God, be honour and glory for ever and ever. *Amen.*

Closing Blessing

Be thou, O Lord, within us to strengthen us, above us to protect us, beneath us to uphold us, before us to guide us, behind us to recall us, round us to fortify us. *Amen.*

SIMPLE SERVICE, WITH HYMNS
29th September 2013

Order of Service

Welcome & Notices (David Beal)

Hymn 172 (Tune: *Easter Song*)
All creatures of our God and King

Brief introduction (David E.)

Hymn 262 (Tune: *St. Cecilia*)
Thy Kingdom come, O God

First reading (David E.) Isaiah Chap. 60, Verses 1–5; 19–20 *(NEB)*

Hymn 354 (Tune: *Pilgrims*)
Hark! Hark, my soul! Angelic songs are swelling

Second reading (Laura) Revelation 21, 1–7; 9–14; 22–25 *(NEB)*

Hymn 258 (Tune: *Richmond*)
City of God, how broad and far

Brief chat (Tony)

Hymn 182 (Tune: *Gott will's machen*)
Father, hear the prayer we offer

Prayers (Peter)

Hymn 379 (Tune: *Nun danket*)
Now thank we all our God

Closing blessing (Philip)

The service will proceed without announcements. All the hymns are in *Hymns Ancient & Modern Revised.*

Thank you for coming. **Please join us in the New Vestry after the service** *for a glass of wine (alternatives available).*

Please use the voting form opposite to list your own favourite hymns for a subsequent service.

Thank you all for coming, and welcome back to David Beal and the Churchwardens, who for one genuine reason or another have been unable to be with us since this time last year.

My thanks as always to everyone who has helped with the planning and will be taking part; it could not be done without you all, from Robert on the keyboard, Laura, Tony and Peter selecting and doing readings and prayers, to everyone who asks for hymns. I am having it easier both this time and next, with Tony giving the Brief Chat today and Philip having got well into drafting something stimulating for 29th December.

We shall miss Clive Seeley, whose funeral was last Tuesday. He was a staunch supporter, he did a reading for us from time to time, and he gave one of the talks in our early years.

I expressed the hope in June that it would still be warm today, and indeed it seemed positively hot this morning as I came back up our road after walking in to collect the Parish Magazines. But whatever weather December brings, we shall look forward to seeing you again then.

Regarding your service sheets today, I should explain that I now have two laser printers, but neither of them is working properly. I started with the old one, but a new (non-HP) toner cartridge wasn't up to the job. So I turned to my newly-acquired second-hand colour printer and thought I'd let it show what it could do. I'm sorry about the background grey streaks and hope to resolve that problem very soon; please just pretend for now either that it's part of the design or that they are printed on greyish paper.

Since last year we have added a brief 'closing blessing' to give a less abrupt ending, after which you are all invited back to the Vestry again for a glass of wine or fruit juice.

Isaiah 60, 1–5; 19–20

Arise, Jerusalem, rise clothed in light; your light has come and the glory of the Lord shines over you.

For, though darkness covers the earth and dark night the nations, the Lord shall shine upon you and over you shall his glory appear; and the nations shall march towards your light and their kings to your sunrise;

Lift up your eyes and look all around: they flock together, all of them, and come to you; your sons also shall come from afar, your daughters walking beside them leading the way.

Then you shall see, and shine with joy, then your heart shall thrill with pride: the riches of the sea shall be lavished upon you and you shall possess the wealth of nations.

264

The sun shall no longer be your light by day, nor the moon shine on you when evening falls; the Lord shall be your everlasting light, your God shall be your glory.

Never again shall your sun set nor your moon withdraw her light; but the Lord shall be your everlasting light and the days of your grieving shall be ended.

Revelation 21, 1–7; 9–14; 22–25

Then I saw a new heaven and a new earth, for the first heaven and the first earth had vanished, and there was no longer any sea. I saw the holy city, Jerusalem, coming down out of heaven from God, made ready like a bride adorned for her husband. I heard a loud voice proclaiming from the throne: "Now at last God has his dwelling among men! He will dwell among them and they shall be his people, and God himself will be with them. He will wipe every tear from their eyes; and there shall be an end to death, and to mourning and crying and pain; for the old order has passed away!"

Then he who sat on the throne said, "Behold! I am making all things new!" And he said to me, "Write this down; for these words are trustworthy and true. Indeed," he said, "they are already fulfilled. For I am the Alpha and the Omega, the beginning and the end. A draught from the water-springs of life will be my free gift to the thirsty. All this is the victor's heritage; and I will be his God and he shall be my son."

Then one of the seven angels that held the seven bowls full of the seven last plagues came and spoke to me and said, "Come, and I will show you the bride, the wife of the Lamb." So in the Spirit he carried me away to a great high mountain, and showed me the holy city of Jerusalem coming down out of heaven from God. It shone with the glory of God; it had the radiance of some priceless jewel, like a jasper, clear as crystal. It had a great high wall, with twelve gates, at which were twelve angels; and on the gates were inscribed the names of the twelve tribes of Israel. There were three gates to the east, three to the north, three to the south, and three to the west. The city had twelve foundation-stones, and on them were the names of the twelve apostles of the Lamb.

I saw no temple in the city; for its temple was the sovereign Lord God and the Lamb. And the city had no need of sun or moon to shine upon it; for the glory of God gave it light, and its lamp was the Lamb. By its light shall the nations walk, and the kings of the earth shall bring into it all their splendour. The gates of the city shall never be shut by day—and there will be no night.

WAS JESUS LITERALLY THE SON OF GOD ?

I expect most of you know the history of how and why the Nicene Creed was put together, but I'll run through it briefly in case anyone doesn't.

When the Emperor Constantine finally established the Eastern-based Roman Empire after a military victory that he believed had been helped by his fighting under the Sign of the Cross, he decided that his Empire should have one religion and that would be Christianity (although he was not himself baptized until he was on his death-bed). However, there were then many versions of Christianity, some of which did not even accept the divinity of Jesus!

Constantine's solution was to call a meeting of the various Churches with instructions to come up with a single statement of what they really believed, and the result was the Nicene Creed as we know it today.

Naturally, this was worded in terms of fourth-century theology and knowledge, and based mainly on the contemporary interpretation of the events recorded in the Gospels. The Bible, for example, describes Jesus literally as "the Son of God", while today's knowledge of genetics tells us that a male child needs the genes from *both* parents, and specifically male ones that he can get only from his father. Does this then mean that God has genes?

You can of course take the easy way out and say that God can do anything, in which case you will sleep peacefully. Or, like me, you can wonder about it at three o'clock in the morning!

What bothers me is that God does not resort to 'unnatural' methods if He can achieve His purposes by what we can all recognize as normal, natural means. The background to Jesus' birth was a long line of descent from the 'line of David', which according to Luke's nativity story would have been through Joseph, which would mean an earthly origin for Jesus' physical body.

Jesus himself is not known to have left us any written records, so all we have are those recorded by someone else in the Gospels. Though when with his Disciples Jesus referred to his "Father in Heaven", he also spoke of "Your Heavenly Father", and when asked "How to Pray" he began his great Prayer with the words, "*Our Father*, who art in Heaven".

This hints that 'Heaven' is somewhere else than Earth, and this may mean 'outside the physical Universe'—which of course makes nonsense of Krushchev's ridiculous statement following sending Uri Gagarin into orbit: "We've been up there [Heaven] and we didn't find God."—showing only that Mr Krushchev was completely ignorant of any theology.

If we are going to resolve my dilemma, perhaps we can see Jesus as *spiritually*, and in his significance for mankind, the Son of God, but as *physically* the son of Joseph?

Tony Hills

Prayers

Jesus said, "Where two or three are gathered together in my Name, there am I in the midst of them."

O Lord, who never failest both to hear and to answer the prayer that is sincere; let not our minds be set on worldly things when we pray, nor our prayers end upon our lips, but send us forth with power to work thy will in the world; through Jesus Christ our Lord. *Amen.*

God of love, whose compassion never fails; we bring to you the sufferings of all mankind; the needs of the homeless; the cry of the prisoner; the pains of the sick and injured; the sorrow of the bereaved; the helplessness of the aged and weak. Strengthen and relieve them, Father, according to their various needs and your great mercy; for the sake of your Son, our Saviour, Jesus Christ. *Amen.*

Praise be to thee, O God, who, through thy Son Jesus Christ, hast revealed thyself to the world. Praise be to thee, O God, that the light of the glorious Gospel of Christ, who is the image of God, has shined upon them that believe. Blessed be the Lord our God, for he has visited and redeemed his people, to give light to them that sit in darkness and in the shadow of death, and to guide our feet into the way of peace. *Amen.*

† Lighten our darkness, we beseech thee, O Lord; and by thy great mercy defend us from all perils and dangers of this night; for the love of thy only Son, our Saviour, Jesus Christ. *Amen.*

O almighty God, who canst bring good out of evil, and makest even the wrath of man to turn to thy praise; teach thy children to live together in charity and peace; and grant, we beseech thee, that the nations of the world may henceforth be united in a firmer fellowship for the promotion of thy glory and the good of all mankind; through Jesus Christ our Lord. *Amen.*

A few moments' silence for your own prayers.

The Lord's Prayer

Praise the Lord, O my soul; while I live I will praise the Lord: yea, as long as I have any being, I will sing praises unto my God.

Closing Blessing

Go forth into the world in peace; be of good courage; hold fast that which is good; render to no man evil for evil; strengthen the faint-hearted; support the weak; help the afflicted; honour all men; love and serve the Lord; rejoicing in the power of the Holy Spirit.

And the blessing of God Almighty, the Father, the Son, and the Holy Spirit, be upon us, and remain with us for ever. *Amen.*

SIMPLE SERVICE, WITH HYMNS
29th December 2013

Order of Service

Welcome & Notices (David Foard)

Hymn 245 (Tune: *Wareham*)
Jesus, where'er thy people meet

Brief introduction (David E.)

Hymn 79 (Tune: *Dix*)
As with gladness men of old

First reading (David E.) Isaiah Chapter 9, Verses 2–7 *(NEB)*

Hymn 189 (Tune: *Belmont*)
Jesu, the very thought of thee

Second reading (Tony) Extract from "In Memoriam" (*Tennyson*)

Hymn 330 (Tune: *Newington*)
Thine for ever! God of love

Brief chat (Philip)

Hymn 708 (*Mission Praise;* words overleaf)
To God be the glory!

Prayers (Peter)

Hymn 165 (Tune: *St. Anne*)
O God, our help in ages past

Closing blessing (Peter)

The service will proceed without announcements. All the hymns except one (words opposite) are in *Hymns Ancient & Modern Revised*.

Thank you for coming. **Please join us in the New Vestry after the service** *for a glass of wine (alternatives available) and a mince pie.*

Please use the voting form overleaf to list your own favourite hymns for a subsequent service.

To God be the glory!

To God be the glory! Great things He hath done;
so loved He the world that He gave us His Son;
who yielded His life an atonement for sin,
and opened the life gate that all may go in.
Praise the Lord, praise the Lord!
Let the Earth hear His voice;
Praise the Lord, praise the Lord!
Let the people rejoice:
O come to the Father,
through Jesus the Son
and give Him the glory;
great things He hath done!

O perfect redemption, the purchase of blood!
To every believer the promise of God;
the vilest offender who truly believes,
that moment from Jesus a pardon receives.
Praise the Lord . . .

Great things He hath taught us, great things he hath done;
and great our rejoicing through Jesus the Son;
but purer, and higher, and greater will be
our wonder, our rapture, when Jesus we see.
Praise the Lord . . .

Frances van Alstyne (1820–1915)

Thank you all for coming, but I have had apologies from David Beal, who is still recovering from Christmas, and the Churchwardens, who have other commitments this evening. David Foard kindly agreed to step in to give the initial welcome and any notices, and to come early and help me move the keyboard into place in the Church, so my thanks to him. We are also without Laura again; she is in Cornwall taking a much needed break from a strenuous first term in full-time teaching.

My thanks as always to everyone who has helped with the planning and will be taking part; it could not be done without you all, from Robert on the keyboard and Tony reading, to everyone who asks for hymns. Especial thanks to Peter this time for selecting the readings and the prayers. Having been very busy all the autumn with Church accounting, I am most grateful to him for doing all this with no effort on my part, and secondly of course to Philip for preparing and giving the Brief Chat.

I predicted a couple of Decembers ago that we should be getting warmer weather for our next service, due at the end of March, only for snowfalls the week before and the week after. So I shall look forward only to lighter evenings and to seeing you all again then.

Your service sheets are not quite perfect, being a bit patchy on the back, but at least they have come out rather better than in September.

After our brief 'closing blessing', do please come back to the Vestry for a drink and a mince pie or two.

Isaiah 9, 2–7

The people who walked in darkness
have seen a great light:
light has dawned upon them,
    dwellers in a land as dark as death.

Thou hast increased their joy and given them great gladness;
they rejoice in thy presence as men rejoice at harvest,
or as they are glad when they share out the spoil;
    for thou hast shattered the yoke that burdened them,
      the collar that lay heavy upon their shoulders,
    the driver's goad, as on the day of Midian's defeat.

All the boots of trampling soldiers
and the garments fouled with blood
shall become a burning mass, fuel for fire.

For a boy has been born to us, a son given to us
　to bear the symbol of dominion on his shoulder;
　　and he shall be called
　　in purpose wonderful, in battle God-like,
　　Father for all time, Prince of peace.
Great shall the dominion be,
　and boundless the peace
bestowed on David's throne and on his kingdom,
to establish it and sustain it
　　with justice and righteousness
　　from now and for evermore.
The zeal of the LORD of Hosts shall do this.

From *In Memoriam* (Tennyson)

Ring out, wild bells, to the wild sky,
The flying cloud, the frosty light.
The year is dying in the night;
Ring out, wild bells, and let him die.

Ring out the old, ring in the new,
Ring, happy bells, across the snow:
The year is going, let him go;
Ring out the false, ring in the true.

Ring out the grief that saps the mind,
For those that here we see no more,
Ring out the feud of rich and poor,
Ring in redress to all mankind.

Ring out a slowly dying cause,
And ancient forms of party strife;
Ring in the nobler modes of life,
With sweeter manners, purer laws.

Ring out the want, the care, the sin,
The faithless coldness of the times;
Ring out, ring out, thy mournful rhymes,
But ring the fuller minstrel in.

Ring out false pride in place and blood,
The civic slander and the spite;
Ring in the love of truth and right,
Ring in the common love of good.

Ring out old shapes of foul disease,
Ring out the narrowing lust of gold;
Ring out the thousand wars of old,
Ring in the thousand years of peace.

Ring in the valiant man and free,
The larger heart, the kindlier hand;
Ring out the darkness of the land,
Ring in the Christ that is to be.

AN ANGLE ON FAITH ... AND *YOU*

Faith is . . . a strong or unshakeable belief in something, especially without absolute proof or evidence!

So, whilst our human relations are with each other — living *proof* — our spiritual one in a religious meaning is, as we know it, with a true but intangible *God*. So to nourish and fortify that faith, a primary channel will be through what forms of prayer and formal worship **work for us**.

Our introduction to a knowledge of God — no matter at what age — *for most*, was largely *acci*dential, or *inci*dental, but certainly providential.

I quote from an un-attributed source:–
Somewhere from inside a place of darkness
Lights a spark that kindles into flame;
Somewhere from the depths of your own being
Comes a light that draws you *on*.
Somewhere from a place that seems to have no ending
There comes a voice: *You know there's no pretending.*

To quote again—this time from Paul's Letter to the Romans (Chapter 5: 1, 2):–

Therefore, since we are justified by faith, we have peace with God through our Lord Jesus Christ, through whom we have obtained access to this Grace in which we stand, and we rejoice in the hope of the Glory of God.

Some opinions have it that, in precise terms of Dogma, Rubrics and Forms of Christian Worship, no service or person is absolutely right (*or* totally wrong!)—inevitably we acquire our own particular preferences, and often *prejudices*—but by trying continually to keep some part of our mind, and spirit, *open* to the variations contained in the *mysteries* of faith . . . that can be most helpful.

On occasions many of us probably feel like 'Doubting Thomas'—that Apostle who expressed his disbelief in Christ's Resurrection, until there was *personal proof*—because if there were *no* doubts . . . there would be no *need* for faith! (Maybe that's a subject for another time?)

So what helps us to sustain our faith in the Lord, through Jesus Christ?

Substantially developed from the teachings of the Bible, of course, but also via the learned thoughts, prayers and practical examples of others—some present and, *many*, past.

Now, one understands that St Ignatius (the one who was a co-founder of the Jesuit order) was renowned for his deep and disciplined approach to prayer, developed in his esteemed 'Spiritual Exercises' (as a means of finding God in *all* things; something touched upon in the Rector's column in January's Parish Magazine!)—based on attention, reverence and devotion, coupled with a practical commitment to works of mercy and the promotion of the Common Good.

To quote from one of his First Principles:–

All the things in this world are gifts from God,
Presented to us so that we can know God more easily,
and make a return of Love more readily.
As a result, we appreciate and use all these gifts of God . . .
. . . insofar as they help us to develop as loving persons.
But, if any of these gifts become the *centre* of our lives, *they displace God*,
and so hinder our growth toward our goal.
In everyday life, then, we must hold ourselves in *balance*
before all of these created gifts.
Insofar as we have a choice
and are not bound by some obligation,
we should not *fix* our *desires* on health or sickness, wealth or poverty,
success or failure, a long life or a short one.
For everything has the potential of calling forth in us . . .
. . . a deeper response to our life in God.
Probably our only desire and our one choice should be this:
"I want and I choose, what better leads,
to God's deepening His life in me."

Simple, sensible—but extremely hard to live up to!

Continuing now with a *Guiding Prayer* (for generosity) by St Ignatius (written in the year 1548):–

Lord, teach me to be generous.
Teach me to serve you as you deserve,
to give and not to count the cost,
to fight and not to heed the wounds,
to toil and not to seek for rest,
to labour and not to ask for reward,
save that of knowing that I do Your Will.   *Amen.*

Rounding off now with a piece extracted, with acknowledgement, from our neighbouring Pulborough Parish Magazine[1]—but which I have entitled, "Now How About *You?*" I say again: "Now how about *You?* (Please *reflect* on how the following applies to *you!*)"

Is anyone happier because you passed this way?
Does anyone remember that you spoke to them today?
The day is almost over, and its toiling time is through,
is there anyone to utter now a kindly word of you?

Can you say in parting with the day that's slipping fast
that you have helped a single person of the many you have passed,
is a single person rejoicing over what you did, or said,
does anyone whose hopes were fading now with courage look ahead?

Did you waste the day or use it, was it well or sorely spent?
Did you leave a trail of kindness, or a scar of discontent?
As you close your eyes in slumber do you think that God would say
that you have earned tomorrow by the way you lived today?

Reflect!

Philip Newman

Prayers
Opening Prayer

To Jesus, redeemer of the peoples, we lift our voices in prayer:

Lord, you are the faithful guide of those who seek you with a pure heart; you came amongst us to usher in your kingdom of peace:

O Lord, encompassed in light as with a cloak, you conquer the darkness of our night:

---

[1] This poem had been found in an old Lancastrian Parish Magazine, in which it was titled "Today and Tomorrow".

O bread eternal, you feed the hunger of your people in desert places:

You change our vessels of water into the gladdening wine of new life:

You are the true host of the marriage feast, welcoming sinners to sit at your table and share your banquet.

Lord Jesus Christ, you are the way, the truth and the life: let us not stray from you who are the way, nor distrust your promises who are the truth, nor rest in anything but you who are the life, for beyond you there is nothing to be desired, neither in heaven nor in earth. *Amen.*

A Christmas Thanksgiving

Blessed are you, Sovereign God, our light and our salvation, to you be glory and praise for ever. To dispel the darkness of our night you sent forth your Son, the firstborn of all creation, to be the Christ, the light of the world. Rejoicing in the mystery of the Word made flesh, we acclaim him Emmanuel, as all creation sings to you: Blessed be God, Father, Son and Holy Spirit.

Opportunity for private prayer:
between Christmas and Epiphany we remember especially . . .

The Church, especially in places of conflict, Church unity . . .

The revelation of Christ to those from whom his glory is hidden . . .

The Holy Land, for peace with justice, and reconciliation, and peace in the world . . .

Refugees and asylum seekers, healing the sick . . .

Homeless people, families with young children . . .

All who travel . . .

A prayer for the New Year

God and Father of our Lord Jesus Christ, whose years never fail and whose mercies are new each returning day: let the radiance of your Spirit renew our lives, warming our hearts and giving light to our minds; that we may pass the coming year in joyful obedience and firm faith; through him who is the beginning and the end, your Son, Christ our Lord, who is alive and reigns with you, in the unity of the Holy Spirit, one God, now and for ever. *Amen.*

A prayer for ourselves

Keep us in peace, O Christ our God, under the protection of your holy and venerable cross; save us from our enemies, visible and invisible, and count us worthy to glorify you with thanksgiving, with the Father and the Holy Spirit, now and for ever, world without end. *Amen.*

The Lord's Prayer

And we close by saying the Grace together.

SIMPLE SERVICE, WITH HYMNS
30th March 2014

Order of Service

Welcome & Notices (David Beal)
Hymn 166 (Tune: *Old 100th*)
All people that on Earth do dwell

Brief introduction (David E.)
Hymn 351 (Tune: *Vox dilecti*)
I heard the voice of Jesus say

First reading (Philip) Exodus Chapter 33, Verses 18–23 *(NEB)*
Hymn 452 (Tune: *In memoriam*)
There's a Friend for little children

Second reading (Laura) Matthew 18, 1–7, 10; 19, 13–15 *(NEB)*
Hymn 210 (Tune: *Petra*)
Rock of ages, cleft for me

Brief chat (Tony)
Hymn 243 (Tune: *Harewood*)
Christ is our Corner-stone

Prayers (Peter)
Hymn 579 (Tune: *Thaxted*)
I vow to thee, my country

Closing blessing (David E.)

The service will proceed without announcements. All the hymns are in *Hymns Ancient & Modern Revised*.

Thank you for coming. **Please join us in the New Vestry after the service** *for a glass of wine (alternatives available).*

Please use the voting form opposite to list your own favourite hymns for a subsequent service.

Thank you all for coming. Remembering the snow we have had at this time of the year, I was careful in December not to predict weather any warmer for this service at the end of March, so it's nice that we do have a very pleasant weekend to go with the lighter evenings.

We are pleased to have David Beal with us this evening, and to have Laura involved again with preparing the service [and doing a reading].

I was very busy all the autumn with Church accounting, and the same pertains this month after a break tackling various other urgent tasks, so my thanks as always to everyone who has helped with the planning, and especially to Tony for doing the talk, leaving me just this introduction and the closing blessing. Unlike a normal service, where hymns may be chosen to go with the readings set for the day, we start with the hymns and then try to think of readings that will go with them. We thought we'd have the story of Moses being hidden in a cleft in the rocks to go with *Rock of Ages*, and weren't quite sure where to find it, but I opened my copy of the Old Testament in what I thought was about the right section, and there it was. For our other readings we went for ones about children for Mothering Sunday, and there's a hymn for children too.

Thanks as always to Robert on the keyboard and the select few who ask for hymns. I imagined when we started that we'd get lots and lots of such requests, but the reverse has turned out to be the case. So if you do fill in one of those forms there's a very good chance of your hymns being selected.

After our brief 'closing blessing', do please come back to the Vestry as usual for a glass of wine or apple juice.

Exodus 33, 18–23

And Moses prayed, "Show me thy glory." The LORD answered, "I will make all my goodness pass before you, and I will pronounce in your hearing the Name JEHOVAH. I will be gracious to whom I will be gracious, and I will have compassion on whom I will have compassion."

But he added, "My face you cannot see, for no mortal man may see me and live." The LORD said, "Here is a place beside me. Take your stand on the rock and when my glory passes by, I will put you in a crevice of the rock and cover you with my hand until I have passed by. Then I will take away my hand, and you shall see my back, but my face shall not be seen."

Matthew 18, 1–7; 10

At that time the disciples came to Jesus and asked, "Who is the greatest in the kingdom of Heaven?" He called a child, set him in front of them, and said, "I tell you this: unless you turn round and become like children, you will never enter the kingdom of Heaven. Let a man humble himself till he is like this child, and he will be the greatest in the kingdom of Heaven. Whoever receives one such child in my name receives me. But if a man is a cause of stumbling to one of these little ones who have faith in me, it would be better for him to have a millstone hung round his neck and be drowned in the depths of the sea. Alas for the world that such causes of stumbling arise! Come they must, but woe betide the man through whom they come!

"Never despise one of these little ones; I tell you, they have their guardian angels in heaven, who look continually on the face of my heavenly Father."

Matthew 19, 13–15

They brought children for him to lay his hands on them with prayer. The disciples scolded them for it, but Jesus said to them, "Let the children come to me; do not try to stop them; for the kingdom of Heaven belongs to such as these." And he laid his hands on the children, and went his way.

WHAT SHOULD WE BELIEVE ?

When the Roman Church is considering whether a person can be recognised as a 'Saint', a form of Court is established to consider the 'pros and cons' of the case and the officer who prepares the case against the elevation is known, I believe, as the Devil's Advocate. I appear to be playing that part in these 'Brief Chats', as I seem to be thinking about difficult areas; that is, areas which cause *me* some concern.

This evening I want to explore the reported actions and statements of Jesus. As far as we know, Jesus did not leave any 'Gospel' himself; we don't even know if he could write, although we might assume that he could as a good Jewish boy who would read in the synagogue. We don't even really know if he considered himself uniquely as the 'Son of God'. He spoke of '*his* heavenly Father', but he also referred to '*the* Father' and even started that great prayer, "*Our* Father, who art in Heaven" when asked by the 'Apostles' how they should pray.

This highlights a point which has rather worried me for some time, which is: What does the description 'The Son of God' mean? It is stated in the Nicene Creed, which we all publicly profess at every Communion service, as: "He was incarnate by the Holy Ghost of the Virgin Mary and was made Man . . . " As I understand the process in Nature, the female egg will need to be fertilized by the introduction of male sperm. This will include the necessary chromosomes to cause the egg to develop into a male child. Has God got chromosomes?

Scientific experimentation has shown that eggs could be activated under laboratory conditions, but initially this would only produce female offspring (remember Dolly the sheep), although I think that a process was eventually perfected to produce a male offspring. Maybe that's how God achieved the Virgin Birth; if we believe what we say, he had to somehow, but how does that make God 'our' father? I play with words but nevertheless I am still uncomfortable about it.

I suppose one can think of God as 'our Father' as He was the Great Creator of the Universe, and I don't mean modelling a human figure out of clay and breathing life into it; rather, in starting the Universe about 13 billion years ago as a multitude of subatomic particles but with the laws already in place ($E=mc^2$) to allow the Universe as we know it today, including ourselves, to evolve. You will note that I am an 'evolutionist' and a 'creationist', although not the literal one that many people still manage to remain, claiming that it was all done in six days in spite of all the evidence against.

I believe that those old boys, not so long ago, perhaps only six or eight thousand years, sat out around their camp fires in the deserts and looked at the fixed stars, and the few that wandered about which we now know to be the planets, and wondered where all this *stuff* (including themselves) came from, and from the information they had they didn't come up with a bad answer.

Getting back to the actions and words of Jesus, they are of course recorded in the Gospels by the Evangelists we know as Matthew, Mark, Luke and John. John stands out well with his wonderful opening: "In the beginning was the Word", which one might describe as 'speculative theology'. Luke, however, begins his Gospel with the statement that he used information received by "eyewitnesses" to the events, which also tells us that he (Luke) did not witness the events himself, thereby condemning his Gospel to the status of 'hearsay' evidence, which as a matter of interest is not accepted as evidence under English Law.

This of course does not necessarily mean that they are not true, rather that our confidence in them might be somewhat lessened. Perhaps we should not necessarily parade them as the 'absolute word of God' or even as exactly what Jesus did say, even in those wonderful words of consecration in the Mass. Sadly, in history, we have tortured and put to death in the cruellest ways possible many thousands of our fellow human beings, because, in words from *The King and I*, they would not believe "that what we do not know is so"!

Should I see a stake being set up in our Churchyard, I think I might keep my head down for a bit . . .

Tony Hills

Prayers

Father, we thank you for the family of the Church. Thank you for those who are true mothers within our Christian family. May they know your blessing and strength as they care for others. *Amen.*

Thank you, Lord, for our mothers. We remember today their loving care, and their ceaseless love for us. May we show them by our gifts, our words and our actions that we love them and care about them too. *Amen.*

God of mercy and love, let us serve you in our world. Loving Lord, let us not stand aside and tolerate the torment and victimization of the vulnerable. Give us strength to act and challenge hatred, and instead bring your justice and mercy. In your name we humbly ask that we may be a channel for your peace and love. *Amen.*

A few moments' silence for your own prayers.

In penitence and faith let us make our prayer to the Father and ask for his mercy and grace.

For your holy people, that they may triumph over evil and grow in grace, **Lord, in your mercy, *Hear our prayer.***

For candidates for baptism and confirmation, that they may live by every word that proceeds from your mouth,
Lord, in your mercy, *Hear our prayer.*

For the leaders of the nations, that you will guide them in the ways of mercy and truth, **Lord, in your mercy, *Hear our prayer.***

For the needy, that they may not be forgotten, nor the hope of the poor be taken away, **Lord, in your mercy, *Hear our prayer.***

For the sick in body, mind and spirit, that they may know your power to heal, **Lord, in your mercy, *Hear our prayer.***

For the poor in spirit, that they may inherit the kingdom of heaven and see you face to face, **Lord, in your mercy, *Hear our prayer.***

The Lord's Prayer

Praise the Lord, O my soul; while I live I will praise the Lord: yea, as long as I have any being, I will sing praises unto my God.

Closing Blessing

May the blessing of almighty God rest upon us and upon all our work; may he give us light to guide us, courage to support us, and love to unite us, now and evermore. *Amen.*

280

SIMPLE SERVICE, WITH HYMNS
29th June 2014

Order of Service

Welcome & Notices (David F.)

Hymn 192 (Tune: *St Peter*)
How sweet the name of Jesus sounds

Brief introduction (David E.)

Hymn 506 (Tune: *Old 104th*)
Disposer supreme, and Judge of the Earth

First reading (Tony) Matthew Chapter 16, Verses 13–28 *(NEB)*

Hymn 487 (Tune: *Melita*)
Eternal Father, strong to save

Second reading (Philip) Matthew Chapter 6, Verses 1–18 *(NEB)*

Hymn 51 (*Mission Praise;* words on page 10. Tune: *Slane*)
Be Thou my vision

Brief chat (David E.)

Hymn 311 (Tune: *Mannheim*)
Lead us, heavenly Father, lead us

Prayers (Peter)

Hymn 372 (Tune: *St Denio*)
Immortal, invisible, God only wise

Closing blessing (David E.)

The service will proceed without announcements. All the hymns except one (words opposite) are in *Hymns Ancient & Modern Revised.*

Thank you for coming. **Please join us in the New Vestry after the service** *for a glass of wine (alternatives available).*

Please use the voting form overleaf to list your own favourite hymns for a subsequent service.

Thank you all for coming to the first of our summer evening services. David Beal and Diane are attending the service at Horsham to mark the retirement of Archdeacon Roger Coombes, so are unable to be with us, but I am pleased to say that we do have Pam. David Foard has kindly agreed to do the Welcome & Notices.

Laura helped us choose the hymns but has a family activity today: my thanks as always to everyone who has helped with the planning. We did check last week's notice sheet to make sure that the readings we selected were not the same as those for this morning, but that was before today's morning readings were adjusted for St Peter and St Paul. However, our first reading does include quite a few more verses.

It's a year since I last did the talk, as Tony has done two and Philip one since last June, for which I am very grateful. This talk, whoever gives it, does not pretend to be a sermon; that's why we call it a brief chat. We are not preaching; far from it, in fact. We are required to love God with all our mind, so we present a few thoughts about what we hope are relevant matters, and probably pose more questions than we answer. All views expressed are our own personal, often unorthodox, opinions. We don't inform David Beal in advance what we are planning to say but we do share it with each other. Fifty years ago I was working in Harlow and at evening services at the Church in the town centre a series of talks were given by lay members of the congregation, and that gave me the idea for doing something similar here at West Chiltington.

Thanks as always to Robert on the keyboard and to our patrons who ask for hymns. We have actually had enough this time for August as well as this evening, but please do keep the requests coming in.

After our 'closing blessing', you are all invited to adjourn with us to the Vestry as usual for a glass of wine or apple juice.

Matthew 16, 13–28

When he came to the territory of Caesarea Philippi, Jesus asked his disciples, "Who do men say that I, the Son of Man, am?" They answered, "Some say John the Baptist, others Elijah, others Jeremiah, or one of the prophets."

"And you," he asked, "who do you say I am?"

Simon Peter answered: "You are the Messiah, the Son of the living God."

Then Jesus said: "Simon son of Jonah, you are favoured indeed! You did not learn that from mortal man; it was revealed to you by my heavenly Father. And I say this to you: You are Peter, the Rock; and on this rock I will build my church, and the gates of death shall never close upon it. I will give you the keys of the kingdom of Heaven; what you forbid on earth shall be forbidden in heaven, and what you allow on earth shall be allowed in heaven."

He then gave his disciples strict orders not to tell anyone that he was the Messiah.

From that time Jesus began to make it clear to his disciples that he had to go to Jerusalem, and there to suffer much from the elders, chief priests and lawyers; to be put to death and to be raised again on the third day. At this Peter took him by the arm and began to rebuke him: "Heaven forbid!" he said. "No, Lord, this shall never happen to you."

Then Jesus turned and said to Peter, "Away with you, Satan; you are a stumbling-block to me. You think as men think, not as God thinks."

Jesus then said to his disciples, "If anyone wishes to be a follower of mine, he must leave self behind; he must take up his cross and come with me. Whoever cares for his own safety is lost; but if a man will let himself be lost for my sake, he will find his true self. For the Son of Man is to come in the glory of his Father with his angels, and then he will give each man the due reward for what he has done. I tell you this: there are some standing here who will not taste death before they have seen the Son of Man coming in his kingdom."

Matthew 6, 1–18

[Jesus continued:–] "Be careful not to make a show of your religion before men; if you do, no reward awaits you in your Father's house in heaven.

"Thus, when you do some act of charity, do not announce it with a flourish of trumpets, as the hypocrites do in synagogue and in the streets to win admiration from men. I tell you this: they have their reward already. No; when you do some act of charity, do not let your left hand know what your right is doing; your good deed must be secret, and your Father who sees what is done in secret will reward you openly.

"Again, when you pray, do not be like the hypocrites; they love to say their prayers standing up in synagogue and at the street-corners, for everyone to see them. I tell you this: they have their reward already. But when you pray, go into a room by yourself, shut the door, and pray to your Father who is there in the secret place; and your Father who sees what is secret will reward you openly.

"In your prayers do not go babbling on like the heathen, who imagine that the more they say the more likely they are to be heard. Do not imitate them. Your Father knows what your needs are before you ask him.

"This is how you should pray:–
'Our Father in heaven,
Thy name be hallowed;
Thy kingdom come,
Thy will be done,
On earth as in heaven.
Give us today our bread for the morrow.
Forgive us the wrong we have done,
As we have forgiven those who have wronged us.
And do not bring us to the test,
But save us from the evil one.'

"For if you forgive others the wrongs they have done, your heavenly Father will also forgive you; but if you do not forgive others, then the wrongs you have done will not be forgiven by your Father.

"So too when you fast, do not look gloomy like the hypocrites: they make their faces unsightly so that other people may see that they are fasting. I tell you this: they have their reward already. But when you fast, anoint your head and wash your face, so that men may not see that you are fasting, but only your Father who is in the secret place; and your Father who sees what is secret will give you your reward."

RELIGION AND IMMORTALITY

Three years ago we were all considering the pros and cons of having women bishops as well as women priests. We had discussions in the PCC and a special meeting of the Deanery Synod at which we were acquainted with the arguments on both sides of the debate and asked to select which one on each side we found the most compelling. I could not help thinking that many of the arguments *against* actually made a good case *for* . . .

But the voting in the General Synod to allow the change fell short of achieving the necessary majority by a small margin. As I understand it, there will be another vote on the topic this year, rather like the Lisbon Treaty a few years ago, when countries that had voted No were sent back to the polls until they voted Yes. It seemed to me after the 2011 result that if we were to pray for guidance in our deliberations we should be ready to be led in a direction in which we had not expected to be travelling.

I mention this now because there is a possible argument against which doesn't seem to have been aired, and might not even have been thought of. That is that women bishops, if they be accepted and appointed, will most definitely be the 'new boys' (if that's not a contradiction in terms) in the Church, anxious not to rock the boat or step out of line with regard to our long traditions of worship and liturgy. Which would be all very well if the Church today were not in desperate need of *rebels*, people who will kindly and gently but firmly draw attention to the Emperor's non-existent clothing. It is only a 'possible' argument because there could of course be appointed a woman Bishop who did fulfil that function and followed in the footsteps of John Robinson and others of the Sixties.

At present even male clergy in the Church of England are required to swear assent to the Thirty-Nine Articles before they can be inducted into a living, so only the laity are free to say what they think about Christian dogma; yet even we are invited, week on week, to "affirm our faith in the words of the Creed". I offered some suggestions a few years ago as to why so many people do not come to Church, and on a further occasion why other people *do* come, but I have been wondering more recently whether we come *because of* the services, or *despite* the services! This feeling was reinforced some weeks ago when someone I knew arrived for what she thought would be the Family Service and was very disappointed that it was the wrong week for it; she didn't find the 10 o'clock inspiring.

At the 8 o'clock, which I settled on a decade or two ago as the service I disliked least, we start with exchanging greetings and follow with what used to be known as the Collect for Purity. No problem with that, or with the reading of Jesus' Summary of the Law, after which it is only natural to confess that we haven't always lived up to this. Sometimes we are first exhorted to 'call to mind our shortcomings', which isn't always easy, not least because quite possibly our most serious errors are ones we are may not have been aware of. Alternatively, we may already have called them to mind in our own prayer before the service, if we can find a quiet time between greeting friends and the bell being rung. The confession prayer is worded in very general terms to be applicable to all of us, and we say "we are heartily sorry and repent of all our sins". After which God (who forgives all who truly repent) is requested to pardon us and keep us "in life eternal". There is a problem here: 'repent' nowadays is synonymous with being 'heartily sorry', but in days gone by it also meant not doing the same sort of things again, which is rather different.

We are spared the Gloria during Advent and Lent; it starts well, and ends well, but addressing Jesus as the "Lamb of God that takes away the sins of the world" is lifted from the words of John the Baptist as recorded in John's Gospel, and reflects the writer's own theological speculations.

Readings, a Psalm [read] and a well-constructed, interesting sermon follow the Creed (already mentioned). Then we turn to prayer for a solid thirteen minutes (I timed it last Sunday). Nothing wrong with the words or the sentiments of the Prayer for the Church, and it can be inspiring, but one's mind can wander on account of their familiarity, and it is too easy to think we have 'done our bit' by asking God to do this, that or the other and forget that God has to act by means of human agents. David Beal has said that all our actions should be underpinned with prayer, but one could also suggest that our prayers should be underpinned with action. It took the encouragement of visiting Stephen Turrell to nudge us (with David's approval) into sending some assistance to our fellow countrymen affected by the winter flooding in addition to 'remembering them in our prayers'.

Jesus gave us a template for prayer and so we include it near the end. Didn't he also say, "Do not go babbling on like the heathen, who imagine that the more they say the more likely they are to be heard"? Finally, after asking the "Lamb of God that takes away the sins of the world" to "have mercy on us" we have what I rather flippantly refer to as the Prayer of Grovelling Access, in which we claim to be worthy of nothing, but in fact request very special treatment on account of God's "great mercies". I can't help contrasting that with Jesus' saying "Why do you keep calling me 'Lord, Lord'—and never do what I tell you?"

The Prayer of Consecration prepares us for Communion, reminding us of Jesus sharing bread and wine with his Disciples for the last time, and asking them to continue the practice in remembrance of him, recorded in Matthew's, Mark's and Luke's Gospels, but not actually in John's. But to this sharing has been added the concept of Jesus' crucifixion as a sacrifice to atone for sin from pre-Christian Jewish theology, making this part of the service into what might uncharitably be described as a magical ritual for having our sins forgiven, *so that we can go to Heaven when we die.*

I was reading recently what a famous American psychologist, William James,[1] had to say in a Postscript to his classic work, *The Varieties of Religious Experience*, published in 1902.[2] In his opinion:–

Religion, in fact, for the great majority of our own race means immortality, and nothing else. God is the producer of immortality, and whoever has doubts of immortality is written down as an atheist without further trial. I have said nothing in my lectures about immortality or the belief therein, for me it seems a secondary point.

The link between religion and immortality is shown clearly in the preamble to the Parable of the Good Samaritan:–

"On one occasion a lawyer came forward to put this test question to him: 'Master, *what must I do to inherit eternal life?*'" Jesus asked him what was written in the Law and he replied, "'Love the Lord your God with all your

---

[1] William James is also mentioned on page 189 for his "Higamous, hogamus" couplet.
[2] p.406. Quoted by Michael Tymn in a Letter to the Editor of the *Journal of the Society for Psychical Research, Vol.77.4* (October 2013), p.265.

heart, with all your soul, with all your strength, and with all your mind; and your neighbour as yourself.' 'That is the right answer,' said Jesus, 'do that *and you will live.*'" But helping the man set upon by thieves is rather different from accepting Jesus' "blood of the new covenant, which is shed for you and for many for the forgiveness of sins". In fact the parable doesn't mention sins at all.

Jesus denounced the rulers of the Church who exploited the poor, but he didn't call his Disciples sinners. They were his 'friends', and though he often had to correct their worldly attitudes he is not recorded as asking them to repent. Could not we, the people of his Church, move on from regarding ourselves as 'miserable sinners' to seeing ourselves, perhaps, more as 'unprofitable servants'?

We need the Communion service; it is good to come to the Altar to share the bread and wine and in doing so to feel closer to God; hence the term Communion. But could not the prayers leading up to this central sacrament dispense with the theological theory of the 'redemptive' aspect of Jesus' "full, perfect and sufficient sacrifice, oblation and satisfaction for the sins of the whole world", which is why it is also termed Eucharist (which means thanksgiving), and instead be made more commemorative of Jesus' whole life, and directed to inspiring us to obey his commands as to how to live and to work in his service? As indeed is included in our final prayer, with its splendid words, "Send us out in the power of thy Spirit to live and work to thy praise and glory." Surely that is more what coming to Church is all about!

While working on this book I read again *Objections to Christian Belief*, recommended in the footnote on page 200. As mentioned, I had attended three of these four lectures in January 1963, as they were intended for all members of the University, and subsequently published for the benefit of lay people in general. Under "Intellectual Objections" J. S. Bezzant comments (p.92) that "the secular outlook of uneducated and unreflective people often makes them feel, when they hear the talk of life after death, that they are being put off their rights in this world by cheques drawn on the bank of heaven, the solvency of which they greatly doubt. . . . So far as I know, if immortality were or should become demonstrable no established fact of science would require revision."

Also relevant, I think, is ongoing work reported by Robb Tilley in the *Australian Journal of Parapsychology* (2002, pp.127–160) on "Poltergeist Disturbances and Hauntings Brought to a Lasting Successful Conclusion" in conjunction with spiritualists and the "spirits (non-physical beings)" said to assist them, relieving the distress these manifestations cause those affected by them to the extent that the Australian Institute of Parapsychological Research, under whose auspices the work was done, has achieved charitable status. *DJE*

Prayers

As we approach the hundredth anniversary of the start of the First World War, and as we recently marked the seventieth anniversary of D-Day, we remember all who have fallen in conflict:–

O God of truth and justice, we hold before you those men and women who died in active service in two World Wars and in later conflicts, and those who are still dying, in Afghanistan and elsewhere. We honour their courage and cherish their memory. We pray that future generations of young people will not be called upon to lay down their lives in armed conflict. Lord, we put our faith in your future; for you are the source of life and hope, now and for ever.
Amen.

A prayer for St Peter and St Paul, the two greatest leaders of the early Church, whose feast falls today:–

Father in heaven, the light of your revelation brought Peter and Paul the gift of faith in Jesus your Son. Through their prayers may we always give thanks for your life given us in Christ Jesus, and for having been enriched by him in all knowledge and love. Through our Lord Jesus Christ, your Son, who lives and reigns with you in the unity of the Holy Spirit, one God, for ever and ever.
Amen.

A few moments' silence for your own prayers.

Lord, you made of Simon Peter, the fisherman, a fisher of human souls: send new preachers in our time so that the multitudes may hear the word. We pray for all who work to spread your word, for those who lead the Church in the world, Archbishop Justin and Pope Francis, and in this village.
Lord, in your mercy, *Hear our prayer.*

Lord, you sent your apostle Paul to preach the Gospel to those who did not know the good news: send your word to all peoples. Strengthen us in studying your word, and in putting into practice your teaching, so that by our lives and examples we may show your love in the world.
Lord, in your mercy, *Hear our prayer.*

The Lord's Prayer

May the Lord bless us, protect us from all evil and bring us to everlasting life.
Amen.

Closing Blessing

The power of the Father, the wisdom of the Son, the love of the Holy Spirit, keep, teach, and guide us for ever.
Amen.

SIMPLE SERVICE, WITH HYMNS

31st August 2014

Order of Service

Welcome, Notices & Brief introduction (David E.)

Hymn 336 (Tune: *Song 34*)
Forth in thy name, O Lord, I go

First reading (David E.) From the Introductory Notice of the Author
of *The Pilgrim's Progress*

Hymn 293 (Tune: *Monks Gate*)
Who would true valour see

Second reading (Philip) Acts, Chapter 16, Verses 11–40 *(NEB)*

Hymn 329 (Tune: *Hereford*)
O thou who camest from above

Third reading (Tony) Extracts from the last chapter of
Part II of *The Pilgrim's Progress*

Hymn 289 (Tune: *Kocher*)
O happy band of pilgrims

Brief chat (David E.)

Hymn 400 (Tune: *St Helen*)
Lord, enthroned in heavenly splendour

Prayers (Peter)

Hymn 296 (Tune: *Cwm Rhondda*)
Guide me, O thou great Redeemer

Closing blessing (Peter)

The service will proceed without announcements. All the hymns are in *Hymns Ancient & Modern Revised.*

Thank you for coming. **Please join us in the New Vestry after the service** *for a glass of wine (alternatives available).*

Please use the voting form opposite to list your own favourite hymns for a subsequent service.

Thank you all for coming to this, the second of our summer evening services. I am combining my usual Introduction with the Welcome & Notices, not only because David Beal is on holiday until late this evening but also because this enables us to fit in a third reading.

As mentioned in the Magazine, we are commemorating John Bunyan this year, although his day was in fact yesterday and we could therefore have waited until 2015. We have picked out some details of the story of his life and a couple of brief extracts from *The Pilgrim's Progress*,[1] but Laura suggested we also had a biblical reading, telling a story that had a parallel with an incident in Bunyan's life.

To compensate for the readings, which are a little longer than usual, I have made my 'Chat' really brief this time. It will be my last until next summer, as Philip has got something all ready for November, when we have been moved forward to the **fourth** Sunday, to accommodate a special Advent Carol Service on 30th at which Bishop Mark will be present, and Tony has been promised the slot in March.

Thanks as always to Robert on the keyboard and to our patrons who ask for hymns, and to everyone who has helped plan the service and/or will be taking part in it.

After our 'closing blessing', you are all invited to adjourn with us to the Vestry as usual for a glass of wine or apple juice, plus a sausage roll or two which Pam has kindly said she would bring us.

FROM "AN INTRODUCTORY NOTICE OF THE AUTHOR"[2]

Born at Elstow in Bedfordshire in 1628, of parents who belonged to the humbler walks of life, [John Bunyan] received little early education worthy of the name; but grew up in the ignorance which was then, and till quite recently, common to his class. At an early age he learned the trade of tinker, and by that occupation earned his livelihood for a few years. Up to the time of his first marriage he lived, if not a desperately profligate, yet a thoroughly Godless and openly wicked life. And though the character and conversation of his wife exerted a restraining influence, and awoke in him some desire for reformation, no real, and but little apparent, change took place until some time afterwards, when he became the subject of converting grace. The deep experiences through which he had passed in connection with this change, combined with his natural gifts, qualified him for profitably addressing others; and he very soon began, in an irregular way at first, to exercise the ministry, which ultimately became his sole occupation, and in which he obtained to a proficiency unsurpassed by any preacher of his time. His preaching, and

[1] Our copy was given to my grandmother for Christmas in 1889, when she was seven.
[2] by Revd William Landels, D.D. (in 2nd Edition, London: S. W. Partridge & Co.)

consequent absence from the parish church, attracted the notice of the ecclesiastical authorities of the neighbourhood, at whose instigation he was thrown into prison for twelve years, where he tagged laces to support his wife and blind child, and conceived and wrote the wonderful allegory by which he has ranked himself for ever among the peers of the intellectual world, and secured for himself an ever-widening and undying fame.

His crime, as we have intimated, was that of absenting himself from the Established Church, and holding meetings where he preached the gospel, and conducted worship in a manner which appeared to him more in accordance than the established service with New Testament principles—one of the worst crimes, in the estimation of the authorities, of which a man could be guilty. On the warrant of a Justice he was apprehended at a meeting in Sansell, and, no bail being found, was thrown into prison to await his trial, which took place seven weeks afterwards. His indictment set forth that "John Bunyan of the town of Bedford, labourer, hath devilishly and perniciously abstained from coming to church to hear Divine service, and is a common upholder of several unlawful meetings and conventicles, to the great disturbance and distraction of the good subjects of this kingdom, contrary to the laws of our sovereign lord the king." On this indictment, without any examination of witnesses, he was found guilty.

Justice Keeling, in a savage tone strangely unbecoming in a judge passing sentence, said, "Hear your judgment: you must be had back to prison, and there lie for three months following. And at three months' end, if you do not submit to go to church to hear Divine service, and leave your preaching, you must be banished from the realm. . . . Jailor, take him away." Bunyan's reply was as worthy of his Christian character, as the judge's manner was unworthy of his exalted office. All that he had to say in answer to such brutal browbeating was, "If I was out of prison today, I would preach again tomorrow, by the help of God!"

His case seems to have given some trouble to the Justices. He was had up before them repeatedly, and always remanded. They were either unwilling or afraid to carry out Justice Keeling's threat of banishment. And as their prisoner would not promise to change his course, they kept him where he was. His friends [and his wife] interceded for him . . . but all their efforts were in vain. The one condition on which his release could be granted was the condition with which the prisoner would not comply.

Without question Bunyan's imprisonment was made conducive for the furtherance of the gospel. The Providence which controls the wrath of man, and makes it contribute to its own purposes, so overruled the malice of his persecutors, as to make it serve the cause which they sought to destroy. Not only may we see the Divine hand, in the fact that Bunyan's imprisonment afforded him leisure for the composition of those works which have made his name immortal; but an overruling Providence is specially seen, in some of the circumstances which facilitated his work. Cruelties such as were perpetrated in other prisons would probably have shortened his days, or at least have rendered writing and study impossible; but in the gaol at Bedford where he was confined, though the place was loathsome in the extreme, the jailor treated the prisoners with such humanity that he incurred the displeasure of the Justices. Bunyan was allowed to visit his family occasionally, and it was on one of his visits that the circumstance occurred which most people would consider peculiarly providential. A neighbouring priest heard of his absence from prison, and immediately despatched a messenger that he might bear witness against the jailor. Meanwhile Bunyan, feeling uneasy at home, had returned to prison sooner than was intended, so that when the messenger demanded, "Are all the prisoners safe?" the jailor could answer "Yes." "Is John Bunyan safe?" "Yes." Bunyan, on being called, appeared; and, said the jailor afterwards, "You may go out when you will, for you know much better when to return than I can tell you." Thus were his health and life preserved, and the man who was forbidden to speak to a few assembled in a peasant's cottage, furnished with facilities for writing a book by which he speaks to millions in every land, and through all succeeding generations; while the men who sought to silence him have been all but forgotten. So do the enemies of the gospel frustrate their own schemes. So does the right live on, emerging into ever-increasing splendour, while the wrong sinks into merited oblivion.

Acts 16, 11–40

So we sailed from Troas and made a straight run to Samothrace, the next day to Neapolis, and from there to Philippi, a city of the first rank in that district of Macedonia, and a Roman colony. Here we stayed for some days, and on the Sabbath day we went outside the city gate by the river-side, where we thought there would be a place of prayer, and sat down and talked to the women who had gathered there. One of them, named Lydia, a dealer in purple fabric from the city of Thyatira, who was a worshipper of God, was listening, and the Lord opened her heart to respond to what Paul said. She was baptized, and her household with her, and then she said to us, "If you have judged me to be a believer in the Lord, I beg you to come and stay in my house." And she insisted on our going.

Once, when we were on our way to the place of prayer, we met a slave-girl who was possessed by an oracular spirit and brought large profits to her owners by telling fortunes. She followed Paul and the rest of us, shouting, "These men are servants of the Supreme God, and are declaring to you a way of salvation!"

She did this day after day, until Paul could bear it no longer. Rounding on the spirit he said, "I command you in the name of Jesus Christ to come out of her," and it went out there and then.

When the girl's owners saw that their hope of gain had gone, they seized Paul and Silas and dragged them to the city authorities in the main square; and bringing them before the magistrates, they said, "These men are causing a disturbance in our city; they are Jews; they are advocating customs which it is illegal for us Romans to adopt and follow."

The mob joined in the attack; and the magistrates tore off the prisoners' clothes and ordered them to be flogged. After giving them a severe beating they flung them into prison and ordered the jailer to keep them under close guard. In view of these orders, he put them in the inner prison and secured their feet in the stocks.

About midnight Paul and Silas, at their prayers, were singing praises to God, and the other prisoners were listening, when suddenly there was such a violent earthquake that the foundations of the jail were shaken; all the doors burst open and all the prisoners found their fetters unfastened. The jailer woke up to see the prison doors wide open, and assuming that the prisoners had escaped, drew his sword intending to kill himself. But Paul shouted, "Do yourself no harm; we are all here!" The jailer called for lights, rushed in and threw himself down before Paul and Silas, trembling with fear. He then escorted them out and said, "Masters, what must I do to be saved?"

They said, "Put your trust in the Lord Jesus, and you will be saved, you and your household."

Then they spoke the word of the Lord to him and to everyone in his house. At that late hour of the night he took them and washed their wounds; and immediately afterwards he and his whole family were baptized. He brought them into his house, set out a meal, and rejoiced with his whole household in his new-found faith in God.

When daylight came the magistrates sent their officers with instructions to release the men. The jailer reported the message to Paul: "The magistrates have sent word that you are to be released. So now you may go free, and blessings on your journey."

But Paul said to the officers: "They gave us a public flogging, though we are Roman citizens and have not been found guilty; they threw us into prison, and are they now to smuggle us out privately? No indeed! Let them come in person and escort us out."

The officers reported his words. The magistrates were alarmed to hear that they were Roman citizens, and came and apologized to them. Then they escorted them out and requested them to go away from the city. On leaving the prison, they went to Lydia's house, where they met their fellow-Christians, and spoke words of encouragement to them; then they departed.

Two brief extracts from Part II of *The Pilgrim's Progress*

We start with part of a conversation between Mr Great-heart and Mr Valiant-for-truth (p.224):–

G-h. Were your Father and mother willing that you should become a pilgrim?

V-f-t. Oh no! They said it was an idle life; and if I myself were not inclined to sloth and laziness, I would never countenance a pilgrim's condition. They told me it was a dangerous way; yea, the most dangerous way in the world, said they, is that which the pilgrims go.

G-h. Did they show wherein this way is so dangerous?

V-f-t. They told me of the Slough of Despond, where Christian was well nigh smothered. They told me that there were archers standing ready in Beelzebub's Castle, to shoot them that should knock at the wicket-gate for entrance. They told me also of the wood, and dark mountains; of the hill Difficulty; of the lions; and also of the three giants, Bloody-man, Maul and Slay-good. They said, moreover, that there was a foul fiend haunted the Valley of Humiliation, and that Christian was by him almost bereft of life. Besides, said they, you must go over the valley of the Shadow of Death, where the hobgoblins are; where the light is darkness; where the way is full of snares, pits, traps and gins. They told me also of Giant Despair; of Doubting Castle, and of the ruin that the pilgrims met with there. Further, they said I must go over the Enchanted Ground, which was dangerous. And that, after all this, I should find a river, over which I should find no bridge, and that the river did lie betwixt me and the Celestial Country. They also told me that this way was full of deceivers, and of persons that lay in wait there, to turn good men out of the path.

G-h. And did none of these things discourage you? (p.226)

V-f-t. No; they seemed but as many nothings to me. I still believed what Mr Tell-true had said, and that carried me beyond them all.

We continue with Mr Valiant-for-truth's crossing of the river (pp.235–6):–

After this it was noised abroad that Mr Valiant-for-truth was taken with a summons by the same post as the other; and had this for a token that the summons was true, "That his pitcher was broken at the fountain". When he understood it, he called for his friends, and told them of it. Then, said he, I am going to my Father's; and though with great difficulty I am got hither, yet now I do not repent me of all the trouble I have been at to arrive where I am. My sword I give to him that shall succeed me in my pilgrimage, and my courage and skill to him that can get it. My marks and scars I carry with me, to be a witness for me, that I have fought his battles who will now be my rewarder. When the day that he must go hence was come, many accompanied him to the river side, into which as he went he said, "Death, where is thy sting?" And as he went down deeper, he said, "Grave, where is thy victory?" *So he passed over, and all the trumpets sounded for him on the other side.*

HOW CAN THE CHURCH TACKLE OUR FALLING NUMBERS ?

David Beal opened the PCC meeting on 8th July with some disturbing statistics reported to the Deanery Synod. Apparently forty per cent of our current stipendiary clergy are due to retire within the next ten years, while ordinations are down by ten per cent. Couple fewer clergy with the tendency of parishes sharing an incumbent to dwindle in numbers and a decline seems inevitable. Now note that in 1980 the average Anglican was 41 years old, but in 2011 the average age was 61, compared with 41 and 45 for the total population, and it is clear that decline has been creeping up on us for a generation. Worse still are the statistics for the youth of today: among all churches, 39% have *no members at all* under the age of 11; 49% none aged between 11 and 15, and 59% none aged from 15–19.

So it is not exactly surprising that women priests, and now bishops, are being made more welcome, or that our Diocesan Bishop is holding a residential Conference over four days next week in Canterbury, for all the clergy in his Diocese, to decide what to do about all this.

How radical are the suggestions going to be, I wonder? Will they start from the premiss that all our Church's doctrine is correct, and our task is just to find better ways of putting it over—with more Alpha courses and perhaps some Beta and Gamma ones to follow? If so, I for one will be more than a little disappointed, having commented in a piece in our May 2010 magazine that "it would be no bad idea if we were . . . to take the whole edifice of our Christian belief system apart, 'brick by brick', examine each one individually, and then reassemble them in a slightly but fundamentally different way".[1]

We would like more people to come to Church, or to see themselves as

---

[1] I had added that my hope that the Church of England might undertake such an examination was not reinforced by what happened with respect to a best-selling book of a couple of decades previously. This was *The Myth of God Incarnate*, published by S.C.M. Press, and no doubt many non-Christian people purchased it because the title suggested that it would reinforce their non-belief. But it was a scholarly work and contained some perceptive observations regarding some of the issues that I felt needed thinking about. The Church of England merely dismissed from its recently set up Doctrine Commission those two of the book's contributors who were on it.

part of our Church, even if they don't come very often. We have at least moved on from the days when people could attend regularly for years yet not be spoken to by anyone; we are welcoming now and even if not quite all of us stay for coffee afterwards we greet each other as friends and I find it pleasant to be in the company of some very nice people.

But I think we need to do something about the services themselves, as I tried to say in June. We don't want to upset our stalwart supporters who have been attending for decades and love it all for its familiarity, or for the beauty of the wording of three and a half centuries ago, so it would be unwise to discard all of those 'bricks' of which our belief system is built. But in putting them back together we need to have more regard for the people currently outside the Church who may feel rather uncomfortable being required to assent to what in essence is dogma that cannot be substantiated. Is our 'faith' really what is prescribed for us as the words of the Creed? Could this be brought 'down to earth' a little?

Could there not be more in the services to stir and encourage us to action, and less recitation of metaphysical assertions, however venerable these may be? And please, please, can we get away from ritual slaughter of sacrificial Lambs? How can killing an animal absolve us from the guilt of our transgressions? Forgiveness, Jesus said, depends on how willing we are to forgive others, and forgiving them *whether they ask us to or not.*

John Bunyan was born in 1628, so he would have been 32 at the time of the Restoration, and 34 when the 1662 BCP was first used in churches. I wonder what he found lacking in Divine service, which would normally have been Mattins, with just an occasional Communion service, and in what way he thought it wasn't sufficiently in accordance with New Testament principles. Maybe it was the sermon? *The Pilgrim's Progress* is biblically based, but its main theme would seem to be that the Christian life requires hard work and perseverance, giving in to no discouragement.

I wonder, too, when he first realized how he could make such good use of his enforced confinement away from the busy world. Perhaps it was during those seven weeks before his case came to Court; familiar as he must have been with how St Paul had written his Epistles from prison.

"He that is down needs fear no fall; he that is poor no pride; he that is humble ever shall have God to be his guide." "I am content with what I have, little be it or much." A very simple, sincere faith. Take Life as it comes, for what appears to be misfortune may be a requisite for a greater good. God moves in a mysterious way, His wonders to perform; and, though we may not appreciate it at the time, He really is working His purpose out, as year succeeds to year.

Prayers

Teach us, O God, to view our life here on earth as a pilgrim's path, and give us grace to tread it courageously in the company of your faithful people. Help us to set our affections on things eternal, not on the passing vanities of this world, and grant that as we journey on in the way of holiness we may bear a good witness to our Lord, and serve all who need our help along the way, for the glory of your name. *Amen.*

God, be with us in every valley; Jesus, be with us on every hill; Holy Spirit, be with us in every stream, every cliff's edge, every green pasture, every mountain and meadow, in the crest of the waves on the sea. Every time we rest, and every time we wake up; God be with us every step we take. *Amen.*

Lord God of compassion, whose will is for peace built on righteousness, we pray for peace in Gaza and Israel; in Iraq; in Syria; in Ukraine; in all corners of the world where there is conflict and violence. We pray for an end to hostilities, for comfort and help for all who suffer, and for reconciliation between those who resort to violence to resolve their differences. We ask this through our Lord Jesus Christ, the Prince of Peace. *Amen.*

In a world of inequality, may we who have plenty live simply so that others may simply live. To those who hunger, give bread, and to us who have bread, give hunger for justice. Help us to acknowledge and grow in the appreciation that all people are made in your image and likeness, and that as brothers and sisters together in Christ, it is through our actions, through what we do and what we say, that his will is done on earth.

Christ has no body now, but ours. No hands, no feet on earth, but ours. Ours are the eyes through which he looks with compassion on this world. We pray in his name that we may have the vision and the strength to do his will. *Amen.*

A few moments' silence for your own prayers.

The Lord's Prayer

At the end of our pilgrimage, bring us, O Lord God, at our last awakening into the house and gate of heaven to enter through that gate and dwell in that house, where there shall be no darkness nor dazzling, but one equal light; no noise nor silence, but one equal music; no fears nor hopes, but one equal possession; no ends nor beginnings, but one equal eternity; in the habitations of your glory and dominion, world without end. *Amen.*

Closing Blessing Be, Lord Jesus, a bright flame before us, a guiding star above us, a smooth path below us, a kindly shepherd behind us: to day, tonight and for ever. *Amen.*

SIMPLE SERVICE, WITH HYMNS
23rd November 2014
Order of Service

Welcome & Notices (David Beal)

Hymn 367 (Tune: *Gwalchmai*)
King of glory, King of peace

Brief introduction (David E.)

Hymn 300 (Tune: *Abridge*)
Be thou my guardian and my guide

First reading (Laura) Psalm 8 *(NEB)*

Hymn 184 (Tune: *Repton*)
Dear Lord and Father of mankind

Second reading (David E.) Acts, Chapter 10, Verses 24–48 *(NEB)*

Hymn 219 (Tune: *Crüger*)
Hail to the Lord's Anointed

Brief chat (Tony)

Hymn 102 (Tune: *Love Unknown*)
My song is love unknown

Prayers (Peter)

Hymn 33 (Tune: *St Clement*)
The day thou gavest, Lord, is ended

Closing blessing (Philip)

The service will proceed without announcements. All the hymns are in *Hymns Ancient & Modern Revised*.

Thank you for coming. **Please join us in the New Vestry after the service** *for a glass of wine (alternatives available).*

Please use the voting form opposite to list your own favourite hymns for a subsequent service.

Thank you all for coming on this damp November evening. If we call this autumn, we could say that we shall not be having a winter service, as we are next due to meet on 29th March 2015, which with any luck might well be Spring. This is the second time we have given up our November fifth Sunday, the first being in 2009, when David, as this year, wanted to hold a special service to mark Advent Sunday.

In preparing for tonight we found ourselves dividing the work. Peter and I chose the hymns, from a welcome abundance of suggestions, and at the end of October Laura managed to find a free morning during her half term, and she put the service together with Tony and me.

The plan was for Philip to give the 'brief chat', but it would not have been new to you, as he sent an early draft to the Editor, who included it in the September Parish Magazine. Tony has taken on the task in his place, boldly tackling a rather unexpected topic, but one that fits the broadly ecumenical tone of tonight's service.

Our thanks, as ever, to everyone who has done anything to help, from Robert on the keyboard to Diane making sure we have the glasses for a drink after the service. Do come back and join us for this as usual.

Psalm 8

O Lord our sovereign,
how glorious is thy name in all the earth!
Thy majesty is praised high as the heavens.
Out of the mouths of babes, of infants at the breast,
    thou hast rebuked the mighty,
silencing enmity and vengeance to teach thy foes a lesson.
When I look up at thy heavens, the work of thy fingers,
    the moon and the stars set in their place by thee,
what is man that thou shouldst remember him,
    mortal man that thou shouldst care for him?
Yet thou hast made him little less than a god,
crowning him with glory and honour.
Thou makest him master over all thy creatures;
thou hast put everything under his feet:
all sheep and oxen, all the wild beasts,
    the birds in the air and the fish in the sea,
    and all that moves along the paths of ocean.
    O Lord our sovereign,
    how glorious is thy name in all the earth!

Acts 10, 24–48

The day after that, Peter arrived at Caesarea. Cornelius was expecting them and had called together his relatives and close friends. When Peter arrived, Cornelius came to meet him, and bowed to the ground in deep reverence. But Peter raised him to his feet and said, "Stand up; I am a man like anyone else."

Still talking with him he went in and found a large gathering. He said to them, "I need not tell you that a Jew is forbidden by his religion to visit or associate with a man of another race; yet God has shown me clearly that I must not call any man profane or unclean. That is why I came here without demur when you sent for me. May I ask what was your reason for sending?"

Cornelius said, "Four days ago, just about this time, I was in the house here saying the afternoon prayers, when suddenly a man in shining robes stood before me. He said: 'Cornelius, your prayer has been heard and your acts of charity remembered before God. Send to Joppa, then, to Simon Peter, and ask him to come. He is lodging in the house of Simon the tanner, by the sea.' So I sent to you there and then; it was kind of you to come. And now we are all met here before God, to hear all that the Lord has ordered you to say."

Peter began: "I now see how true it is that God has no favourites, but that in every nation the man who is God-fearing and does what is right is acceptable to him. He sent his word to the Israelites and gave the good news of peace through Jesus Christ, who is Lord of all. I need not tell you what happened lately all over the land of the Jews, starting from Galilee after the baptism proclaimed by John. You know about Jesus of Nazareth, how God anointed him with the Holy Spirit and with power. He went about doing good and healing all who were oppressed by the devil, for God was with him. And we can bear witness to all that he did in the Jewish countryside and in Jerusalem. He was put to death by hanging on a gibbet; but God raised him to life on the third day, and allowed him to appear, not to the whole people, but to witnesses whom God had chosen in advance—to us, who ate and drank with him after he rose from the dead. He commanded us to proclaim him to the people, and affirm that he is the one who has been designated by God as judge of the living and the dead. It is to him that all prophets testify, declaring that everyone who trusts in him receives forgiveness of sins through his name."

Peter was still speaking when the Holy Spirit came upon all who were listening to the message. The believers who had come with Peter, men of Jewish birth, were astonished that the gift of the Holy Spirit should have been poured out even on Gentiles. For they could hear them speaking in tongues of ecstasy and acclaiming the greatness of God.

Then Peter spoke: "Is anyone prepared to withhold the water for baptism from these persons, who have received the Holy Spirit just as we did ourselves?"

Then he ordered them to be baptized in the name of Jesus Christ. After that they asked him to stay with them for a time.

IN DEFENCE OF ISLAM

By the way, I must emphasize that the contents of my 'Brief Chats' are thoughts about various aspects of our Christian faith that puzzle me personally, and I would have thought puzzled other people as well, concerning their interpretation. I am not preaching.

You might think that with the current behaviour of some Muslims a defence of their religion would not be possible when they think the way they do and carry out the actions they do.

Islam, together with Judaism and Christianity, makes up the three religions that are known collectively as 'The Religions of the Book', and that Book is of course the Old Testament. Muslims also strongly respect the teachings and life of Jesus and recognize him as a great prophet but not 'The Son of God'. They share with their Jewish brethren certain restrictions on what can be eaten, and they pray at regular times throughout the day. Also, they do not drink alcohol and do not eat proscribed foods such as pork.

The religion of Islam was of course started in the sixth century by the Prophet Muhammad, who believed that he had a direct experience of God (Allah), who effectively dictated their holy book, the Koran, to him.

Muhammad had immediate success in attracting many converts to the new religion, which expanded rapidly throughout the area.

However, Islam and Christianity clashed with the first Crusade, which was called for by the Pope in an attempt to crush Islam by force of arms. Many of those who responded were knights who were 'landless' as a result of the practice of inheritance by 'primogeniture' (i.e. the eldest son inherits the whole estate and its titles). Younger sons were 'landless' and depended on the generosity of their elder brothers! Thus, Crusades seemed a 'godsend' to these young scions, who could see the possibilities of cutting out estates in the Middle East; that is, Islamic lands! It is not surprising that the Muslims resisted what they considered to be an invasion of their natural lands by these 'Christian robbers'. These lands, of course, included the 'Holy Land' of Israel.

In many respects the behaviour of the 'Crusaders' was disgraceful; they 'sacked' the city of Constantinople (now Istanbul), doing irreparable damage to a historic city that had contributed so much to the early development of

Christianity. For example, the Nicene Creed, which we repeat during our Communion service to affirm our faith, was conceived at the command of the Emperor Constantine, after whom the city was named.

Richard I spent most of his reign on crusade, really because he loved fighting, and eventually died as the result of an arrow wound that turned septic, not an unusual development for the time. The 'Holy Land' was never fully taken over by the Christians and to this day remains a holy place for all three faiths, and sadly is still a place of conflict, which is highlighted by the current battle across the border in Syria. This situation was really started by the artificial formation of Israel as a Jewish state to which the Jews displaced by the Second World War emigrated.

Another aspect of Islam which we have suddenly become conscious of is that of Jihad. Should Muslims become aware that 'Islam' is being attacked, they are bound to defend it, and that is 'Jihad'.

Some Muslims are of the opinion that civilization (Western-type), with its concept of freedom of speech and actions such as allowing women to walk unprotected in public, etc., is in fact worthy of Jihad; hence the occasional attacks that we have suffered from extremists — and what we can do to stop these I just don't know, and nor does anyone else!

Tony Hills

Prayers

[JEWISH PRAYER] O Lord, ruler of the world, even while the Earth was without form you were King, and you will still reign when all things are brought to an end. You are supreme and you will never be equalled. You are power and might: there is neither beginning nor end in you.   *Amen.*

[PRAYER FROM HAWAII] Father of all mankind, make the roof of my house wide enough for all opinions, oil the door of my house so it opens easily to friend and stranger, and set such a table in my house that my whole family may speak kindly and freely around it.   *Amen.*

Lord, behold our family here assembled. We thank thee for this place in which we dwell; for the love that unites us; for the peace accorded us this day; for the hope which we expect the morrow; for the health, the work, the food, and the bright skies, that make our life delightful; for our friends in all parts of the earth and our friendly helpers in this foreign isle. Let peace abound in our small community. Purge out of every heart the lurking grudge. Give us grace and strength to forbear and to persevere. Give us courage, gaiety and the quiet mind.   *Amen.*
[ROBERT LOUIS STEVENSON, 19TH CENTURY]

Yesterday was the feast day of St Cecilia, the Patron Saint of Music, and on Tuesday we commemorate Isaac Watts, prolific hymn writer.

Lord, we thank you for the gift of music, for the hymns we sing to express our praise and adoration, for the joy of live music. And we give thanks too for the loyal and devoted service of Peter Knowles, who has played the organ in our Church for more than sixty years. For all these we give thanks in your name. *Amen.*

This is our song, O God of all nations,
a song of peace for lands afar, and ours.
This is our hope, the country where our hearts are.
This is our hope, our dream, and our shrine.
But other hearts in other lands are beating
with hopes and dreams that are the same as ours.
Our country's skies are bluer than the ocean,
the sunlight beams on clover leafs and pine;
but other lands have sunlight too, and clover,
and other skies are just as blue as ours.
O hear our prayer, thou God of all the nations,
a prayer of peace for other lands and ours.

[AUTHOR UNKNOWN] *Amen.*

A few moments' silence for your own prayers.

The Lord's Prayer

Unto the King, eternal, immortal, invisible, the only wise God, be honour and glory for ever and ever. *Amen.*

Closing Blessing

May the blessing of almighty God rest upon us and upon all our work; may he give us light to guide us, courage to support us, and love to unite us, now and evermore. *Amen.*

SIMPLE SERVICE, WITH HYMNS
29th March 2015

Order of Service

Welcome & Notices (David Beal)

Hymn 766 (Tune: *Praise My Soul*)
Praise, my soul, the King of heaven

Brief introduction (David E.)

Hymn 163 (Tune: *Sing Hosanna*)
There's a man riding in on a donkey

First reading (Robert) "The Donkey" *by G. K. Chesterton*

Hymn 628 (Tune: *Rievaulx*)
Father of heaven, whose love profound

Second reading (Tony) Luke, Chapter 20, Verses 27–40 *(NEB)*

Hymn 810 (Tune: *Moscow*)
Thou, whose almighty word

Brief chat (David E.)

Hymn 765 (Tune: *Lobe den Herren*)
Praise to the Lord, the Almighty, the King of creation

Prayers (Philip)

Hymn 735 (*Mission Praise;* words on page 25. Tune: *Finlandia*)
We rest on Thee, our shield and our defender

Closing blessing (David E.)

The service will proceed without announcements. All the hymns are in *Ancient & Modern (2013 Edition)* except the last one, which is in *Mission Praise* (words opposite).

Thank you for coming. **Please join us in the New Vestry after the service** *for a glass of wine (alternatives available).*

Please use the voting form overleaf to list your own favourite hymns for a subsequent service.

As always, thank you all for coming. We met last on a dark, damp November evening. A week over four months on, here we are welcoming the start of Summer Time, with warmer weather to look forward to, and the next fifth Sunday is the end of May, and the one after that in August.

In preparing for tonight we have been unusually short-staffed. Peter, sadly, decided to call it a day in November, after eleven years of giving tremendous help and encouragement; and Laura couldn't make a meeting during her half term, but anyway we were loath to distract her in this vital term in her teaching career.

Tony and I have chosen the hymns and planned the service, and we are most grateful to Philip for taking over the prayers, and to Robert for doing a reading as well as providing our music. I must apologize that my talk will touch very sketchily on just a few aspects of a vast subject, but I can provide much further information to anyone who is interested in it.

Do come back and join us as usual for a drink after the service. This time we have even brought our own glasses for you to use.

The Donkey

When fishes flew and forests walked
And figs grew upon thorn,
Some moment when the moon was blood
Then surely I was born;

With monstrous head and sickening cry
And ears like errant wings,
The devil's walking parody
On all four-footed things.

The tattered outlaw of the earth,
Of ancient crooked will;
Starve, scourge, deride me: I am dumb,
I keep my secret still.

Fools! For I also had my hour;
One far fierce hour and sweet:
There was a shout about my ears,
And palms before my feet.

Gilbert Keith Chesterton

Luke 20, 27 – 40

Then some Sadducees came forward. They are the people who deny that there is a resurrection. Their question was this: "Master, Moses laid it down for us that if there are brothers, and one dies leaving a wife but no child, then the next should marry the widow and carry on his brother's family. Now, there were seven brothers: the first took a wife and died childless; then the second married her, then the third. In this way the seven of them died leaving no children. Afterwards the woman also died. At the resurrection whose wife is she to be, since all seven had married her?"

Jesus said to them, "The men and women of this world marry; but those who have been judged worthy of a place in the other world and of the resurrection from the dead, do not marry, for they are not subject to death any longer. They are like angels; they are the sons of God, because they share in the resurrection. That the dead are raised to life again is shown by Moses himself in the story of the burning bush, when he calls the Lord, 'the God of Abraham, Isaac and Jacob'. God is not God of the dead but of the living; for him they are all alive."

At this some of the lawyers said, "Well spoken, Master." For there was no further question that they ventured to put to him.

A BRIEF OUTLINE OF THE PARANORMAL

Nearly forty-four years ago, when I was helping at their summer camp in North Wales with the Scouts from the tiny Hertfordshire village of High Wych, we joked that telling ghost stories round the camp file (not that we actually did) would represent "Dave 'talking shop' ". That was because I was then the holder of a studentship in what is known as psychical research. The study of the psychic is frowned on in evangelical circles as 'the work of the Devil', and treated with scornful scepticism by the 'orthodox' scientific establishment, while those who take an active, unbiased interest in it find a mass of puzzles and enigmas.

If something happens which defies explanation in terms of currently known science, we call it 'paranormal'. Someone involved with the field and aware of its problems once defined a psychic phenomenon as one that could neither be debunked nor conclusively be proved to be paranormal!

My interest was kindled in my sixth-form years by a book I borrowed from the library entitled *Explorations of a Hypnotist*. With a good subject, a hypnotist can draw out long-lost memories from early life, and this one took his subjects right back to the time of birth, and found that some took on a different personality as if from a former life, exhibiting knowledge, such as an acquaintance with astronomy, that the subject did not normally possess. Though intriguing, this technique is not regarded as providing reliable evidence for reincarnation, as it is so difficult to rule out the more normal means of acquiring such information, coupled with the capacity for dramatization that we all possess.

My grandmother had moved in 1960 from her house in Folkestone to a flat near the sea in Hove, to be near to where we then lived. A neighbour lent her a book ostensibly about communication with the departed, entitled *Beyond the Horizon*. On the back cover was a panel about "The Churches' Fellowship for Psychical Study", for whom James Clarke (London) published it in 1961. It seemed to me that if an organization connected with the Church was prepared to endorse this sort of thing, it couldn't all be the work of the Devil! The author, Grace Rosher, had lost a friend of long standing through his sudden death just before he was going to sail from his home in Vancouver to visit her in England, and one day she was sitting with her pen in her hand after having addressed a letter when she heard a voice telling her to leave her hand there and see what happened. She didn't expect anything to happen, but the pen started to move and scribed a message from her friend. Thus began some very interesting communications by what is known as 'automatic writing'.

Our second reading today is from Jesus' days in Jerusalem after Palm Sunday. Jesus affirms quite clearly that "the dead are raised to life again". Life after physical death, therefore, is not something that commenced only with the Resurrection of Jesus on Easter Day.

We don't often hear the orthodox doctrine of our own resurrection propounded, although it must have been commonly believed in earlier times. After death we shall sleep in our graves until the Last Day, and then be raised back to life and reassembled like what happened in the Valley of Dry Bones. Members of congregations were laid to rest facing their minister. Those of us then deemed fit for Heaven will spend the rest of eternity sitting on clouds playing harps, not a very attractive prospect. But certainly more acceptable than being consigned to the fires of hell.

What Grace's friend Gordon described was rather different, and others ostensibly communicating through good mediums have conveyed something similar, even though they feel, in the words reported of one of them, that they "appear to be standing behind a sheet of frosted glass, which blurs sight and deadens sound, dictating feebly to a reluctant and somewhat obtuse secretary." On death you find yourself in a world so similar to our own that you may not even realize that you have died, until perhaps you meet some people you knew who 'passed on' before you. And in the 'next world' there is still work to be done that involves helping other people.

Some people have so nearly died, as the result of an accident or when undergoing an operation, that they seem to have had a glimpse of the life beyond, while seeing their body on the operating table or being attended to by ambulance workers; though to all appearances unconscious they have listened to conversations or seen things that they should not have been aware of. Told to go back as it was not their time they have subsequently been revived, but with a new attitude to life and a reduced fear of death.

Some children have memories of what seem to be former lives; when taken to visit where they claim to have lived they recognize 'relatives' and various details of their former 'home environment'. Many cases have been studied, with care taken to exclude more prosaic explanations. It does seem to me that one life on this earth is not much when compared with the whole of eternity, if we are indeed immortal beings. We may all have experienced other lives, even if we have no memories of them.

In common with religion, the study of mediumship and the paranormal is very much concerned with what life is all about.

Hamlet saw death as "To sleep, perchance to dream"; Lewis Carroll's *An Easter Greeting to Every Child Who Loves 'Alice'* puts it the other way:–[1]

Surely your gladness need not be the less for the thought that you will one day see a brighter dawn than this—when lovelier sights will meet your eyes than any waving trees or rippling waters—when angel-hands shall undraw your curtains, and sweeter tones than ever loving Mother breathed shall wake you to a new and glorious day—and when all the sadness, and the sin, that darkened life on this little earth, shall be forgotten like the dreams of a night that is past! *Easter 1876.*

If, as this passage suggests, life itself is a 'dream' that somehow we all share, is it fanciful to see our inner selves as more 'real' than the physical world in which we live and move and have our being, in the same way that any dreamer is more substantial than the world of his or her dreams?

I decided to pursue my interest in psychical research after having spent some six years after graduation working in an industrial research laboratory.

I joined the Churches' Fellowship in 1969 and was able to meet Miss Rosher, but this was some twelve years after her writing had commenced and towards the end of her life. I served on two of the Fellowship's committees in the 1970s. Although I missed seeing her doing this writing, she had attended a meeting of one of those committees and members had seen her pen writing while simply resting against her closed fist.

I held the Studentship mentioned for two years, and later printed and published a book on my research project (*The Mediumship of the Tape Recorder*, 1978). That was after I had taken up printing, having failed to find any further funded research opportunities.

As I mentioned in my talk, anyone taking an active unbiased interest in the subject is liable to find a mass of puzzles and enigmas. Often things are not what they may seem at first sight, and this has been reflected in my attitude to religion, as readers may have noticed. But that there is something worthy of investigation is beyond doubt.

[1] In my (c.1948) *Through the Looking-Glass,* pp.189–191. London: Ward Lock & Co.

Prayers

Almighty God, our creator and preserver, we thank thee for the springtime, in which thou art renewing the face of the earth and quickening all things. Thou who carest for the trees and flowers, revive and renew our life, that we may bring forth the fruit of good works, as disciples of him who came to quicken in human hearts the seed of eternal life; through Jesus Christ our Lord.
Amen.

Almighty God, the Giver of all good gifts, grant unto us a courteous spirit, a forgiving temper and an unselfish heart. Bestow upon us the spirit of self-sacrifice and cheerfulness, of hope and endurance. Increase in us the love of truth, of candour and of honour. Grant us courage to do what is right and, rejoicing in thee, to persevere unto the end; through Jesus Christ our Lord.
Amen.

O Lord God, whose will and joy it is that thy children love one another; bless our friendships, that they may be made happy and kept pure by thine unseen presence, now and at all times; through Jesus Christ our Lord. *Amen.*

Heavenly Father, in your Son Jesus Christ you have given us a true faith and a sure hope. Strengthen this faith and hope in us all our days, that we may live as those who believe in the communion of saints, the forgiveness of sins and the resurrection to eternal life; through Jesus Christ our Lord.   *Amen.*

We thank you, O God, for the pleasures you have given us through our senses; for the glory of thunder, for the mystery of music, the singing of birds and the laughter of children.

We thank you for the delights of colour, the awe of the sunset, the wild roses in the hedgerows, the smile of friendship.

We thank you for the sweetness of flowers and the scent of hay.

Truly, O Lord, the earth is full of your riches!   *Amen.*

A few moments' silence for your own prayers.

The Lord's Prayer.

Unto the King, eternal, immortal, invisible, the only wise God, be honour and glory for ever and ever.   *Amen.*

Closing Blessing

May the blessing of almighty God rest upon us and upon all our work; may he give us light to guide us, courage to support us, and love to unite us, now and evermore.   *Amen.*

SIMPLE SERVICE, WITH HYMNS

31st May 2015

Order of Service

Welcome & Notices (David Beal)

Hymn 754 (Tune: *Hannover*)
O worship the King, all glorious above

Brief introduction (David E.)

Hymn 679 (Tune: *St Stephen*)
In Christ there is no East or West

First reading (Tony) Luke, Chapter 6, Verses 20–38; 46–49 *(NEB)*

Hymn 775 (Tune by Karen Lafferty)
Seek ye first the kingdom of God

Second reading (Clive) Luke, Chapter 11, Verses 1–13 *(NEB)*

Hymn 685 (Tune: *St Matthias*)
Jesu, my Lord, my God, my all

Brief chat (David E.)

Hymn 706 (Tune: *Monkland*)
Let us, with a gladsome mind

Prayers (Philip)

Hymn 748 (Tune: *Thornbury*)
O Jesus, I have promised

Closing blessing (David E.)

The service will proceed without announcements. All the hymns are in *Ancient & Modern (2013 Edition)*.

Thank you for coming. **Please join us in the New Vestry after the service** *for a glass of wine (alternatives available).*

Please use the voting form opposite to list your own favourite hymns for a subsequent service.

As always, thank you all for coming. We met last on Palm Sunday, welcoming the start of Summer Time, expecting warmer weather to look forward to, but so far all we can say is that it is somewhat less cold. The next fifth Sunday is in August, so let's hope that by then we shall have had some of that warmer weather, as we certainly did last year.

Tony and I were joined by Laura in choosing the hymns, but on our own for planning the service, which we finished doing only yesterday. Once again we are most grateful to Philip for taking on the prayers, and Clive this time for doing a reading. Robert has been diligently practising the hymn tunes, which we think you will find more familiar than one or two of the hymns we shall be singing to them.

David Burnett kindly scanned for me the cartoon strip on the back of the service sheet; it's there [on p.313] because it gave me an idea for my talk.

Do come back and join us as usual for a drink after the service. We now have our own glasses for you to use, which makes things easier than having to remember to ask to borrow the Church ones.

Luke 6, 20 – 38; 46 – 49

Then turning to his disciples, Jesus began to speak:–

"How blest are you who are poor; the kingdom of God is yours.

"How blest are you who now go hungry; your hunger shall be satisfied.

"How blest are you who weep now; you shall laugh.

"How blest you are when men hate you, when they outlaw you and insult you, and ban your very name as infamous, because of the Son of Man. On that day be glad and dance for joy; for assuredly you have a rich reward in heaven; in just the same way did their fathers treat the prophets.

"But alas for you who are rich; you have had your time of happiness.

"Alas for you who are well-fed now; you shall go hungry.

"Alas for you who laugh now; you shall mourn and weep.

"Alas for you when all speak well of you; just so did their fathers treat the false prophets.

"But to you who hear me I say:–

"Love your enemies; do good to those who hate you; bless those who curse you; pray for those who treat you spitefully. When a man hits you on the cheek, offer him the other cheek too; when a man takes your coat, let him have your shirt as well. Give to everyone who asks you; when a man takes what is yours, do not demand it back. Treat others as you would like them to treat you.

"If you love only those who love you, what credit is that to you? Even sinners love those who love them. Again, if you do good only to those who do good to you, what credit is that to you? Even sinners do as much. And if you lend only where you expect to be repaid, what credit is that to you: even sinners lend to each other if they are to be repaid in full. But you must love your enemies and do good; and lend without expecting any return, and you will have a rich reward: you will be sons of the Most High, because he himself is kind to the ungrateful and wicked. Be compassionate as your Father is compassionate.

"Pass no judgement, and you will not be judged; do not condemn, and you will not be condemned; acquit, and you will be acquitted; give, and gifts will be given you. Good measure, pressed down, shaken together, and running over, will be poured into your lap; for whatever measure you deal out to others will be dealt to you in return."

"Why do you keep calling me 'Lord, Lord' — and never do what I tell you? Everyone who comes to me and hears what I say, and acts upon it — I will show you what he is like. He is like a man who, in building a house, dug deep and laid the foundations on rock. When the flood came, the river burst upon that house, but could not shift it, because it had been soundly built. But he who hears and does not act is like a man who built his house on the soil without foundations. As soon as the river burst upon it, the house collapsed, and fell with a great crash."

Luke 11, 20 – 38; 46 – 49

Once, in a certain place, Jesus was at prayer. When he ceased, one of his disciples said, "Lord, teach us to pray, as John taught his disciples."

He answered, "When you pray, say,

'Father, thy name be hallowed;
Thy kingdom come.
Thy will be done,
On earth as in heaven.
Give us each day our bread for the morrow.
And forgive us our sins,
For we too forgive all who have done us wrong.
And do not bring us to the test,
But save us from the evil one.' "

312

He added, "Suppose one of you has a friend who comes to him in the middle of the night and says, 'My friend, lend me three loaves, for a friend of mine on a journey has turned up at my house, and I have nothing to offer him'; and he replies from inside, 'Do not bother me. The door is shut for the night; my children and I have gone to bed; and I cannot get up and give you what you want.' I tell you that even if he will not provide for him out of friendship, the very shamelessness of the request will make him get up and give him all he needs. And so I say to you, ask, and you will receive; seek, and you will find; knock, and the door will be opened. For everyone who asks receives, he who seeks finds, and to him who knocks, the door will be opened.

"Is there a father among you who will offer his son a stone when he asks for bread, or a snake when he asks for fish, or a scorpion when he asks for an egg? If you then, bad as you are, know how to give your children what is good for them, how much more will the heavenly Father give the Holy Spirit to those who ask him!"

WASTED ON THE CHURCH ?

It's now twelve years since the idea of a service based on hymns was put to Kevin, although it was a further six months before we had the first one. That was because Kevin had said we could have the fifth Sunday, but avoid August, as that was the Bank Holiday weekend and people would be away. Even so, it was touch and go, as the friend who had been interested in helping found himself busy with domestic concerns and had to withdraw, and I only just thought of asking Peter Evans on the last day before I needed to get an announcement into the Parish Magazine. Had he not been at home that very afternoon and had he not been so encouraging, the idea might never have got off the ground.

It helped a lot that Peter and I thought the same way about what we were doing. We put together a very simple service, for the simple reason that we thought that Christianity is—or should be—a very simple religion. Simple, that is, to state, and simple to understand, even if it is by no means always simple to put into practice.

Although the hymns were the most important part, the way we filled the gaps between them was intended to be constructive as well. Our hope was that we should in due course attract not only church members who liked singing hymns, but friends, relatives, neighbours and other people of good will who might not otherwise think of darkening the church's door. In other words, what we might now call an 'outreach' project.

Kevin said before our first hymn service that he didn't think there was time for an address, and we filled the slot by splitting a long second reading. But noting that Kevin had let David Hammond and Sally Levett address other services, I thought I would have a go myself at our second one. Was it just coincidence that there was a sharp drop in numbers at our third service? Or the result of having one on a Bank Holiday weekend? Attendance did improve again later, fortunately.

Undertaking to say something has two consequences. The obvious one is that though there are times when one's thoughts seem to flow readily to the keyboard, there are others when they most certainly do not. Solutions have varied between having a third reading and letting someone else do the talk.

from
THE POP
ANNUAL
published
by
THE DAILY
GRAPHIC
(193?)

Only slightly less obvious is that one can't speak about anything without at least giving it some considered thought, especially necessary subsequent to Anne Barnes's kind suggestion that the talks be sent to the Parish Magazine, to reach several hundred people instead of just twenty.

This may run counter to what I suspect many of us do. We come to Church, as this is what we are used to doing on Sunday mornings, meet people we know, take part in the service, perhaps stay for coffee, and go back home, confident that we have done our bit for the day.

Done our bit? Well, we've had our sins forgiven, taken part in a ritual to 'keep us in life eternal' and asked God to do all sorts of things, from healing the sick, to guiding our leaders into acting responsibly, to sorting out the troubles of the world. But will this be done by some sort of magic, or will ordinary people like you and me each be inspired to put in his or her own little contribution?

I was walking home from the 8 o'clock some weeks ago, and thinking of the cartoon strip on the previous page, and wondering if a case could be made for saying, 'Wonderful religion, Christianity'. 'Yes, wasted on the Church!'

When our Diocesan Strategy was unveiled last Sunday, I was less than impressed to hear (if I caught the words correctly) that we were exhorted to persuade outsiders to come and join us to enjoy our wonderful liturgy, as personally I have developed reservations concerning this liturgy, with its metaphysical assertions about Jesus, recited as indisputable facts when they can be no more than theological speculation, that we are all required to assent to in order to 'affirm our faith'. If we want thinking people of good will to come to Church, we should at least try to meet them half way and not insist that they accept all the doctrine about Jesus that developed in the first centuries of the Christian era as his followers were striving to make sense of the events of his life and their implications. That all this doctrine is dear to the hearts of our Church leaders can be seen from the disputes down the ages between Catholics, Protestants and the Orthodox Churches. Jesus' teaching was so radical and so contrary to the prevailing mentality of self-interest and retaliation, of observing rules of religious observance as an end in themselves, that he needed divine status to lend authority to any promotion of that teaching. Such status was evidenced by his undoubted healing gifts, and the remarkable fact of his resurrection. But do we now need to take on board all the theological assertions in the Gospel of John, credit Jesus with having 'made' the world, and ask him, as the 'Lamb of God that takes away the sins of the World' to have mercy on us? On this Trinity Sunday, I am happy to follow Jesus as a Man who showed us all how to live, and went about doing good—God's work—because, as the Gospels record, he was 'led by the Holy Spirit'. I may be 'theologically naïve'; but I want to see things simply.

People do in fact come to Church to attend baptisms, weddings and funerals. These services have a different structure from our regular ones, and may well appear to outsiders to have more of a purpose to them, in addition to their social aspects. It has been suggested that attending a funeral is one of the most unselfish things we do, as there is no way that the deceased can reward us for our trouble. No way? I have had so many positive experiences associated with attending funerals that these have made me wonder whether there might be some way that they can (I mean other than through a legacy).

"To know, love, follow Jesus" is a worthy aim provided we remember his "If you love me, keep my commandments". The Christian religion needs to be tried, and if it is tried it can be self-reinforcing, in that when we set out to do something for somebody else we can sometimes, or even often, find ourselves given unexpected assistance. Life is an experience, and we can only begin to learn what it is all about by observing what actually happens, or in other instances doesn't happen, as the case may be. If everything seems to be going wrong, hang on, don't despair, for there may be some reason why this was needed for something else to go right. It's one thing to read of Jesus' saying that we should not worry about tomorrow, as tomorrow will take care of itself, but when one encounters instances of this sort of thing happening in one's own life, it does provide assurance for future occasions that we should not worry, as things really will work out right in the end. So long as we go on pursuing what we sincerely believe to be right, we are made aware that we are looked after.

I have come across a very interesting comment on Jesus' "story of the Friend at Midnight, who comes knocking at the door asking for three loaves so that he can entertain an unexpected guest. Jesus . . . asks what makes the central character get out of bed to do as he is asked. He won't do it, says Jesus, just for friendship's sake; he does it because he'd be ashamed not to. . . . Jesus recognizes . . . that one of the strongest of all motives for action is our need to live up to our own ego-ideal—that is, my sense of myself as a person who can be relied upon to live up to certain moral standards. To function as a person, it seems, I need to maintain *my own self-respect,* and this rules out certain kinds of pretence, laziness, deceitfulness and so on in my dealings with others."

Our conscience is usually thought of as providing a restraining guide against what we should *not* be doing. But it can also have a positive role: when the idea of some kindness or act of generosity comes to mind, our conscience can be very insistent that we carry on and actually do it.

It is natural as a member of any organization to want to work to its benefit. But we must be careful that we act collectively in the same way that we should act individually; thus if as Christians we seek to be kind and generous, we must avoid being collectively mean and grasping. Some of what the Church has done collectively in past ages is so appalling that it could not be regarded as Christian at all. What gives us hope are the acts of genuine reconciliation between former foes, such as we have seen recently in Northern Ireland. If we are unhappy about what our Church does or doesn't do, should we simply leave, or stay and work to improve things? Jesus was faced with such a problem, and it might be said that his answer was to distil the wisdom of those who had gone before, simplify their teaching and explain clearly to everyone who would listen what was essential and what was not, using memorable stories to make his points.

Prayers

A PRAYER OF ST RICHARD OF CHICHESTER

Thanks be to thee, our Lord Jesus Christ, for all the benefits which thou hast won for us, for all the pains and insults thou hast borne for us. O most merciful Redeemer, Friend and Brother, may we know thee more clearly, love thee more dearly, follow thee more nearly, day by day. *Amen.*

We praise and bless thy holy name, O Lord, for all those who have laboured to serve the cause of freedom and good government in this land, and for all who have striven to uphold the sanctity of the home and family; for all who have sought to bless mankind by their sacrifice and service, and for all who have given their lives to enlarge the bounds of thy Kingdom on earth. For all the prophets, patriarchs and martyrs, and for all obscure and humble saints, we bless and praise thy holy name, through Jesus Christ our Lord. *Amen.*

O God, our heavenly Father, help us always to be of a good courage. Let us not be disheartened by our difficulties, never doubting thy love nor any of thy promises. Give us grace that we may encourage others and always do our best to make life easier for those who need a friendly word or helping hand; for the sake of Jesus Christ our Lord. *Amen.*

Be present, O merciful God, and protect us through the silent hours of this night, so that we who are fatigued by the changes and chances of this fleeting world may repose upon thy eternal changelessness: through Jesus Christ our Lord. *Amen.*

A few moments' silence for your own prayers.

The Lord's Prayer.

† The grace of our Lord Jesus Christ, the love of God, and the fellowship of the Holy Spirit, be with us all, this night and for evermore. *Amen.*

Closing Blessing

O God, the King of righteousness, lead us, we pray thee, in the ways of justice and of peace; inspire us to break down all tyranny and oppression, to gain for every man his due reward and from every man his due service; that each may live for all, and all may care for each, in the Name of Jesus Christ. *Amen.*[1]

---

[1] The quotation on page 315 was from Don Cupitt's *Jesus and Philosophy*, page 42.

SIMPLE SERVICE, WITH HYMNS

30th August 2015

Order of Service

Welcome & Notices

Hymn 1 (Tune: *Morning Hymn*) Verses 1–4, 8
Awake, my soul, and with the sun

Brief introduction (David E.)

Hymn 167 (*Mission Praise;* words overleaf. Tune: *Sing Hosanna*)
Give me oil in my lamp, keep me burning

First reading (Robert) Ecclesiasticus, Chapter 6, Verses 5–17 *(NEB)*

Hymn 794 (Tune: *Dominus Regit Me*)
The King of love my Shepherd is

Second reading (David E.) "The Battle of Britain" by Peter Simpson

Hymn 631 (Tune: *Duke Street*)
Fight the good fight with all thy might

Brief chat (Tony) "Henry VIII and Rome"

Hymn 664 (Tune: *St Peter*)
How sweet the name of Jesus sounds

Prayers (Philip)

Hymn 128 (Tune: *Aberystwyth*)
Jesu, lover of my soul

Closing blessing (David E.)

The service will proceed without announcements. All the hymns are in *Ancient & Modern (2013 Edition)* except the second one, for which we are using the words from *Mission Praise* (shown opposite).

Thank you for coming. Please join us in the New Vestry after the service for a glass of wine (alternatives available).

Please use the voting form overleaf to list your own favourite hymns for a subsequent service.

Give me oil in my lamp, keep me burning

Give me oil in my lamp, keep me burning
Give me oil in my lamp, I pray;
Give me oil in my lamp, keep me burning
Keep me burning till the break of day.
Sing hosanna, sing hosanna,
Sing hosanna, to the King of kings!
Sing hosanna, sing hosanna,
Sing hosanna to the King!

Make me a fisher of men, keep me seeking,
Make me a fisher of men, I pray;
Make me a fisher of men, keep me seeking,
Keep me seeking till the break of day.
Sing hosanna, sing hosanna,
Sing hosanna, to the King of kings!
Sing hosanna, sing hosanna,
Sing hosanna to the King!

Give me joy in my heart, keep me singing,
Give me joy in my heart, I pray;
Give me joy in my heart, keep me singing,
Keep me singing till the break of day.
Sing hosanna, sing hosanna,
Sing hosanna, to the King of kings!
Sing hosanna, sing hosanna,
Sing hosanna to the King!

Give me love in my heart, keep me serving,
Give me love in my heart, I pray;
Give me love in my heart, keep me serving,
Keep me serving till the break of day.
Sing hosanna, sing hosanna,
Sing hosanna, to the King of kings!
Sing hosanna, sing hosanna,
Sing hosanna to the King!

Anyone who came this morning will have noticed that not only do we not have David Beal with us, but we don't even have a Churchwarden to welcome you and give out any notices. My thanks to Stephen Turrell for giving us a good 'plug' at the 8 o'clock, the most enthusiastic we have ever had. And John Peal said he would mention us at the 10 o'clock. Do take a 'pew sheet' home for its notices if you didn't get one this morning.

As always, thank you all for coming. When we met on Palm Sunday, welcoming the start of Summer Time, we had been expecting warmer weather in May, but all we could say was that it was somewhat less cold. Now here we are in August; we have indeed had some warmer weather, in July, but this month has been wetter. November will once again see us taking an earlier Sunday than the fifth, to allow David to hold a Carol Service on Advent Sunday.

Tony and I chose the hymns from lists kindly supplied by Viv and Robert, and we finally planned the service only yesterday. Once again we are most grateful to Philip for conducting the prayers, and Robert for doing a reading as well as diligently practising the hymn tunes. I thank Tony for taking on the talk this time, and David Burnett for scanning a picture of the subject of this talk to go on our front cover. That leaves me free to do our second reading, which is one that Philip found for us. I am always amazed that people are very ready to pray for God's help, yet so reticent to acknowledge that they have actually had it; this account helps to redress that imbalance.

Do come back and join us as usual for a drink after the service. This part of the evening has been easier to prepare for since we acquired our own glasses and so no longer have to borrow the Church ones.

Ecclesiasticus 6, 5 – 17

Pleasant words win many friends,
and an affable manner makes acquaintance easy.

Accept a greeting from everyone,
but advice from only one in a thousand.

When you make a friend, begin by testing him,
and be in no hurry to trust him.

Some friends are loyal when it suits them
but desert you in time of trouble.

Some friends turn into enemies
and shame you by making the quarrel public.

Another sits at your table,
but is nowhere to be found in time of trouble;

320

when you are prosperous, he will be your second self
and make free with your servants,
but if you come down in the world, he will turn against you
and you will not see him again.
Hold your enemies at a distance,
and keep a wary eye on your friends.
A faithful friend is a secure shelter;
whoever finds one has found a treasure.
A faithful friend is beyond price;
his worth is more than money can buy.
A faithful friend is an elixir of life,
found only by those who fear the Lord.
The man who fears the Lord keeps his friendships in repair,
for he treats his neighbour as himself.

"THE BATTLE OF BRITAIN"

The Battle of Britain is deemed officially to have begun on 10th July 1940. Central to the German invasion plan was the incapacitating of the RAF prior to the crossing of the Channel by German troops.

A crucial period in the ensuing weeks was 13th–16th August. These were the four days during which Goering hoped to deliver a decisive blow against the RAF, enabling the German seaborne invasion to proceed unhindered. The most intense day of the whole of the Battle of Britain was 15th August, with the Luftwaffe flying 1,786 sorties, in particular targeting the airfields and radar stations. On this day the Germans lost 75 aircraft and the RAF 34. The Germans were inflicting much damage, but, in God's providence, the desired knockout blow against the RAF was not materializing.

The next phase of the Battle began on 24th August, and British losses were mounting. Come 6th September the situation had become desperate, with 289 RAF planes shot down in the previous fortnight, along with 171 seriously damaged. Around 300 pilots had also been lost, and newly trained pilots without adequate experience were being forced prematurely into the heat of the battle.

Then, however, Hitler ordered a change of tactics, and instead of pressing home its advantage against the airfields, the Luftwaffe began an all-out attack on London on 7th September.

Here we observe an amazing and unpredictable outworking of God's providence. What happened was not mere tactical error, but the direct hand of the God who ordains the outcome of battles. The Lord was intervening, answering and anticipating the solemn pleas for help uttered to Him by many in the nation, for on Sunday 8th September there was a second National Day of Prayer, which again had been called for by the King. This day of intercession was once more heavily supported up and down the land. Churches were filled, as the people cried out to God for deliverance. Yet again there were vast queues of people forming snake-like shapes in the roads and squares around Westminster Abbey. The words of King Solomon at the completion of the Jerusalem temple were proving their eternal significance:–

If thy people go out to battle against their enemy, whithersoever thou shalt send them, and shall pray unto the LORD toward . . . the house that I have built for thy name: Then hear thou in heaven their prayer and their supplication, and maintain their cause. [1 Kings 8.44–45]

A particularly severe and crucial push was made by the Luftwaffe on 15th September, when the German bombers had more fighter support than ever before. Yet, despite the enemy's huge numbers, many of their aircraft failed to reach their targets in London, hindered as they were by the RAF's Spitfires and Hurricanes. Sixty German planes were shot down upon this day, and this was enough to ensure that the Luftwaffe failed yet again.

In the previous two weeks the weather conditions in the English Channel had been very poor for the time of year, making conditions quite unsuitable for the invasion barges to be launched. In God's providence these concurring circumstances caused Hitler, on 17th September, to postpone the invasion of Britain indefinitely. It is appropriate in this context to quote the words of Psalm 18:–

I will call upon the LORD, who is worthy to be praised: so shall I be saved from mine enemies . . . For thou has girded me with strength unto the battle: thou has subdued under me those that rose up against me.
[Psalm 18.3,39]

The Air Chief Marshal, Sir Hugh Dowding, declared, "I pay homage to those gallant boys who gave their all that our nation might live. I pay tribute to their leaders and commanders; but I say with absolute conviction that I can trace the intervention of God, not only in the battle itself, but in the events which led up to it, and that if it had not been for this intervention, the battle would have been joined in conditions which, humanly speaking, would have rendered victory impossible."

Pastor Peter Simpson
Cheering Words, September 2015, pp.134–135

Included by permission of Andrew Toms, Editor, and David Oldham, Publisher

HENRY VIII AND THE CHURCH OF ROME

Our beautiful old Church of St Mary has stood on her hill for something like 1,000 years and apart from the addition of the spire has not changed very much during that time. If we were allowed to peep in during the early stages, we would have found the main congregation standing or kneeling, with some seating around the walls for the aged and ill, hence 'weakest to the wall'. There is evidence that a Rood Screen stood at the end of the choir, behind which the magic of the Mass would be said or sung as it still is today, although most of us tend to call it 'Holy Communion' rather than Mass. Some people may not recognize the word 'Rood' used in this way, but it is the representation of Christ on the Cross supported by St Mary and St John, as we see in the window behind the Altar.

Up to the time of Henry VIII, the Church was under Papal authority, with the Pope trying to work with the King of the time where possible, but this fell to pieces with Henry and as is often the case Henry's trouble was women. The story is a bit complicated but worth telling. Henry was a truly God-fearing man, convinced that all the things that happened were the Will of God (if they were not God's will, they would not happen).

Henry was not the heir to the throne of Henry VII, as he had an elder brother, Arthur, and Arthur had married (by arrangement) Catherine of Aragon, who brought with her a substantial dowry. However, Arthur died young and Henry, who was probably fascinated by this mature princess, was loath to send either her or her dowry back to Aragon. He wanted both.

Because Catherine had first been the wife of his brother Arthur, the Pope was approached and granted what was called a dispensation, giving leave for the marriage. But the only child conceived in twenty years of marriage was a daughter, Mary, later known to us as 'Bloody Mary' because of the many prosecutions and executions carried out in her name.

In Henry's mind it was obvious that it was not God's Will for them to have a male heir, and therefore what was wrong had to be corrected. So the Pope (the next one) was approached again. Henry wanted him to say that the old Pope had been wrong to let him marry Catherine. But the new Pope was in the power of the Emperor Charles V, who was a nephew of Queen Catherine, so he dared not do as the King desired. By then Henry had become interested in one of Catherine's ladies, Anne Boleyn, and had already had an affair with Anne's sister, Mary.

Henry had been given the title of 'Defender of the Faith' (still used by our own Sovereign) and, as such, questioned why Rome should be involved. At that time the European intelligentsia were in the middle of their own revolt against the authority of Rome (Martin Luther, etc.) and strongly supported

Henry's approach. Henry therefore proclaimed his own annulment, but this was at the price of a complete break with Rome, although still continuing with many Catholic aspects as defined in the Creed.

So Henry defied the Pope, and permitted no more money to be paid to him as had been done for centuries. He put away his wife Catherine, and took the new wife whom he desired, Anne Boleyn, who became the mother of Queen Elizabeth I. Nor was Henry content simply to break away from Rome, for he dealt very severely with church men in England, closing the monasteries and confiscating their wealth. . . . But though his ways were those of a tyrant, yet all Protestants hold that he did well to free the land from the spiritual rule of the Pope.

These days the relationship between the Church of England and Rome is much closer. We have even seen the Pope and our Archbishop worshipping together in the same Church. Who knows what the future will be?

Tony Hills

Prayers

Gratitude in the summer for the cosseting of the sun, for the play and sparkle of water, for the gentle rain, for the ripening of the grain, for the shade of the woodland, for the quiet sunsets, for the long and lingering twilight and for the nectar of night.

Almighty and everlasting God, who hast graciously given to us the fruits of the earth in their season, we yield thee humble and hearty thanks for these thy bounties, beseeching thee to give us grace rightly to use them, to thy glory and the relief of those that need. Through Jesus Christ our Lord. *Amen.*

O Lord, our heavenly Father, be with us in our homes. Make us to be loving and patient in our own families, forgiving others, as we remember how much we ourselves need to be forgiven. Keep us from all hastiness of temper, and all want of thoughtfulness for others in little things. Make us more ready to give than to receive; and grant that in our homes the holy law of love may reign, bringing to us a foretaste of thy Kingdom, where thy love shall be the everlasting joy of thy people for ever. Through Jesus Christ our Lord. *Amen.*

O God of our life, there are days when the burdens we carry chafe our shoulders and weigh us down; when the road seems dreary and endless, the skies grey and threatening, when our lives have no music in them and our hearts are lonely, and our souls have lost their courage. Flood the path with light, we beseech thee; turn our eyes to where the skies are full of promise; tune our hearts to brave music; give us the sense of comradeship with heroes and saints of every age; and so quicken our spirits that we may be able to encourage the souls of all who journey with us on the road of life; to thy honour and glory. *Amen.*

A few moments' silence for your own prayers.

The Lord's Prayer.

Go forth into the world in peace; be of good courage; hold fast that which is good; render to no man evil for evil; strengthen the faint-hearted; support the weak; help the afflicted; honour all men; love and serve the Lord; rejoicing in the power of the Holy Spirit.

And the blessing of God Almighty, the Father, the Son, and the Holy Spirit, be upon us, and remain with us for ever. *Amen.*

Closing Blessing

May the blessing of almighty God rest upon us and upon all our work; may he give us light to guide us, courage to support us, and love to unite us, now and evermore. *Amen.*

SIMPLE SERVICE, WITH HYMNS

22nd November 2015

Order of Service

Welcome & Notices

Hymn 704 (Tune: *Luckington*)
Let all the world in every corner sing

Brief introduction (David E.)

Hymn 675 (Tune: *Bishopthorpe*)
Immortal Love for ever full

First reading (Robert) Luke, Chapter 16, Verses 1–15 *(NEB)*

Hymn 75 (*Mission Praise;* overleaf. Tune: *Land of Hope and Glory*)
Christ is surely coming

Second reading (Tony) Matthew, Chapter 20, Verses 1–16 *(NEB)*

Hymn 650 (Tune: *Faithfulness*) [words on page 254]
Great is thy faithfulness, O God my Father

Brief chat (David E.)

Hymn 676 (Tune: *St Denio*)
Immortal, invisible, God only wise

Prayers (Philip)

Hymn 41 (Tune: *Helmsley*)
Lo, he comes with clouds descending

Closing blessing (Tony)

The service will proceed without announcements. All the hymns are in *Ancient & Modern (2013 Edition)* except the third one, for which we are using the words (and music) from *Mission Praise* (shown opposite).

Thank you for coming. Please join us in the New Vestry after the service for a glass of wine (alternatives available).

Please use the voting form overleaf to list your own favourite hymns for a subsequent service.

Christ is surely coming

Christ is surely coming, bringing His reward,
Alpha and Omega, First and Last and Lord:
root and stem of David, brilliant Morning Star –
    Meet your Judge and Saviour, nations near and far;
    meet your Judge and Saviour, nations near and far!

See the holy city! There they enter in,
all by Christ made holy, washed from every sin:
thirsty ones, desiring all He loves to give,
    Come for living water, freely drink, and live;
    come for living water, freely drink, and live!

Grace be with God's people! Praise His holy name!
Father, Son, and Spirit, evermore the same:
hear the certain promise from the eternal home:
    Surely I come quickly! – Come, Lord Jesus, come;
    Surely I come quickly! – Come, Lord Jesus, come!

Words from Revelation 22   *Christopher Idle (b.1938)*

Music: Edward Elgar (1857–1934)

arranged Robin Sheldon

As always, thank you all for coming. It is your support that has been encouraging us to continue, so that after twelve years here we are on the fiftieth of these simple services.

Last year we had a damp but mild day in November, and with a break to March we could almost say we had missed a winter service. However, that doesn't seem to be the case today, and we wonder what the end of January will bring, before our break to May, to be followed by July and October, which should be warm again.

Sadly, this year we have been without the two younger members of our team, with Peter Evans calling it a day last November, and Laura, having fully qualified as a teacher, moving away to be nearer her current school in Croydon. I am very grateful to Tony for helping choose the hymns from those requested, and later plan the service. I was more than a little concerned that we might not be ready in time for this one, but we managed to put in a concerted effort towards the end of last week.

Once again we are most grateful to Philip for conducting the prayers, selected by Tony from a printout of all the ones we have had so far, and to Robert for taking on a reading as well as diligently practising all the hymn tunes. Do come back and join us as usual for a drink after the service.

Luke 16, 1–15

He said to his disciples, "There was a rich man who had a bailiff, and he received complaints that this man was squandering the property. So he sent for him, and said, 'What is this that I hear? Produce your accounts, for you cannot be manager here any longer.'

"The bailiff said to himself, 'What am I to do now that my employer is dismissing me? I am not strong enough to dig, and too proud to beg. I know what I must do, to make sure that, when I have to leave, there will be people to give me house and home.' He summoned his master's debtors one by one. To the first he said, 'How much do you owe my master?' He replied, 'A thousand gallons of olive oil.' He said, 'Here is your account. Sit down and make it five hundred; and be quick about it.' Then he said to another, 'And you, how much do you owe?' He said, 'A thousand bushels of wheat', and was told, 'Take your account and make it eight hundred.' And the master applauded the dishonest bailiff for acting so astutely. For the worldly are more astute than the other-worldly in dealing with their own kind.

"So I say to you, use your worldly wealth to win friends for yourselves, so that when money is a thing of the past you may be received into an eternal home.

"The man who can be trusted in little things can be trusted also in great; and the man who is dishonest in little things is dishonest also in great things. If, then, you have not proved trustworthy with the wealth of this world, who will trust you with the wealth that is real? And if you have proved untrustworthy with what belongs to another, who will give you what is your own?

"No servant can be the slave of two masters; for either he will hate the first and love the second, or he will be devoted to the first and think nothing of the second. You cannot serve God and Money."

The Pharisees, who loved money, heard all this and scoffed at him. He said to them, "You are the people who impress your fellow-men with your righteousness, but God sees through you; for what sets itself up to be admired by men is detestable in the sight of God."

Matthew 20, 1–16

"The kingdom of Heaven is like this. There was once a landowner who went out early one morning to hire labourers for his vineyard; and after agreeing to pay them the usual day's wage he sent them off to work. Going out three hours later he saw some more men standing idle in the market-place. 'Go and join the others in the vineyard,' he said, 'and I will pay you a fair wage'; so off they went.

"At noon he went out again, and at three in the afternoon, and made the same arrangement as before. An hour before sunset he went out and found another group standing there; so he said to them, 'Why are you standing about like this all day with nothing to do?' 'Because no one has hired us', they replied; so he told them, 'Go and join the others in the vineyard.'

"When evening fell, the owner of the vineyard said to his steward, 'Call the labourers and give them their pay, beginning with those who came last and ending with the first.' Those who had started work an hour before sunset came forward, and were paid the full day's wage. When it was the turn of the men who had come first, they expected something extra, but were paid the same amount as the others. As they took it, they grumbled at their employer: 'These late-comers have done only one hour's work, yet you have put them on a level with us, who have sweated the whole day long in the blazing sun!'

"The owner turned to one of them and said, 'My friend, I am not being unfair to you. You agreed on the usual wage for the day, did you not? Take your pay and go home. I choose to pay the last man the same as you. Surely I am free to do what I like with my own money. Why be jealous because I am kind?' Thus will the last be first, and the first last."

FOUR VERY INTERESTING BOOKS

Not so long ago, Tony would borrow books on religion from our local library, and let me have a read of any he found interesting. Thus I came to see John Dickson's *Jesus: A Short Life*[1] and to read it right through on a Saturday afternoon in the summer of 2009. Impressed with its content, I purchased my own copy and subsequently twenty more from a Christian bookshop in Petersfield at a modest discount to sell or give to friends. In May 2010, during a visit to a cousin in Yorkshire, I had the chance to browse round a second-hand-book shop in Helmsley on a damp day, and acquired a few more interesting books, including one by John Robinson entitled *The New Reformation?*, which I mentioned in my talk in October that year. Another was Don Cupitt's *Taking Leave of God,* which was published by SCM Press in 1980. In June 2010, when in Cambridge for a College function, I had time to visit the large bookshop in Trinity Street and there in the Theology section was another book by Cupitt, *Jesus & Philosophy*, published by SCM in 2009, nearly thirty years later. Naturally, I was intrigued by the opportunity to discover how the author's thinking had developed over those three decades. At £17.99 I nearly left it unpurchased, but on the way back to my car to come home I realized that I still had enough cash with me, so I returned for it!

Don Cupitt in 1980 was Dean of Emmanuel College, and I am sure you would find it helpful if I take a few moments to explain what that means. The Dean is a clergyman responsible for the spiritual life of his or her College, as a Chaplain might be. In my day as an undergraduate we had a Chaplain as well, but the Dean was the senior. In the case of most other clergy, the local (or perhaps Diocesan) Bishop is what is known as the 'Ordinary' and has responsibility for their appointment (or dismissal), but, perhaps for historical reasons, in the case of Cambridge colleges the College Council is the Ordinary. The Dean would also be elected to a College Fellowship, and be expected to take part in teaching duties in the University, normally in the Theology Faculty. Cupitt started lecturing on Christian Ethics in 1962, and held a teaching post in the Philosophy of Religion from 1968 until retiring for health reasons in 1996.

As you can imagine, there will be a wide variation in the views and fields of scholarship among College Deans. The Dean of my College (Gonville & Caius) was Canon Hugh Montefiore, a Jew converted to Christianity during his schooldays, who in 1963 (at the end of my third year), moved on to be Vicar of Great St Mary's, the University Church, succeeding Canon J. E. Fison, who had been made Diocesan Bishop of Salisbury.[2]

---

[1] Lion Hudson, Oxford, 2008. Extracts quoted on page 331 are Copyright © 2008 John Dickson and reproduced by permission of Lion Hudson Ltd.
[2] Hugh Montefiore is also mentioned on pages 168–169 and 200.

The present Dean of Caius is Revd Dr Cally Hammond, a classicist who worked in academic life in Oxford and Cambridge, as well as seven years in full-time ministry in rural parishes. I met her briefly during a visit in 2011 and purchased her paperbacks, *Joyful Christianity* (SPCK 2009) and *Passionate Christianity* (2007), which had been reviewed in a College magazine.

I am not sure when I started doing a little reading at bedtime; just a quarter-hour or so does take one's mind away from concerns of the day. It was no later than August 2014, when we devoted one of these services to John Bunyan, and I realized that I had never read *The Pilgrim's Progress*.

During recent months I have worked through both those books by Don Cupitt at least twice, and when a year or so ago I printed out the four pages of his official website I discovered that I had come across his work many years ago as well. He was a contributor to the symposium under the title *The Myth of God Incarnate*, again published by the SCM Press (1977). I had borrowed the book from a friend, then bought my own copy, which I lent to another friend in 1985 and never had back, so I am not sure which part was his. Then in 1984 there was a four-part BBC television series, *The Sea of Faith*, which our then rather fundamentalist Rector, Jim Reeves, denounced one Sunday, prompting me to write to the Parish Magazine to thank him for drawing attention to it, as it had proved very interesting!

The website noted that Cupitt's "notoriety peaked in . . . the early 1980s" with *Taking Leave of God* making him "in the eyes of the Press an atheist and perhaps 'the most radical theologian in the world'. He survived, partly because the then Archbishop of Canterbury and the then Master of Emmanuel defended his right to put forward his views." The Archbishop then would have been Robert Runcie, a Caius graduate.

Those views are supported by detailed examination of the relevant writings of philosophers down the ages, and argued with due academic rigour, which is hard to fault. But occasionally Cupitt makes a dogmatic statement that is contrary to what I personally believe. For example, he dismisses the paranormal out of hand, in contrast to Hugh Montefiore, who after his retirement wrote a well-researched, fair and up-to-date assessment, *The Paranormal: A Bishop Investigates* (Upfront, Leicestershire, 2002). So while Cupitt's present Life Fellowship of his Cambridge College could be described as the good fortune of giving him a very secure base for his studies, in this respect at least it could possibly also be a misfortune. For despite the fact that the Society for Psychical Research was founded in 1882 with the active participation of Cambridge dons, the current academic atmosphere there has such a strong bias against the study of the paranormal that even their own Cavendish Professor of Physics, Brian Josephson, F.R.S., has been sidelined on occasion for taking an interest in the subject.

Cupitt's thesis in *Taking Leave of God* was "that the law written on stone tablets must be changed for a law written directly in men's hearts." In *Jesus & Philosophy* he says the Kingdom of God is Blake's Jerusalem, "the dream of a good society that inspires old-fashioned leftists". In other words, "It is a secular hope, the age-old dream of a good society here on this earth." He sees Jesus as "no sort of religious conservative, and no sort of swivel-eyed apocalyptist. He was a secular moral teacher, battling to raise our moral awareness; battling to get all the negative emotions out of human relationships . . . not only 'envy, hatred, malice and all uncharitableness', and not only 'lust, oppression, crime', but much more, for he carries his satirical attack on the ethics of law so far as to ridicule our most basic everyday ideas of justice and desert. Now that really *is* extreme." We have picked a couple of readings to illustrate that last point.

Cupitt's accounts of Jesus' teachings in his later book are drawn from an American study known as the 'Jesus Seminar', which between 1985 and 1993 assessed all the known sources reporting his sayings and finally assembled them in 1995 "into a very carefully composed *Gospel of Jesus*,[1] which reflects the state of the best available traditions about Jesus as they may have stood in about the year 50 or 60." He dismisses the Gospel stories about his life as a largely fictional framework in which the sayings could be recounted: Mark's Gospel "clearly follows the usual pattern of the life of an ancient oriental holy man."

Enter John Dickson, an Australian historian, who quotes none of Cupitt's references, but instead a good number of historical studies from the present century. In his Introduction, he says that "the general public's perception of what experts think about the Jesus of history is massively skewed by voices from the margins of the scholarly playing field. Nowadays the public could be forgiven for thinking that *most* scholars think *most* of the details of Jesus' life are either unknown to us or completely contrary to what Christians find in their treasured Gospels. Neither is true, as we shall see." Dickson stresses 'the randomness of history', which he likens to a game of 'joining the dots'. "Unfortunately, the dots of history are usually unnumbered and very incomplete." This randomness "should caution us against assuming what kind of evidence we ought to possess for the life of Christ. A principle of historical enquiry I learnt early on in my studies states: *absence of evidence does not equal evidence of absence* . . . Just because historians cannot find documentary or archaeological corroboration for an event or person does not mean that the event never occurred or the person never existed." In fact, as his book reveals, we do know a considerable amount about Jesus' life, not only from the biblical records but also from contemporary writings.

---

[1] R. W. Funk and the Jesus Seminar, Polebridge Press, Santa Rosa, CA, 1999.

332

Cally Hammond's writing is also scholarly and closely reasoned, but she works with what is recorded in the Bible. In *Passionate Christianity* she struggles with the events of Good Friday,[1] and how they came to be interpreted by St Paul and the early Church. Just a couple of quotations show that this is not easy:–

"We were slaves to sin and Christ bought us back with the price of his own blood. If we push this image to its natural human conclusion, it would suggest that the ransom was paid to Satan, not to God. This is what some of the early Christians thought, although eventually the Church abandoned that idea . . . Still, this is a valuable reminder that there are limits to how far even biblical metaphors, like ransom and redemption, can take us." (pp.70–71).

"The death of Jesus undoes death. His perfect offering of himself once for all, the lamb of God without spot or blemish, himself both priest and victim, changes reality . . . the death of Jesus should not be understood as a metaphorical or figurative sacrifice (giving up what we value for the sake of some greater good) but as literal sacrifice (the ritual letting of blood of a living creature, and participation in its flesh, through which a union with the divine is brought about)." (p.77).

I don't know what you make of those passages, but to me they show quite clearly that while at least some aspects of religion may be divinely inspired, theology is very definitely man-made. Comparing Jesus being crucified to the 'lamb without blemish' that the Israelites were commanded to kill, cook and eat before their exodus from Egypt seems so contrived that I find it hard to imagine anyone endorsing such a notion, let alone a Cambridge academic.[2] It was very sensible to ensure that everyone had a good meal before setting out on a long and arduous journey, whatever its later ritual significance. Whereas death by crucifixion resulted mainly from being unable to breathe properly without constant painful effort, not loss of blood from a few puncture wounds.

So theology might well be described as Man's attempt to make sense of the incomprehensible. But I have a sneaking feeling that making sense of the incomprehensible is something you are all going to have to do with this talk of mine. Trying to convey in the space of ten minutes or so the essence of four quite different books may well have been a challenge too far, but there is a lot of very interesting material in all of them for me to consider attempting to distil from them something more lucid for January.

---

[1] See also brief mention on p.207.

[2] If Dr Hammond were to reply to this rather unfair stricture, no doubt she would refer me to the whole of this chapter, in which she goes to some lengths to explain how "The reconciling of the world to God could only happen through Jesus Christ, because only he was both true God and true man." (p.70).

Prayers

O Lord, support us all the day long of this troublous life, until the shadows lengthen and the evening comes, and the busy world is hushed, and the fever of life is over, and our work is done. Then in thy mercy grant us a safe lodging, a holy rest, and peace at the last; through Jesus Christ our Lord. *Amen.*

A PRAYER OF ST FRANCIS OF ASSISSI

Lord, make us instruments of thy peace. Where there is hatred, let us give love; where there is injury, pardon; where there is discord, union; where there is doubt, faith; where there is despair, hope; where there is darkness, light; where there is sadness, joy; for thy mercy and for thy truth's sake.   *Amen.*

God of love, whose compassion never fails; we bring to you the sufferings of all mankind; the needs of the homeless; the cry of the prisoner; the pains of the sick and injured; the sorrow of the bereaved; the helplessness of the aged and weak. Strengthen and relieve them, Father, according to their various needs and your great mercy; for the sake of your Son, our Saviour, Jesus Christ.   *Amen.*

Almighty God, who canst bring good out of evil, and makest even the wrath of man to turn to thy praise; teach thy children to live together in charity and peace, and grant that the nations of the world may be united in a firmer fellowship for the promotion of thy glory and the good of all mankind; through Jesus Christ our Lord.   *Amen.*

† Lighten our darkness, we beseech thee, O Lord; and by thy great mercy defend us from all perils and dangers of this night; for the love of thy only son, our Saviour, Jesus Christ.   *Amen.*

A few moments' silence for your own prayers.

The Lord's Prayer.

Go forth into the world in peace; be of good courage; hold fast that which is good; render to no man evil for evil; strengthen the faint-hearted; support the weak; help the afflicted; honour all men; love and serve the Lord; rejoicing in the power of the Holy Spirit.

And the blessing of God Almighty, the Father, the Son, and the Holy Spirit, be upon us, and remain with us for ever.   *Amen.*

Closing Prayer (after final hymn)

Unto the King, eternal, immortal, invisible, the only wise God, be honour and glory for ever and ever.   *Amen.*

SIMPLE SERVICE, WITH HYMNS
31st January 2016

Order of Service

Welcome & Notices (David Beal)

Hymn 358 (Tune: *Be still*) [words are on page 44]
Be still, for the presence of the Lord

Brief introduction (David E.)

Hymn 94 (Tune: *Dix*)
As with gladness men of old

First reading (Clive Cole) Luke, Chapter 8, Verses 1–18 *(NEB)*

Hymn 96 (Tune: *Epiphany*)
Brightest and best of the sons of the morning

Second reading (David E.) Some extracts from *Jesus and Philosophy*

Hymn 236 (Tune: *Carlisle*)
Breathe on me, Breath of God

Brief chat (David E.) Comments on Cupitt's *Jesus and Philosophy*

Hymn 294 (Tune: *Quam Dilecta*)
We love the place, O God

Prayers (Philip)

Hymn 103 (Tune: *Was Lebet*)
O worship the Lord in the beauty of holiness

Closing blessing (David E.)

The service will proceed without announcements. All the hymns are in *Ancient & Modern (2013 Edition)*.

Thank you for coming. **Please join us in the New Vestry after the service** *for a glass of wine (alternatives available).*

Please use the voting form opposite to list your own favourite hymns for a subsequent service.

As always, thank you all for coming.

From 2014 to 2015 we could almost say we had missed a winter service, with a damp but mild day in November, and then a break to the start of Summer Time at the end of March. Although today is mild again, our November service coincided with the first cold day of this winter, which kept a few people away. We can now look forward to May, July and October, which should be warm and light again.

As in November, I was very concerned that we might not be ready in time, but Tony's stalwart help and support have made a big difference, and it has been heartening to be able to rely on Philip for conducting the prayers, and to have Clive to do a reading. However, though Robert has been diligently practising all the hymn tunes from when Tony helped me choose them from your requests early in December, sadly, he is not able to be with us this evening. For the last fortnight he has been troubled with a nasty virus, probably flu, and daren't risk passing this on to any of you. This will be the first time we have been without his help since Peter Knowles handed over to him in October 2005. We are most grateful, therefore, to David Beal for stepping in at very short notice to undertake the necessary accompaniment on his guitar.

We have an unusual second reading today, resulting from my promise in November to say something more lucid about the books I had told you about in my talk. I have restricted myself to just one book instead of four, and rather than intersperse quotations from it with my own comments I have put all the quotations first into a longish reading, and will present some thoughts on them afterwards as my much briefer chat.

Once again we invite you all to join us for a drink after the service.

Luke 8, 1 – 18

After this he went journeying from town to town and village to village, proclaiming the good news of the kingdom of God. With him were the Twelve and a number of women who had been set free from evil spirits and infirmities: Mary, known as Mary of Magdala, from whom seven devils had come out, Joanna, the wife of Chuza a steward of Herod's, Susanna, and many others. These women provided for them out of their own resources.

People were now gathering in large numbers, and as they made their way to him from one town to another, he said in a parable:–

"A sower went out to sow his seed. And as he sowed, some seed fell along the footpath, where it was trampled on, and the birds ate it up. Some seed fell on rock and, after coming up, withered for lack of moisture. Some seed fell in among thistles, and the thistles grew up with it and choked it. And some of the seed fell into good soil, and grew, and yielded a hundredfold."

As he said this he called out, "If you have ears to hear, then hear."

His disciples asked him what this parable meant, and he said, "It has been granted to you to know the secrets of the kingdom of God; but the others have only parables, in order that they may look but see nothing, hear but understand nothing.

"This is what the parable means. The seed is the word of God. Those along the footpath are the men who hear it, and then the devil comes and carries off the word from their hearts for fear they should believe and be saved. The seed sown on rock stands for those who receive the word with joy when they hear it, but have no root; they are believers for a while, but in the time of testing they desert. That which fell among thistles represents those who hear, but their further growth is choked by cares and wealth and the pleasures of life, and they bring nothing to maturity. But the seed in good ground represents those who bring a good and honest heart to the hearing of the word, hold it fast, and by their perseverance yield a harvest."

FROM CUPITT'S *JESUS AND PHILOSOPHY*

I ended my talk in November with the thought that in January I might be able to distil something more lucid from the books I had discussed. It seemed wiser this time to keep to a single author, and I'll take Don Cupitt as the one who has given us the most to think about. I set out to select and quote some briefish key passages, but as this would still make my talk much too long, I have assembled the quotations into our second reading, leaving any comments on them to my 'brief chat'.

Cupitt's speciality was ethics, or morality, a different aspect of religion from biblical study but an equally essential one. Ethics, he says, is difficult to think about clearly, because "we are trying to follow and understand the complex shifting texture of human relationships."

In the past, moral principles were commonly seen as laws. In the Jewish, Christian and Islamic traditions God is seen as absolute Monarch at the cosmic level. His will for his creation is expressed in natural law, in the natural moral law, and in a body of revealed divine moral commandments. Against such a background all major moral wrongdoing was regarded as a sin against *God*, rather than as an offence against a wronged *fellow human*. It was not the *neighbour* whom you had to worry about, . . . whereas *God* was certainly the one chiefly offended and the one with all the power to detect and punish your sin. It was therefore above all necessary to confess your sins very frequently to God, and not to your neighbour, and to obtain absolution from God, and not from your neighbour, and that is exactly what believers did. . . . Only in the second half of the twentieth century were most Roman Catholic and other Western service books revised to incorporate the modern sense that many of our sins are sins against our neighbours and perhaps against society generally, as well as against God.

To make ethics interesting again we need to sharpen up and to make central the controversy that I believe is still the hinge of ethics today. The 'right wing' view emphasizes our 'vertical' relationship to the Moral Standard, seen as being real, unchanging and authoritative. It is the Law, known by conscience. It calls for conscientious and dutiful discharge of our obligations, for an iron will and for strict self-control. On this view the relation to one's fellow human being is secondary. The neighbour is merely the one to whom and for whom we do our duty, and that is all. . . . The alternative view puts all the emphasis upon the 'horizontal' relationship to the fellow human. Its organ of moral knowledge is not the conscience, but rather the heart. It sums up the two chief commandments of the Law, love God and love your neighbour, in the *second*, because this moral outlook is non-metaphysical. Everything has come down into the 'horizontal' temporally flowing world of human life, which is now seen as the field of morality and of human feeling. Self-transcendence is now not a matter of conscientiously living under a Law that is imposed upon one from Above, but rather of a heightened self-awareness that enables us to recognize and to shake off those things in ourselves that make it difficult for us to love and be loved freely.

What made possible the emergence of this new and strongly humanistic ethic of philanthropic feeling, social reform and self-improvement? The familiar answer is surely the correct one: the triumph of the new mechanistic world-picture in the work of Newton suddenly made the universe seem very chilly and non-human. There is no purposiveness out there, and no ready-made moral order built into the way the world goes. All the old 'realist' or objectivist moral theories had suddenly been shown to be just untrue. There is no readymade moral framework, laid on for us at cosmic level, which asks of us only obedient conformity. On the contrary, the universe is cold and non-moral; so cold that we humans find thrust upon us the sole responsibility for building the moral order that we are to live by.

This second type of ethic . . . derives from the old biblical dream of the future establishment of a fully free and good society on earth at the end of time. The dozen or so chief passages about this topic . . . in the Hebrew Bible . . . all describe a world in which the common people enjoy a full span of life, in peace, justice and prosperity. . . And the dream is 'Jerusalem', or in New Testament terms, 'the Kingdom of God'.

The great prophet in antiquity of our modern radical humanist ethic, of . . . our desire to see human beings fully 'free at last', was a neglected Jewish teacher, Jesus of Nazareth. He fell into severe neglect very early, because barely twenty years after his death a great religion began to grow up around his name. . . . It made him into the personification of his own teaching, it made of him therefore himself just one more sovereign lawgiver and around him it rebuilt authoritarian, mediated religion—and so eventually became a standing denial of his original message. But mercifully a few of his own sayings and ideas survived.

Jesus' idea was that a morality of law that defines and observes moral rules precisely, that establishes an elaborate network of reciprocal rights and duties, and that says "Keep all these rules punctiliously and the Kingdom of God will come"—such a morality is utterly unbearable. . . . There cannot be a good and humanly fulfilling society unless everyone is willing on occasion to be ecstatically generous, as when someone donates an organ to a stranger or is willing to go to the aid of a victim of misfortune *anonymously*. Like purity, morality shouldn't be seen as being a matter of what gets put into us; it depends on what comes out of us.

Considering that he is supposed to be the founder of the greatest and most influential of the world's religions, it is a shock to realize that Jesus has no teaching about 'spirituality'. By that I mean that among his teachings there is virtually nothing that presupposes the absolute primacy of the individual's inner and secret relation to God, and that describes ways of purifying ourselves and getting closer to God. It's true that Jesus has the well-loved and beautiful sayings about not letting ourselves fall a prey to undue anxiety. But the bald fact is that he does not teach any system of stages on one's journey into God. . . . His overriding interest is in the space between one human being and another, and in the manifold ways in which that space can be blocked or clouded by an utterly amazing range of 'reactive' or 'negative' emotions and conventional barriers.

Jesus offers an interpretation of what he regards as the destructive core of all the very worst negative emotions. According to him, it is a seething sense of injustice and a desire for vengeance. . . . We know too well that many ordinary people will campaign relentlessly for decades in order to get what they describe as 'justice'—that is, retribution—on behalf either of themselves or of a very seriously wronged relative.

Jesus' remedy, in a surprising number of his major parables and sayings, is to launch a remarkable and disturbing satirical attack upon the ordinary person's desire for, and indeed *concept of*, justice. We are intended to see the wrongness, the mean-spiritedness of the elder brother in the parable of the Prodigal Son, and of the day-labourers in the parable of the Vineyard who have put in the full day's work that they agreed upon that very morning. These characters, and others like them in Jesus' teaching, are too mean-spirited ever to be pleased by someone else's unmerited good fortune. They actually think that the good fortune of that other is tantamount to *an injustice to themselves.*

We cannot hope to check the poisonous destructive effects of [these negative reactions] by an ethic of law and strict justice alone. A touch of pure 'grace' or gratuitous generosity of spirit is needed. In our own world the point is very familiar to negotiators who are struggling to make peace between two communities who have been bitterly hostile to each other for centuries. Each community clings tenaciously to its own story of cherished grievances, justified retaliation and so on. To make peace, you must persuade many people who have bad memories to be almost supernaturally 'big' and generous, and you must go beyond justice. It's a lot to ask, but it has to be done. On this point, the great originality and power of Jesus as a moral teacher has been recognized around the world by many people who have no liking at all for Christianity.

To me, the human and conventional character of modern ethics is exhilarating. It breathes the air of pure moral freedom that since the Second World War has enabled us to bring about huge moral changes. Better health and longer lives for the common people, at least in the developed countries. More care about the environment. Great advances in the social and economic emancipation of women and many other groups. That we humans have in many ways done so well shows that the new only-human and emotivist approach to ethics is at least as good as the old objectivist ethics ever was. And I have claimed that Jesus of Nazareth was a remote and very remarkable pioneer of our modern humanism. As a *man* he has been and still is so influential as almost to justify the division of all history into the periods before and after him.

But there is a serious sense in which the Kingdom-dream seems to be impossible. It seems to be economically impossible. We cannot all live like holy vagabonds, and we cannot *all* of us sell up everything we have. Who would there be to sell *to*? There has to be settled life, there has to be land tenure, there has to be economic exchange, and of course there has to be Piers Plowman, toiling away in the fields every day and carrying the rest of the world on his back. And in view of all this, is it not obvious that there will have to be some sort of compromise between the two moralities? The old theological morality of religious law binds everyone into maintaining the existing social order, while the dream morality is kept as 'pie in the sky' and as a distant hope of future blessedness. The compromise might be justifiable— so long as the Dream is not idle, but genuinely influential and productive.

Since around 1680–1720 the liberal democratic state has gradually come to perform the traditional Corporal Works of Mercy on a vast scale, and today actually implements much of Jesus' programme. In the post-Christian epoch, as the Church has slowly died, the state has become startlingly Christian. The state's ethics today is much more Christian than is the official ethics of the churches. But the secure and highly esteemed public-service side of the culture that delivers the emergency services, welfare benefits and all the rest to the people has become a sort of new 'church', which is actually supported by heavy taxes levied upon the private sector—bankers, businessmen, managers and ordinary workers who actually generate the wealth. It all bears an eerie resemblance to the relationship between the religious and secular realms in the Middle Ages.

This leads me to end by proposing a new, reformulated distinction, between lawlike morality-systems that seek to validate and support the existing social order, and our very long-lived, slow-acting indelible Dream of a world in which human relationships are far, far better than they usually are now. This dream of a radically better world has been enormously influential amongst us, especially during the last few centuries, and it has generated a huge number of spin-offs. We owe it, most of all, to Jesus of Nazareth.

SOME COMMENTS ON CUPITT'S BOOK

There is much to comment on in what I quoted from Don Cupitt's *Jesus and Philosophy*, and of course in the rest of his book as well.

He has a footnote saying that some early Christian writers saw Jesus as 'himself the Kingdom', "and it could be that this is the correct interpretation of Jesus' own chosen way of life and his symbolic actions. He *intends* to act out a kingdom which is always coming into being as he goes along, and as others join it and do the sort of things he does." This ties in with our first reading, which starts with Jesus proclaiming the good news of the kingdom of God. In the parable that follows, the gospel, or good news, is that the kingdom is the result of people hearing *and acting on* the word of God.

In what I quoted in November, Cupitt is scornful about all the Gospel narratives and suggests that only the early records of Jesus' sayings are to be relied on. I think this is unfair, not least because what Jesus did was so unusual and remarkable that it would have been long remembered by his disciples who witnessed them, notably Peter, whom tradition regards as the main source of information for Mark's Gospel.

He is also very doubtful about the healing miracles, and describes Jesus touching the sick as a symbolic action: "The touch of a royal or other charismatic person was felt in prescientific times to be powerfully therapeutic, because it symbolized social acceptance and love" and likens this to Diana, Princess of Wales, shaking hands with an AIDS victim. But by all accounts the lepers, blind people and others whom Jesus touched recovered from their ailments, while as far as we know the AIDS victim did not. It was surely Jesus' fame far and wide as a healer that drew all the crowds to follow him, and consequently to hear his teaching. There are people today with a gift for healing, despite present-day Cambridge academics having closed their minds to all aspects of the 'paranormal'.

Continuing on the academic theme, Cupitt cites the scientific work of Newton and others after him in challenging the metaphysics of religious people; they "made the universe seem very chilly and non-human". Any religion is ultimately concerned with what life is all about and inevitably will generate its own metaphysics, its concept of how things are, so that what it requires its adherents to do can be made to seem reasonable. The Hebrews actually did quite well in getting the order of how life evolved right, even though they were a bit out on the time-scale. As they did not have telescopes they had little idea of the vastness of the universe. But rather like present-day scientists who shy away from anything that might challenge their mechanistic world-view, Church leaders stuck to their old concepts and refused to look through Galileo's telescope.

Cupitt traces his "modern radical humanistic ethic" to "a neglected Jewish teacher, Jesus of Nazareth". Neglected because the religion that grew up around his name rebuilt the authoritarian morality that he had sought to supplant. Unfortunately, that is how things happen in this life; nothing is so simple and straightforward as we might like it to be. Were it not for that "great religion", misguided as Cupitt reckons it to have been, would we now have any record of Jesus' own sayings and ideas at all? Without the Crucifixion there could have been no Resurrection, and was it not the latter which galvanized the scattered Disciples back into action, and ultimately led to Christianity as we know it? It left his followers in no doubt that Jesus was a truly remarkable person, and though that meant his being worshipped for himself as well as for the God whose will he sought to proclaim, it gave authority to all his teachings, and reason for them to be recorded for the benefit of future generations.

It is undoubtedly regrettable that down the ages there has been so much argument among followers of this "great religion" concerning its metaphysical assertions and speculations. Beliefs so strongly held have led to unbelievable cruelty exacted on people who did not share them, all in the name of a loving God! This certainly goes back to the parallel with codes of civil laws, with their prescribed penalties for non-compliance.

Some observances start as what has been learnt by experience. It is very sensible to wash one's hands before handling food. Only long usage made this into a ritual observance, never to be omitted.

I am sorry that Cupitt welcomes the decline of Church Christianity, talking about "the post-Christian epoch". Surely a local Church, at its best, and I mean the people who are part of it and not the building, can and should be a microcosm of the Kingdom-dream that he longs for? A body of people who not only care for each other, but also reach out to the people of the town or village where they live?

On the other hand, I can't resist a comment on the "much more Christian ethics of the state". We are indeed so fortunate in being looked after so well. We are provided with 'benefits' to enable us to live if we are unable to work, but complain that they are unfair or insufficient. We have free, or nearly free, medical facilities, but complain that we can't get to see a doctor, or that the one we saw failed to see what was wrong with us. The daily news often suggests that we are a nation of whingers.

To end on a personal note, I considered myself fortunate to have been a Scout when I was a boy. While the Ten Commandments were nearly all negative, the Scout Law and Promise were very positive. Even better, the provisions were not obligatory; you had only to promise to do your best to observe them. And as a leader you were reminded to allow that some boys' best wasn't necessarily going to be as good as that of others.

Prayers

Teach us, good Lord, to serve thee as thou deservest; to give and not to count the cost; to fight and not to heed the wounds; to toil and not to seek for rest; to labour and not to ask for any reward save that of knowing that we do thy will. *Amen.*

A PRAYER OF ST FRANCIS OF ASSISSI

Lord, make us instruments of thy peace. Where there is hatred, let us give love; where there is injury, pardon; where there is discord, union; where there is doubt, faith; where there is despair, hope; where there is darkness, light; where there is sadness, joy; for thy mercy and for thy truth's sake. *Amen.*

O merciful Father, whose will it is that we should love one another, give us grace that we may fulfil it. Make us gentle, courteous and forbearing. Direct our lives so that we may each look to the good of the other in word and deed; and hallow all our friendships by the blessing of thy Spirit, for his sake who loved us and gave himself for us, Jesus Christ our Lord. *Amen.*

Almighty God, our creator and preserver, we thank thee for the springtime, in which thou art renewing the face of the earth and quickening all things. Thou who carest for the trees and flowers, revive and renew our life, that we may bring forth the fruit of good works, as disciples of him who came to quicken in human hearts the seed of eternal life; through Jesus Christ our Lord. *Amen.*

A few moments' silence for your own prayers.

The Lord's Prayer.

May the love and friendship of Jesus go with us now and his Spirit abide with us for ever. *Amen.*

Closing Blessing

May the Lord bless us and keep us; the Lord make his face to shine upon us and be gracious to us; the Lord lift up the light of his countenance upon us and give us peace, this night and for evermore. *Amen.*

SIMPLE SERVICE, WITH HYMNS

29th May 2016

Order of Service

Welcome & Notices (Pam)

Hymn 422 (Tune: *Hyfrydol*)
Alleluia, sing to Jesus!

Brief introduction (David E.)

Hymn 746 (Tune: *St Anne*)
O God, our help in ages past

First reading (David E.) Philippians, Chapter 4, Verses 6–14 *(NEB)*

Hymn 706 (Tune: *Monkland*)
Let us, with a gladsome mind

Second reading (Tony) 2 Corinthians, Chapter 12, Verses 1–10 *(NEB)*

Hymn 587 (Tune: *Amazing grace*) [words on p.38]
Amazing grace (how sweet the sound)

"A New Day, A New Direction – This is my Testimony" (*Jane Burton*)

Hymn 739 (Tune: *Nun danket*)
Now thank we all our God

Prayers (Philip)

Hymn 748 (Tune: *Thornbury*)
O Jesus, I have promised

Closing blessing (David E.)

The service will proceed without announcements. All the hymns are in *Ancient & Modern (2013 Edition)*.

Thank you for coming. **Please join us in the New Vestry after the service** *for a glass of wine or apple juice.*

Please use the voting form opposite to list your own favourite hymns for a subsequent service.

As always, thank you all for coming, especially on as nice a day as this in the middle of a Bank Holiday weekend. David Beal has sent his apologies; in fact he might normally have gone away for the whole week at half term, but decided to stay for this morning's services as it was only last week that he told everyone he would be moving to Billingshurst.

Our thanks to Pam for being with us to start us off with any notices.

It's good to be back to light evenings and we can now look forward to July and October, which should be warm and light as well.

It's also good to have Robert back on the keyboard; he had to miss our January service when he was troubled with a nasty virus, probably flu. David Beal stepped into the breach to accompany all our hymns on his guitar, which he was able to link up to our sound system, and we also had some Choir members to help keep us in tune. Thanks again to Tony, for his help with the planning, and to Philip for doing the prayers.

This service is very special on account of something completely different in respect of what we call our 'Brief Chat'. We have a guest speaker and, as you will have seen from the service sheet, she is going to present what she calls her Testimony, which you might say is how a very talented young person suddenly found her life going in an unexpected direction, and received the help and inspiration she needed to continue.

I am not going to spoil her story by saying anything less enigmatic, but I can tell you that she and I met a few weeks ago after attending the funeral of a dear friend; she vaguely remembered my face but not my name; and I recalled her name as someone Tony and I had met in 2010.[1]

Whereas I am at the Don Cupitt end of the theological spectrum, Jane is very much at the Billy Graham end, and as her mother went to hear him a couple of months before she was born she can claim to have been 'born again' when she came into this world! Later in life she met the famous preacher; uncertain of what to say to him she mentioned a name—of someone who turned out to be Billy Graham's best friend!

Jane has been on the staff at the Big Church Day Out at Wiston this weekend, but has slipped away a little early to be with us this evening. At her request I have printed some copies of her talk for any of you who would like to have one or more to pass on to friends or relatives.

Once again we invite you all to come back and join us for a drink after the service.

---

[1] Later checking of records revealed that this was actually in 2009.

Philippians 4, 6–14

The Lord is near; have no anxiety, but in everything make your requests known to God in prayer and petition with thanksgiving. Then the peace of God, which is beyond our utmost understanding, will keep guard over your hearts and your thoughts, in Christ Jesus.

And now, my friends, all that is true, all that is noble, all that is just and pure, all that is lovable and gracious, whatever is excellent and admirable—fill all your thoughts with these things.

The lessons I taught you, the tradition I have passed on, all that you heard me say or saw me do, put into practice; and the God of peace will be with you.

It is a great joy to me, in the Lord, that after so long your care for me has now blossomed afresh. You did care about me before for that matter; it was opportunity that you lacked. Not that I am alluding to want, for I have learned to find resources in myself whatever my circumstances. I know what it is to be brought low, and I know what it is to have plenty. I have been very thoroughly initiated into the human lot with all its ups and downs—fullness and hunger, plenty and want. I have strength for anything through him who gives me power. But it was kind of you to share the burden of my troubles.

2 Corinthians 12, 1–10

I am obliged to boast. It does no good; but I shall go on to tell of visions and revelations granted by the Lord. I know a Christian man who fourteen years ago (whether in the body or out of it, I do not know—God knows) was caught up as far as the third heaven. And I know that this same man (whether in the body or out of it, I do not know—God knows) was caught up into paradise, and heard words so secret that human lips may not repeat them. About such a man as that I am ready to boast; but I will not boast on my own account, except of my weaknesses.

If I should choose to boast, it will not be the boast of a fool, for I should be speaking the truth. But I refrain, because I should not like anyone to form an estimate of me which goes beyond the evidence of his own eyes and ears. And so, to keep me from being unduly elated by the magnificence of such revelations, I was given a sharp pain in my body which came as Satan's messenger to bruise me; this was to save me from being unduly elated. Three times I begged the Lord to rid me of it, but his answer was: "My grace is all you need; power comes to its full strength in weakness." I shall therefore prefer to find my joy and pride in the very things that are my weakness; and then the power of Christ will come and rest upon me. Hence I am well content, for Christ's sake, with weakness, contempt, persecution, hardship and frustration; for when I am weak, then I am strong.

A NEW DAY, A NEW DIRECTION – THIS IS MY TESTIMONY
by Jane Burton[1]

Heavy rain was falling and visibility was poor as four of us rode back to London from a party in High Wycombe. It was 2.30 in the morning. When I got into the car, I didn't know that the driver had had too much to drink. As we sped along, the driver did not see the signs directing traffic onto the filter road. Up ahead an oil tanker had overturned, spilling oil. With the mixture of oil and rain, the road had become like a sheet of ice. The car slid down a 50-foot slope, hitting a lamppost on the way. The impact forced the wheels and the doors to fall off, and I was thrown out. Amazingly this saved my life. The driver was killed instantly. (The other passengers suffered minor injuries. *DJE*)

My neck was fractured in two places, also two bones in my wrist. My knee and right hand were badly cut. I had a fractured skull and remained unconscious for nearly a week. When I finally awoke I had total amnesia for two weeks. I couldn't remember that at age 22 I was already well established in a successful career as a dancer.

When I was three years old, I had started dancing lessons. When I was seven, my family moved and my new dance teacher told my mother that I had great talent and should take up dancing as a career.

At age 11 I was sent to Bush Davies School, located about 30 miles south of London. It is a boarding school specializing in dance training as well as offering the usual academic studies. I worked hard for five years, training in all styles of dance, including ballet, jazz, contemporary and tap. I passed all the ballet and modern exams, and was one of four students at the top of the ballet class. All four of us went for further training at the Royal Ballet School in London. In the middle of my second year I heard about a private audition with the London Festival Ballet Company. I auditioned, was offered the job, and a few days later I was performing in *Swan Lake*.

After a year with Festival Ballet, I turned to free-lance work. Although I enjoyed ballet, I wanted the freedom to perform the other styles of dance that I'd trained for. In the following years I danced with numerous companies all over Europe expanding my repertoire to include jazz and contemporary as well as ballet. I also sang and danced with an Italian Operetta Company as well as five Operas at Covent Garden Opera House. In between all of this I managed to fit in three television series, which was all period dance.

As soon as my career started, I stopped going to church. I had been reared in the church, but now I didn't think that I needed Jesus. My life seemed great without him.

---

[1] Compiled in conjunction with the author and published internationally by *Decision*.

Then the accident happened. Although most of my memory eventually returned during the next twelve months, I was left with constant back pain, frequent headaches, a painful knee and brain damage. To prevent the recurrence of epileptic fits I was allowed no physical activity that was more strenuous than walking.

I had to face the truth that I would never resume my career as a dancer. This made me rebel against God. I couldn't understand why He had allowed this to happen. What was the point of being alive if I couldn't dance?

Ten months after the accident I was sent to a psychiatric hospital where I was treated for suicidal depression. While there, a Christian friend visited me. He gave me the book, *Joni*, by Joni Eareckson Tada. It tells the true story of a young woman who, at the age of 17, broke her neck in a diving accident. Though a quadriplegic she has become a wonderful servant of Christ. If God could use Joni, maybe He could use me too, and I realized that He had saved my life for a reason. I knelt by my bed and committed my life to Christ.

When I was released from the hospital, I began attending my parents' church. There I responded to an altar call and publicly accepted Jesus Christ as my Lord and Saviour.

Emotional healing came slowly as my anger and bitterness lingered for another couple of years. I was grieving over the loss of my career. Eventually I was able to dance again but I had to accept I would never again achieve professional status. I was in constant physical pain and unable to hold any job down for any length of time.

Soon after this commitment another friend told me about the Arts Centre Group. This is an organization set up by a small group of professional artists who are Christian. After a few months of regular meetings with other Christian dancers we decided to form a dance group that would communicate the Gospel message visually through dance and mime. We named it "Springs". Now it is considered "Europe's foremost professional Christian dance company"!

In December 1979, I emigrated to Australia, where I became involved in the Christian Dance Fellowship of Australia as a teacher. Two years later I became a founder member of another Christian dance group. We called it "Prepare" [Isaiah 40:3 "Prepare ye the way of the Lord"] and this time I was their teacher, choreographer, and dancer. I also went to Vision Bible College in Sydney.

My bitterness began to disappear as I came to realize that I had gifts other than dancing, and that God could use me to reach people who needed to hear the Good News of Jesus Christ. While in Sydney, I did volunteer work through a church. I worked at a day-care centre for the elderly where I frequently had the opportunity to tell people that Jesus loves them. In telling them of Jesus' love, I became even more convinced of his love for me!

After nearly five years in Australia, I returned to London, where I struggled through long periods of unemployment. But early in 1990 I began teaching dance to children aged 3 to 12 at a YMCA youth hostel in Wimbledon. I also took on the position of membership administrator at the same hostel. I loved my work.

At my church I did volunteer work, such as helping in the kitchen or on the welcome desk during the week. And on Sundays I was either teaching in the children's Sunday school or ushering in the Church service. I'm also a voluntary visitor at a hospice for terminally ill cancer patients. I talk with the patients and sometimes I read to them from the Bible and pray with them. I always leave feeling blessed.

I also have what I call a 'car ministry'. I give people rides to and from the airport, or I help them move maybe from hostel to house. Sometimes I take people around London sightseeing. This gives me an opportunity to witness to my faith. One girl told me that while I was taking her to see the sights in London, she could see Christ in me and she decided that she too wanted to give her life to the Lord!

I am continually finding opportunities to communicate the love of Christ to other accident victims. Because I am able to relate to how they are feeling, I can open up to them and tell them how God loved me and saved my life and healed me. I have also been able to be a support to other dancers who have suffered injuries. At the Arts Centre Group where I work voluntarily, I am known as the 'encourager'!

I feel humbled and privileged that God is able to use me to help others. This might not have been possible had I not struggled through physical and emotional pain, depression and rejection. It is still hard sometimes to accept my limitations and also my singleness, but, like the Apostle Paul, I am learning to be content in whatever situation I find myself.

Philippians 4:11 and 4:13 – I can do everything through Him who gives me strength.

As soon as I wake up in the morning and often throughout the day, I praise God for His goodness to me. Sometimes I don't feel like praising God, but I find that an attitude of thankfulness gets me through the difficult times.

One of the most difficult problems I've had over many of these years has been learning how to forgive the man who was driving that car. I cannot remember his name and have no way of finding it. I have no memory of his appearance or how he behaved. I would find it easier if he was still alive or if I had known him before that fatal night. How many times have I honestly said "I forgive you" and then the next day cursed him because I'm in pain or in some emotional upset.

I happened to watch *The Hour of Power*, which is broadcast on television every Sunday from the Crystal Cathedral in Los Angeles. They had a guest who ran a 'Forgiveness Ministry'. I really feel that the Holy Spirit spoke to me as I suddenly realized that I was thankful that I had broken my neck. If I had broken my leg, yes my career would have ended, but would anyone write a book about breaking their leg and as a result commit their life to Christ? I doubt it! So I now Praise God for Joni's books as I would not be walking with the Lord as I am now without having suffered a broken neck.

Now I consider my career to be one of serving Christ. My goal is to be bold about my faith, and to win non-believers to the Lord. Recently I had the opportunity to dance at a church service. This was new to many in the congregation, and I found that barriers dropped as people said they sensed the Holy Spirit working through me.

Paul's words in 2 Corinthians 12:9 are especially meaningful to me: "I begged the Lord to rid me of [the pain in my body], but his answer was: 'My grace is all you need; power comes to its full strength in weakness.' I shall therefore prefer to find my joy and pride in the very things that are my weakness; and then the power of Christ will come and rest upon me."

Although I am weak, I thank the Lord that He didn't allow me to die in the accident, but that He gave me a new life . . . a life through which He is able to demonstrate His power and glorify His name.

ladyjanehaha@yahoo.co.uk   *publ. February 1991 from information supplied 1988/89*[1]

---

[1] *David Ellis writes:–* When compiling this book I asked Jane about what she had done since her Testimony was published. She told me that she had many messages from people who had derived inspiration for themselves, and a couple offering her work involving her dancing expertise – one from Anchorage in Alaska and one from Slovakia. The former fell through from no fault of hers or of the organization, but simply because they lost their funding; the latter required a visa that would have taken many months to obtain. She lived in West London for eleven years, doing voluntary work at All Souls' Church, Langham Place. Having gone on mission to Egypt twice in 1985, she loved that country so much that she visited the Coptic Church in Kensington for some tuition in Arabic. Besides fluency in languages she also has a gift in Networking, involving introducing people from her wide circle of contacts to each other, often with a very productive outcome. She became involved with the dramatization of *The Life of Christ* at Wintershall in 2009, the year she met Tony and me (for details visit **www.wintershall.org.uk**), as well as *The Passion* in Trafalgar Square. In 2010, during 'The Feeding of the 5000', she noticed a Coptic Priest sitting in the audience, and spoke to him in Arabic! At the end she introduced him to a Chinese Missionary who was also based in Brighton. As a result *The Passion* has been presented, over the Easter weekend, every year in various places in Brighton.

Prayers

Jesus said, "Where two or three are gathered together in my Name, there am I in the midst of them."

O Lord, who never failest both to hear and to answer the prayer that is sincere; let not our minds be set on worldly things when we pray, nor our prayers end upon our lips, but send us forth with power to work thy will in the world; through Jesus Christ our Lord. *Amen.*

O Lord, we do not pray for tasks equal to our strength; we ask for strength equal to our tasks.

O Almighty and everlasting God, we praise thy holy Name for all the blessings, known and unknown, which we have this day received from thy bounty, beseeching thee still to continue thy fatherly care over us, and to give us such a sense of thy mercies that we may show forth our thankfulness by a humble, holy and devout life, in Jesus Christ our Lord. *Amen.*

Our Father, as we turn to the comfort of our rest, we remember those who must wake that we may sleep; bless those who watch over us at night, the firemen and police, and all who carry on through the hours of darkness the restless commerce of men on land and sea. We thank thee for their faithfulness and sense of duty; we pray thee for pardon, if our selfishness or luxury adds to their nightly toil. Grant that we may realize how dependent the safety of our loved ones and the comforts of life are on these our brothers, so that we may think of them with love and gratitude, and help to make their burden lighter; for the sake of Jesus Christ our Lord. *Amen.*

O God, our Father, by whose will we dwell together in families, let thy blessing rest upon our homes. Bless our parents, our children, and all the members of our families. Give them health and strength of soul and body, and unite us all in love for thee; through Jesus Christ our Lord. *Amen.*

A few moments' silence for your own prayers.

The Lord's Prayer.

May the Lord lead us when we go, and keep us when we sleep, and talk with us when we wake; and may the peace of God, which passeth all understanding, keep our hearts and minds in Jesus Christ our Lord. *Amen.*

Closing Blessing

The power of the Father, the wisdom of the Son, the love of the Holy Spirit, keep, teach, and guide us for ever. *Amen.*

SIMPLE SERVICE, WITH HYMNS
31st July 2016

Order of Service

Welcome & Notices
 Hymn 613 (Tune: *Richmond*)
  City of God, how broad and far

Brief introduction (David E.)
 Hymn 537 (Tune: *England's Lane*)
  For the beauty of the earth

First reading (Clive) Luke, Chapter 24, Verses 13–43 *(NEB)*
 Hymn 128 (Tune: *Aberystwyth*)
  Jesu, lover of my soul

Second reading (David E.) "The Story of a Hymn"
 Hymn 584 (Tune: *Michael*)
  All my hope on God is founded

Brief chat (Tony) "The Turin Shroud"
 Hymn 10 (Tune: *Eventide*)
  Abide with me; fast falls the eventide

Prayers (Philip)
 Hymn 594 (Tune: *Finlandia*)
  Be still, my soul: the Lord is on your side

Closing blessing (David E.)

The service will proceed without announcements. All the hymns are in *Ancient & Modern (2013 Edition)*.

Thank you for coming. **Please join us in the New Vestry after the service** *for a glass of wine or apple juice.*

Please use the voting form opposite to list your own favourite hymns for a subsequent service.

As always, thank you all for coming, again on a pleasant summer day. I love this time of the year, when we can arrive and get home afterwards in the daylight. David Beal will be home on Wednesday, after his two weeks away and his and Mary's wedding anniversary on Tuesday.

Clive offered to do a reading this time, which we have gratefully taken up, and thanks once again to Philip for doing the prayers, plus Robert, as usual, for his work on the keyboard, which involves a lot of rehearsing. But especial thanks to Tony this time, not only for taking on the talk and joining me on the planning, but also for drafting the prayers for Philip rather than just choosing some from the many we have used previously.

We had something completely different in respect of what we call our 'Brief Chat' last time, when Jane Burton came and presented her Testimony and told us how it had encouraged people over the years. It was very welcome for Tony and me not to have to put something together ourselves at what proved to be a very busy time. We had longer to work on Tony's talk, but that does mean that we are using it well past the relevant time of the year, and the same goes for the reading to go with it. This is a longish one that we have actually used before, when we had a service on Easter Day in 2013. However, all the other items, apart from this introduction, are shorter than usual.

When we started these services, the idea of letting people choose a number of hymns each was that it increased the chance of a hymn being asked for by more than one person. That actually happened this time, but we did not immediately notice this! However, we were able to get David Burnett to amend our list of hymns in the July magazine to include it. In case you are unfamiliar with *All my hope on God is founded* Robert will play the whole verse through for you first.

Once again we invite you all to come back and join us for a drink after the service.

Luke 24, 13–43

That same day two of them were on their way to a village called Emmaus, which lay about seven miles from Jerusalem, and they were talking together about all these happenings. As they talked and discussed it with one another, Jesus himself came up and walked along with them; but something held their eyes from seeing who it was.

He asked them, "What is it that you are debating as you walk?"

They halted, their faces full of gloom, and one, called Cleopas, answered, "Are you the only person staying in Jerusalem not to know what has happened there in the last few days?"

"What do you mean?" he said.

"All this about Jesus of Nazareth," they replied, "a prophet powerful in speech and action before God and the whole people; how our chief priests and rulers handed him over to be sentenced to death, and crucified him. But we had been hoping that he was the man to liberate Israel. What is more, this is the third day since it happened, and now some women of our company have astounded us: they went early to the tomb, but failed to find his body, and returned with a story that they had seen a vision of angels who told them he was alive. So some of our people went to the tomb and found things just as the women had said; but him they did not see."

"How dull you are!" he answered. "How slow to believe all that the prophets said! Was the Messiah not bound to suffer thus before entering upon his glory?" Then he began with Moses and all the prophets, and explained to them the passages which referred to himself in every part of the scriptures.

By this time they had reached the village to which they were going, and he made as if to continue his journey, but they pressed him: "Stay with us, for evening draws on and the day is almost over."

So he went in to stay with them. And when he had sat down with them at the table, he took bread and said the blessing; he broke the bread, and offered it to them. Then their eyes were opened, and they recognized him; and he vanished from their sight. They said to one another, "Did we not feel our hearts on fire as he talked with us on the road and explained the scriptures to us?"

Without a moment's delay they set out and returned to Jerusalem. There they found that the Eleven and the rest of the company had assembled, and were saying, "It is true: the Lord has risen; he has appeared to Simon." Then they gave their account of the events of their journey and told how he had been recognized by them at the breaking of the bread.

As they were talking about all this, there he was, standing among them. Startled and terrified, they thought they were seeing a ghost. But he said, "Why are you so perturbed? Why do questionings arise in your minds? Look at my hands and feet. It is I myself. Touch me and see; no ghost has flesh and bones as you can see that I have."

They were still unconvinced, still wondering, for it seemed too good to be true. So he asked them, "Have you anything here to eat?"

They offered him a piece of fish they had cooked, which he took and ate before their eyes.

N.B. For technical information about the tests on the Turin Shroud (p.356) and the quotation from the Italian physicist, we are indebted to an article by Frank Viviano, published on the web by *National Geographic* on 17 April 2015.

THE STORY OF A HYMN

This is billed as a reading, of something I saw in the Pulborough Parish Magazine a year or two ago, but though I searched through my dusty copies of back numbers for at least an hour and a half on Friday evening I was unable to locate the copy concerned. Most probably it had been put somewhere else on account of that article! So I shall just have to rely on my probably rather imperfect memory of it.

The author is given as Henry Francis Lyte (1793–1847), so he was no more than 54 when he died. He was a local minister, somewhere, I think, in the West Country, perhaps Somerset, but he also wrote a few hymns, including *Praise, my soul, the King of heaven*. His health had declined and he was aware that he might not have much longer to live, but he thought he could make the trip to Lourdes, the place in France renowned for its healing powers.

Maybe it was at Eastertide that he was reminded of our first reading, and of what those two disciples said to Jesus when they got to Emmaus, as the Authorized Version put it: "Abide with us; for it is toward evening, and the day is far spent." Perhaps the parallel with his own life struck him as this too seemed to be coming rapidly to its evening. So he penned a few verses on that theme and how he felt about things, little knowing that with a memorable tune composed by someone who was then only 24, it would become such a well-known hymn that even a crossword clue could be based on it in the 21st Century. We shall sing it after Tony's talk.

THE TURIN SHROUD

During the late 1950s and early 1960s considerable interest was shown in an ancient piece of linen cloth which was held in Turin Cathedral.

The cloth is about fourteen feet long by three feet in width.

The many dark 'stains' on the cloth correspond to a human male body which bears the marks of wounds associated with the scourging and execution by crucifixion as described in the Bible to have been suffered by Jesus Christ!

Over the years, this cloth had passed through many hands before finally reaching Turin Cathedral, where on certain occasions it has been exhibited for adoration by the faithful.

The body had been laid on the Shroud such that half of this could then be folded back to cover the face and body of the deceased. Stains left by the body could be clearly seen but it was not until photography had been invented and a photograph taken of it in 1898 that scientific interest in it was aroused.

Before the invention of digital imaging in modern times, photography was a two-stage process. The action of light on a silver compound in the camera caused it to darken and this could be made into a permanent image by processing with the appropriate chemicals. As the brightest parts of the image came out darkest, the result, in early days on a glass plate and later on celluloid film, was known as a negative. A positive was then made by shining light through this negative and focusing it on light-sensitive paper. The excitement of this first photograph resulted from the examination of the original negative, which showed the image of the man in a very positive way! There were even scratches on the forehead that might have come from the crown of thorns placed on Jesus' head!

Twentieth-century scientists were eager to use techniques at their disposal to examine the Shroud and a team of 33 experts was granted five days' access in 1978. They brought seven tons of equipment and worked night and day. They found no evidence of artificial pigments and showed that the bloodstains were composed of haemoglobin. The image was very thin, penetrating to only a thirtieth of the diameter of a single thread.

In 1983 the Shroud's ownership was legally transferred to the Catholic Church and in 1988 the Vatican allowed small samples from a corner of the fabric to be removed for carbon-14 dating tests. Several laboratories working independently found that the material dated to the years between 1260 and 1390, which tallied with the first appearance of the Shroud in 1353. These results have been challenged but robustly defended. No one has come up with any way of producing anything like the image by artificial means, so how could a medieval forger have done it anyway?

So for the last 118 years the argument has been going on between the believers and the sceptics! I of course would like it to be believable and felt fairly comfortable to accept that the Shroud was not a fake, as photography had not been invented until well after the Shroud was 'made', so a 'negative' had never been seen. However, printing for books was relatively known much earlier and to achieve a readable printed page the type had to be set up as a negative. This of course does not 'prove' that the Shroud is a fake, only that one cannot prove that it is not.

An Italian physicist who is a leading expert on the Shroud has said that he thinks it unlikely that science will provide a full solution to the many riddles posed: "A leap of faith over questions without clear answers is necessary— either the 'faith' of sceptics, or the faith of believers."

What does the Shroud tell us if it is genuine? For a start, it would be the only photo-portrait we have of Jesus. Secondly, it tallies with the biblical accounts, not only concerning the wounds inflicted on Jesus but also of the post-resurrection appearances of Jesus, those that strive to make it clear that it was not a ghost that his disciples were meeting again. One wonders what will be revealed if it becomes possible to do DNA tests on the bloodstains . . .

Prayers

Lord, we live in a time when many people do not find time for you! Many of them believe that the wonders of the Universe which Science has shown us can be used as the basis of an attack on religious faith when in fact they enhance it.

Lord, please give comfort to those who are sick. Where possible, help in their recovery, but if recovery is not to be, help them accept your will with a calm and settled mind.   *Amen.*

Please, Lord, bless your divided Church throughout the 'world' and help us to accept with love those who interpret your teachings in a manner slightly different from our own approach.   *Amen.*

Please comfort those who have 'lost' a loved one, whether this loss is recent or long-standing.   *Amen.*

Please help those who so willingly give their time in the smooth running of your Church here in West Sussex, our Rector, Churchwardens and those who form the various committees that are necessary for the running of this Church and the wider community.   *Amen.*

Bless our Rector, David, and his family as he prepares to leave us and takes up his new post within the Diocese. Please help those who will choose David's replacement as our Rector and will continue to 'steer' the good people of West Chiltington.   *Amen.*

A few moments' silence for your own prayers.

The Lord's Prayer.

Unto the King, eternal, immortal, invisible, the only wise God, be honour and glory for ever and ever.   *Amen.*

Closing Blessing

May the blessing of almighty God rest upon us and upon all our work; may he give us light to guide us, courage to support us, and love to unite us, now and evermore.   *Amen.*

SIMPLE SERVICE, WITH HYMNS
30th October 2016

Order of Service

Welcome & Notices

Hymn 758 (Tune: *St Gertrude*)
Onward, Christian soldiers

Brief introduction (David E.)

Hymn 754 (Tune: *Hanover*)
O worship the King, all glorious above

First reading (Clive) "How Christian is the Family?" *by David Burnett*

Hymn 652 (Tune: *Cwm Rhondda*)
Guide me, O thou great Redeemer

Brief chat (Philip) "Putting the World to Rights"

Hymn 645 (Tune: *Dambusters' March*)
God is our strength and refuge

Further Comments (David E.) "Influences on the Family"

Hymn 629 (Tune: *Sussex*)
Father, hear the prayer we offer

Prayers (Tony)

Hymn 735 (*Mission Praise;* words on page 25. Tune: *Finlandia*)
We rest on Thee, our shield and our defender

Closing blessing (David E.)

The service will proceed without announcements. All the hymns are in *Ancient & Modern (2013 Edition)* except the last one, which is in *Mission Praise* (words opposite).

Thank you for coming. **Please join us in the New Vestry after the service** *for a glass of wine (alternatives available).*

Please use the voting form overleaf to list your own favourite hymns for a subsequent service.

Well, we are now at the end of October, for the first time since 2011, and like then the weather is still quite mild. As always, thank you all for coming, and 'the team' for your efforts, including Robert for his sterling work on the keyboard, both on the hymns and on music before and after the service.

We have a very unusual format this time, which started when I saw that Philip had done a talk a year ago which we had never used. He had written it in response to David Burnett's Editorial in the May 2015 Parish Magazine, so rather than quote what David had said we decided that the simplest solution would be to have David's piece as a reading.

David was talking about Christianity and the family, and commented that there wasn't much mention of family life in Christian literature, or of Jesus' family life in the New Testament, so we decided to omit a biblical reading altogether, which made room for a second chat after Philip's talk.

My especial thanks to Tony this time, not only for joining me on the planning, but also for taking on the prayers in Philip's place and drafting the opening ones as well as choosing some from the many we've used previously.

Once again we invite you all to come back and join us for a drink after the service.

HOW CHRISTIAN IS THE FAMILY?

Virtually every Christian I have known has thought of the family as being a very Christian idea. We may not have invented it but we certainly approve of it. But how Christian is the family?

From what is known of culturally primitive people (mostly small 'lost' tribes in the jungles of the Amazon or small South East Asian islands) they live as small tribes or extended families of about 30 not seriously divided into nuclear families; a sort of commune with a strong loyalty.

Something similar seems implied in Genesis as in the story of Abram (who was renamed Abraham by God), who was nomadic. A similar structure probably survived into Greek and Roman times where duty to family was often the supreme moral imperative. A similar impulse is detectable in English society in the days of Jane Austen, though more nuclear and less tribal. The family was 'nature's insurance policy' where wealth and hence freedom from destitution depended on the family. Hence the importance of arranged marriages. Think of *Pride and Prejudice*, where the family fortune was entailed away from daughters and the consequent huge importance of at least one daughter making a 'good marriage', since achieving that protected all the rest from ruin.

As we passed through Victorian times families became more nuclear but, in the absence of state benefits, family membership was your best chance of surviving bad luck.

During the 20th century state benefits such as unemployment benefit and the old age pension grew in size and scope. This has been accompanied by the steady disintegration of even the nuclear family and it is hard to resist the idea that family disintegration was perhaps caused by the rise of state benefits. The main social bond was no longer the family one but that between the state and the isolated individual. Put simply, our society lost its granularity and became atomised.

Interestingly, although I assume early Christians shared their local family-oriented culture, there is not much reference to it in Christian literature. The occurrence of apostles, hermits and the like points to an emphasis on a God/man relationship rather than a family one.

We (Christians) still like the idea of a strong and stable nuclear family, whatever the above says. It provides some protection in times of sickness and unemployment. Perhaps even more important is the stability and protection afforded to children if father and mother stay together (and don't quarrel). There have been any number of studies showing that the children of long-term relationships do better in later life.

'Middle class' families do well because they are stable. Poorer families, more dependent on state benefits and more short-term, do badly. Put brutally, stable families are good, unstable/single parent families are bad. Christian views are projected in things like nativity plays and crib scenes. Rather embarrassingly the New Testament does not make much of Jesus' family life, though his bond with his mother Mary is clear. Perhaps to Gospel writers a strong sense of family — like the law of gravity — was too obvious to need stating.

This is not to pick on single parents (usually mothers) or on gays, who might indeed make very good parents, but these arrangements are not seen as ideal. We are learning to live with divorce and cohabitation on the grounds of making the best of a difficult situation, of not making things worse than they already are.

In fact the whole area of sexual behaviour has become rather a grey one. The old certainties have been set aside but no new ones have emerged to put in their place. In a sense we know what we like but are afraid to criticise what differs from it. Perhaps in the absence of Biblical certainties we do not want to let cultural (not necessarily Christian) beliefs harden into hostile judgemental condemnations. We still have a duty to love our fellows.

An example of the sort of thing I am thinking of is the move to women priests and bishops. Quite a few people I have talked to are not enthusiastic about this development but are trying to come to terms with change.

David Burnett

PUTTING THE WORLD TO RIGHTS

The May 2015 Parish Magazine Editorial was on the broad spectrum of Christian marriage, and the wider family. This raised so many 'trigger points' for me.

I borrow from George Carey (103rd Archbishop of Canterbury) and his book, *Know the Truth—A Memoir*. His boyhood family background was:–

. . . like so many a Church of England family . . . the Church of England we did *not* attend (like many families), although we were not grafted into the institutional Church, we still felt deeply Christian.

A fair description, one imagines, of where we are nowadays as well?

At best!

He adds:–

. . . as with so many social trends the reasons for the decline in Church-going are more prosaic than are sometimes realized.

Most people do not leave institutions (the Church, the Family) because they no longer *believe*, but because they no longer have a sense of belonging.

The contours of the World have changed.

The transformation of small towns into industrial centres fed by changes in ready transport—train, car, 'plane—have had their impact on community life, and correspondingly on our sense of where 'home' is located. *[This ends my quotation from George Carey.]*

From all this, it does seem that the parochial/close-knit family, established over many centuries, has indeed suffered a *huge* blow to its position in present society.

Our Magazine's Editor raised some thought-provoking observations regarding problems besetting the established, and, as might be termed, our 'Host population'. It seems to me to need to become more like some of this country's immigrant communities, in the especial context of re-inventing (!), yes, re-inventing Marriage, and the proper meaning of 'Family'!

Undeniably there has been a diminishing of the passing on of family traditions between generations. There *was* a time when children inherited their parents' occupations, went to the same schools as they did, became members of similar organizations, shopped at comparable retail outlets, cooked in the style of Mother, supported the football club where their father was a fan—and, in adulthood, lived 'around the corner' from the family home.

What *has*, perhaps, seemed to have happened is that the economy has flourished through providing a diversity of products, services and, above all, choice.

The expansion of secondary, and especially university, education has been partly to fulfil the need for high-grade, transferable skills. New generations have tended to embrace eagerly these material changes—*un* surprisingly. Their reliance on their family roots and parochiality consequently borders on the fleeting!

As an aside, one wonders whether this is the direct cause of the withering of much-loved local dialects—an erosion not culturally for the good, one feels.

Interestingly, too, that Editorial makes the point that perhaps the beginning of this perceived decaying of social obligation started to materialize noticeably in the 1960s.

"The death of deference" is surely well said by the Editor!

With hindsight, those 'Swinging Sixties' came into being and begat the era of deference to *fashion*—almost generally.

The author of this talk offers a long-held theory that at that time, over half a century ago, there occurred a *considerable social shift.* [*Pause*] This was the cessation of National Service, when the great bulk of young men in the UK were conscripted into the military at age 18, during the period of the two National Service Acts of Parliament, 1939 to 1962.

Consequent on the abandonment of National Service, the subsequently 'liberated' youth of these Isles (from those early 60s) maybe helped the developing overall lack of respect for traditional niceties, manifesting its eventual self into much ill-discipline within British society.

Thereafter the ongoing latter half of the 20th century progressively saw the vogue of 'co-habiting'—another aspect of the erosion of traditional civilized society, subsequently accepted rather feebly by the national community! Allied to this, although in a far less harmful way, feminism decreed that the forms of address, Mrs and Miss, often now had a new abbreviation: Ms! (cynically, perhaps Ms brought with it some mystique?)

The term 'good manners' now seems to be rather archaic—both in words and, sadly, deeds. All part of the aforesaid 'death of deference'!

These past, say, five decades have of course produced a quite vast improvement in the quality of life in the United Kingdom—*materialistically*. I repeat, *materialistically*! But, sadly, at the overall expense of social discipline and respect. Satan's powerful weapons, selfishness and greed, seem increasingly to have established themselves, even being exemplified by a few standard-setting politicians!

'Vandalism' has become an over-used word, seemingly accepted (with a sigh and a 'tut-tut') as a 'sign of the times', by the community in general.

Our news media have appeared to condone social disrespect as it broadly became fashionable—*and very newsworthy*—so must surely accept a lot of the blame for the withering niceties and decency standards of public life right down to the present day. Dare I venture to suggest but, again perceivably, *almost* supporting despicable deeds for their constant *newsworthiness!*

Hereabouts I suspect most strongly that most of you, who have so far listened patiently, have indulged the earnest hope that there will be a magical outcome—indeed 'Putting the World to Rights'?

But there, no one except the Creator has the divine power of restoring our society 'at a stroke' to, say, the more perceivable and satisfactory moral tones largely obeyed by the community overall until soon after the middle of the last century.

Perhaps, a forward move towards the renewal of decency standards can only be led by an enlightened hierarchy within the print/airwave media, which reaches (even preaches) to almost everyone, obviously?

Our schools, too, have an extremely large part to play in teaching good manners—today's curricula are so very much in need of a complete overhaul in the teaching of social niceties, it would seem.

A Parliamentary lead just has to come from central government—initially by a brave party manifesto (yes, all this takes time) — directly to teacher-training colleges, school governors and local civic authorities.

Oh, there's so much more to be done, rather than, as has been the case, merely sitting back and muttering 'tut-tut'!

Concluding now, hoping for a parallel upsurge in the teachings of Christianity (semi-cynically, yes, we are still a Christian nation), particularly in consequent attitudes to one's fellow human beings; this needs, at the same time, direct orchestration (again following an appropriately enlightened party political manifesto — yes, that time/long-term factor, again); to repeat, *orchestration* from Parliament, together with appropriate Ecclesiastical Outreach.

Were this to begin to materialize—a goodly number of years hence, one fears—then the Christian Church, that fulcrum of theoretical, proper social behaviour, will again be able to rekindle the strong, ubiquitous faith it breeds.

In this House of God, it is appropriate to say Amen!

[Pause]   *Thank you for listening!*

Philip Newman

364

INFLUENCES ON THE FAMILY

Philip suggests that there was a considerable social shift in the middle of the twentieth century with the cessation of National Service. Both he and Tony were involved with this, serving in the RAF, but I missed it by a couple of years. Had I been required to enlist, I should have joined the Royal Navy, not least on account of my having learnt in the Scouts some skills that sailors also needed. As we moved from home to home because of Dad's career in the bank, I attended four secondary grammar schools; all had cadets but only in the final two of these was it possible to 'join up' and be a Scout as well. In those days the masters running them had seen wartime involvement in their respective Services.

I was a member of my first Scout Troop for only seven months until we moved, but it was very well run and provided a lasting vision of how good Scouting could be. The next one had a young and popular leader but he got married and moved away, leaving a trio of young Patrol Leaders (and my 'Second') to keep it going while a new Scoutmaster was sought.

I hadn't thought of myself as a potential Scouter, but got involved with two Hertfordshire Groups when I was working in Harlow, Essex. I helped with summer camps for the Scout Troops and ran sections for the boys over Scout Troop age. This by way of introduction to my quoting a few paragraphs from a paper I wrote early in 1977, prior to my moving back to West Chiltington and helping with a Scout Troop in Pulborough, and then finding myself running it single-handed from the spring of 1979 to the summer of 1980. The paper was inspired by my rather idealistic conception of how good Scouting could be and the idea of quoting some of it is intended to give a contemporary—well, forty years ago— complement to Philip's talk. *So, to quote some extracts:–*

Whether parents come to us or not, we should visit them, to see for ourselves how the boy is treated in his home environment. Parents do not always admit their sons' potential or understand how they respond to a challenge to try something difficult and see if they can master it.

There are no problem children, it has been said, only problem (i.e. incompetent) parents. It has been said that Scouting can be the biggest single influence on a boy's life, outside his home. Sometimes one wonders whether it isn't the biggest single influence, full stop. How often the boy from a broken or unhappy home can find in the happy, stable atmosphere of the Scout Troop and in the companionship and fun of camping with his Patrol some of the friendship, love and encouragement to his own self-confidence that he doesn't get at home.

One can hardly talk about parents and the home without thinking of the influence of television. This acts in two ways: what we see on it and the fact that we watch it at all. Many programmes are excellent, informative and stimulating, or provide entertainment in the best sense of that word. It is good to know what is going on in the world, but the habit of watching rather than taking part may make us spectators rather than participators in life itself. What I think is insidious is the steady output of fictional programmes which portray life and personal relationships as the author sees them, depicting selfishness and unkindness, often for the sake of weak humour. That's life, of course, but the viewer may say to himself, 'that is how to behave', and the influence of television on human behaviour may become negatively educational. [Tony's candidate for lowering standards in the Fifties is the establishment of ITV.]

Scouting is active and requires individual participation and involvement, which should militate against our members being spectators only, and every evening taken up with Scout meetings and constructive Scout activities means one fewer evening sitting in front of the telly.

It has been well said that Scouting's great appeal to a boy is that its activities represent 'legalized mischief'. This can be interpreted as saying that boys can do the adventurous and exciting things that their parents would be unwilling to let them do unsupervised, with wise and competent leadership to make sure that they have as much freedom as considerations of their safety will allow.

Robert Baden-Powell understood boys and knew how to get the best out of them. He could talk to them without talking down to them and he made religion simple enough for a boy to understand its true meaning. By 'playing the game of Scouting' a boy could teach himself how to live a good and useful life, and could teach other boys to do the same.

In Scouting we have fun, but we also have a tremendous opportunity to develop personal relationships and adult–boy exchange of ideas and experience such as is found nowhere else, with leaders relating to each other and to the boys as brother to brother.

Subsequent to my Scouting career I became involved with a national society, founded in Arundel in 1972, which campaigned for improved standards in English. A petition supported by some well-known people was presented to the Secretary of State for Education calling for the return of formal grammar teaching to schools. We decried the modern trend in education for not correcting children's mistakes in case it hurt their feelings. My candidate for the trends Philip so decries would be the change to so-called progressive education, coupled with sweeping away the grammar schools, whose pupils in the Sixties could compete on even terms for university places with those from the public schools, and made British education the pride of the world. Equality of opportunity can so easily give way to equality of attainment.

Prayers

O Lord, we thank you for the love and comradeship of this congregation that brings us together, each to give you worship in our own way. We ask you to comfort those who for some reason are in distress and, if possible, to lighten their load. If this cannot be done, please give them renewed courage to bear their load. Please guide our Bishops and those responsible for finding a Rector to serve us in future years.

We ask you to bless all who live in our village, especially those who have no contact with our Church and those who believe that modern scientific discoveries leave no room for theology, rather than seeing that these are only how the Lord achieved his ends!

O Lord, we do not pray for tasks equal to our strength; we ask for strength equal to our tasks. *Amen.*

We praise and bless thy holy name, O Lord, for all those who have laboured to serve the cause of freedom and good government in this land, and for all who have striven to uphold the sanctity of the home and family; for all who have sought to bless mankind by their sacrifice and service, and for all who have given their lives to enlarge the bounds of thy Kingdom on earth. For all the prophets, patriarchs and martyrs, and for all obscure and humble saints, we bless and praise thy holy name, through Jesus Christ our Lord. *Amen.*

O Lord God, whose will and joy it is that thy children love one another; bless our friendships, that they may be made happy and kept pure by thine unseen presence, now and at all times; through Jesus Christ our Lord. *Amen.*

O Lord, support us all the day long of this troublous life, until the shadows lengthen and the evening comes, and the busy world is hushed, and the fever of life is over, and our work is done. Then in thy mercy grant us a safe lodging, a holy rest, and peace at the last; through Jesus Christ our Lord. *Amen.*

A few moments' silence for your own prayers.

The Lord's Prayer

May the blessing of almighty God rest upon us and upon all our work; may he give us light to guide us, courage to support us, and love to unite us, now and evermore. *Amen.*

Closing Blessing

Accept, O God, our offerings of praise and thanksgiving. Forgive, we pray thee, all that is imperfect in our worship, and help us to glorify and enjoy thee for ever; through Jesus Christ our Lord. *Amen.*

SIMPLE SERVICE, WITH HYMNS
29th January 2017

Order of Service

Welcome & Notices (Pam)

Hymn 589 (Tune: *Angel Voices*)
Angel-voices ever singing

Brief introduction (David)

Hymn 580 (Tune: *Rhuddlan*) [Words are on page 156]
Judge eternal, throned in splendour

First reading (Robert) Luke, Chapter 16, Verses 1–15 *(NEB)*

Hymn 649 (Tune: *Heathlands*)
God of mercy, God of grace

Second reading (Tony) Ephesians, Chapter 6, Verses 10–24 *(NEB)*

Hymn 810 (Tune: *Moscow*)
Thou, whose almighty word

Brief chat (David)

Hymn 784 (Tune: *Morning Light*)
Stand up, stand up for Jesus

Prayers (Philip)

Hymn 265 (*Hymns A & M Revised;* words overleaf. Tune: *Aurelia*)
From Greenland's icy mountains

Closing prayer (David)

The service will proceed without announcements. All the hymns are in *Ancient & Modern (2013 Edition)* except the last one, which is in *Hymns Ancient & Modern Revised* (words opposite).

Thank you for coming. **Please join us in the New Vestry after the service** *for a glass of wine (alternatives available).*

Please use the voting form overleaf to list your own favourite hymns for a subsequent service.

From Greenland's Icy Mountains

From Greenland's icy mountains,
  From India's coral strand,
Where Afric's sunny fountains
  Roll down their golden sand,
From many an ancient river,
  From many a palmy plain,
They call us to deliver
  Their land from error's chain.

What though the spicy breezes
  Blow soft o'er Java's isle,
Though every prospect pleases
  And only man is vile:
In vain with lavish kindness
  The gifts of God are strown;
The heathen in his blindness
  Bows down to wood and stone.

Can we, whose souls are lighted
  With wisdom from on high,
Can we to men benighted
  The lamp of life deny?
Salvation! O salvation!
  The joyful sound proclaim,
Till each remotest nation
  Has learned Messiah's name.

Waft, waft, ye winds, his story,
  And you, ye waters, roll,
Till, like a sea of glory,
  It spreads from pole to pole;
Till o'er our ransomed nature
  The Lamb for sinners slain,
Redeemer, King, Creator,
  In bliss returns to reign.

Bishop R. Heber (1783–1826)
Music: S. S. Wesley (1810–76)

We missed a winter service in 2015, going four months from a mild November to the end of March, but it's rather welcome to have a warmer weekend for our January service than the icy weather of last week, not least because the Church boiler has been out of action recently.

As always, thank you all for coming. Tony and I planned the service, and we are grateful to Philip for leading the prayers again, and to Robert for doing a reading as well as providing our music. Our thanks, too, to Pam for her encouragement, and for coming along to start us off.

Tony and I couldn't resist marking the totally unexpected and bizarre termination of my Treasurership of this Church with the parable of the unjust steward.[1]

The next fifth Sunday is 30th April, and there is the usual form on the service sheet for your choice of hymns for this, but I cannot promise that it will happen, as I am taking a break to do other things, one of which will be to assemble our talks from these services into book form. Peter Evans decided to call it a day after 46 services (11 years), but we have now done no less than 55, which I certainly did not contemplate when we had our first one on Advent Sunday in 2003.[2]

Returning to the present, may I extend our usual invitation to all of you to come out to the New Vestry to enjoy a drink after this service. We started this at the end of August in David Beal's second year with us; he and Mary had just returned from holiday and provided something to eat at the Rectory, and we supplied the drinks. We had a very good attendance!

---

[1] I should like to assure readers that my stewardship was not being questioned, and my accounts, including those for my final twelve months, and the five Annual Reports I assembled in the 3½ years when I was Treasurer, have satisfied three Independent Examiners, including a firm of accountants. I am uncertain as to exactly why our two lady Churchwardens, backed up during the interregnum by our lady Rural Dean and lady Archdeacon, decided to dispense with my services, having persuaded an elderly predecessor to take up the role again, but it could well have been related to my refusal to sign the PCC up to a commercial giving website the previous summer (see discussion in the penultimate paragraph of my January talk, on p. 373). It had been a very time-consuming role, so I have appreciated the reduced call on my time, but it left me feeling so sad about our Church administration that I had no desire to put any more time in, commenting that if I felt like attending a Church service I could always go to Pulborough. It was a bit further to walk, but that has not been a problem. *DJE*

[2] So this turned out to be our final service; in retrospect the correct decision even if the actual reason was an unfortunate one. We were all getting older, and putting on the services, even just four or sometimes five a year, represented a lot of work. And the two 5's of our 55 total match well with the 5 of Fifth Sundays!

Luke 16, 1–15

He said to his disciples, "There was a rich man who had a bailiff, and he received complaints that this man was squandering the property. So he sent for him, and said, 'What is this that I hear? Produce your accounts, for you cannot be manager here any longer.'

"The bailiff said to himself, 'What am I to do now that my employer is dismissing me? I am not strong enough to dig, and too proud to beg. I know what I must do, to make sure that, when I have to leave, there will be people to give me house and home.' He summoned his master's debtors one by one. To the first he said, 'How much do you owe my master?' He replied, 'A thousand gallons of olive oil.' He said, 'Here is your account. Sit down and make it five hundred; and be quick about it.' Then he said to another, 'And you, how much do you owe?' He said, 'A thousand bushels of wheat', and was told, 'Take your account and make it eight hundred.' And the master applauded the dishonest bailiff for acting so astutely. For the worldly are more astute than the other-worldly in dealing with their own kind.

"So I say to you, use your worldly wealth to win friends for yourselves, so that when money is a thing of the past you may be received into an eternal home.

"The man who can be trusted in little things can be trusted also in great; and the man who is dishonest in little things is dishonest also in great things. If, then, you have not proved trustworthy with the wealth of this world, who will trust you with the wealth that is real? And if you have proved untrustworthy with what belongs to another, who will give you what is your own?

"No servant can be the slave of two masters; for either he will hate the first and love the second, or he will be devoted to the first and think nothing of the second. You cannot serve God and Money."

The Pharisees, who loved money, heard all this and scoffed at him. He said to them, "You are the people who impress your fellow-men with your righteousness, but God sees through you; for what sets itself up to be admired by men is detestable in the sight of God."

Ephesians 6, 10 – 24

Finally then, find your strength in the Lord, in his mighty power. Put on all the armour which God provides, so that you may be able to stand firm against the devices of the devil. For our fight is not against human foes, but against cosmic powers, against the authorities and potentates of this dark world, against the superhuman forces of evil in the heavens.

Therefore, take up God's armour; then you will be able to stand your ground when things are at their worst, to complete every task and still to stand. Stand firm, I say. Buckle on the belt of truth; for coat of mail put on integrity; let the shoes on your feet be the gospel of peace, to give you firm footing; and, with all these, take up the great shield of faith, with which you will be able to quench all the flaming arrows of the evil one. Take salvation for helmet; for sword, take that which the Spirit gives you — the words that come from God.

Give yourselves wholly to prayer and entreaty; pray on every occasion in the power of the Spirit. To this end keep watch and persevere, always interceding for all God's people; and pray for me, that I may be granted the right words when I open my mouth, and may boldly and freely make known his hidden purpose, for which I am an ambassador—in chains. Pray that I may speak of it boldly, as it is my duty to speak.

THE INTERNET – SERVANT OR MASTER ?

Several years ago, Malcolm Bennett kindly asked me if I would be interested in joining the local Rotary. Quite some years further back still, our then next-door neighbour persuaded me to come to his Branch in London and give a talk, not surprisingly, given my long interest, on the paranormal. On our way there in his car, he explained that membership of the Rotary was by invitation, and they selected the people recognized in their location as the best exemplars of the different trades. So I was a bit surprised to be invited to join in West Chiltington, as I am by no means the best printer even in our village; my first reaction was that I was loath to join an organization that was willing to accept me as a member!

However, I did accept an invitation to come along to one of their meetings and enjoyed a splendid evening meal at West Chiltington Golf Club, and just as it happened the talk was a very interesting one about the atom-smashing research installation at CERN at Geneva. They had a problem in that they needed to get large amounts of data to their colleagues around the world as quickly as possible, so they invented a communication set-up that would be capable of doing this. Which in due course became known as the Internet, and that's what I thought I'd say a few words about today.

Back at the beginning of this century telecommunications allowed one to send photocopies over the telephone lines by means of a fax machine and a modem, and not long after that we had a dial-up system that could send what came to be called e-mails. But the internet enabled the setting up of files that anyone else could access, and there ensued the 'dot.com bubble' of every commercial enterprise setting up its own 'web site', not all of which turned out to be profitable. If you left your computer on dial-up, or used it in this mode for any length of time, that left your phone line engaged with respect to receiving normal phone calls, so the next stage was the development of 'broadband', which allowed you to do both at the same time. So far so good, but by then the Internet had changed from a way to distribute data to an interlocking network of commercial interests.

I selected our second reading as it included St Paul's statement "For we wrestle not against flesh and blood, but against principalities, against powers, against the rulers of the darkness of this world, against spiritual wickedness in high places", as the AV puts it. Well, do we? Just a few decades ago our Church bowed before the altar of Political Correctness, a movement that appealed to everyone's better nature but was driven by people with an Agenda that wasn't necessarily Christian. Today it has been commented that 'taking offence' has become very popular; notably, I would add, taking offence on behalf of groups of other people who might not actually have taken offence themselves.

Websites to advertise one's own activities or products serve a useful purpose, and indeed I set up one myself for an association I was working for in 2009, and this proved quite productive, but other people were more inventive and saw their potential for making money. Boris Johnson wrote a few years ago in the *Daily Telegraph* commending the founders of the Facebook site for "creating wealth", but that was inaccurate as what they were actually doing was redistributing it. You only create wealth by such activities as agriculture, mining or generating hydro-electric power. The website is 'free' to the people who use it, but not to all the commercial enterprises who need to advertise on it to keep up with their competitors.

Just before the Iraq War in 2003, I read in the aforementioned paper a piece about the "poor, deprived children of Iraq". Why were they said to be deprived? Because they did not have Internet access! Some fourteen years later, a connection to high-speed fibre-optic broadband has been elevated almost to the status of a human right.

The computer companies achieved a massive coup in persuading the Government to install computers in schools. When you see on television even a primary-school class, the pupils all have their little laptops on their desks. I was a little surprised at this, as I had read previously of a trial run that was not entirely successful. The children were asked to scour the web for information about crocodiles, which it seems they managed without difficulty. But the information was not much use to them, as they had yet to be taught to read. Even more of a problem is the necessity for parents to purchase computers to enable their offspring to do their homework, as that leaves the children to spend time online unsupervised, up to some 20 hours a week so it seems, and that hasn't always been beneficial for them.

We also have the Twitter website, catering for everyone's passion for expressing their opinions. To say that some of these are ill-advised and do more harm than good would be stating the obvious. I am tempted to enquire of ITV whether Facebook and Twitter, being commercial sites, actually pay them to plug them day in, day out on Meridian news. "Or you can send us a tweet". They won't be getting one from me, or Tony (he gave me his computer as he didn't want to bother with one any more).

The relentless advance of technology can be very tiresome if one can do all one needs to do with the equipment one already has. Apparently the software people can't leave a good operating system or word-processing program alone, but must always be adding to or changing it. Sooner or later one is obliged to purchase new equipment because though what one has still works perfectly it is no longer compatible with one's internet access or, in the case of a printer, 'supported' by availability of supplies or parts if a repair is needed. But I have yet to come across any protest that this might not be 'fair trading'.

My thesis today is that the Internet is a principality, or power, that we should at least consider wrestling against if we do not consider all its aspects to be beneficial. Like fire, it can be very useful, but also, like fire, it can be destructive. It is not good to read of teenagers killing themselves because they are not getting enough 'likes' on their Facebook page, or of the many instances of internet bullying. Just where would Isil be without YouTube to show their executions on, or the web to 'radicalize' people to join them? So what is the Church doing about it, apart from getting in on the act themselves? I'm afraid I've made myself unpopular with some of our Church people by declining to support 'giving' websites, which no doubt generate a nice income for themselves by catering for people's laziness, or their passion for 'clicking' away their money by computer. A closer look at what using them entails reveals that actually they are more bother than they are worth, but that of course represents my personal opinion, as indeed does the whole of this talk!

But just think that if our own country's businesses stopped advertising on Facebook and Twitter, both these sites would soon wither away . . .

Prayers

ST PATRICK'S BREASTPLATE

May the strength of God pilot us.
May the power of God preserve us.
May the wisdom of God instruct us.
May the hand of God protect us.
May the way of God direct us.
May the shield of God defend us.
May the host of God guard us against the snares of evil and the
    temptations of the world.
May Christ be with us, Christ before us, Christ in us, Christ over us.
May thy salvation, O Lord, be always ours, this day and for evermore.

Amen.

O Father, who hast declared thy love to men by the birth of the holy Child at Bethlehem; help us to welcome him with gladness and to make room for him in our common days; so that we may live at peace with one another, and in goodwill with all thy family; through the same, thy Son Jesus Christ our Lord. *Amen.*

O Lord we pray thee to raise up leaders of the people who will fear thee and thee alone, whose delight shall be to do thy will and work thy work: that the heart of this people may be wise, its mind sound, and its will righteous; through Christ our Lord. *Amen.*

A few moments' silence for your own prayers.

The Lord's Prayer

Go forth into the world in peace; be of good courage; hold fast that which is good; render to no man evil for evil; strengthen the faint-hearted; support the weak; help the afflicted; honour all men; love and serve the Lord; rejoicing in the power of the Holy Spirit.

And the blessing of God Almighty, the Father, the Son, and the Holy Spirit, be upon us, and remain with us for ever. *Amen.*

Closing Prayer

We praise thee, O God, for the healthful delights of this season; for mirth quickening the blood, uniting us with others and refreshing us for work; for joy that heightens all our life and doubles our powers. Help us, we beseech thee, to share these blessings with others, kindling their hearts by our gladness; through Jesus, the Christ Child, our King. *Amen.*

APPENDIX

Hymns with Words Included

Schedule of Talks[1]

---

[1] The talks were given by David Ellis except where indicated otherwise.

And as this volume goes at last to the printers, I record my thanks to Betty Markwick for some helpful suggestions and for meticulously checking the final text and thereby finding a few typos that, despite my careful reading, I had failed to notice myself! *DE*

Poems Included

Other Items Included [1]

---

[1] When we planned these services we did not envisage publication of all the readings we had made use of; inevitably there is still one for which we have no record of its source, so we apologize for our failure to acknowledge this. There are two we were unable to obtain permission to include, and for one of these we put in something else.